GONE PRO
ALABAMA

Crimson Tide Athletes Who Became Pros

2ND EDITION

Steve Millburg

CLERISY PRESS

Gone Pro Alabama

For further information, contact the publisher at:

Clerisy Press
306 Greenup Street
Covington, KY 41011
clerisypress.com

a division of Keen Communications, Birmingham, Alabama

CATALOGING-IN-PUBLICATION DATA IS AVAILABLE FROM THE LIBRARY OF CONGRESS

ISBN-13: 978-1-57860-525-5; eISBN 978-1-57860-526-2

Distributed by Publishers Group West
Printed in the United States of America
Second edition, first printing
Editor: Tim Jackson, Crimson Clover Creative
Cover design: Scott McGrew
Interior design: Annie Long and Donna Collingwood

Cover photo © groveb
Image on p. 323 courtesy of horia varlan through Creative Commons
    license on Flickr; image on p. 347 courtesy of adil113 through
    Creative Commons license on Flickr.
All other photographs credited as noted.

TABLE OF CONTENTS

Acknowledgments

First, thank you to Bob Sehlinger and Molly Merkle of Menasha Ridge Press for giving me this opportunity, and for not killing me at several post-deadline points during the creation of this book. I'm sure the thought crossed your minds. And I wouldn't have blamed you.

Thanks to University of Alabama Athletics for research and photography assistance—and especially to all of the athletes, coaches, staff members, and others who have created such an amazing sports legacy. I'm proud and humbled to be able to tell your stories.

Thanks to Brad Green of the Paul W. Bryant Museum for digging up wonderful archival photos.

Thanks to the amazingly resourceful Megan Daily for tracking down photography and sharing insights about her great-grandfather, "Football Freddy" Sington.

Thanks to Cary Estes and Rubin Grant; you both helped me more than you know.

Thanks to Pamela P. Smith for the sharp eyes and sharp advice.

Thanks to Tim Jackson for catching my stupid mistakes. If you missed any, I'll take the blame. Maybe.

Thank you to my late father, Gene Millburg, the finest man I've ever known. He taught me to try to do the right thing always, in sports and in everything else.

Thanks to Taylor Rogers Scott, Paul Rogers, and C. J. Duke, my stepchildren, for adding so much to my life.

And a most heartfelt thank you to Pamela, my wife, for everything.

About Gone Pro

Welcome to *Gone Pro,* a series of books that celebrates college athletes who have continued their sporting exploits in the professional ranks or the Olympics. Each book focuses on a single college or university. The one you're holding, the very first in the series, salutes the storied sports legacy of the Crimson Tide of the University of Alabama.

In it, we applaud, with a biographical sketch or at least a listing of basic information, every Alabama athlete, male or female, who has performed in a top-level professional league or the Olympic Games. Some stars, of course, get more notice than others. You can catch up with old (or not-so-old) favorites, relive (or find out about) the glory days gone by, and maybe even learn something you didn't know about the exalted Bear Bryant.

Perhaps this book is your introduction to the world of "Roll, Tide!" courtesy of a true believer who wants to induct you into the ranks of the Crimson Tide faithful. Don't worry that we'll throw a bunch of numbers at you. We include some key statistics, but we're much more interested in telling stories about everyone from the Bear (see page 37) and Joe Namath (see page 136) to the great blind golfer Charley Boswell (see page 342) and diminutive Olympics medalist-turned-cop Terin Humphrey (see page 376).

Even for the avid fan, we can pretty much guarantee surprises. Did you know about Ray Abruzzese (see page 82), the obscure second-stringer who helped alter the course of pro football in the 1960s? Or Arthur "Tarzan" White (see page 167), the free-spirited 1930s and '40s lineman who took up pro wrestling in the off-seasons and continued climbing into the ring until he was 60 years old? Or Jackie Hayes (see page 226), the major league second baseman who mysteriously lost his eyesight in midcareer, came home to Clanton, Alabama, and spent 12 years as Chilton County tax collector?

Do you know who recently tied Bear Bryant's record of six national championships as an Alabama head coach? Here's a hint: They call her The Pink Lady (see page 363). And what is rabble-rousing former Alabama Governor George Wallace (see page 411) doing in a book about pro athletes?

We'll let you read on and find out. Coach Bryant used to say, "Don't talk too much or too soon." We've already talked enough, and the very beginning of a book is too soon to get long-winded.

Website

Your Gone Pro experience doesn't have to end when you've finished the book. You can extend it indefinitely by hanging out at the Gone Pro website, **www. GoneProBooks.com.** Click on over for regular updates about Crimson Tiders in the pro ranks, advance excerpts from new books in the series, and more.

Tell Us More

We hope this book stirs warm memories and tells you some things you didn't know about Alabama's athletic heroes. But there's always more to learn and more to tell. If we missed something about one of your favorites, we'd like to know about it. Please contact us at:

Gone Pro
PO Box 43673
Birmingham, AL 35243
steve@goneprobooks.com

You can also reach us through the website, **www.GoneProBooks.com.**

Introduction

Suddenly, the Crimson Tide is awash with national championships.

In football, Alabama has so many that it can't keep track of them all. The athletics department claims 15. A National Collegiate Athletic Association list credits Alabama with winning or sharing 13 national titles. For an explanation of the discrepancy, see "National Championships" in the Football chapter, page 53.

Until 2012, the only other Alabama sport with a national championship was gymnastics. The gymnasts added their sixth title, and second in a row, in 2012. Then, within a two-week span in late spring 2012, the women's golf team seized its first title, followed by the softball team. The men's golf team nearly added a fifth crown, losing on the last hole to a 30-foot birdie putt, but came back to decisively win the national championship in 2013.

Who says Alabama's just a football school?

In the history of University of Alabama sports, which dates back to 1892, thousands of athletes have represented the Crimson Tide. In this book, we address only 539—the best of the best. They're the ones who have gone pro, moving on to compete at the highest level.

In order to keep the book to a manageable size, we define "gone pro" as competing either at the top professional rank of a sport or in the Olympic Games. In other words, we're talking about major leaguers here. This book tells their stories.

Here's the breakdown by sport of those 539 athletes whom you'll be getting to know better:

306 Football *(National Football League, American Football League, All-America Football Conference, Canadian Football League)*

 62 Baseball *(American League, National League)*

 58 Swimming and Diving *(men and women; Olympics)*

 32 Track and Field *(men and women; Olympics)*

 31 Basketball *(men and women; National Basketball Association, Women's National Basketball Association)*

 26 Golf *(men and women; PGA Tour, LPGA Tour)*

 13 Softball *(National Pro Fastpitch)*

7 Tennis *(ATP Tour, Davis Cup, Olympics)*

2 Fighting *(pro boxing, mixed martial arts)*

1 Gymnastics *(Olympics)*

1 Triathlon *(Olympics)*

As the numbers indicate, football is kind of big at Alabama. Dismantling Notre Dame, 42–14, in the 2012 season BCS National Championship Game gave Alabama its third national football championship in four years, a feat last accomplished by, believe it or not, Notre Dame in 1946, 1947, and 1949. But Alabama also posted national championships over the past three seasons from its gymnastics team, softball team, and men's and women's golf teams. The powerhouse gymnastics and softball teams annually contend for the national attendance titles in their respective sports. In the Southeastern Conference, the men's basketball team ranks second only to hoops-obsessed Kentucky in all-time victories. Some great athletes have represented Alabama in a wide variety of pro sports.

Many have chosen fascinating careers after their playing days—everything from professional wrestling to politics (not that there's necessarily a lot of difference between the two). We've done our best to answer that "whatever happened to . . . ?" question for you as well.

SPORTS AND SEASONS

Alabama competes on an intercollegiate basis in eight men's and 11 women's sports. Here's a quick sketch of each, including when Alabama took up the sport and when it's in season:

Baseball (men)

BEGAN: July 1, 1892. Baseball was Alabama's first intercollegiate sport.
SEASON: February–May; conference and NCAA tournaments through the College World Series in mid-June.

Basketball (men and women)

BEGAN: 1913 for men, 1974 for women. **SEASON:** Early November–late February or early March; postseason tournaments extend another month.

Cross-Country (men and women)

BEGAN: University records go back only to the start of Southeastern Conference competition, which was 1935 for men and 1983 for women. Alabama almost certainly began intercollegiate competition before then.
SEASON: September–November.

Football (men)

BEGAN: 1892. **SEASON:** Late August or early September–early December, plus possibility of a December conference championship and usually a January bowl game.

Golf (men and women)

BEGAN: 1951 for men, 1974 for women. **SEASON:** September–October, February–April; conference and NCAA tournaments mid-April to late May or early June.

Gymnastics (women)

BEGAN: 1975. **SEASON:** January–mid-March; conference and NCAA tournaments late March through April.

Rowing (women)

BEGAN: 2005. **SEASON:** October–November, March–May.

Soccer (women)

BEGAN: 1986. **SEASON:** August–late October or early November; conference and NCAA tournaments November–December.

Softball (women)

BEGAN: 1997. **SEASON:** February–early May; conference and NCAA tournaments into early June.

Swimming and Diving (men and women)

BEGAN: 1959 for men, 1974 for women. **SEASON:** October–January or early February; conference and NCAA tournaments February–March.

Tennis (men and women)

BEGAN: 1949 for men, 1975 for women. **SEASON:** September–November, January–April; conference and NCAA tournaments April–May.

Track and Field (men and women)

BEGAN: University records are incomplete, but men were competing at least as early as 1921. Records for women go back only to the start of Southeastern Conference competition in 1981. **SEASON:** January–April; conference and NCAA tournaments early May–early June.

Volleyball (women)

BEGAN: 1974. **SEASON:** August–November; NCAA tournament in December.

Alabama Club Sports

Club sports are allowed to use the university name and some facilities but are not officially sponsored—or, usually, funded—by the university. Because students create and operate the teams, the lineup of sports can change from year to year. Here's the most recent list:

• Badminton	• Equestrian Sports	• Table Tennis
• Baseball	• Ice Hockey	• Team Handball
• Basketball (wheelchair)	• Kayaking	• Tennis
• Bass Fishing	• Lacrosse	• Triathlon
• Bowling	• Paintball	• Ultimate
• Climbing	• Racquetball	• Volleyball
• Cricket	• Rowing	• Water Polo
• Cycling	• Rugby	• Waterskiing
• Disc Golf	• Soccer	• Wrestling

FACILITIES

Bryant-Denny Stadium (Football)

OPENED: 1929; expanded in 1937, 1950, 1961, 1966, 1988, 1998, 2006, and 2010. **SEATING CAPACITY:** 101,821 (originally 12,000). **SURFACE:** grass.

Bryant-Denny Stadium became Alabama's largest sports facility in terms of seating capacity when it reached 92,138 seats in 2006.
Credit: Garry Thompson

George Hutcheson Denny, University of Alabama president from 1912 until 1935 (and on an interim basis in 1941–42), lent his name to both what was originally called Denny Stadium and to the campus bell tower, Denny Chimes. In 1975, the State Legislature added football coach Bear Bryant's name, making the football facility officially Bryant-Denny Stadium.

Periodic expansions, including a flurry of four starting in 1988, have made it the fifth-largest stadium in the country by seating capacity and second-largest in the Southeastern Conference.

The 2006 upgrade included the addition of the Walk of Champions outside the stadium. It contains bronze statues of the five football coaches who have led Alabama to a national championship. The original likenesses were of Wallace Wade, Frank Thomas, Bear Bryant, and Gene Stallings. After current coach Nick Saban's team won the 2009 championship, his statue was unveiled in April 2011.

Top 10 College Football Stadiums (ranked by seating capacity)

109,901 Michigan Stadium (Michigan), Ann Arbor, Michigan

106,572 Beaver Stadium (Penn State), University Park, Pennsylvania

102,455 Neyland Stadium (Tennessee), Knoxville, Tennessee

102,329 Ohio Stadium (Ohio State), Columbus, Ohio

101,821 Bryant-Denny Stadium (Alabama), Tuscaloosa

100,119 Darrell K. Royal-Texas Memorial Stadium (Texas), Austin, Texas

93,607 Los Angeles Memorial Coliseum (Southern California), Los Angeles

92,542 Rose Bowl (UCLA), Pasadena, California

92,746 Sanford Stadium (Georgia), Athens, Georgia

92,542 Tiger Stadium (LSU), Baton Rouge, Louisiana

Southeastern Conference Football Stadiums (ranked by seating capacity)

102,455 Neyland Stadium (Tennessee), Knoxville, Tennessee

101,821 Bryant-Denny Stadium (Alabama), Tuscaloosa

92,746 Sanford Stadium (Georgia), Athens, Georgia

92,542 Tiger Stadium (LSU), Baton Rouge, Louisiana

88,548 Ben Hill Griffin Stadium (Florida), Gainesville, Florida

87,451 Jordan-Hare Stadium (Auburn), Auburn, Alabama

82,600 Kyle Field (Texas A&M), College Station, Texas

80,250 Williams-Brice Stadium (South Carolina), Columbia, South Carolina

72,000 Donald W. Reynolds Razorback Stadium (Arkansas), Fayetteville, Arkansas

71,004 Farout Field (Missouri), Columbia, Missouri

67,606 Commonwealth Stadium (Kentucky), Lexington, Kentucky

60,580 Vaught-Hemingway Stadium (Mississippi), Oxford, Mississippi

55,082 Davis Wade Stadium (Mississippi State), Starkville, Mississippi

40,550 Vanderbilt Stadium (Vanderbilt), Nashville, Tennessee

<blockquote>

Namesmanship

In 2008, Alabama alumnus James M. Fail donated money to have the visitors' locker room at Bryant-Denny Stadium named The Fail Room. He explained, "I figured it was the most appropriate opportunity I would ever have to use my name."

</blockquote>

Thomas-Drew Practice Fields (Football)

The famous tower where Bear Bryant perched during football practice, surveying the proceedings from above, still stands alongside the Thomas-Drew Practice Fields. Three full-size grass fields and an artificial-turf field with just one end zone make up the facility. A privacy fence screens the goings-on from the public—and scouts from other teams. The fields date back decades and bear the names of mid–20th-century coaches Frank Thomas and Harold "Red" Drew (see page 41).

Hank Crisp Indoor Facility
(Football, Baseball, Soccer, Softball)

OPENED: 1986; renovated 2009.

When the weather is bad, the football, baseball, soccer, or softball team can practice in climate-controlled comfort in the Hank Crisp Indoor Facility, named in 1991 for a former Alabama basketball, baseball, and track coach, football assistant, and athletics director (see page 274). Cameras suspended from the ceiling allow coaches to analyze plays from overhead.

Legion Field, Birmingham (formerly used for Football)

OPENED: 1927; renovated in 1934, 1948, 1961, 1965, 1977, 1991, and 2005. **SEATING CAPACITY:** 71,594 (originally 21,000). **SURFACE:** FieldTurf artificial turf.

Some of Alabama's greatest games, including every Iron Bowl battle against Auburn from 1948 through 1988, took place at Legion Field. Alabama used to play several home games there every season, especially the big draws, because Legion Field had the most seats of any stadium in the state.

With its 1998 expansion, Bryant-Denny Stadium on campus surpassed Legion Field in seats. And Legion, once the self-proclaimed Football Capital of the South, was not well-maintained. Alabama's last game there was in 2003.

The stadium was named for the American Legion. Like Bryant-Denny, it was expanded several times, reaching a peak capacity of 83,091 in 1991. In 2004, the 9,000-seat upper deck was found to be structurally deficient. Rather than pay for repairs, the City of Birmingham removed the upper deck in 2005. Maintenance has continued to be minimal. The main tenant, the University of Alabama at Birmingham football team, would love to build an on-campus stadium, and the city has periodically floated the idea of new domed stadium at another location. Legion Field's future seems, at best, cloudy.

Coleman Coliseum (Men's Basketball, Gymnastics)

OPENED: 1968; renovated in 2005 and 2009; Coleman Auxiliary Volleyball Extension added in 1996. **SEATING CAPACITY:** 15,383 for basketball (originally 15,043), 15,075 for gymnastics, 16,000 for concerts.

Coleman Coliseum covers two acres of land, and its main arena encompasses almost 100,000 square feet of space.
Credit: Wikimedia Commons

Originally Memorial Coliseum, the facility was renamed in 1988 in honor of Jeff Coleman, longtime business manager for Alabama athletics and alumni director. It has been the home of the women's basketball team and the volleyball team in the past as well as a venue for commencements, political rallies, concerts, operas, ballets, and Broadway shows. Among those who have performed at Coleman are Elvis Presley, Tom Petty, Ray Charles, Bob Dylan, Reba McIntyre, Jay Leno, Hank Williams Jr., and the Grateful Dead.

The CAVE (Coleman Auxiliary Volleyball Extension; basically a rectangular box, like an old-time high-school gym) was added in 1996 as a practice facility for basketball and volleyball. In 2000, the volleyball team started playing matches there, with the tightly packed, vocal crowds creating a nice home-court advantage. In 2011, the volleyball team moved to a remodeled Foster Auditorium.

Another part of the Coleman Coliseum Annex, the Frances Smith Gymnastics Practice Facility, got a summer 2012 upgrade that included new crimson matting and, in the training room, new hot and cold therapy tubs. The facility also includes a comprehensive video analysis system.

Foster Auditorium (Women's Basketball, Volleyball)

OPENED: 1939; renovated and reopened in 2011. **SEATING CAPACITY:** 3,800.

Foster Auditorium was part of a flurry of construction from 1936 through 1939 that added 14 buildings to campus. The majestic, white-columned auditorium was the largest. In 1942, it was named for university president Richard Foster, who had died in office the year before.

The auditorium was the Coleman Coliseum of its time, a multipurpose building for graduations, concerts, lectures, meetings, boxing matches, intramural sports, and, at various times, men's and women's basketball, volleyball, and gymnastics.

Because it was also used for registration, it was the site of the June 11, 1963, "Stand in the Schoolhouse Door" by then-Governor George Wallace (see page 411). Wallace protested the enrollment of two black students by symbolically blocking the entrance. After a confrontation involving U.S. Deputy Attorney General Nicholas Katzenbach and the National Guard, Wallace stepped aside, having played out his little bit of political theater.

The building was declared a National Historical Landmark in 2005, even as it fell into disuse and disrepair. A $15 million rejuvenation allowed it to

The entrance to Foster Auditorium now overlooks Malone-Hood Plaza and the Autherine Lucy Clock Tower.
Credit: Wikimedia Commons

reopen in February 2011 as the home of women's basketball and volleyball. The renovation included the addition outside the main entrance of Malone-Hood Plaza, named after the students whom Wallace attempted to block, with a 40-foot Autherine Lucy Clock Tower, named after the university's first black student, who attended Alabama for three days in 1956.

Sewell-Thomas Stadium (Baseball)

OPENED: 1948; renovated in 1996 and 2001. **SEATING CAPACITY:** 6,571 (originally 2,000). **OUTFIELD DISTANCES FROM HOME PLATE:** 325 feet at the left- and right-field lines, 365 to right center and left center, 400 feet to center field.

Those who contend that Alabama is definitely a football school can point to its baseball stadium, which was named for a football coach. Frank Thomas (see page 41) compiled a 115-24-7 football record with two national championships (depending on how you count; see "National Championships" in the Football chapter, page 53) from 1931 through 1942 and 1944 through 1946. He was also athletics director.

Thomas, who smoked cigars even during games, developed heart problems and high blood pressure. He had to resign as football coach after the 1946 season because he could stand for only brief periods, but he stayed on as athletics director. So it's understandable that when Alabama opened its new baseball stadium in 1948, affection for a sick old coach (just 49 years old) carried the day. The university named the stadium Frank Thomas Field.

In 1978, Alabama added the name of Joe Sewell (see page 239), its baseball coach from 1964 through 1969 and the only Hall of Fame baseball player Alabama has produced. Major and minor renovation projects have enlarged, updated, and improved the stadium over the years. A video board was added in 2007. In September 2013, the university trustees approved a massive, $30 million rebuild of the stadium, to begin after the 2013–14 season.

Rhoads Stadium (Softball)

OPENED: 2000; expanded three times. **SEATING CAPACITY:** 3,940 (originally 1,500). **OUTFIELD DISTANCES FROM HOME PLATE:** 200 feet at the left- and right-field lines, 220 feet to center field.

One of the finest softball stadiums anywhere draws the biggest crowds in women's collegiate softball. Alabama and Arizona annually battle for the lead in softball attendance. In 2013, the Crimson Tide's fans crushed the Wildcats'. Alabama beat its own year-old national record, drawing 93,332 to 32 home games. The average of 2,916 also broke a national record, set by Alabama in 2011. Arizona's 2013 total was 57,615 for 27 home games, an average of 2,134. Season-ticket holders have filled all of Alabama's permanent grandstand seats for several years.

When Thomas Field (now Sewell-Thomas Stadium) opened in 1948, it seated 2,000.
Credit: David Smith

The stadium was officially renamed in 2011 for Ann Rhoads, a longtime Alabama softball booster, and her late husband, John. Ann pledged a $1.2 million donation plus another $2.5 million after her death to promote the softball team and other women's sports.

Alabama Aquatics Center
(Men's and Women's Swimming and Diving)

OPENED: 1981; renovated in 2002. **SEATING CAPACITY:** 1,500 (main venue). **MAIN POOL:** 50 meters by 25 yards. **TRAINING POOL:** 25 yards.

In 2001, the University of Alabama named the main pool the Don Gambril Olympic Pool after its most successful swimming and diving coach (see page 354). Appropriately, it's considered a "fast" pool. The Aquatic Center also includes a smaller training pool (25 yards, eight lanes). The main pool has two 1-meter diving boards, two 3-meter boards, and 5-meter and 10-meter diving platforms.

Alabama Soccer Stadium (Soccer)

OPENED: 2004. **SEATING CAPACITY:** 1,500.

The Soccer Stadium has a nice hand-me-down from Bryant-Denny Stadium: a giant high-definition video scoreboard, removed from the football stadium during a renovation.

Alabama Tennis Stadium (Men's and Women's Tennis)

OPENED: 2004. **SEATING CAPACITY:** 2,000. **COURTS:** 12 hard courts.

The overhead seating faces all 12 courts. In 2012, the university added the adjacent Roberta Alison Baumgardner Tennis Facility, an indoor facility with six hard courts for use during inclement weather.

Sam Bailey Track and Field Stadium
(Men's and Women's Outdoor Track and Field)

OPENED: 1975; renovated in 2006 and 2012. **SEATING CAPACITY:** 4,500.

In 2012, the biggest renovation since the stadium opened turned it into what track and field Coach Dan Waters called "a championship-caliber facility." Just about every inch, from the surface to the stands and press box, got an upgrade. The redesigned nine-lane track is wider and has a high-performance Benyon BSS-2000 surface. An infield redesign involved relocation or realignment of the shot put, jumps, and other areas. The stadium also received permanent lights for the first time. "With the way everything is configured now and with the addition of the lights, we can run an efficient and fan-friendly meet," said Waters, who became men's and women's track and field coach in May 2011. "We can run a meet in four hours now instead of it being an all-day grind like it could be in the past."

The $4.2 million renovation demonstrates the commitment by the late athletics director Mal Moore (see page 20) to making Alabama a championship contender in all varsity sports, not just football. "It's a beautiful facility that is also highly functional," Waters said. "We took every inch of that space that we could and used it to the very best of our ability. I think the facility and everything that has gone into it makes a very definite statement that at the University of Alabama, we take our track and field very seriously."

Appropriately, Sam Bailey, the stadium's namesake, was also known for supporting the full array of Crimson Tide sports while in the athletics department. Bailey came with Bear Bryant to Alabama in 1958 as the assistant coach in charge of freshman football. In 1969, he became assistant athletics director, handling most of the duties of running the department so Bryant could concentrate on coaching. Bailey spent 30 years at Alabama. He died of lung cancer in Tuscaloosa in 1990, age 67.

Birmingham Crossplex
(Men's and Women's Indoor Track and Field)

OPENED: 2011. **SEATING CAPACITY:** 4,000.

The University of Alabama holds its indoor track and field meets at the Birmingham Crossplex, an indoor track, volleyball, and swimming facility in Birmingham. The track can be hydraulically banked or left flat, depending on the scheduled events.

Ol' Colony Golf Course (Men's and Women's Golf)

OPENED: 2000. **DESIGNER:** Jerry Pate.

Ol' Colony Golf Course, a Tuscaloosa County–owned public facility, also acts as the home course for the Alabama men's and women's golf teams. Jerry Pate, the best pro golfer the Crimson Tide has produced, designed it with the golf teams in mind. *Golf Digest* named it one of the country's top five new public courses in 2001. The site was once a farm for a mental institution named Boy's Colony.

Jerry Pate Golf Center (Men's and Women's Golf)

OPENED: 2004.

Alabama's home course is the public Ol' Colony Golf Course, but the $1 million Jerry Pate Golf Center there is a private practice facility just for the Crimson Tide men's and women's golfers. It was named for Pate, the Ol' Colony course designer and Alabama's most successful pro golfing alum. It features indoor and outdoor practice facilities, including a driving range, putting greens, chipping and hitting areas with practice bunkers and six target greens, and a swing analysis studio.

Henry Pritchett Running Park (Cross-Country)

OPENED: 1959 as the University Golf Course; became Harry Pritchett Running Park in 2003.

The former golf course was converted for cross-country use in 2003. The park can accommodate cross-country courses of 5,000, 6,000, 8,000, and 10,000 meters. The surface is grass and the terrain rolling.

Black Warrior River (Rowing)

Alabama lists the Black Warrior as the "facility" for its rowing team. A pretty darn good facility, in fact. According to the athletics department website, "It is one of the best practice and competitive courses in the nation, . . . with high banks, long, protected straightaways, and minimal current." The river also provides several excellent viewing areas, including the university-owned Park at Manderson Landing, which is near the finish line for most rowing events.

The university plans a "state-of-the-art" boathouse that would include a restaurant and a walking bridge to campus. So far, the land has been acquired.

RIVALRIES

Alabama has one great rival, and every sports fan in America knows what school it is. The rivalry plays out every Thanksgiving weekend in the football war known as the Iron Bowl. There, and in every other sport in every other venue, Crimson Tide athletes, coaches, and fans yearn for nothing other than to beat Auburn.

Individual sports programs have developed their own secondary rivalries over the years, although none approach the passions stirred by the great in-state foe. In football, the Third Saturday in October used to bring the annual Alabama-Tennessee grudge match. The game is still played, and it still represents a great rivalry. But the vagaries of Southeastern Conference divisional scheduling have meant that it now occurs on Approximately the Third Saturday in October, Give or Take a Week, which just doesn't have the same ring.

Some memorable bowl games and an annual regular-season series through the 1980s and into 1990 have turned Penn State into a significant football rival. Recent national championship battles with LSU as well as Alabama coach Nick Saban's past job as the head coach there have made games against the Tigers into something special.

Other rivalries have developed within the Southeastern Conference. In gymnastics, Alabama and Georgia have battled for not only regional but also national supremacy for three decades. Fueling the fire was the personal animosity between Alabama coach Sarah Patterson and former Georgia coach Suzanne Yoculan, who retired in 2009. In volleyball, games against LSU and Arkansas take on an extra edge.

Still, if you added together the intensities of all of the other rivalries, they wouldn't come close to the fervor behind "beat Auburn!"

CONFERENCE AFFILIATIONS

The Beginning: Southern Intercollegiate Athletic Association

In 1894, two years after it began playing intercollegiate sports (baseball and football), Alabama became a founding member of the Southern Intercollegiate Athletic Association, one of the first college conferences. The other original members were Auburn (then the Agricultural and Mechanical College of Alabama), Georgia, Georgia Tech (then the Georgia School of Technology), North Carolina, Sewanee (The University of the South), and Vanderbilt.

Invited to join the following year, 1895, as charter members were Clemson, Cumberland, Kentucky, LSU, Mercer, Mississippi, Mississippi State (then known as Mississippi A&M), Rhodes (then known as Southwest Presbyterian University), Tennessee, Texas, Tulane, and the University of Nashville (then known as Peabody Normal School; it ceased operations in 1909).

Most of the conference's larger schools defected in 1921 because of a dispute over whether freshmen should be eligible to play. The larger schools opposed freshman eligibility; the smaller schools favored it. The SIAA continued as a small-school conference until it disbanded in 1942.

Transition: Southern Conference

In February 1921, Alabama joined seven other members of the SIAA in splitting off to form the Southern Conference. Fellow SIAA defectors were Auburn, Clemson, Georgia, Georgia Tech, Kentucky, Mississippi State, and Tennessee. Also joining the new conference were Maryland, North Carolina, North Carolina State (then known as North Carolina College of Agriculture and Mechanic Arts), Virginia, Virginia Tech (then officially known as Virginia Agricultural and Mechanical College and Polytechnic Institute), and Washington and Lee.

In 1922, six more SIAA refugees joined: Florida, LSU, Mississippi, South Carolina, Tulane, and Vanderbilt. Sewanee came aboard in 1923, followed by Virginia Military Institute in 1924 and Duke in 1929.

From the beginning, that was a sprawling aggregation. Geographically, it was especially unwieldy in the days before routine air travel and interstate highways. The Southern Conference soon spawned two of today's most prominent sports leagues, the Southeastern Conference and the Atlantic Coast Conference.

Southeastern Conference Sports

The Southeastern Conference sponsors championships in 9 men's and 12 women's sports (counting indoor and outdoor track and field separately). Alabama competes in all of them except equestrian, a women's-only sport involving horseback riding skill. It's the newest SEC sport, added for the 2012–13 season. Competing schools are Auburn, Georgia, South Carolina, and Texas A&M. The official SEC sports are:

- Baseball (men's)
- Basketball (men's and women's)
- Cross-Country (men's and women's)
- Equestrian (women's)
- Football (men's)
- Golf (men's and women's)
- Gymnastics (women's)
- Soccer (women's)
- Softball (women's)
- Swimming and Diving (men's and women's)
- Tennis (men's and women's)
- Track and Field
  - Indoor (men's and women's)
  - Outdoor (men's and women's)
- Volleyball (women's)

The last original member, Virginia Tech, left in 1965. But the Southern Conference didn't die. It's still an NCAA Division I league. In football, its members compete in the Football Championship Subdivision, formerly called Division IAA.

Current conference members are Appalachian State, The Citadel, Davidson, Elon, Furman, Georgia Southern, North Carolina-Greensboro, Samford, Tennessee-Chattanooga, Western Carolina, and Wofford. In 2014, Appalachian State and Georgia Southern plan to move to the Sun Belt Conference, Davidson plans to move to the Atlantic 10 Conference, and Elon plans to move to the Colonial Athletic Association. Planning to join the Southern Conference in 2014 are East Tennessee State and Mercer, both from the Atlantic Sun Conference, and Virginia Military Institute, from the Big South Conference. VMI is currently an associate member in wrestling. Other wrestling-only associate members are Campbell, Gardner-Webb, and Southern Illinois-Edwardsville. Appalachian State is expected to remain an associate member in wrestling and men's soccer.

Final Home: Southeastern Conference

Today's most dominant college sports conference—especially in football—began in December 1932. Alabama and the other 12 Southern Conference members that lay west and south of the Appalachian Mountains broke off to form the Southeastern Conference.

Ten original members have stayed the course: Alabama, Auburn, Florida, Georgia, Kentucky, LSU, Mississippi, Mississippi State, Tennessee, and Vanderbilt. Of the other founders:

Sewanee departed in 1940, later de-emphasized athletics, and now competes in the Division III Southern Athletic Association.

Georgia Tech left in 1964 and is now a member of the Atlantic Coast Conference.

Tulane left in 1966 and now is part of Conference USA.

In 1991, the SEC swiped Arkansas from the once-mighty Southwest Conference (now defunct) and South Carolina from the Metro Conference. In 2011, it plucked Texas A&M and Missouri from the Big 12 Conference.

SEC schools compete in Division I—and, in football, in the Football Bowl Subdivision, formerly Division IA. For football purposes, the league is divided into Eastern and Western divisions, with the division winners playing for the conference championship at the end of the season.

Alabama competes in the Western Division, along with Arkansas, Auburn, LSU, Mississippi State, Mississippi, and Texas A&M. The Eastern Division consists of Florida, Georgia, Kentucky, Missouri, South Carolina, Tennessee, and Vanderbilt. (Yes, we know that Columbia, Missouri, home of the Eastern Division's Missouri Tigers, lies west of all but two of the Western Division teams, Arkansas and Texas A&M. The conference, mindful of traditional rivalries, had to make some geographic compromises while shoehorning Missouri and Texas A&M, the two newest members, into the divisional structure.)

ATHLETICS DIRECTORS

Athletics directors are like referees. They generally draw attention only when they make a mistake—such as hiring the wrong coach.

In today's athletics departments, with their multimillion-dollar budgets, athletics directors are CEOs of what amounts to a medium-size company. Getting and keeping a good one is crucial. And the demands of the job are such that it's now rare for a high-profile coach to double as athletics director, as was typical back when Bear Bryant did exactly that.

The Wallace Wade Era

We know practically nothing about Alabama's first athletics director, in 1916–20, except that we love his name: B. L. "Loonie" Noojin. Charles Bernier succeeded him for three years, and then came a titan.

Wallace Wade, who played guard for Brown from 1914 through 1916, arrived at Alabama in 1923 as head football coach and athletics director after only two years as an assistant coach (at Vanderbilt). He turned out to be a brilliant hire. In eight years, he won three national championships. When he departed unexpectedly for Duke after his third national title in 1930, Alabama again gave the AD job to a head coach—but not a head football coach.

The Hank Crisp Era

Hank Crisp was head basketball coach and an assistant football coach when he added "athletics director" to his list of titles in 1930. He did just fine in his first stint, 1930–40, hiring the man who would be Alabama's second great football coach, Frank Thomas. During his second stint (1954–1957), however, he hired Ears Whitworth (see "The Ears Whitworth Error . . . er, Era," page 42).

The Frank Thomas Era

Crisp turned the athletics director job over to football coach Frank Thomas in 1940. Thomas was a fine coach, winning national championships in 1934 and 1941 (though the 1941 claim is dubious; see "National Championships," page 53). As an administrator, he had to deal with the disruptions of World War II and then with his own failing health that forced him to give up coaching after the 1946 season. He stayed as athletics director until 1952. In retrospect, perhaps having an increasingly ill man in charge of the athletics department had something to do with the lean football years of the 1950s.

The Bear Bryant Era

Pete Cawthorn succeeded Thomas for three years before Crisp returned to the job. The Ears Whitworth debacle made both the football coach and athletics director posts available to a man who needs no introduction, Paul "Bear" Bryant. He ran the athletics department with gruff benevolence and a genuine desire to see all sports, not just football, succeed. One of his hires is still winning national championships today: gymnastics coach Sarah Patterson (see page 363).

The Hootie Ingram Era

After Bear Bryant died in 1983, Ray Perkins donned the mantles of both football coach and athletics director. He wore

Frank Thomas statue,
Alabama campus
Credit: The George F. Landegger Collection of Alabama Photographs in Carol M. Highsmith's America, Library of Congress, Prints and Photographs Division

Bear Bryant statue,
Alabama campus
Credit: Clara Williams

them uncomfortably. When he left in 1987, the jobs were split—permanently, one suspects. Former Alabama quarterback Steve Sloan became athletics director and hired Bill Curry as football coach, which never really worked out. Then, in 1989, another former Alabama player became athletics director: Cecil "Hootie" Ingram, who had been doing the same job at Florida State.

Ingram hired Gene Stallings to coach football, which worked out quite well, at least at first. Stallings' 1992 team won the national championship. But a series of NCAA rules violations under his and Stallings' watch led to a reprimand from the NCAA, and Ingram resigned in 1995.

The Mal Moore Era

After Hootie Ingram's departure, the Alabama administration passed over assistant athletics director, longtime assistant coach, and former Bear Bryant quarterback Mal Moore in favor of outsider Bob Bockrath. An outsider Bockrath remained, right through his departure in 1999, which was followed the next year by the firing of the football coach that he'd hired, Mike DuBose.

This time, Moore got his chance. In 1999, he got the AD job.

He made some missteps in the area of football coaches—Dennis Franchione, Mike Price, Mike Shula. But Moore brought stability to the athletics department. And he learned from his mistakes. After Shula's firing, Moore went for the best coach available, Nick Saban—who, as the Miami Dolphins' head coach, was theoretically not even available.

Moore hired him anyway in 2007. Coincidentally or not, that's the same year the Alabama Sports Hall of Fame inducted Moore.

Three national championships later (2009, 2011, 2012), everybody was happy. Until March 2013. Moore had been hospitalized the previous August with an irregular heartbeat, but he went home after two days. As far as the public knew, everything was fine at the athletics director's corner office in the Mal M. Moore Athletic Facility. But on March 20, the news that serious lung problems had forced Moore to retire stunned Crimson Tide Nation. Ten days later, the surprise turned to grief. Moore died at the Duke University Medical Center in Durham, North Carolina. He was 73.

Moore was an exceptional leader of Alabama's athletics program, but everyone who knew him insists that he was an even better human being. (See "Mal Moore, Nick Saban's Secret Weapon," page 22.) In tribute, Alabama players for the 2013 season wore a decal on the backs of their helmets that read simply "MAL"—all capital letters, with the "A" printed in the trademark

Alabama script. To replace him, at least as athletics director, the university hired a close friend and former teammate, Bill Battle, who was head coach at Crimson Tide rival Tennessee for seven years, beginning in 1970 at age 28. After being forced out at Tennessee following the 1976 season, he launched a very successful career in the business world. Among other things, he founded The Collegiate Licensing Company, the country's largest licenser and marketer of collegiate trademarks. The company's first client was the University of Alabama.

Alabama Athletics Directors

B. L. "Loonie" Noojin, 1916–20	Steve Sloan, 1987–89
Charles A. Bernier, 1920–23	Thomas Jones, 1989 (interim)
Wallace Wade, 1923–30	Cecil "Hootie" Ingram, 1989–95
Hank Crisp, 1930–40, 1954–57	Glen Tuckett, 1995–96 (interim)
Frank Thomas, 1940–52	Bob Bockrath, 1996–99
Pete Cawthon, 1952–54	Finus Gaston, 1999 (interim)
Paul "Bear" Bryant, 1957–83	Mal Moore, 1999–2013
Ray Perkins, 1983–87	Bill Battle, 2013

ALL-AMERICA, ALL-CONFERENCE, ALL-WHAT?

You won't see a lot of mention in this book of All-America, All-Conference, or other All-Whatever lists. Nor do we cite many Player of the Year, Coach of the Year, or similar awards. We don't mean to slight anyone. But All-America and other such designations have proliferated to such an extent that what was once an honor has become almost an entitlement. If you have a halfway decent season, somebody somewhere will put you on an All-America team— even if it's the second team. Or the third.

In football, the NCAA recognizes All-America teams selected by the Associated Press, American Football Coaches Association, Football Writers Association of America, *Sporting News*, and Walter Camp Football

continued on page 27

Mal Moore, Nick Saban's Secret Weapon

Mal Moore was such a nice guy that people focused on his personality and overlooked his accomplishments. Even many of the most fanatic Alabama fans don't realize how profoundly he improved Crimson Tide athletics.

He did get off to a shaky start as athletics director (see page 20). But by the sudden, heartbreaking end of his 14-year tenure in March 2013, he had presided over eight national championships in four different sports (football, gymnastics, women's golf, softball) as well as 19 Southeastern Conference titles (football, basketball, baseball, gymnastics, men's and women's golf, men's cross-country, softball) and more than $240 million in capital improvements to University of Alabama athletics facilities.

Mal Moore
Credit: Official White House Photo by Lawrence Jackson

During most of that time, he dealt every day with deep personal tragedy.

In 1999, when Moore succeeded Bob Bockrath as athletics director, his department's annual budget was $36 million. When Moore died on March 30, 2013, the budget exceeded $100 million. *Sports Business Journal* and *Sports Business Daily* posthumously named him the college athletics director of the year. Moore's deft handling of the logistics and business sides of Alabama sports left Nick Saban and the other Crimson Tide coaches free to concentrate on coaching.

Bear Bryant was both head football coach and athletics director from the time he arrived at Alabama in 1958 until he retired as coach following the 1982 Liberty Bowl. That dual role, once the norm in college sports, had grown uncommon by then. Today, it's about as rare as letting a quarterback call his own plays. Among Bryant's contemporaries, Coach Darrell Royal at Texas also wore both hats. Dan Devine at Missouri, Frank Broyles at Arkansas, and John McKay at Southern California added the athletics directorship during the last few years of their coaching tenures. But Auburn Coach Shug Jordan had Jeff Beard as athletics director, Mississippi's Johnny Vaught had Tad Smith, Ohio State's Woody Hayes had Dick Larkins, Notre Dame's Ara Parseghian had Moose Krause, Michigan's Bo Schembechler had Don Canham, and Penn State's Joe Paterno had Ernie McCoy.

Even in that simpler era, no one man, not even the Bear, could really handle two such demanding jobs at a high-profile institution like Alabama. Bryant himself implied as much when he turned over many of the athletics director's day-to-day responsibilities to Sam Bailey (see page 13) after the football team slipped to a record of 6-5 in 1969.

What if Bryant had had his own Mal Moore—a full-time athletics director? Would Saban be chasing not a mark of six Bryant national championships at Alabama, but maybe seven? Eight? More? It's impossible to know, but fun to speculate.

Moore never aspired to run the athletics department. He wanted Bryant's other job: head football coach. He played at Alabama as a backup quarterback for Bryant, sparingly, accumulating enough game time to earn a varsity letter only in 1962, his senior year. In 1964, he became a graduate assistant coach under Bryant. In 1971, he moved up to quarterbacks coach. In 1976, Bryant appointed Moore as Alabama's first-ever offensive coordinator.

"He didn't panic," said Cecil "Hootie" Ingram, the athletics director who, in 1994, hired Moore as associate athletics director in charge of fund-raising. "He was always cool. Calling plays for Coach Bryant can put a lot of ice water in your veins."

Moore loved coaching, especially at Alabama. But when the Bear retired after the 1982 season, Moore not only didn't get the top job, but he also lost the job he had. New Coach Ray Perkins brought in his own crew of assistants.

Moore became an assistant coach at Notre Dame in 1983, then coached for four years as an assistant to Gene Stallings with the Cardinals of the National Football League, first in St. Louis and then, after the team moved, in Phoenix. When Stallings became the Alabama head coach in 1990, Moore came back to Tuscaloosa as assistant head coach and quarterbacks coach.

Mal Moore, Nick Saban's Secret Weapon (continued)

Back in 1968, when the handsome young assistant coach's career was beginning to take off, he had married a beautiful special-education teacher from Tuscaloosa named Charlotte Davis. By all accounts, the honeymoon never ended.

During the 1993 season, Moore started getting calls to come home in the middle of the day. The phone began ringing more frequently, eventually almost hourly. Charlotte was diagnosed with Alzheimer's disease. She was only 55 years old. Moore couldn't fulfill the responsibilities of coaching and care for her at the same time. So in 1994 he gave up one of his loves in order to tend to the other—the one whom he had vowed to cherish in sickness and in health. Ingram's offer for him to move into fundraising gave Moore the flexible hours he needed.

Charlotte spent the last several years of her life at LaRocca Nursing Home in Tuscaloosa. Every single day that he was in town, Moore visited her.

"Someone asked why he would visit every day if she didn't know who he was," said Lyman Hardy, former director at LaRocca. "He answered, 'But I know who she is.' That's just the perfect example of what you should see in a marriage. He was such a good soul, a kind and decent man."

During a 2009 interview with Don Kausler Jr. of the *Birmingham News*, Moore's eyes filled with tears as he revealed, "She's not said my name in 10 years." His Charlotte finally slipped completely away from him on January 18, 2010. She was 71. She and Mal had been married for 41 years.

Saban, in a university statement released upon Moore's death, said, "We can talk about all the championships Mal has been involved with, but I think what will be remembered most was the man he was. He always put the best interests of others ahead of his own, he carried himself as a first-class gentleman, and he helped bring out the best in those around him.

"Mal was an outstanding leader in terms of all he did for Alabama athletics. Most importantly, he was a great friend to me and my family. Mal was the number one reason we decided to make the move to Tuscaloosa."

When Moore began working to lure Saban to Alabama in late 2006, Saban, then coaching the Miami Dolphins, decided he wasn't interested. He picked up the phone to tell his wife. "I called Terry and said, 'I don't think I'm going to talk to these guys,' and she said, 'Oh, Mal is already here. We've been talking for an hour.'"

Moore's fund-raising prowess prepared the way for Saban's success. "The administration before him had recognized the needs," said Paul Bryant Jr., son of the legendary coach and president of the university's Board of Trustees, "but they hadn't been able to project that to the alumni and supporters of the university."

Moore got the message across, and the wallets began opening. "Our facilities may have been the worst in the conference," he said later. "It was very difficult for our coaches to recruit. We knew what had to be done."

And he did it: two renovations of the football stadium; a renovation of the indoor practice facility used by the football, baseball, soccer, and softball teams; two renovations of the auditorium used for men's basketball games and gymnastics meets; an upgrade to the gymnastics practice facility; a major renovation of the women's basketball and volleyball facility; a renovation of the baseball stadium; the construction and three rapid-fire expansions of the softball stadium; a renovation of the swimming and diving center; the construction of the soccer stadium; the construction of the outdoor and indoor tennis facilities; two renovations of the track and field stadium; the construction of the golf teams' home course and practice facility; the conversion of a former golf course into a cross-country running park; and the creation of the Sarah Patterson Champions Plaza to honor national championship–winning teams and coaches in all sports.

It's no accident that Alabama's first national titles in any sport besides football and gymnastics occurred on Moore's watch. The 2011–12 academic year brought an astonishing four championships, in football, gymnastics, softball, and women's golf. The following year, the football team again reached the pinnacle, and the men's golf team added its own title, two months and three days after Moore's death.

Dennis Pursley, whom Moore hired as swimming and diving coach before the 2012–13 season, said, "I've spent my entire career working with college coaches around the country and hearing them sing the blues that their athletics directors were one-track football people, but Coach Moore wasn't that way. . . . He's the reason that we have the environment we do at the university and the athletics department, where everyone supports one another and cares what happens in all the sports across the board."

Mal Moore, Nick Saban's Secret Weapon (continued)

At the same time, in any competitive enterprise, loyalty can go too far. Bryant began telling confidants that he wanted to retire a couple of years before he finally hung up his houndstooth hat. But he said he couldn't quit because too many people depended on him for jobs. It may be sacrilegious to say this, but if people can keep their jobs only as long as you're around, then perhaps they shouldn't really be on the payroll. Moore built a skilled athletics staff, changed coaches when he needed to, and conveyed the message that at Alabama, there was no such thing as a minor sport.

Softball Coach Patrick Murphy recalled the damp June night at the 2012 Women's College World Series in Oklahoma City when Alabama won its first-ever national softball championship. "When he went up to the World Series last year and stood out in the rain with everybody else, it meant a lot to everyone in the program. Not just to that team but the kids on all 17 teams."

On the day he stepped down, Moore met with Bill Battle, the man who was to succeed him. Moore's lungs were failing. They would give out entirely 10 days later. But Battle said his old friend summoned the energy to sketch out everything that he thought still needed to be accomplished at the school to which he had devoted so much of his life.

On April 5, 2013, a cool, cloudy day with spring flowers in bloom, Moore came home to tiny Dozier (population 391), the South Alabama town where his heroics as a high-school quarterback in the 1950s earned him the opportunity to play for the Crimson Tide. He had always kept in touch with his family and childhood friends. They welcomed him back for the last time, with fond sorrow, and laid him to rest in a private graveside ceremony.

That day, Priscilla Kimbro, who had been a cheerleader all those years ago when Moore starred at now-closed Dozier High, summed up the feelings of the town, and of all the Crimson Tide faithful: "He was just a good guy."

Foundation. Of those, the AFCA, FWAA, and *Sporting News* pick only a first team. The Walter Camp Foundation, which traces its roots back to the first All-America selections in 1889, picks a first team and a second team. The AP picks first, second, and third teams.

If all five selectors list you on the first team, you're a "unanimous" All-America selection. If three of the five do so, you're a "consensus" pick.

Those five are not the only organizations that publish an All-America football team. Others who get in on the fun include (at the moment, anyway), *Sports Illustrated, Pro Football Weekly,* ESPN, CBS Sports, *College Football News,* Scout.com, SB Nation, college football preseason preview writer Phil Steele, and Yahoo! Sports, not to mention lots of individual newspapers and lesser-known websites.

And that's just the Division I Football Bowl Subdivision (formerly Division IA). It doesn't include the Division I Football Championship Subdivision (formerly Division IAA) or Division II or III, or the National Association of Intercollegiate Athletics, or the Academic All-America recognition bestowed by the College Sports Information Directors of America.

So when we see someone described as an All-American, we're not sure what that means. According to whom? First, second, or third team? Consensus? Unanimous? We're similarly uncertain about such designations as Player of the Year and Coach of the Year.

Therefore, we try to steer clear of this thicket as much as we can. We think you'll enjoy reading about the players in this book, regardless of whether they made somebody's All-Something list.

TITLE IX AND WOMEN'S SPORTS

Some 40 years after the federal law popularly known as Title IX was enacted, it still stirs passions—for and against.

The 1972 law reads, in part: "No person in the United States shall, on the basis of sex, be excluded from participation in, be denied the benefits of, or be subjected to discrimination under any education program or activity receiving Federal financial assistance."

Virtually every U.S. college and university receives federal funds. In effect, Title IX has forced most schools to provide intercollegiate athletic opportunities for women in proportion to their representation in the student body. Basically, if a college with a 50-50 gender split among students fields men's teams that total 100 athletes, then it more or less has to field women's teams that total 100 athletes as well.

No one disputes that Title IX has greatly increased the opportunities for and numbers of female collegiate athletes. Critics say it has also reduced opportunities for and numbers of male collegiate athletes. If our hypothetical school with the 50-50 gender split among the general student body has slots for 100 male athletes but for only 50 female athletes, it can either add women's sports or cut men's sports, or both.

Often, it's easier and cheaper to cut men's sports, especially if they're "nonrevenue" sports—in other words, if the costs to field the team exceed the income generated from ticket sales and other revenue sources. Except for football and basketball, most sports at most universities are nonrevenue.

Without Title IX, would Alabama have both men's and women's varsity soccer teams, instead of the current lineup of varsity women's soccer and club men's soccer? It's impossible to say for sure. Maybe.

But without Title IX, would Alabama have started a women's gymnastics team in 1975? Maybe not. And if not, it would have missed out on six national championships and an atmosphere for home meets at Coleman Coliseum that rivals football Saturdays for energy and excitement. That would have been a shame.

When his Alabama softball team won the Southeastern Conference championship in May 2012—en route to a national championship—coach Patrick Murphy said, "It's the 40th anniversary of Title IX, so to have this type of crowd and this type of media presence for women's softball is just incredible in my mind."

THE MILLION DOLLAR BAND

In 2003, the John Philip Sousa Foundation bestowed on Alabama's Million Dollar Band the Sudler Trophy, awarded annually at that time (now every other year) to a college or university marching band that has demonstrated top musical and marching ability over a period of years. No band can win more than once.

The ensemble began as a military band in 1914. It got its name in 1922, when an Atlanta sportswriter, during a 33–7 thrashing of Alabama by Georgia Tech, said to Alabama alumnus W. C. Pickens, "You don't have much of a team. What do you have at Alabama?"

Pickens replied, "A million-dollar band."

The Million Dollar Band performs at the 2010 Alabama–Penn State football game in Tuscaloosa.
Credit: Matthew Tosh

Or at least that's one version of the story. Everybody does agree that Colonel Carleton K. Butler (he received the honorary title from the campus ROTC in 1935) built the band to its current national prominence during his 1935–69 tenure as director. Today, with more than 400 students as members, the band is the largest single organization on campus.

GIMME AN . . .

If you've ever seen a cheerleading competition on TV, then you know that cheerleading these days deserves status as a sport all its own. Today's cheer and dance routines involve some incredibly athletic (and dangerous) moves. Alabama warns potential cheerers: "In addition to practice, the cheerleaders are required to attend weightlifting/workout sessions."

The university has two cheerleading squads, plus Big Al, the elephant mascot. The Crimson Squad (a minimum of 11 men and 9 women) cheers for all home and away football games and men's basketball games. The White Squad (a minimum of 20 women) cheers for women's basketball games, gymnastics meets, volleyball games, and all home football games. Members of both squads can try out for the team that Alabama sends to competitions. In 2011, the Crimson Tide cheer squad won the College Cheerleading and Dance Team National Championships, hosted by Universal Cheerleaders Association in Orlando, Florida.

Big Al is such a busy guy that it takes five students to meet all of his costumed commitments.

Alabama mascot Big Al got his name from a student vote.
Credit: Wikimedia Commons

RED LINES, CRIMSON TIDES, AND ELEPHANTS

More than a century ago, newspaper writers often referred to the University of Alabama football team as the "Crimson White," after the school colors. Or the team was simply called "the varsity."

Then sportswriters came up with a more imaginative moniker, "The Thin Red Line." That was a reference to an 1853 Crimean War battle. A small, red-coated British regiment, strung out in a thin line only two men deep (instead of the usual four), held off a charge by a much larger Russian cavalry force.

Whether sportswriters actually knew their Crimean War history is debatable, but you have to admit it was a pretty cool nickname. In 1907, Hugh Roberts of the *Birmingham Age-Herald* came up with something even cooler. That year's Alabama-Auburn game took place in a sea of mud. Roberts described the Alabama men surging like a Crimson Tide against their heavily favored opponents, holding Auburn (then formally known as the Alabama Polytechnic Institute) to a 6-6 tie.

That was the last Alabama-Auburn game until 1948, but the new nickname caught on. Zipp Newman, an influential writer and sports editor at the *Birmingham News,* took a liking to the name and helped popularize it.

In 1930, elephants entered the picture. *Atlanta Journal* sportswriter Everett Strupper covered the Alabama-Mississippi game that year. Alabama coach Wallace Wade played his second team for the entire first quarter. Then, Strupper wrote, "At the end of the quarter, the earth started to tremble, there was a distant rumble that continued to grow. Some excited fan in the stands bellowed, 'Hold your horses, the elephants are coming,' and out stamped the Alabama varsity. It was the first time that I had seen it and the size of the entire eleven nearly knocked me cold, men that I had seen play last year looking like they had nearly doubled in size."

Obviously, Strupper was a pretty excitable guy. What, one wonders, would he have called today's 350-pound linemen? Mammoths? Whales? Anyway, he and other writers began referring to the Alabama linemen as "Red Elephants," and the name stuck.

RAMMER JAMMER

Generally viewed with distaste by administrators but beloved by fans, the Rammer Jammer cheer remains a fixture at the end of Alabama victories, especially big ones. If the loser is, for example, the Auburn Tigers, the cheer goes:

Hey, Tigers!
Hey, Tigers!
Hey, Tigers!
We just beat the hell outta you!
Rammer jammer, yellowhammer,
Give 'em hell, Alabama!

The Rammer-Jammer was a student humor and literary magazine published from 1924 until 1956, and the woodpecker known as the yellowhammer or northern flicker is Alabama's state bird.

Before we go on to talk about the sport that Bear Bryant invented, or at least perfected, let's hear that other favorite Alabama cheer one time from everybody:

ROOOOLLLLLLLLLL TIIIIIIIIIIIIIIIIIDE!

FOOTBALL

Do we really need to tell you about Alabama football? More to the point, can we tell you anything about Alabama football that you don't already know?

We think so. Otherwise, we wouldn't have gone to all the trouble of creating this book.

We count 306 Crimson Tide football players who have gone on to play at least one game in the National Football League, American Football League, All-America Football Conference, or Canadian Football League (as of the 2012 NFL season). This chapter contains capsule biographies of 158 of those players, plus a chart sketching out the college and pro careers of the other 148.

You already know many of the greats, of course: Joe Namath, Ken Stabler, Cornelius Bennett, Dwight Stephenson, Ozzie Newsome—and, going further back, Bart Starr, Lee Roy Jordan, even Dixie Howell and the astonishing Don Hutson. But you may not know which of those greats almost didn't even make it to the pros (see page 159). Or which one you should follow on Twitter (see page 136). Or which one said recently, "I can honestly say I enjoy doing what I'm doing now more than when I was a player" (see page 86).

We hope you'll also enjoy getting to know some players you've lost track of or maybe have never even heard of. There's the tight end who had a brief but, for a football player, appropriate movie career (see page 140); the old coach who came out of an 11-year retirement at age 70 to take over the football team at a community college (see page 140); the fullback who, facing a slow-developing, fatal illness, told an interviewer, "I'm at peace. I don't want to die, but I'm not afraid to. I look at it as a new adventure" (see page 162).

We've also pulled together some historical perspective on NCAA football in general and Alabama football in particular. If that's not your thing, feel free to skip ahead to the player bios. As long as you don't mind missing the real story behind Alabama's worst football coach—and some numbers that affirm the genius of the Crimson Tide's best.

DIVISIONS AND SUBDIVISIONS

The National Collegiate Athletic Association splits its football-playing members into three divisions—or, depending on how you count, four. They are:

- **Division I, which generally consists of the major football schools. It is subdivided into:**

   The Football Bowl Subdivision, formerly known as Division IA and commonly (if clumsily) called Division I FBS.

The Football Championship Subdivision, formerly known as Division IAA and commonly (if equally clumsily) called Division I FCS.

- **Division II, in which the schools tend to be smaller.**

- **Division III, in which the schools are usually smaller yet.**

The big-time programs play in Division I FBS—124 schools as of 2013. (One additional university, Georgia State, is scheduled to achieve full membership in 2014, and four more in 2015: Appalachian State, Georgia Southern, North Carolina-Charlotte, and Old Dominion.) That's Alabama's subdivision. It's the only NCAA sport or subdivision that does not have a postseason playoff to determine its national champion, although that will change with the new four-team playoff plan that's scheduled to begin with the 2014 season. Division I FBS had not previously had a playoff out of deference to the postseason bowl games. Since the first one, the 1902 Rose Bowl, their numbers have increased to 35 as of 2013.

The NCAA anoints no official champion in this top division. Various ratings groups make their selections at the end of the year. Most prominent are the Associated Press poll of sportswriters and a coaches poll that has been conducted by several different entities (currently *USA Today*). Sometimes they agree; sometimes they don't.

Starting with the 1992 season, an alliance of postseason bowl games and major conferences plus powerful independent Notre Dame has attempted to create a de facto national championship, using various polls and computer ranking systems to pick what it thinks are that season's two best teams. Since 1998, the alliance has been known as the Bowl Championship Series.

The coaches poll agreed to vote the BCS champion number one in its final ranking. The AP poll did not. Since the BCS system started, it has differed only once, favoring Southern California in 2003 instead of BCS champion LSU. Still, because of arguments over its selection process, the BCS system seems to have made little, if any, progress toward the goal of crowning a universally acknowledged national champion.

Division I FCS schools (125 in 2013) have a 24-team championship playoff that begins in late November. As of 2013, the FCS consisted of 124 teams, including four—Appalachian State, Georgia Southern, North Carolina-Charlotte, and Old Dominion—that will move to the FBS in 2015. Abilene Christian and Incarnate Word will join the FCS in 2014, and East Tennessee

State and Kennesaw State in 2015. The national championship game takes place in early January. Both FCS and FBS schools are allowed a maximum of 85 players on scholarship. But all FBS scholarships are full rides. FCS schools get the equivalent of only 63 full scholarships to divide up.

Two FCS conferences don't participate in the tournament. The Ivy League de-emphasized football in 1945 because of academic concerns. The Southwestern Athletic Conference, made up of 10 historically black colleges and universities, splits its schools into two divisions and plays a conference championship game. Both that contest and the Bayou Classic, an annual postseason battle between SWAC members Grambling and Southern, take place during the FCS tournament.

In Division II, 168 schools play football as of 2013, with Limestone and Paine scheduled to join the fun in 2014. Division II teams are allowed to offer the equivalent of up to 36 full scholarships.

In Division III, 233 schools played football in 2013, with Southern Virginia scheduled to become a full competitor in 2014. The Newport News Apprentice School in Virginia also plays a Division III schedule, but it does not grant degrees, so the Apprentice Builders are not actually members of the NCAA or any other collegiate sports organization. Members of Division III do not offer athletic scholarships. Their 32-team tournament also begins in mid-November and ends with the championship in mid-December.

Some smaller colleges and universities are members of the National Association of Intercollegiate Athletics. Of its 265 members (as of 2013), 84 play football. Southeastern University of Lakeland, Florida, is scheduled to become the 85th in 2014.

And then there's the Collegiate Sprint Football League. Formerly known as the Eastern Lightweight Football League and before that the Eastern 150-pound Football League, it dates back to 1934. It currently has eight members: Penn, Princeton, Cornell, Navy, Army, Mansfield University, Post University, and Franklin Pierce University. At those schools, sprint football is a varsity sport. It follows the familiar college football rules, but players must weigh no more than 172 pounds and have a minimum body fat of 5 percent (to discourage excessive weight loss). Those with less than 5 percent body fat may weigh no more than 165 pounds.

There's no postseason tournament. Regular-season records determine the league champion.

Fabled football coach Paul "Bear" Bryant liked to watch pregame warm-ups while leaning against a goalpost, looking as if he owned the stadium. Which, for all practical purposes, he did.

Credit: Paul W. Bryant Museum/The University of Alabama

HEAD COACHES

One man casts a giant shadow over the head-coaching position at Alabama, even though at least three other titans have also held the job. "His nickname was Bear," said one of his star players, Joe Namath (see page 136). "Now imagine a guy that can carry the nickname Bear."

No need to imagine. Three decades after his death (Has it really been that long?), Alabama fans retain vivid memories of the tall, gravel-voiced colossus in a houndstooth hat: Paul "Bear" Bryant.

During Bryant's 25 years in charge of Alabama football, the game was changing rapidly. He changed with it—much more than most fans probably remember. Early in his Alabama tenure, he preferred small, fast linemen. But when the behemoths become dominant, he got some of his own and dominated right back. He liked to run the ball, but he also won with such pass-oriented quarterbacks as Joe Namath and Ken Stabler. (As a player Bryant was, after all, an end.)

In the early 1970s, he switched with just a month's preparation to the then-novel wishbone formation. If he were coaching today, he'd have his quarterback running the spread offense out of the shotgun formation. Or maybe he'd invent something even better. In any case, we know one thing: he'd be winning.

Alabama's biggest change during Bryant's tenure, with the broadest implications, came in 1970: integration. Some say the wily Bear scheduled a home game against Southern California in 1970 because he knew that Southern Cal's black athletes would embarrass the all-white Crimson Tide. They did indeed; African-American running back Sam Cunningham gained 135 yards and scored two touchdowns as the Trojans beat the Tide, 42–21, at Birmingham's Legion Field. Jerry Claiborne, a former Bryant assistant coach, famously said, "Sam Cunningham did more to integrate Alabama in 60 minutes than Martin Luther King did in 20 years."

Well . . . that's insulting to the memory of King's tireless work and suffering. And, though not many knew it yet, Bryant had already integrated Alabama's football team. Alabama freshman-team receiver Wilbur Jackson, the first African-American offered a scholarship at the University of Alabama, watched the Southern Cal game from the stands. (Freshmen were not eligible for varsity play at the time.)

The next year's Alabama team that took on Southern Cal in a season-opening rematch in Los Angeles included both Jackson, who had switched to running back, and African-American John Mitchell, a defensive end. Alabama, running a wishbone offense that Bryant had secretly installed, got revenge, 17–10.

Integration came not soon enough for some, too soon for many. Just seven years previously, on Alabama's campus, Governor George Wallace had made his segregationist "Stand in the Schoolhouse Door" (see page 411). That same year, a church bombing in Birmingham killed four African-American girls.

Bryant was such a commanding figure in Alabama that he could have forced integration earlier. Whether it would have been accepted at that point by the Alabama public is another question. Whatever the merits of his timing, Bryant prepared carefully so that when integration did come, it would be seen as a success.

Bryant's most dominant decade in coaching was his last, the 1970s, when his teams won three national championships and an incredible eight Southeastern Conference titles. He won his last national championship in 1979 at age 66. He never let the game pass him by.

The Beginning

In the first four decades of Alabama football, no coach stayed more than four years. The very first coach, E. B. Beaumont, may also have been the first to get fired for losing to Auburn (then the Agricultural and Mechanical College of Alabama). His team went 2-2 but ended the season by falling to Auburn, 32–22. The university yearbook said, "We were unfortunate in securing a coach. After keeping him for a short time, we found that his knowledge of the game was very limited. We therefore got rid of him."

Another one-season coach, G. H. Harvey (some sources say George Roy Harvey) remains the only man ever to coach both Alabama and Auburn. His 1901 Alabama team went 2-1-2; his record while coaching Auburn in 1893 was 2-0-2.

In 1923, things changed.

The Wallace Wade Era

Wallace Wade has a stadium named after him. But it's not at Alabama. It's at Duke.

Alabama won a bidding war with Kentucky for Wade's services as football coach in 1923. He had been an assistant for two years at Vanderbilt, helping the Commodores compile a record of 15-0-2. In his first season, the Crimson Tide went 7-2-1 and finished second in the Southern Conference. In his second season, the Tide went 8-1 and won the conference title. In his third season, Alabama went 10-0 and won its first national championship.

That 1925 season and its climax, the 20–19 Rose Bowl victory over heavily favored Washington, jolted American sportswriters and fans into taking Southern football seriously. Alabama laid claim to another national championship the following year. And another in 1930.

And then, after the 1930 season, Wade quit.

He shocked the football world by moving to Durham, North Carolina, to coach Duke. Today, that would be like moving from Alabama's football program to, well, Duke's. Wade didn't explain the move, but he continued his success. He won no more national championships, but his Duke teams had a record of 110-36-7 in 16 seasons.

Wade took three years off from football during World War II to enlist, at age 49, in the Army. He saw combat in the Battle of Normandy and the Battle of the Bulge, then returned to coach Duke from 1946 through 1950. He was commissioner of the Southern Conference from 1951 through 1960. In 1967, Duke renamed its football stadium Wallace Wade Stadium. Wade died in Durham in 1986. He was 94.

After his retirement, Wade told an interviewer that he left Alabama in order to direct a total athletics program, including intramural sports. He wanted to incorporate sports into the collegiate experience for all students. He thought that a private university such as Duke offered a better opportunity to do that without the pressure from government officials sometimes found at public universities such as Alabama.

Wade, Frank Thomas, Bear Bryant, and Gene Stallings are the four Alabama coaches in the College Football Hall of Fame (see page 179). They plus Harold "Red" Drew, Ray Perkins, and, as of 2013, Nick Saban are also in the Alabama Sports Hall of Fame.

Alabama coach Wallace Wade mysteriously left for Duke after the 1930 season, explaining himself only years afterward. This is his statue in Walk of Champions Plaza on campus.

Credit: The George F. Landegger Collection of Alabama Photographs in Carol M. Highsmith's America, Library of Congress, Prints and Photographs Division

The Frank Thomas Era

Alabama's first great coach, Wallace Wade, hired the second great coach, Frank Thomas, to succeed him. Thomas had a remarkable career, posted a sterling record as head coach, and yet wound up as something of a tragic figure.

Thomas played quarterback under legendary coach Knute Rockne at Notre Dame from 1920 through 1922. His roommate and best friend was George "The Gipper" Gipp. At Alabama, he coached Bear Bryant as well as Alabama's greatest pro player ever, Don Hutson (see page 112), Bryant's teammate and close friend. He also hired Bryant as an assistant coach in 1936.

Thomas ranks second to Bryant in career victories with 115. Over his 15-year coaching career at Alabama, his teams allowed an astonishing average of only 6.3 points per game. Not many coaches can boast a lower average of points per game than wins per season (7.7 in Thomas's case). He won four Southeastern Conference championships and, according to Alabama's reckoning, two national titles (though the claim for 1934 is stronger than for 1941).

A heart condition and high blood pressure forced him to coach most of the 1946 team's practices from a trailer because he could no longer stand for long periods. He stepped down as head coach after that season but clung to his other job as athletics director until 1952. He died in 1954, age 55.

The Red Drew Era

When Frank Thomas's health forced him to relinquish the reins as head football coach, he—in his capacity as athletics director—reached over to the University of Mississippi to hire his replacement, Harold "Red" Drew.

Drew had one year of big-time coaching experience: 1946, when his Mississippi team went 2-7. In nine other years of coaching at Trinity College in Connecticut, Birmingham-Southern College in Birmingham, and the University of Chattanooga (now Tennessee-Chattanooga), he had managed just five winning seasons.

He started well enough in 1947, taking the Crimson Tide to an 8-3 record and a Sugar Bowl berth—though Alabama lost the bowl to Texas, 27–7. But frustration soon set in. Under Drew, the Tide would threaten to slip into mediocrity (records of 6-4-1 and 6-3-1 in 1948–49) then redeem itself (9-2 in 1950 with a 34–0 pasting of Auburn), then stumble again (5-6 in 1951).

A 4-5-2 season in 1954 that included a 28–0 loss to Auburn finally sealed his doom. Unfortunately, it caused Alabama to lurch from inconsistency to disaster.

Drew died in 1979 in Tuscaloosa, age 84.

The Ears Whitworth Error . . . er, Era

It wasn't his fault. That, at least, was the conclusion of *Birmingham Weekly* in 2009, when it examined the much-reviled 1955–57 tenure of Jennings Bryan "Ears" Whitworth as Alabama football coach.

Whitworth debuted with an 0-10 season in 1955—one of only two winless campaigns ever for Alabama. (The team went 0-4 in 1895.) His record didn't get much better in 1956 and 1957: 2-7-1 each year, with shutout losses in 1957 to LSU, Texas Christian, Tennessee, Tulane, and, most unforgivably, Auburn (40–0). Whitworth's three-year mark: 4-24-2.

Matt Hooper of *Birmingham Weekly* blamed not Whitworth but rather his boss, athletics director Hank Crisp. Hooper wrote that even after becoming athletics director in 1954, Crisp had retained his longtime position as line coach. In other words, one of head coach Red Drew's subordinates that year was also his boss. "Since he wanted to continue this unusual arrangement for the foreseeable future," Hooper wrote, "Crisp needed to find a coach he could easily manipulate."

Whitworth was, like his head-coaching successor, Bear Bryant, an Arkansas boy—from Blytheville, 60 miles north of Memphis. He lettered for the Crimson Tide in 1930 and 1931 as a tackle and sometime kicker. His extra-point kick capped the scoring in Alabama's 24-0 victory over Washington State in the 1931 Rose Bowl.

After his playing career, Whitworth stayed on the sideline as an assistant coach for Alabama, LSU, and Georgia (and as baseball coach for the Crimson Tide and the Bulldogs). As head football coach at Oklahoma A&M (now Oklahoma State) from 1950 through 1954, he did pretty well at a school not known for football prowess. After three losing seasons, he led the 1953 team to a 7-3 record, which tied for the Missouri Valley Conference championship. He stayed a winner, barely, the next season at 5-4-1.

Crisp offered Whitworth his dream job under nightmare conditions. Ears (one glance at a photo shows why the nickname was inevitable) could become head coach at his alma mater, but he had to retain his predecessor's assistant coaches—especially his boss-cum-line coach. It also turned out that shaky recruiting by Drew had left Alabama short of good players. And the

After starting his Alabama coaching career 0-14, Ears Whitworth wept as his players carried him off the field following his first win, 13–12, over Mississippi State on October 27, 1956.

Credit: Paul W. Bryant Museum/The University of Alabama

Tide, thanks to Crisp's scheduling, played a crushingly strong set of rivals. Of Alabama's 10 opponents in Whitworth's rookie year, eight were ranked in the Associated Press top 20 poll at some time during the season.

So, yeah, Whitworth wasn't a very good coach. But it's a business axiom that managers must put subordinates in positions where they can succeed. Whitworth's boss, Hank Crisp, failed to do that. The two of them did make at least one positive contribution to Alabama's football legacy. They both departed after the 1957 season, clearing the way for Bryant to take full control of the program as both football coach and athletics director.

Whitworth returned to coaching in 1959 as an assistant at Georgia. The Bulldogs opened the season by beating Alabama, 17–3, finished by shutting out Missouri, 14–0, in the Orange Bowl, and posted a 10-1 record. In March 1960, Whitworth died of a heart attack at his home just before a scheduled recruiting trip. He was 51.

The Bear Bryant Era

To appreciate the brilliance of Paul "Bear" Bryant (as if you didn't already), check the surprisingly short list of players he sent to the pros.

Bryant coached the Crimson Tide from 1958 through 1982. To get a rough idea of the talent level he worked with, let's see how many Alabama players began National or American Football League careers from 1960 through 1984. And let's compare that 25 years' worth of players—who collectively won six national championships—with players of the next 25-year period, 1985–2009, who combined for just a single national championship. The latter stretch of years includes players from the great Gene Stallings teams but also the less-stellar squads of Ray Perkins, Bill Curry, Mike DuBose, Dennis Franchione, and Mike Shula.

During the Bryant Era, 64 Alabama players were good enough for the pros. During the 25 Years After Bryant Era, 116 Alabama players went on to the pros—almost twice as many. In other words, Bryant won by coaching less-skilled young men to play above their talent level.

Former college and NFL coach Bum Phillips supposedly said of Bryant, "He can take his'n and beat your'n, and take your'n and beat his'n." Bryant could also get his'n to play better than your'n, even if your'n were better athletes.

Look at Bryant's first great Alabama team. The 1961 edition of the Crimson Tide won the national championship with an 11-0 record, including a Sugar Bowl victory over ninth-ranked Arkansas. The smothering defense allowed only 25 total points all year. But how in the world did quarterback Pat Trammell, ends Tommy Brooker and Bill Battle, and running backs Cotton Clark, Butch Wilson, and Mike Fracchia operate an offense that averaged 27 points per game? Fracchia, the fullback, led the team in rushing yards with 652. Brooker led in pass receptions with 12 for all of 183 yards. Center Lee Roy Jordan (see page 118) and tackle Billy Neighbors (see page 137) anchored a great offensive line, but still.

Bryant got the absolute most out of every individual's talent. He got his players to work harder than anybody else. And he got everyone to play together as a team. That formula, simple to state but devilishly difficult to execute, made him the greatest college football coach of all time.

Bryant announced his retirement from coaching after the 1982 regular season, which his team finished with a record of 7-4. He won his last game, the 1982 Liberty Bowl, 21–15 over Illinois. Twenty-eight days later, he died of a heart attack. He was 69.

The Gene Stallings Era

Alabama AB (After Bryant) wasn't sure what it wanted. It tried Ray Perkins, one of "Bear's Boys" (he had played end, Bryant's position, under Bryant in 1964–66). But he had the bad taste to post Alabama's first losing season since Ears Whitworth. It tried Bill Curry, who wasn't one of Bear's Boys. But he couldn't beat Auburn.

Finally, it decided to replicate Bryant as closely as possible by hiring tall, craggy, gruff Gene Stallings, who had played for Bryant at Texas A&M and coached for him at Alabama.

That worked out nicely. Stallings beat Auburn—five times in seven seasons. He beat just about everyone else too. He compiled a record of 70-17-1 (though not officially; more on that in a moment). His winning percentage of .810 isn't too far behind Bear's .824. And in 1992, Stallings fashioned one of the greatest defensive college teams of all time into a 13-0 national champion. In the title game, the 1993 Sugar Bowl, Alabama left favored Miami (Florida) looking dazed. The final score was 34–13.

Stallings coached three more Southeastern Conference Western Division champions before his retirement at the end of the 1996 season—in 1993, 1994, and 1996. But none of them could beat Florida in the SEC title game. And the 1993 team, which went 9-3-1, now has an official record of 1-12 because of NCAA accusations that Stallings and athletics director Hootie Ingram were implicated in falsifying the eligibility of cornerback Antonio Langham (see page 102).

His 1992 national championship team earned Gene Stallings a bronze statue in the University of Alabama's Walk of Champions Plaza.

Credit: The George F. Landegger Collection of Alabama Photographs in Carol M. Highsmith's America, Library of Congress, Prints and Photographs Division

Nevertheless, Stallings restored Alabama to the first rank of college football. Alabama fans were grateful, especially given what happened during the subsequent decade.

The Nick Saban Era

Has Alabama found a new Bear? (See "Who's Better, Saban or the Bear?" on page 71.)

The Crimson Tide turned to Nick Saban after the 2006 season out of something approaching desperation. Mike DuBose and Mike Shula had each posted two losing seasons, and Shula never beat Auburn in four tries. Dennis Franchione left Alabama for Texas A&M after just two years. (Isn't that supposed to work the other way around?) Mike Price didn't even get to coach a real game before he was sent packing after an incident involving an exotic dancer. NCAA sanctions vacated wins in what would end up being three straight seasons, and restricted bowl appearances and scholarships.

Nick Saban may be a great coach, but he could learn something from Bear Bryant about headgear.
Credit: Wikimedia Commons

To the rescue came Saban, formerly a not especially liked rival during his 2000–04 stint as head coach at LSU. Alabama's eight-year, $32 million contract lured him away from the Miami Dolphins, where he had found the National Football League frustrating. His Dolphins teams went 9-7 and 6-10, the latter being Saban's only losing record as a head coach.

Crimson Tide fans consider the money well spent. In six seasons through 2012, Saban has produced five consecutive 10-win seasons and an incredible three national championships. Like Bear Bryant, he seems capable of putting his team in the title hunt just about every year. He even has a winning record

(4-2) against Auburn. And, after the 13-1 national title season of 2012, he has passed the Bear in winning percentage, leading .839 to .824 and trailing only the perfect 1.000 mark that Allen McCants achieved in 1897 by winning the one Alabama game he ever coached.

But those straw hats? Not nearly as cool as houndstooth.

Head Coaching Records

(In chronological order, including record and winning percentage; a tie counts as half a win, half a loss, per NCAA practice)

YEARS	COACH	RECORD	WINNING %
1892	E. B. Beaumont	2-2-0	.500
1893–95, 1902	Eli Abbott	7-13-0	.350
1896	Otto Wagonhurst	2-1-0	.667
1897	Allen McCants	1-0-0	1.000
1898	no team because of a trustees rule against off-campus athletic competition		
1899	W. A. Martin	3-1-0	.750
1900	M. Griffin	2-3-0	.400
1901	G. H. Harvey	2-1-2	.600
1903–04	W. B. Blount	10-7-0	.588
1905	Jack Leavenworth	6-4-0	.600
1906–09	J. W. H. Pollard	21-4-5	.783
1910	Guy Lowman	4-4-0	.500
1911–14	D. V. Graves	21-12-3	.625
1915–17	Thomas Kelly	17-7-1	.700
1918	no team (World War I)		
1919–22	Xen C. Scott	29-9-3	.744
1923–30	Wallace Wade	61-13-3	.812
1931–42, 1944–46	Frank Thomas	115-24-7	.812
1943	no team (World War II)		
1947–54	Harold Drew	54-28-7	.643
1955–57	J. B. Whitworth	4-24-2	.167

YEARS	COACH	RECORD	WINNING %
1958–82	Paul W. Bryant	232-46-9	.824
1983–86	Ray Perkins	32-15-1	.677
1987–89	Bill Curry	26-10-0	.722
*1990–96	Gene Stallings	70-17-1	.810
1997–2000	Mike DuBose	24-23-0	.511
2001–02	Dennis Franchione	17-8-0	.680
*2003–06	Mike Shula	26-23-0	.531
2006	Joe Kines (interim)	0-1-0	.000
*2007–12	Nick Saban	68-13-0	.839

Note: Officially, because of penalties for infractions, the NCAA lists Stallings's record as 62-25-0, Shula's as 10-23-0, and Saban's as 63-12-0.

(Ranked by victories)

RECORD	WINNING %	COACH	YEARS
232-46-9	.824	Paul W. Bryant	1958–82
115-24-7	.812	Frank Thomas	1931–46
*70-17-1	.810	Gene Stallings	1990–96
*68-13-0	.839	Nick Saban	2007–12
61-13-3	.812	Wallace Wade	1923–30
54-28-7	.643	Harold Drew	1947–54
32-15-1	.677	Ray Perkins	1983–86
29-9-3	.744	Xen C. Scott	1919–22
26-10-0	.722	Bill Curry	1987–89
*26-23-0	.531	Mike Shula	2003–06
24-23-0	.511	Mike DuBose	1997–2000
21-4-5	.783	J. W. H. Pollard	1906–09
21-12-3	.625	D. V. Graves	1911–14
17-8-0	.680	Dennis Franchione	2001–02
17-7-1	.700	Thomas Kelly	1915–17
10-7-0	.588	W. B. Blount	1903–04
7-13-0	.350	Eli Abbott	1893–95, 1902
6-4-0	.600	Jack Leavenworth	1905
4-4-0	.500	Guy Lowman	1910

RECORD	WINNING %	COACH	YEARS
4-24-2	.167	J. B. Whitworth	1955–57
3-1-0	.750	W. A. Martin	1899
2-1-0	.667	Otto Wagonhurst	1896
2-1-2	.600	G. H. Harvey	1901
2-2-0	.500	E. B. Beaumont	1892
2-3-0	.400	M. Griffin	1900
1-0-0.	1.000	Allen McCants	1897
0-1-0	.000	Joe Kines	2006

Note: Officially, because of penalties for infractions, the NCAA lists Stallings's record as 62-25-0, Saban's as 63-12-0, and Shula's as 10-23-0.

(Ranked by winning percentage; a tie counts as half a win, half a loss, per NCAA practice)

WINNING %	RECORD	COACH	YEARS
1.000	1-0-0	Allen McCants	1897
.839	*68-13-0	Nick Saban	2007–12
.824	232-46-9	Paul W. Bryant	1958–82
.812	115-24-7	Frank Thomas	1931–46
.812	61-13-3	Wallace Wade	1923–30
.810	*70-17-1	Gene Stallings	1990–96
.783	21-4-5	J. W. H. Pollard	1906–09
.750	3-1-0	W. A. Martin	1899
.744	29-9-3	Xen C. Scott	1919–22
.722	26-10-0	Bill Curry	1987–89
.700	17-7-1	Thomas Kelly	1915–17
.680	17-8-0	Dennis Franchione	2001–02
.677	32-15-1	Ray Perkins	1983–86
.667	2-1-0	Otto Wagonhurst	1896
.643	54-28-7	Harold Drew	1947–54
.625	21-12-3	D. V. Graves	1911–14
.600	6-4-0	Jack Leavenworth	1905
.600	2-1-2	G. H. Harvey	1901
.588	10-7-0	W. B. Blount	1903–04

WINNING %	RECORD	COACH	YEARS
.531	*26-23-0	Mike Shula	2003–06
.511	24-23-0	Mike DuBose	1997–2000
.500	4-4-0	Guy Lowman	1910
.500	2-2-0	E. B. Beaumont	1892
.400	2-3-0	M. Griffin	1900
.350	7-13-0	Eli Abbott	1893–95, 1902
.167	4-24-2	J. B. Whitworth	1955–57
.000	0-1-0	Joe Kines	2006

Note: Officially, because of penalties for infractions, the NCAA lists Saban's record as 50-11-0, Stallings's as 62-25-0, and Shula's as 10-23-0.

DEEEE-FENSE

What kind of game did Bear Bryant's teams play? Well, Alabama has led the NCAA seven times in scoring defense. Bryant coached the first four of those teams. Here's the list:

- **1961:** 2.2 points per game
- **1966:** 3.7
- **1975:** 6.0
- **1979:** 5.3
- **2005:** 10.7 (coach Gene Stallings)
- **2011:** 8.8 (coach Nick Saban)
- **2012:** 10.9 (coach Nick Saban)

HEISMAN TROPHY

Running back Mark Ingram (see page 113) finally won Alabama's first Heisman Trophy for his 2009 season, 117 years after Alabama began playing football and 74 years after Jay Berwanger of the University of Chicago won the initial Heisman in 1935.

Heisman Trophy winners have not generally become stars after they've gone pro. Through the 2012 season, there have been 77 individual Heisman winners (Ohio State's Archie Griffin won twice in 1974 and 1975). We're counting Southern California's Reggie Bush, although the Heisman folks don't. Bush voluntarily gave up his 2005 award after his improper dealings with an agent triggered NCAA sanctions against Southern Cal.

Of the 77 winners, only eight have been inducted into the Pro Football Hall of Fame: Doak Walker (SMU, 1948), Paul Hornung (Notre Dame, 1956), Roger Staubach (Navy, 1963), O. J. Simpson (Southern Cal, 1968), Tony Dorsett (Pittsburgh, 1976), Earl Campbell (Texas, 1977), Marcus Allen (Southern Cal, 1981), and Barry Sanders (Oklahoma State, 1988).

New York's Downtown Athletic Club originated the award as the DAC Trophy to honor the best player east of the Mississippi River. In 1936, John Heisman, the club's athletic director and a pioneer college player and coach, died. That year, the club renamed the trophy after him and expanded eligibility nationwide.

Running back Mark Ingram won the Heisman Trophy and a national championship in the same season.
Credit: Executive Office of the President

The September 11, 2001, terrorist attacks damaged the club's building. In 2002, it declared bankruptcy. The Yale Club of New York City took over presentation of the award for 2002 and 2003. Since 2004, The Heisman Trust has administered the trophy selection and presentation.

In the ranking of schools with the most Heisman winners, Ingram's win puts Alabama in a 21-way tie for 18th. Here's the list:

7	Notre Dame	2	Georgia	1	BYU
7	Ohio State	2	Miami (Florida)	1	Chicago
*7	Southern California	2	Navy	1	Colorado
5	Oklahoma	2	Texas	1	Houston
3	Army	2	Texas A&M	1	Iowa
3	Auburn	2	Wisconsin	1	LSU
3	Florida	2	Yale	1	Minnesota
3	Michigan	**1**	**Alabama**	1	Oklahoma State
3	Nebraska	1	Baylor	1	Oregon State
2	Florida State	1	Boston College	1	Penn State

Chris Samuels shakes hands with U.S. Admiral Timothy J. Keating before the 2008 Pro Bowl game. Behind them is Washington Redskins long snapper Ethan Albright.

Credit: U.S. Navy photo by Mass Communication Specialist 1st Class James E. Foehl

1 Pittsburgh	**1** Southern Methodist	**1** Texas Christian
1 Princeton	**1** Stanford	**1** UCLA
1 South Carolina	**1** Syracuse	

Note: Southern Cal's total includes the 2005 trophy awarded to Reggie Bush and later vacated. Bush voluntarily gave up the award after his improper dealings with agents triggered NCAA sanctions against Southern Cal.

OTHER INDIVIDUAL AWARDS

"At Alabama," Bear Bryant supposedly growled, "our players do not win Heisman trophies. Our teams win national championships."

It's true that Bryant-coached teams won six national championships but never had a winner of a Heisman Trophy—or, for that matter, any other individual college-football award. Since his reign, however, Tide players have picked up some individual hardware. And two of them have proven that individual awards and national titles can coexist. In the championship season of 2009, Mark Ingram won the Heisman, and Rolando McClain (see page

131) won the Lambert Award and Butkus Award, both given to the year's top college linebacker.

Alabama's other winners of major individual collegiate awards are:

CORNELIUS BENNETT, Lombardi Award for top lineman or linebacker, 1986

DERRICK THOMAS, Butkus Award, 1988

ANTONIO LANGHAM, Jim Thorpe and Jack Tatum awards for best defensive back 1993

CHRIS SAMUELS, Outland Trophy for best interior lineman, 1999

ANDRE SMITH, Outland Trophy, 2008

BARRETT JONES, Outland Trophy, 2011

NATIONAL CHAMPIONSHIPS

Alabama's football team has won 15 national championships. Or 13. Or 19. It depends on who's counting.

The university counts 15, for the 1925, 1926, 1930, 1934, 1941, 1961, 1964, 1965, 1973, 1978, 1979, 1992, 2009, 2011, and 2012 seasons. The NCAA counts 13, leaving out 1934 and 1941 and considering the 1926, 1930, 1961, 1964, 1965, 1973, and 1978 titles to be shared by one or more other schools.

The NCAA list reflects the opinions of six "major selectors": the Associated Press, United Press International, *USA Today* and its partners (primarily CNN and ESPN), the National Football Foundation, the Football Writers Association of America, and, since 1998, the Bowl Championship Series rankings. To determine champions from the pre–AP poll era (before 1936), the NCAA relies on retroactive polls conducted by the College Football Researchers Association, Helms Athletic Foundation, and National Championship Foundation.

But at least 29 other individuals or organizations have attempted to authoritatively rank college football teams over the years. At least one of those selectors ranked Alabama as the best in the nation in 1945, 1966, 1975, and 1977. Add those four to the 15 that the university counts, and you're up to 19 national championships.

Let's look more closely at the NCAA list and the nonconsensus titles.

Who Are the Champions?

The NCAA keeps a semiofficial "Championship History" list for major colleges going back to 1869, when two games were played. (Rutgers beat

Princeton, 6–4, and then Princeton beat Rutgers, 8–0.) However, the NCAA itself does none of the rankings. It just compiles the opinions of major polls and other selecting organizations.

No national championship was awarded for 1871 because no college football games were played that year.

Yale has the most national championships (won outright or shared) with 18, followed by Princeton at 15, and Alabama and Notre Dame tied at 13. Yale and Princeton built up a lot of their lead in the very early years when they were about the only schools playing football. Literally. In 1869, Princeton was one of two schools fielding teams, in 1870, one of three; in 1872, one of five, along with Yale.

The NCAA's list confines itself to what we call today the NCAA Division I Football Bowl Subdivision teams. For years before the FBS, or even the NCAA, existed it tries to pick the equivalent schools of the day. Here are the title teams, ranked by number of national championships won outright or shared:

18 Yale	4 Penn State	1 Chicago
15 Princeton	4 Texas	1 Clemson
13 Alabama	3 Army	1 Colorado
13 Notre Dame	3 California	1 Georgia
9 Michigan	3 Cornell	1 Iowa
9 Southern California	3 Florida	1 Lafayette
8 Harvard	3 Georgia Tech	1 Maryland
7 Ohio State	3 Illinois	1 Mississippi
7 Oklahoma	3 Michigan State	1 Stanford
6 Minnesota	2 Auburn	1 Syracuse
5 Miami (Florida)	2 Florida State	1 Texas Christian
5 Nebraska	2 Tennessee	1 UCLA
5 Pittsburgh	2 Texas A&M	1 Washington
4 LSU	1 Arkansas	
4 Pennsylvania	1 Brigham Young	

Alabama is the only school to have more than two streaks of two or more consecutive championships. The Crimson Tide has four such back-to-back titles, in 1925–26, 1964–65, 1978–79, and 2011–12. Yale has the longest consecutive-championships streak—five years—but it happened during the Hayes,

Garfield, and Arthur presidential administrations (1880–84). Here are the schools with streaks, ranked by number of years of consecutive championships:

5 Yale 1880–84	**2 Alabama 1925–26, 1964–65, 1978–79, and 2011–12**	**2** Nebraska 1970–71 and 1994–95
4 Michigan 1901–04	**2** Army 1944–45	**2** Notre Dame 1929–30 and 1946–47
4 Princeton 1869–73 (not counting 1871, when no games were played)	**2** Cornell 1921–22	**2** Oklahoma 1955–56 and 1974–75
3 California 1920–22	**2** Harvard 1898–99 and 1912–13	**2** Penn State 1911–12
3 Minnesota 1934–36	**2** Michigan State 1965–66	**2** Southern California 1931–31 and 2003–04
3 Princeton 1878–80	**2** Minnesota 1940–41	**2** Yale 1876–77 and 1891–92
3 Yale 1886–88		

The Case for 15 Titles

Alabama claims 15 football national championships, for the 1925, 1926, 1930, 1934, 1941, 1961, 1964, 1965, 1973, 1978, 1979, 1992, 2009, 2011, and 2012 seasons. The National Collegiate Athletic Association includes 13 of those titles in its semiofficial list of champions:

1925	**1978** (shared with Southern California)
1926 (shared with Stanford)	**1979**
1930 (shared with Notre Dame)	**1992**
1961 (shared with Ohio State)	**2009**
1964 (shared with Arkansas and Notre Dame)	**2011**
1965 (shared with Michigan State)	**2012**
1973 (shared with Notre Dame)	

Again, the NCAA is merely listing champions as determined by others, not officially recognizing any championships. But how is it that the NCAA and Alabama lists differ? If you're up for an exploration of the minutiae of football ratings, read on.

The two most widely recognized selection methods are the polls of sportswriters and coaches. The Associated Press began polling sportswriters in 1936. The coaches poll began in 1950. It has been conducted by United Press International (1950–90), *USA Today*/Cable News Network (1991–96), *USA Today*/ESPN (1997–2005), and *USA Today* by itself (2006–present). Since 1998, the winner of the Bowl Championship Series postseason bowl Championship Game has automatically been recognized as the national champion by the coaches poll. The AP voters have reserved the right to make up their own minds.

During much of their existence, the AP poll and the coaches poll awarded championships before the postseason bowl games (1936–1964 and 1966–67 for AP, 1950–73 for the coaches). If a poll's champion lost its bowl game, that opened the door for other schools to claim the title.

A number of other individuals and organizations have bestowed mythical national championships over the years. Some have relied on mathematical formulas, others on polls of their membership or of other selectors. Many of those individuals and organizations have further confused the issue by awarding retroactive national championships—applying their formulas or polling to seasons that preceded the formulas' or polls' creation.

Here's a breakdown of Alabama's shared (or disputed; pick your terminology) championships, including some that the university doesn't actually claim:

1926: For this season, University of Illinois economics professor Frank G. Dickinson introduced his mathematical formula for determining the best college football team. Dickinson used his system to name champions from 1926 through 1940. At the request of Notre Dame coach Knute Rockne, he also retroactively figured the 1924 and 1925 champions (Notre Dame and Dartmouth, respectively). The system awarded points for victories, defeats, and ties against "strong" and "weak" teams. Dickinson's first national champion was the 1926 Stanford team, which finished the regular season 10-0. After the season, Stanford played Alabama (9-0) in the Rose Bowl. Stanford scored a touchdown in the first quarter; Alabama finally answered with a touchdown with a minute to go in the game. Final score: 7–7. Dickinson's awarding of the championship to Stanford was the only contemporary ranking. Since then, the Billingsley Report and Poling System formulas and College Football Researchers Association poll have retroactively picked Alabama. The Helms Athletic Foundation and National Championship Foundation polls retroactively called it a tie between Alabama and Stanford. The Sagarin Ratings formula retroactively called it a tie between Stanford and Michigan (7-1). Football historian Parke H. Davis retroactively selected Lafayette (9-0)—which was a legitimate football power at the time. And the Boand System and Houlgate System formulas retroactively chose Navy (9-0-1).

1930: The raters at the time—Dickinson, Boand, Houlgate, and the Dunkel System, all based on mathematical formulas—agreed that 10-0 Notre Dame was the national champion. Retroactively, Billingsley, Helms, the National Championship Foundation, and Poling agreed. (That was coach Knute Rockne's last team; he died in an airplane crash on March 31, 1931.) Two other retroactive systems, the College Football Researchers Association and Sagarin, preferred the 10-0 Alabama team. Davis called it a tie between the two. The Crimson Tide thrashed Washington State, 24-0, in the Rose Bowl, college football's only postseason game.

1934: Alabama went 10-0 and thumped Stanford, 29–13, in the Rose Bowl on January 1, 1935. Dunkel, Houlgate, and the formula-based Williamson System, which had appeared in 1933, all thought that made the Crimson Tide the national champion. Boand, Dickinson, and the new Likenhous formula liked 8-0 Minnesota instead. Retroactively, Poling favored the Tide, while Billingsley, the College Football Researchers Association, Helms, and Sagarin supported the Golden Gophers. That postseason, incidentally, was the first in which the Rose Bowl had company. The first Orange, Sugar, and Sun bowls took place on January 1, 1935, though the Sun Bowl matched two high-school teams that year before becoming a college contest in 1936. The Cotton Bowl debuted on January 1, 1937.

1941: Minnesota, 8-0, was the consensus national champion. Houlgate was the only rating system that picked Alabama, 9-2. The contemporary Williamson and the retroactive Berryman formulas chose Texas, 8-1-1. Alabama's claim to this, the most controversial national title on the university's official list, can be traced to one man: Wayne Atcheson, Alabama's sports information director from 1983 to 1987. In his annual media guides, Atcheson started listing five earlier championships (in 1925, 1926, 1930, 1934, and 1941) in addition to the six that Bear Bryant had accumulated. Before then, the university had never published an authoritative list. Atcheson, who became director of the Billy Graham Library in Charlotte, North Carolina, and is now library awareness representative at the Billy Graham Evangelistic Association, explained his reasoning to the *Birmingham News* in 2010. Alabama finished third in the Southeastern Conference in 1941 and 20th in the Associated Press poll. It lost 14–0 at home to SEC champion Mississippi (8-1-1) and 7–0 late in the season at Vanderbilt (8-2). Atcheson said you need to balance the Mississippi State loss in the rain and the close loss to Vanderbilt against victories over Georgia (8-1-1), Tennessee (8-2), Miami (8-2), and, in the Cotton Bowl, Southwest Conference champion Texas A&M (9-2, including the bowl loss). By the end of the season, he said, the Crimson Tide was the best in the land.

"Texas A&M was the hottest team in America," Atcheson said, "and Alabama just soundly defeated them, even though the score was just 29-21." Um, in its last two regular-season games, Texas A&M lost to Texas, 23–0, and eked out a 7-0 win over Washington State. In the Cotton Bowl, Alabama did run up a 29-7 lead in the fourth quarter before inserting its third string, but A&M had 309 yards in total offense compared with Alabama's 75. The Crimson Tide won because it intercepted seven Aggie passes and recovered five fumbles. Is that enough for a national championship? Atcheson and the late Los Angeles PR man and football statistician Deke Houlgate have said yes.

1945: Alabama doesn't claim this one, but the National Championship Foundation poll retroactively selected 10-0 Alabama as the 1945 national champion. Every other rater, contemporary or retroactive, favored the 9-0 Army team. The final AP poll had Navy, 7-1-1, second and Alabama third. The poll was taken before the bowl games. Neither of the service academies played in a bowl. Alabama beat Southern California, 34–14, in the Rose Bowl.

1961: This time, Alabama was the consensus champion after an 11-0 season that included a 10–3 Sugar Bowl victory over Arkansas. Only the Football Writers Association of America poll and the Poling System formula preferred Ohio State. The Buckeyes opened the season with a 7–7 tie at home in Columbus against Texas Christian, which finished the season 3-5-2. Ohio State then won its other eight regular-season games, qualifying for a Rose Bowl invitation. However, the university faculty council voted 28–25 not to accept the invitation, saying the school was overemphasizing athletics at the expense of academics. Poling used a mathematical formula, but the Football Writers derived their rankings from a poll of their members. You have to wonder whether some writers voted for Ohio State out of sympathy—or protest.

1964: After Alabama's 10-0 regular season, both the AP sportswriters poll and UPI coaches poll picked the Crimson Tide as national champion. But Alabama lost, 21–17, to number three Texas in the Orange Bowl. Tide quarterback Joe Namath, with an injured left knee, didn't start. With the Tide trailing 14-0 in the second quarter, Namath limped into the game and engineered a comeback that fell just short when Texas stopped his quarterback sneak on fourth and goal from the one-yard line with time running out. Namath was named the game's most valuable player. Meanwhile, second-ranked Arkansas beat sixth-ranked Nebraska, 10–7, in the Cotton Bowl. The Football Writers of America and several other raters that waited until after the bowl games chose Arkansas (11-0) as national champion. Dunkel named 9-1 Michigan. The DeVoid System, *Football News*, and the National Football Foundation chose Notre Dame, also 9-1.

1965: This time, Alabama benefited from the bowl results. At the end of the regular season, the AP and UPI polls had 10-0 Michigan State ahead of 8-1-1 Alabama. But the AP decided to take one final poll after the bowl games. (It reverted to pre-bowl polling in 1966–67 before permanently switching to post-bowl polling in 1968. UPI followed suit in 1974.) After the 1965 season, the seventh-ranked AP team, UCLA, upset Michigan State, 14–12, in the Rose Bowl. Unranked LSU (the polls included only the top 10) beat second-ranked Arkansas, 14–7, in the Cotton Bowl. And fourth-ranked Alabama rolled over third-ranked Nebraska, 39–28, in the Orange Bowl. So the AP voters selected Alabama as the champion. The Football Writers Association of America, also voting after the bowls, declared Alabama and Michigan State co-champions. All other contemporary raters and most of the retroactive raters favored Michigan State.

1966: Alabama doesn't claim this one either, but Berryman and Sagarin retroactively figured that 11-0 Alabama, the 34–7 victor over sixth-ranked Nebraska in the Sugar Bowl, deserved the national championship. This was the year that Notre Dame and Michigan State, then ranked one-two (in that order) in the two major polls, played to an epic 10–10 tie on November 19. Notre Dame coach Ara Parseghian played conservatively to preserve the tie after the Fighting Irish got the ball on their own 30-yard line with 70 seconds to play. Both AP and UPI, polling before the bowl games, had Notre Dame first and Michigan State second, each with a 9-0-1 record, and Alabama third. Neither Notre Dame nor Michigan State played in a bowl. An entire book, *The Missing Ring: How Bear Bryant and the 1966 Alabama Crimson Tide Were Denied College Football's Most Elusive Prize* by Keith Dunnavant, argues that the poll voters should have awarded Alabama a third straight national championship.

1973: Bill Davis's missed extra-point kick in the fourth quarter of the Sugar Bowl kept Alabama from achieving a consensus national championship. After the regular season, the AP sportswriters ranked Alabama (11-0) first and Notre Dame (10-0) second. The final UPI coaches poll, taken after the regular season but before the bowl games, had Alabama on top and the Fighting

Irish at number four. The two teams, playing each other for the first time, met in a Sugar Bowl for national bragging rights. Notre Dame prevailed, 24–23, on a fourth-quarter field goal after Davis missed the extra point following Alabama's final touchdown. Notre Dame earned the top ranking in the final AP poll, released after the bowls. The Football Writers Association of America and the National Football Foundation also crowned Notre Dame as the national champion. A few minor selectors favored Michigan, Ohio State, or Oklahoma, each 10-0-1. The following season, UPI, capitulating to common sense, added a final coaches poll after the bowl games.

1975: Matthews Grid Ratings declared that, according to its mathematical formula, Alabama (11-1) was the best team in college football. No one else paid any attention—including Alabama, which doesn't claim this as one of its championships. The major selectors agreed that Oklahoma, also 11-1, deserved the national championship.

1977: This is the last of four seasons (along with 1945, 1966, and 1975) in which one or two little-known selectors gave Alabama a national championship that not even Alabama acknowledges. Retroactively, the College Football Researchers Association thought Alabama deserved the top ranking over consensus national champion Notre Dame. In the postseason, fifth-ranked Notre Dame beat top-ranked Texas, 38–10, in the Cotton Bowl, sixth-ranked Arkansas beat second-ranked Oklahoma, 31–6, in the Orange Bowl, and third-ranked Alabama beat eighth-ranked Ohio State, 35–6, in the Sugar Bowl. Alabama, Notre Dame, Arkansas, Texas, and Penn State all finished 11-1; Oklahoma finished 10-2, and Ohio State went 9-3. The final AP and UPI polls had Notre Dame first and Alabama second.

1978: Alabama finished 11-1 and beat top-ranked Penn State, 14–7, in a thrilling Sugar Bowl that featured a famous fourth-quarter goal-line stand. The Crimson Tide claimed the top spot in the AP, Football Writers Association of America, and National Football Foundation polls. The UPI coaches poll went for 12-1 Southern California. Why? Because the Trojans were the team that gave Alabama that single loss, an early-season 24–14 thrashing at Legion Field in Birmingham. Southern Cal's loss came three weeks later at Arizona State, which finished the season 9-3 and unranked by AP. So Alabama can make a pretty strong case that, by season's end, it was America's best college football team.

BOWL GAMES

Alabama has played in more postseason bowl games than any other university, 60—and won more than any other university, 35. (We're including the 2006 Cotton Bowl victory over Texas Tech that the NCAA later vacated because of violations of NCAA rules regarding textbooks.)

The Crimson Tide's first five postseason appearances all took place in the Rose Bowl from 1926 through 1938. Alabama won three of those games, including "The Football Game That Changed the South"—the 20-19 win over heavily favored Washington that earned a huge dose of national respect for Southern football in general and Alabama football in particular. It's hard to believe today, but back then, with major media centers on the East and West Coast and no television coverage, Southern football received little notice in the national press.

Alabama's Complete List of Bowl Games

YEAR	GAME	FINAL SCORE
1926	ROSE BOWL	**Alabama** 20, Washington 19
1927	ROSE BOWL	**Alabama** 7, **Stanford** 7
1931	ROSE BOWL	**Alabama** 24, Washington State 0
1935	ROSE BOWL	**Alabama** 29, Stanford 13
1938	ROSE BOWL	**California** 13, Alabama 0
1942	COTTON BOWL	**Alabama** 29, Texas A&M 21
1943	ORANGE BOWL	**Alabama** 37, Boston College 21
1945	SUGAR BOWL	**Duke** 29, Alabama 26
1946	ROSE BOWL	**Alabama** 34, Southern California 14
1948	SUGAR BOWL	**Texas** 27, Alabama 7
1953	ORANGE BOWL	**Alabama** 61, Syracuse 6
1954	COTTON BOWL	**Rice** 28, Alabama 6
1959	LIBERTY BOWL	**Penn State** 7, Alabama 0
1960	BLUEBONNET BOWL	**Alabama** 3, **Texas** 3
1962	SUGAR BOWL	**Alabama** 10, Arkansas 3
1963	ORANGE BOWL	**Alabama** 17, Oklahoma 0
1964	SUGAR BOWL	**Alabama** 12, Mississippi 7
1965	ORANGE BOWL	**Texas** 21, Alabama 17
1966	ORANGE BOWL	**Alabama** 39, Nebraska 28

YEAR	GAME	FINAL SCORE
1967	SUGAR BOWL	**Alabama** 34, Nebraska 7
1968	COTTON BOWL	**Texas A&M** 20, Alabama 16
1969	LIBERTY BOWL	**Colorado** 47, Alabama 33
1970	BLUEBONNET BOWL	**Alabama** 24, **Oklahoma** 24
1972	ORANGE BOWL	**Nebraska** 38, Alabama 6
1973	COTTON BOWL	**Texas** 17, Alabama 13
1973	SUGAR BOWL	**Notre Dame** 24, Alabama 23
1975	ORANGE BOWL	**Notre Dame** 13, Alabama 11
1975	SUGAR BOWL	**Alabama** 13, Penn State 6
1976	LIBERTY BOWL	**Alabama** 36, UCLA 6
1978	SUGAR BOWL	**Alabama** 35, Ohio State 6
1979	SUGAR BOWL	**Alabama** 14, Penn State 7
1980	SUGAR BOWL	**Alabama** 24, Arkansas 9
1981	COTTON BOWL	**Alabama** 30, Baylor 2
1982	COTTON BOWL	**Texas** 14, Alabama 12
1982	LIBERTY BOWL	**Alabama** 21, Illinois 15
1983	SUN BOWL	**Alabama** 28, SMU 7
1985	ALOHA BOWL	**Alabama** 24, Southern California 3
1986	SUN BOWL	**Alabama** 28, Washington 6
1988	HALL OF FAME BOWL	**Michigan** 28, Alabama 24
1988	SUN BOWL	**Alabama** 29, Army 28
1990	SUGAR BOWL	**Miami** 33, Alabama 25
1991	FIESTA BOWL	**Louisville** 34, Alabama 7
1991	BLOCKBUSTER BOWL	**Alabama** 30, Colorado 25
1993	SUGAR BOWL	**Alabama** 34, Miami 13
1993	GATOR BOWL	**Alabama** 24, North Carolina 10
1995	CITRUS BOWL	**Alabama** 24, Ohio State 17
1997	OUTBACK BOWL	**Alabama** 17, Michigan 14
1998	MUSIC CITY BOWL	**Virginia Tech** 38, Alabama 7
2000	ORANGE BOWL	**Michigan** 35, Alabama 34, OT
2001	INDEPENDENCE BOWL	**Alabama** 14, Iowa State 13
2004	MUSIC CITY BOWL	**Minnesota** 20, Alabama 16
*2006	COTTON BOWL	**Alabama** 13, Texas Tech 10
2006	INDEPENDENCE BOWL	**Oklahoma State** 34, Alabama 31

YEAR	GAME	FINAL SCORE
2007	**INDEPENDENCE BOWL**	**Alabama** 30, Colorado 24
2009	**SUGAR BOWL**	**Utah** 31, Alabama 17
2010	**BOWL CHAMPIONSHIP SERIES NATIONAL CHAMPIONSHIP**	**Alabama** 36, Texas 21
2011	**CAPITAL ONE BOWL**	**Alabama** 49, Michigan State 7
2012	**BCS NATIONAL CHAMPIONSHIP**	**Alabama** 21, LSU 0
2013	**BCS NATIONAL CHAMPIONSHIP**	**Alabama** 42, Notre Dame 14

Note: Victory vacated per NCAA ruling

All-Time Alabama Bowl Game Records

- **Aloha Bowl:** 1-0
- **Bowl Championship Series National Championship:** 3-0
- **Blockbuster Bowl:** 1-0
- **Bluebonnet Bowl:** 0-0-2
- **Citrus/Capital One Bowl:** 2-0
- ***Cotton Bowl:** 7-4
- **Fiesta Bowl:** 0-1
- **Gator Bowl:** 1-1
- **Hall of Fame Bowl:** 0-1
- **Independence Bowl:** 2-1
- **Liberty Bowl:** 2-2
- **Music City Bowl:** 0-2
- **Orange Bowl:** 4-4
- **Outback Bowl:** 1-0
- **Rose Bowl:** 4-1-1
- **Sugar Bowl:** 8-5
- **Sun Bowl:** 3-0
- ***Overall: 35-22-3**

Note: Includes 2006 Cotton Bowl victory that was vacated per NCAA ruling

Top 20 Schools by Bowls Played

***60 Alabama 35-22-3**	44 LSU 22-21-1	37 Auburn 22-13-2
51 Texas 27-22-2	44 Penn State 27-15-2	35 Clemson 17-18-0
49 Nebraska 24-25-0	***43 Ohio State 20-23-0	35 Texas Tech 13-21-1
**49 Southern California 32-17-0	42 Florida State 26-14-2	34 Miami (Florida) 18-16-0
49 Tennessee 25-24-0	42 Michigan 20-22-0	34 Mississippi 22-12-0
48 Georgia 27-18-3	41 Georgia Tech 23-18-0	34 Texas A&M 15-19-0
46 Oklahoma 27-18-1	40 Florida 20-20-0	
	39 Arkansas 13-23-3	

* *Includes 2006 Cotton Bowl victory that was vacated per NCAA ruling*

** *Includes 2005 Orange Bowl victory and 2006 Rose Bowl loss that were vacated per Bowl Championship Series ruling*

*** *Includes 2011 Sugar Bowl victory that was vacated per NCAA ruling*

Top 20 Schools by Bowl Wins

*35-22-3 **Alabama**	25-24-0 Tennessee	***20-23-0 Ohio State
**32-17-0 Southern California	24-25-0 Nebraska	18-16-0 Miami (Florida)
27-18-3 Georgia	23-18-0 Georgia Tech	17-18-0 Clemson
27-18-1 Oklahoma	22-13-2 Auburn	15-17-0 Notre Dame
27-15-2 Penn State	22-21-1 LSU	15-8-0 Oklahoma State
27-22-2 Texas	22-12-0 Mississippi	15-19-0 Texas A&M
26-14-2 Florida State	20-20-0 Florida	15-16-1 Washington
	20-22-0 Michigan	

* Includes 2006 Cotton Bowl victory that was vacated per NCAA ruling

** Includes 2005 Orange Bowl victory and 2006 Rose Bowl loss that were vacated per Bowl Championship Series ruling

*** Includes 2011 Sugar Bowl victory that was vacated per NCAA ruling

THE IRON BOWL

Alabama does, of course, have one other "bowl game" on its schedule that in the hearts of the fans may transcend even a national championship contest in importance: its annual battle with in-state mega-rival Auburn. For four decades, the two teams met at Legion Field in the iron and steel city of Birmingham, so the game became known as the Iron Bowl.

The two schools have been arguing ever since their first-ever meeting on February 22, 1893, at Lakeview Park, a baseball field in Birmingham. Auburn (then the Agricultural and Mechanical College of Alabama) won, 32–22. Press reports said 226 Auburn fans and 220 Alabama fans attended. Alabama considered it the last game of the 1892 season (the inaugural season of football for both teams). Auburn considered it the first game of the 1893 season.

After the 1907 game—a 6–6 tie, the only tie of the rivalry—the schools disagreed over player expenses and whether "neutral" officials should be imported. They didn't play again until 1948. The series resumed after threats by the State Legislature to withhold funding otherwise. Alabama and Auburn decided to hold the game in Birmingham because it had the state's biggest stadium, then–45,000-seat Legion Field. The schools would split the tickets evenly. To symbolically ratify the agreement, students from the two schools held a ceremony at what is now Birmingham's Linn Park in which they literally buried a hatchet.

By 1987, Auburn's Jordan-Hare Stadium had more seats (and was in better repair) than Legion Field. Starting in 1989, Auburn began playing its home games of the series at Jordan-Hare (except for one game at Legion Field in 1991). By 1998, Bryant-Denny Stadium's capacity also exceeded that of Legion Field. In 2000, Alabama moved its own Iron Bowl home games to Bryant-Denny.

The players take the game as seriously as the fans and try fiercely to beat their archrivals. But the crucible of the game also forges an unlikely respect, even camaraderie, between the two teams. It's evident in the interteam mingling on the field afterward. Players from both sides linger, not quite ready to let go of the transcendent experience they have created together. Each has become a member of a very exclusive fraternity. Having given their all in a brutally physical game against a foe who has done exactly the same thing, they can't help but share a bond.

And now, the Iron Bowl has done the seemingly impossible: It has taken on even more significance. For the past four seasons, 2009 through 2012, the victor has gone on to win the national championship. In fact, every Alabama and Auburn national champion, including the teams anointed by only one or two obscure selectors (see The Case for 15 Titles, page 55), has also won the Iron Bowl in its championship year—except, obviously, during the period from 1908 through 1947 in which the schools didn't play each other. Frankly, it's not surprising. If a championship-quality team can survive the crucible of the Iron Bowl, then it can handle just about anything.

Iron Bowl Scores

YEAR	TEAMS/SCORE	YEAR	TEAMS/SCORE
1893 (Feb.)	**Auburn** 32, Alabama 22	**1905**	**Alabama** 30, Auburn 0
1893 (Nov.)	**Auburn** 40, Alabama 16	**1906**	**Alabama** 10, Auburn 0
1894	**Alabama** 18, Auburn 0	**1907**	Alabama 6, **Auburn** 6
1895	**Auburn** 48, Alabama 0	**1948**	**Alabama** 55, Auburn 0
1900	**Auburn** 53, Alabama 5	**1949**	**Auburn** 14, Alabama 13
1901	**Auburn** 17, Alabama 0	**1950**	**Alabama** 34, Auburn 0
1902	**Auburn** 23, Alabama 0	**1951**	**Alabama** 25, Auburn 7
1903	**Alabama** 18, Auburn 6	**1952**	**Alabama** 21, Auburn 0
1904	**Auburn** 29, Alabama 5	**1953**	**Alabama** 10, Auburn 7

YEAR	TEAMS/SCORE
1954	**Auburn** 8, Alabama 0
1955	**Auburn** 26, Alabama 0
1956	**Auburn** 34, Alabama 7
1957	**Auburn** 40, Alabama 0
1958	**Auburn** 14, Alabama 8
1959	**Alabama** 10, Auburn 0
1960	**Alabama** 3, Auburn 0
1961	**Alabama** 34, Auburn 0
1962	**Alabama** 38, Auburn 0
1963	**Auburn** 10, Alabama 8
1964	**Alabama** 21, Auburn 14
1965	**Alabama** 30, Auburn 3
1966	**Alabama** 31, Auburn 0
1967	**Alabama** 7, Auburn 3
1968	**Alabama** 24, Auburn 16
1969	**Auburn** 49, Alabama 26
1970	**Auburn** 33, Alabama 28
1971	**Alabama** 31, Auburn 7
1972	**Auburn** 17, Alabama 16
1973	**Alabama** 35, Auburn 0
1974	**Alabama** 17, Auburn 13
1975	**Alabama** 28, Auburn 0
1976	**Alabama** 38, Auburn 7
1977	**Alabama** 48, Auburn 21
1978	**Alabama** 34, Auburn 16
1979	**Alabama** 25, Auburn 18
1980	**Alabama** 34, Auburn 18
1981	**Alabama** 28, Auburn 17
1982	**Auburn** 23, Alabama 22
1983	**Auburn** 23, Alabama 20

YEAR	TEAMS/SCORE
1984	**Alabama** 17, Auburn 15
1985	**Alabama** 25, Auburn 23
1986	**Auburn** 21, Alabama 17
1987	**Auburn** 10, Alabama 0
1988	**Auburn** 15, Alabama 10
1989	**Auburn** 30, Alabama 20
1990	**Alabama** 16, Auburn 7
1991	**Alabama** 13, Auburn 6
1992	**Alabama** 17, Auburn 0
1993	**Auburn** 22, Alabama 14
1994	**Alabama** 21, Auburn 14
1995	**Auburn** 31, Alabama 27
1996	**Alabama** 24, Auburn 23
1997	**Auburn** 18, Alabama 17
1998	**Alabama** 31, Auburn 17
1999	**Alabama** 28, Auburn 17
2000	**Auburn** 9, Alabama 0
2001	**Alabama** 31, Auburn 7
2002	**Auburn** 17, Alabama 7
2003	**Auburn** 28, Alabama 23
2004	**Auburn** 21, Alabama 13
2005	**Auburn** 28, Alabama 18
2006	**Auburn** 22, Alabama 15
2007	**Auburn** 17, Alabama 10
2008	**Alabama** 36, Auburn 0
2009	**Alabama** 26, Auburn 21
2010	**Auburn** 28, Alabama 27
2011	**Alabama** 42, Auburn 14
2012	**Alabama** 49, Auburn 0

Iron Bowl Records

Overall: Alabama leads, 42–34–1
Most consecutive wins: Alabama, 9 (1973–81)
Shutouts: Alabama 16, Auburn 8
Most consecutive shutouts: Alabama, 4 (1959–62)
Highest score: Alabama, 55 (Auburn 0, 1948)

Iron Bowl Records by Coaches (in chronological order)

0-1 E. B. Beaumont, 1892
1-3 Eli Abbott, 1893–95, 1902
0-1 M. Griffin, 1900
0-1 G. H. Harvey, 1901
1-1 W. B. Blount, 1903–04
1-0 Jack Leavenworth, 1905
1-0-1 J. W. H. Pollard, 1906–07
5-2 Harold "Red" Drew, 1948–54
0-3 J. B. Whitworth, 1955–57
19-6 Paul W. Bryant, 1958–82
2-2 Ray Perkins, 1983–86
0-3 Bill Curry, 1987–89
5-2 Gene Stallings, 1990–96
2-2 Mike DuBose, 1997–2000
1-1 Dennis Franchione, 2001–02
0-4 Mike Shula, 2003–06
4-2 Nick Saban, 2007–12

(Ranked by victories)

19-6 Paul W. Bryant, 1958–1982
5-2 Harold "Red" Drew, 1948–54
5-2 Gene Stallings, 1990–96
4-2 Nick Saban, 2007–12
2-2 Ray Perkins, 1983–86
2-2 Mike DuBose, 1997–2000
1-0 Jack Leavenworth, 1905
1-0-1 J. W. H. Pollard, 1906–07
1-1 W. B. Blount, 1903–04
1-1 Dennis Franchione, 2001–02
1-3 Eli Abbott, 1893–95, 1902
0-1 E. B. Beaumont, 1892
0-1 M. Griffin, 1900
0-1 G. H. Harvey, 1901
0-3 J. B. Whitworth, 1955–57
0-3 Bill Curry, 1987–89
0-4 Mike Shula, 2003–06

(Ranked by winning percentage; a tie counts as half a win, half a loss, per NCAA practice)

1.000 1-0, Jack Leavenworth, 1905		**.500** 1-1, Dennis Franchione, 2001–02
.760 19-6, Paul W. Bryant, 1958–82		**.250** 1-3, Eli Abbott, 1893–95, 1902
.750 1-0-1, J. W. H. Pollard, 1906–07		**.000** 0-1, E. B. Beaumont, 1892
.714 5-2, Harold "Red" Drew, 1948–54		**.000** 0-1, M. Griffin, 1900
.714 5-2, Gene Stallings, 1990–96		**.000** 0-1, G. H. Harvey, 1901
.667 4-2, Nick Saban, 2007–12		**.000** 0-3, J. B. Whitworth, 1955–57
.500 2-2, Ray Perkins, 1983–86		**.000** 0-3, Bill Curry, 1987–89
.500 2-2, Mike DuBose, 1997–2000		**.000** 0-4, Mike Shula, 2003–06
.500 1-1, W. B. Blount, 1903–04		

FOOTBALL GOES PRO

Professional football dates back at least to 1892, when the Allegheny Athletic Association paid former star Yale guard William "Pudge" Heffelfinger $500 to play in a game against the Pittsburgh Athletic Club. We feel certain that a few bucks were slipped into a few players' pockets well before then.

But a national football league (though it wasn't very "national" in the beginning) didn't coalesce until 1920. The founding meeting took place at a Hupmobile auto dealership in Canton, Ohio, which is why the Pro Football Hall of Fame is in Canton.

The league began as the American Professional Football Conference, then after a month became the American Professional Football Association. In 1922, the name changed to National Football League.

Two charter members still exist: the Chicago Bears (originally the Decatur Staleys of Decatur, Illinois, sponsored by starch-maker Staley Manufacturing Co.) and the Arizona Cardinals (then the Chicago Cardinals, later the St. Louis Cardinals and Phoenix Cardinals). The oldest team still in its original location is the Green Bay Packers, founded in 1919 but not a member of the league until 1921.

The other founding NFL teams were the Akron (Ohio) Pros, Buffalo (New York) All-Americans, Canton (Ohio) Bulldogs, Chicago Tigers, Cleveland Tigers, Columbus (Ohio) Panhandles, Dayton (Ohio) Triangles, Detroit

Heralds, Hammond (Indiana) Pros, Muncie (Indiana) Flyers, Rochester (New York) Jeffersons, and Rock Island (Illinois) Independents. That lineup gives you some idea of why pro football was considered a distinctly minor sport during its first couple of decades.

Teams entered and left the league, dissolved and re-formed, but the league itself persevered. Before the 1933 season, the NFL split into Eastern and Western divisions, with the division winners meeting in the NFL Championship Game. That provided an attention-getting season finale—much superior to the earlier practice of awarding the championship to the team with the best regular-season record, which was complicated by league instability that meant that some teams played several more games than others.

NFL rosters included several black players from the beginning, but they were all purged before the 1927 season. The league reintegrated after World War II. The Cleveland (now St. Louis) Rams wanted to move to Los Angeles in 1946, and the stadium, the Los Angeles Coliseum, required the team to accept black players.

In 1935, partly as a reaction to the bidding war over the services of Alabama star Don Hutson (see page 112), the league instituted an annual draft of free-agent players. It was the first of its kind, since copied by just about every other major professional team sport.

By the end of World War II, the NFL had become a player on the national sports scene. Star quarterbacks such as Bob Waterfield of the Rams, Sid Luckman of the Bears, and Slinging Sammy Baugh of the Washington Redskins captured the public's attention. (So did Detroit Lions halfback Byron "Whizzer" White, later a U.S. Supreme Court justice.)

But what really elevated the NFL to its current position as the preeminent American sports institution debuted in the late 1950s: widespread television broadcasts. The national broadcast of the 1958 NFL Championship Game between the Baltimore Colts and New York Giants has particularly been credited with lighting the fuse of the NFL popularity rocket. In "The Greatest Game Ever Played," young quarterback Johnny Unitas led the Colts to a 23-17 victory in sudden-death overtime, completing 12 passes to end Raymond Berry—still a record for most championship game catches by one receiver.

Over the years, other leagues rose to challenge the NFL, such as an early version of the American Football League in 1936–37 and, more seriously, the All-America Football Conference in 1946–49. The NFL reacted by stealing some of their best teams (the AFL's Cleveland Rams) or merging in a way that essentially stole some of their best teams (the AAFC's Cleveland Browns, now the Baltimore Ravens; San Francisco 49ers; and Baltimore Colts, which folded after one season and were succeeded in 1953 by a new Baltimore Colts franchise that is now the Indianapolis Colts).

In 1960, a bigger threat emerged: a new American Football League. It began play in 1960 with teams in Dallas, New York, Houston, Denver, Los Angeles, Buffalo, Boston, and Oakland, California. It started drafting the same college players as the NFL—and signing some of the biggest stars, most famously Alabama quarterback Joe Namath (see page 136). It negotiated a TV deal with NBC worth $36 million—big bucks at the time. Viewers liked the AFL's wide-open, high-scoring style.

By 1966, the NFL was ready to sue for peace. Starting with the 1970 season, the NFL and AFL combined in a true merger, encompassing every team from both leagues. Competing leagues continued to form—the World Football League in 1974–75, the United States Football League in 1983–85, the XFL in 2001. The NFL largely ignored them, and they went away.

The NFL itself tried creating a new league to expand into new markets. In 1991, it launched the World League of American Football, later known as the World League, NFL Europe, and NFL Europa, a mostly (and eventually exclusively) European developmental league. It lasted until June 2007 without either developing many NFL players or igniting a frenzy of European fan interest in American football.

Today, the NFL consists of 32 teams organized into two conferences (National Football Conference and American Football Conference). Each conference consists of four divisions (East, North, South, West) of four teams each.

Moves of established franchises to new cities by owners in search of greener (as in the color of money) pastures occasionally rankle fans in the spurned locale. And there's a glaring hole in the NFL map: there's no team in the nation's second-largest city, Los Angeles.

But by all measures of popularity—polls, TV ratings, income—the NFL ranks at the top of American sport.

WHO'S BETTER, SABAN OR THE BEAR?

Has Nick Saban surpassed Bear Bryant to become the best college football coach in history?

Not so long ago, no Alabama fan would have dared suggest that any mortal could ever usurp Bryant's place of primacy in the college coaching pantheon. But Saban's stunning success since he came to Tuscaloosa has led some to boldly advance his case, while keeping a nervous eye on the heavens for incoming thunderbolts.

Saban (see page 46) won't surpass the Bear's total of 323 victories as a college head coach. (Well, probably; see "Could Saban Out-Win Bryant?" on page 72.) Saban has spent too much time as a college and National Football League assistant coach to rack up a historic college win total under his own name. But after the 13-1 national title season of 2012, he has passed the Bear in winning percentage, leading .839 to .824 and trailing only the perfect 1.000 mark that Allen McCants achieved in 1897 by winning the one Alabama game he ever coached.

And no coach in the history of college football has posted a multiyear stretch of such thorough dominance against such tough competition as

In 2011, Alabama added Nick Saban's statue to its Walk of Champions.
Credit: Patriarca12

Could Saban Out-Win Bryant?

To pass Bear Bryant's total of 323 victories as a college football head coach, Nick Saban would have to maintain his current pace at Alabama for 14 and a half seasons. Could he do it?

Saban entered the 2013 season with 159 wins (crediting him for the purposes of this discussion with the five 2007 victories vacated because of textbook-related NCAA infractions carried over from his predecessor's regime). He was 61 years old; his birthday is October 31. During his first six years at Alabama, he averaged 11 wins a year—actually, 11 and a third. At that pace, he'd pass Bryant with his sixth victory of the 2027 season, which would occur shortly before his 76th birthday on October 31.

Is that possible? No coach has ever maintained such an average over 14 years. But Bobby Bowden almost did. From 1987 through 2000, his Florida State teams averaged 10.86 wins a year. Bowden's teams played an average of 12 and a quarter games a season during that stretch. Saban's Alabama teams have averaged 13 and a half. The four-team championship playoff that's scheduled for implementation following the 2014 season will add yet another game for the two national championship semifinalists.

Would Saban coach into his mid-70s? Could he keep the competitive fires stoked that long? We'll see.

What about Bryant's record of 232 victories at Alabama? Frank Thomas is second with 115, Gene Stallings third with 70, and Saban fourth with, after the 2012 season, 68. So Saban needs 165 to pull ahead. If he maintains his current Alabama pace, he'd tie Bryant with, believe or not, that same sixth victory of 2027 that would give him career win number 324.

Saban has during his past five years at Alabama. From 2008 through 2012, his Crimson Tide team:

- Completed the regular season undefeated and ranked number one before falling to Florida, 31–20, in the Southeastern Conference Championship Game and finishing 12-2.

- Won a national championship.

- Reached the midpoint of the season ranked number one before suffering its first loss and finishing 10-3.

- Won a national championship.
- Won a national championship.

For most coaches, the "worst" of those five seasons would be a career year.

On the other hand, Bryant (see page 37) strode atop the sport of college football longer than any other coach in history. From the 1940s to the 1980s, from leather helmets and the single-wing formation to armor-like padding and the wishbone, he stayed on top of his game.

It's almost impossible for a coach to remain driven, flexible, and innovative for that long. Burnout creeps in. Or complacency. A coach sticks a little too long with the system, or the assistant coaches, that got him to the top. The Bear never let that happen. His last full decade, the 1970s, was also his best (a record of 103-16-1, a winning percentage of .863, and three national championships). No other coach of his stature can say that. He dominated in the one-platoon era, when players stayed on the field for both offense and defense, and he dominated in the unlimited-substitution era of offensive and defensive specialists. No other coach can say that, either. Over the long haul, nobody was better.

The arc of his Alabama career does include a modest dip. After going 11-0 in 1966, Alabama slipped to 8-2-1, 8-3, 6-5, and 6-5-1 over the next four seasons. That downturn coincided with the waning years of racial segregation in the Southeastern Conference, the last major conference to integrate. Bryant, who had pushed for integration at both Kentucky and Texas A&M before coming to Alabama, added black players to the Alabama team in 1971—and went 11-1.

So Bryant still leads in what we might call career value. But in peak value—a sustained run of excellence over a shorter span of seasons—we think Saban has pulled ahead.

Here's another way to look at the "who's better" question: Bryant won six national championships, all at Alabama, in 1961, 1964, 1965, 1973, 1978, and 1979. (See "Coaches' National Championships," page 77.) Saban has won four so far, three at Alabama (2009, 2011, 2012) and one at LSU (2003). Of Bryant's championships, the NCAA considers only one (1979) to be "unanimous"; all three of Saban's Alabama championships, but not his LSU title, are considered unanimous. (If you want to immerse yourself in the details of national championship arguments, see "National Championships," page 53.)

Winning a national championship doesn't mean you're a great coach, as Gene Chizik (career head coaching record: 38-38) demonstrated at Auburn

College Football's Biggest Winners

Officially, Bear Bryant ranks third in victories among major-college coaches. With 323 overall wins, he trails Bobby Bowden, with 377 wins, and Glenn "Pop" Warner, with 336.

If you go by what actually happened on the field, Bryant remains in third with 323 wins, and Florida State legend Bowden still has 377. But Penn State's Joe Paterno leads them both with 409. Warner slips to fourth with 318 wins, or possibly 319. Here's the explanation for the discrepancies:

- To be eligible for the official NCAA list of top major-college winners, coaches must have spent 10 years leading a Football Bowl Subdivision school or its equivalent. However, the NCAA still counts the victories those coaches achieved at lower-level four-year institutions—for example, Bowden's 31 wins at Howard College (now Samford University).

- Paterno won 409 games at Penn State, but the NCAA vacated 111 of them because of the child sex abuse scandal at the school.

- The NCAA credits Warner with 18 wins as coach of Iowa State from 1895 through 1899, but few others do—not even Iowa State itself. So in our "real list" below, we won't either. In each of those years, Warner led Iowa State in preseason drills, then left to coach Georgia (1895–96), Cornell (1897–98), or Carlisle Indian Industrial School (1899) once the actual season started.

- Historians differ over whether Carlisle's 1908 record was 11-2-1 or 10-2-1. The NCAA goes with the latter, which would give Warner 318 victories if you remove the 18 Iowa State wins.

after his 2010 national title. But almost every great coach has at least one. The biggest name never to finish a season on top is Bo Schembechler, head coach at Miami of Ohio (1963–68) and Michigan (1969–89). His 1985 Michigan team came closest, ending at number 2 with a 10-1-1 record.

Other notables who have never won a national title, at least according to the semiofficial NCAA championship list, include Barry Alvarez of Wisconsin; Frank Beamer of Murray State and Virginia Tech; Earle Bruce of Tampa, Iowa State, Ohio State, Northern Iowa, and Colorado State; Fritz Crisler of

Minnesota, Princeton, and Michigan; Doug Dickey of Tennessee and Florida; Bobby Dodd of Georgia Tech; Terry Donahue of UCLA; Frank Howard of Clemson; Frank Kush of Arizona State; Mark Richt of Georgia—and Frank Thomas of Chattanooga (now Tennessee-Chattanooga) and Alabama. (For a discussion of the 1934 and 1941 national championships that Alabama claims on Thomas's behalf, see National Championships, page 53.)

Those in a position to know claim that Saban is practically the second coming of Bryant. "I'm a diehard Nick Saban fan, because he's teaching the same things that Coach Bryant taught 50 years ago to us guys about honesty and integrity and discipline and teamwork and those kind of things," said Lee Roy Jordan, who starred as a center and linebacker on Bryant's 1961 title team (see page 118). Jordan was speaking at a 2013 fund-raiser in Mobile, Alabama.

"He's teaching these guys, just like Coach Bryant always said, the game of life, not just the game of football. If you apply those things in your life and your profession, you'll be successful no matter what business you're in."

Dennis Homan, a star wide receiver for Bryant in the 1960s (see page 109), said in 2012, "Coach Saban is a lot like Coach Bryant. Talking about finishing, talking about teamwork and dedication, pride. It's a 'we' thing; it's not a 'me' thing. He's got the players buying into that, and that's the reason we've been successful."

Both coaches maintained strong ties to their former players. Bryant's boys marveled at how warm and fatherly he could be to his alumni—especially compared to how terrifying he had seemed when he was their coach. He developed one of his closest post-Alabama friendships with quarterback Joe Namath (see page 136), whom he had repeatedly disciplined and even famously suspended.

"We pride ourselves on the fact that our players come back a lot," said Saban at the 2013 Southeastern Conference Media Days. "A lot have been successful. We even have players that have been unsuccessful and suspended and come back and make an impact on our players when they realize that what they did is not the way to go, and they can affect somebody else in a positive way."

Affecting somebody in a positive way is what all coaches try to do. The best try to do it both on and off the field. Nobody has done it better than Bryant and Saban. Between the two in that very important arena, we'll have to call it a tie.

Top 10 Winningest Coaches

■ Official NCAA List (Through 2012)

377 Bobby Bowden, Samford, West Virginia, Florida State	**258** Frank Beamer, Murray State, Virginia Tech
336 Glenn "Pop" Warner, Georgia, Iowa State, Cornell, Carlisle, Pittsburgh, Stanford, Temple	**257** LaVell Edwards, Brigham Young
	255 Tom Osborne, Nebraska
323 **Paul "Bear" Bryant, Maryland, Kentucky, Texas A&M, Alabama**	**249** Lou Holtz, William & Mary, North Carolina State, Arkansas, Minnesota, Notre Dame, South Carolina
314 Amos Alonzo Stagg, Springfield, Chicago, Pacific	**238** Woody Hayes, Denison, Miami (Ohio), Ohio State
298 Joe Paterno, Penn State	

■ The Real List (Through 2012)

409 Joe Paterno	**258** Frank Beamer
377 Bobby Bowden	**257** LaVell Edwards
323 **Paul "Bear" Bryant**	**255** Tom Osborne
318 Glenn "Pop" Warner	**249** Lou Holtz
314 Amos Alonzo Stagg	**238** Woody Hayes

■ Just FBS Wins (Wins while coaching a Football Bowl Series or equivalent school, through 2012)

409 Joe Paterno, Penn State	**257** LaVell Edwards, Brigham Young
346 Bobby Bowden, West Virginia, Florida State	**255** Tom Osborne, Nebraska
323 **Paul "Bear" Bryant, Maryland, Kentucky, Texas A&M, Alabama**	**249** Lou Holtz, William & Mary, North Carolina State, Arkansas, Minnesota, Notre Dame, South Carolina
318 Glenn "Pop" Warner, Georgia, Iowa State, Cornell, Carlisle, Pittsburgh, Stanford, Temple	**234** Bo Schembechler, Miami (Ohio), Michigan
314 Amos Alonzo Stagg, Springfield, Chicago, Pacific	**230** Mack Brown, Tulane, North Carolina, Texas

Coaches' National Championships

**NCAA Football Bowl Subdivision teams or equivalent
(Based on a semiofficial NCAA list; the list shows two or more teams
sharing the championship in some years)**

6 Paul "Bear" Bryant, Alabama (solo, 1979; shared, 1961, 1964–65, 1973, 1978)

6 Fielding Yost, Michigan (solo, 1901–02; shared, 1903–04, 1918, 1923)

5 Bernie Bierman, Minnesota (solo, 1934–36, 1940–41)

5 Woody Hayes, Ohio State (solo, 1968; shared, 1954, 1957, 1961, 1970)

4 Frank Leahy, Notre Dame (solo, 1943, 1946–47, 1949)

4 John McKay, Southern California (solo, 1962, 1967, 1972; shared, 1974)

4 Knute Rockne, Notre Dame (solo, 1924, 1929; shared, 1919, 1930)

4 Nick Saban, LSU (shared, 2003), Alabama (solo, 2009, 2011–12)

3 Walter Camp, Yale (solo, 1888, 1891–92)

3 Percy Haughton, Harvard (solo, 1913; shared, 1910, 1912)

3 Howard Jones, Yale (solo, 1909), Southern California (solo, 1931–32)

3 Tom Osborne, Nebraska (solo, 1994–95; shared, 1997)

3 Bill Roper, Princeton (solo, 1906; shared, 1911, 1922)

3 Darrell Royal, Texas (solo, 1963, 1969; shared, 1970)

3 Andy Smith, California (solo, 1920; shared, 1921–22)

3 Barry Switzer, Oklahoma (solo, 1975, 1985; shared, 1974)

3 Wallace Wade, Alabama (solo, 1925; shared, 1926, 1930)

3 Glenn "Pop" Warner, Pittsburgh (solo, 1916; shared, 1918), Stanford (shared, 1926)

3 Bud Wilkinson, Oklahoma (solo, 1950, 1955–56)

3 Bob Zuppke, Illinois (shared, 1919, 1923, 1927)

2 Earl "Red" Blaik, Army (solo, 1944–45)

2 Bobby Bowden, Florida State (solo, 1993, 1999)

*2 Pete Carroll, Southern California (solo, 2004; shared, 2003)

2 Duffy Daugherty, Michigan (shared, 1965–66)

2 Bob Devaney, Nebraska (solo, 1971; shared, 1970)

2 Gil Dobie, Cornell (shared, 1921–22)

2 Dennis Erickson, Miami (Florida) (solo, 1989; shared, 1991)

2 Bill Hollenback, Penn State (shared, 1911, 1912)

2 Urban Meyer, Florida (solo, 2006, 2008)

2 Ara Parseghian, Notre Dame (shared, 1966, 1973)

2 Joe Paterno, Penn State (solo, 1982, 1986)

2 George Woodruff, Pennsylvania (solo, 1895, 1897)

1 George Adams-George Stewart, Harvard (solo, 1890)

■ *NCAA Football Bowl Subdivision teams or equivalent (continued)*

1 William Alexander, Georgia Tech (solo, 1928)

1 Mack Brown, Texas (solo, 2005)

1 Dana X. Bible, Texas A&M (shared, 1919)

1 Paul Brown, Ohio State (solo, 1942)

1 Frank Broyles, Arkansas (shared, 1964)

1 Lloyd Carr, Michigan (shared, 1997)

1 Gene Chizik, Auburn (solo, 2010)

1 Larry Coker, Miami (Florida) (solo, 2001)

1 Charles Daly, Army (solo, 1914)

1 Parke H. Davis, Lafayette (shared, 1896)

1 Dan Devine, Notre Dame (solo, 1977)

1 Benjamin Dibblee, Harvard (solo, 1899)

1 Paul Dietzel, LSU (shared, 1958)

1 Vince Dooley, Georgia (solo, 1980)

1 LaVell Edwards, Brigham Young (solo, 1984)

1 Forest Evashevski, Iowa (shared, 1958)

1 Bob Fisher, Harvard (shared, 1919)

1 W. Cameron Forbes, Harvard (solo, 1898)

1 Danny Ford, Clemson (solo, 1981)

1 Phillip Fulmer, Tennessee (solo, 1998)

1 John Heisman, Georgia Tech (solo, 1917)

1 A. R. T. Hillenbrand, Princeton (shared, 1903)

1 Lou Holtz, Notre Dame (solo, 1988)

1 Don James, Washington (shared, 1991)

1 Jimmy Johnson, Miami (Florida) (solo, 1987)

1 T. A. D. "Tad" Jones, Yale (shared, 1927)

1 Ralph "Shug" Jordan, Auburn (shared, 1957)

1 Harry Kipke, Michigan (solo, 1933)

1 William Knox, Yale (solo, 1907)

1 Johnny Majors, Pittsburgh (solo, 1976)

1 Bill McCartney, Colorado (shared, 1990)

1 Malcolm McBride, Yale (solo, 1900)

1 Sol Metzger, Pennsylvania (shared, 1908)

1 Dutch Meyer, Texas Christian (solo, 1938)

1 Les Miles, LSU (shared, 2003)

1 Clarence "Biggie" Munn, Michigan State (solo, 1952)

1 Robert Neyland, Tennessee (solo, 1951)

1 Homer Norton, Texas A&M (solo, 1939)

1 Bernie Oosterbaan, Michigan (solo, 1948)

1 William Rhodes, Yale (solo, 1894)

1 John Robinson, Southern California (shared, 1978)

1 Bobby Ross, Georgia Tech (shared, 1990)

1 Red Sanders, UCLA (shared, 1954)

1 Howard Schnellenberger, Miami (Florida) (solo, 1983)

1 Ben Schwartzwalder, Syracuse (solo, 1959)

1 Al Sharpe, Cornell (solo, 1915)

1 Steve Spurrier, Florida (solo, 1996)

1 Amos Alonzo Stagg, Chicago (solo, 1905)

1 **Gene Stallings, Alabama (solo, 1992)**

1 Bob Stoops, Oklahoma (solo, 2000)

1 Jock Sutherland, Pittsburgh (solo, 1937)

1 Jim Tatum, Maryland (solo, 1953)

1 Joe Thompson, Pittsburgh (shared, 1910)

1 Jim Tressel, Ohio State (solo, 2002)

1 John Vaught, Mississippi (shared, 1960)

1 Murray Warmath, Minnesota (shared, 1960)

1 Carl "Cap" Williams, Pennsylvania (shared, 1904)

1 Edgar Wingard, LSU (shared, 1908)

*2004 Bowl Championship Series title vacated because of NCAA sanctions involving running back Reggie Bush

Note: The NCAA also lists national championships for Princeton in 1869–70, 1872–73, 1878–79, 1880 (shared with Yale), 1885, 1889, 1893, and 1896 (shared with Lafayette); Yale in 1874, 1876–77, 1880 (shared with Princeton), 1881–84, and 1886–87; and Harvard in 1875, but those teams were led by their captains and had no formal coach.

The Most Solo Championships

NCAA Football Bowl Subdivision teams or equivalent
(Based on a semiofficial NCAA list of solo and shared championships)

4 Frank Leahy, Notre Dame, 1943, 1946–47, 1949

3 Bernie Bierman, Minnesota, 1934–36

3 Walter Camp, Yale, 1888, 1891–92

3 Howard Jones, Yale, 1909; Southern California, 1931–32

3 John McKay, Southern California, 1962, 1967, 19712

3 Nick Saban, Alabama, 2009, 2011–12

3 Bud Wilkinson, Oklahoma, 1950, 1955–56

2 Earl "Red" Blaik, Army, 1944–45

2 Bobby Bowden, Florida State, 1993, 1999

2 Urban Meyer, Florida, 2006, 2008

2 Tom Osborne, Nebraska, 1994–95

2 Joe Paterno, Penn State, 1982, 1986

2 Knute Rockne, Notre Dame, 1924, 1929

2 Darrell Royal, Texas, 1963, 1969

2 Barry Switzer, Oklahoma, 1975, 1985

2 George Woodruff, Pennsylvania, 1895, 1897

2 Fielding Yost, Michigan, 1901–02

1 George Adams-George Stewart, Harvard, 1890

1 William Alexander, Georgia Tech, 1928

1 Mack Brown, Texas, 2005

1 Paul Brown, Ohio State, 1942

1 Paul "Bear" Bryant, Alabama, 1979

*1 Pete Carroll, Southern California, 2004

1 Gene Chizik, Auburn, 2010

1 Larry Coker, Miami (Florida), 2001

1 Charles Daly, Army, 1914

1 Bob Devaney, Nebraska, 1971

1 Dan Devine, Notre Dame, 1977

1 Benjamin Dibblee, Harvard, 1899

1 Vince Dooley, Georgia, 1980

1 LaVell Edwards, Brigham Young, 1984

1 Dennis Erickson, Miami (Florida), 1989

1 W. Cameron Forbes, Harvard, 1898

1 Danny Ford, Clemson, 1981

1 Phillip Fulmer, Tennessee, 1998

1 Percy Haughton, Harvard, 1913

1 Woody Hayes, Ohio State, 1968

1 John Heisman, Georgia Tech, 1917

1 Lou Holtz, Notre Dame, 1988

1 Jimmy Johnson, Miami (Florida), 1987

1 Harry Kipke, Michigan, 1933

■ *NCAA Football Bowl Subdivision teams or equivalent (continued)*

1 Harry Kipke, Michigan, 1933	**1** Ben Schwartzwalder, Syracuse, 1959
1 William Knox, Yale, 1907	**1** Al Sharpe, Cornell, 1915
1 Johnny Majors, Pittsburgh, 1976	**1** Andy Smith, California, 1920
1 Malcolm McBride, Yale, 1900	**1** Steve Spurrier, Florida, 1996
1 Dutch Meyer, Texas Christian, 1938	**1** Amos Alonzo Stagg, Chicago, 1905
1 Clarence "Biggie" Munn, Michigan State, 1952	**1 Gene Stallings, Alabama, 1992**
1 Robert Neyland, Tennessee, 1951	**1** Bob Stoops, Oklahoma, 2000
1 Homer Norton, Texas A&M, 1939	**1** Jock Sutherland, Pittsburgh, 1937
1 Bernie Oosterbaan, Michigan, 1948	**1** Jim Tatum, Maryland, 1953
1 William Rhodes, Yale, 1894	**1** Jim Tressel, Ohio State, 2002
1 Bill Roper, Princeton, 1906	**1 Wallace Wade, Alabama, 1925**
1 Howard Schnellenberger, Miami (Florida), 1983	**1** Glenn "Pop" Warner, Pittsburgh, 1916

**2004 Bowl Championship Series title vacated because of NCAA sanctions involving running back Reggie Bush*

OUR ALABAMA ALL-STARS: FOOTBALL

(based on their pro careers)

Quarterback: **BART STARR**

Running back: **SHAUN ALEXANDER**

Wide receiver: **DON HUTSON**

Tight end: **OZZIE NEWSOME**

Offensive guard: **JOHN HANNAH**

Offensive tackle: **CHRIS SAMUELS**

Center: **DWIGHT STEPHENSON**

Kicker: **TOMMY BROOKER**

Safety: **ROMAN HARPER**

Cornerback: **MIKE WASHINGTON**

Linebacker: **DERRICK THOMAS**

Defensive end: **MARTY LYONS**

Defensive tackle: **JESS RICHARDSON**

Nose tackle: **BOB BAUMHOWER**

Punter: **CHRIS MOHR**

Kick-punt returner: **JAVIER ARENAS**

Held back by injuries and bad coaching decisions at Alabama, Bart Starr became one of the greatest National Football League quarterbacks ever.
Credit: Paul W. Bryant Museum/The University of Alabama

Best overall: **DON HUTSON** created the position of modern receiver and set more records than anyone else in National Football League history. Plus, "The Alabama Antelope" is such a cool nickname.

PLAYER BIOS

College years are years receiving a varsity letter unless otherwise noted.

Pro years are years actually played through the 2012 season.

AAFC: All-America Football Conference	**USFL:** United States Football League
AFL: American Football League	**WFL:** World Football League
ArFL: Arena Football League	**WL:** World League
CFL: Canadian Football League	**WLAF:** World League of American Football
NFL: National Football League	**HOF:** Hall of Fame
UFL: United Football League	**MVP:** Most Valuable Player

RAY ABRUZZESE ■ *Defensive Back-Punt Returner-Kick Returner-Long Snapper*

COLLEGE: 1960–61 . . . . **AFL:** 1962–66

Little remembered today, Ray Abruzzese nevertheless greatly influenced the course of professional football. Abruzzese was a 6-1, 195-pound halfback and defensive back for Alabama at the beginning of the Bear Bryant era. He played more on defense than offense, and he also returned punts and kicks.

He finished his college career on a high note, playing for the 1961 national championship team, which went 11-0 and beat Arkansas, 10–3, in the Sugar Bowl. Along the way, he acquired as a roommate a highly touted young quarterback whom Bryant had recruited in 1960: Joe Namath.

In 1964, Namath (see page 136) was deciding between the St. Louis Cardinals of the established National Football League and the New York Jets of the fledgling American Football League. He told the Jets he wanted to play with his old Crimson Tide roommate.

Abruzzese was then a member of the AFL's Buffalo Bills.

The Bills obligingly traded Abruzzese, and Namath picked the Jets. His star power gave the AFL credibility and helped lead to the AFL-NFL merger in 1966.

Abruzzese played sparingly for two years with the Jets before retiring from football. He moved to Fort Lauderdale, Florida, as a partner with Namath in the Bachelors III restaurant-bar there and continued in the business with other area establishments. He died in Fort Lauderdale in 2011, age 73.

SHAUN ALEXANDER ■ *Running Back*

COLLEGE: 1996–99 . . . . **NFL:** 2000–08, 3 Pro Bowls; Alabama Sports HOF, Bert Bell Award

Only in football would someone 5-11 and 225 pounds be considered small. But that's what they said about Shaun Alexander after both high school and college: maybe a little small. The University of Alabama and the Seattle Seahawks took chances on him anyway. Boy, are they glad they did.

Alexander holds more than a dozen Alabama records, including those for most touchdowns in a season (24 in 1999), most rushing yards in a game (291 against LSU in 1996), and most career rushing yards (3,565). He could have left for a rich pro contract after his junior season, but he and star offensive lineman Chris Samuels (see page 150) decided to return together because of their love for Alabama.

In 2000, Alexander's rookie year with the Seahawks, he gained only 313 yards on 64 carries playing behind veteran Ricky Watters. The next year, he exploded, gaining 1,318 yards and leading the league with 14 rushing touchdowns (adding two more receiving TDs). It was the first of five straight years of more than 1,100 yards rushing and more than 15 total touchdowns.

Shaun Alexander signs autographs during 2006 Seattle Seahawks pre-season training.
Credit: Tom McDonald, Jason Fierle

After missing the National Football League rushing title by a single yard in 2004, Alexander reached his career peak in 2005. He led the league with 1,880 rushing yards and an NFL-record 28 touchdowns. He won the Bert Bell Award as the league's player of the year. The Seahawks finished the regular season with a league-best 13-3 record and reached the Super Bowl. They lost to the Pittsburgh Steelers, 21–10, although Alexander was the game's leading rusher with 95 yards on 20 carries.

Injuries started to slow him in 2006. After the 2007 season, the Seahawks released him. He caught on in 2008 with the Washington Redskins but played just four games.

Alexander was known throughout his career as a smiling, positive person. He and his wife, Valerie, who live in the Washington, DC, area, speak frequently

continued on next page

about their born-again Christian faith and their advocacy of sexual abstinence outside marriage. In 2011, Alexander was inducted into the Alabama Sports Hall of Fame. And in this era of video games, he holds another major distinction: he was the first person to be featured on the covers of both the leading college and pro football video games, *NCAA Football 2001* and *Madden 2007*. In early 2013, Alexander attended the NFL Hollywood Boot Camp at Universal Studios and revealed that he planned to try writing movies. Stay tuned.

MARK ANDERSON ■ *Defensive End*

COLLEGE: 2002–05 . . . . **NFL:** 2006–12

Charging into the National Football League as a pass-rushing specialist (he's among Alabama's career top 10 in tackles for loss), Mark Anderson recorded 12 quarterback sacks, eighth in the league, his rookie year. His Chicago Bears reached the Super Bowl (losing, 29–17, to the Indianapolis Colts). But Anderson, 6-4 and 255 pounds, couldn't duplicate that performance in

JAVIER ARENAS ■ *Cornerback-Punt Returner-Kick Returner*

COLLEGE: 2006–09 . . . .
NFL: 2010–12

Javier Arenas began 2010 by helping Alabama beat Texas, 37–21, at the Rose Bowl in Pasadena, California, for the national championship. That summer, he signed a four-season, $3.798 million contract with the National Football League's Kansas City Chiefs. Not a bad year. The stocky Arenas, 5-9 and 195 pounds, returned punts and kicks, played extensively as an extra defensive back in nickel and dime coverages, and became a starting cornerback halfway through the 2012 season, recording a career-high 60 tackles. In 2011 he even scored a touchdown lining up as quarterback on a play near the goal line. Before the 2013 season, the Arizona Cardinals plucked him from the Chiefs in a trade designed to upgrade their pass coverage.

At Alabama, Javier Arenas set a Southeastern Conference record with seven career punt returns for touchdowns.

Credit: Jeffrey Beall

> ## How Times Have Changed
>
> Half a century ago, Tommy Brooker (see page 89) led Alabama's undefeated 1961 national championship team in pass receptions—with 12. Of course, the offense didn't have to do much. The defense gave up a total of only 25 points in 11 games.

subsequent years. The Bears cut him after four games in 2010. The Houston Texans immediately picked him up for the balance of the season.

In 2011, the New England Patriots signed Anderson as a free agent. He rebounded with a 10-sack season and added another 1.5 sacks in the Patriots' 21–17 Super Bowl loss to the New York Giants. That earned him a four-year, $19.5 million contract with the Buffalo Bills. Unfortunately, a left-knee injury in game five of 2012 required season-ending surgery, and the Bills released Anderson in the offseason. Fortunately, even though at press time he was looking for another team, $7.9 million from that big contract was guaranteed.

MARK BARRON ■ *Safety*

COLLEGE: 2008–11 . . . . **NFL:** 2012

A standout safety for two national championship teams at Alabama (2009 and 2011), Mark Barron became the Crimson Tide's highest-drafted defensive back ever when the Tampa Bay Buccaneers grabbed him in the seventh round of the 2012 National Football League draft.

Barron offers both size (he's 6-1 and 213 pounds) and speed, and turned in a solid rookie year at strong safety with 89 tackles, 72 of them unassisted. Still, the Buccaneers gave up the most passing yards in the NFL. So after the 2012 season they acquired free safety Dashon Goldson and cornerback Darrelle Revis, both former All-Pros, and got rid of every holdover defensive backfield starter—except Barron.

The Mobile, Alabama, native was happy to still be a Buc. "There are some things I still want to improve on," Barron said. "I'm a lot more comfortable; I will say that."

He's also a bit more financially comfortable. He worked out a deal with Revis to switch to uniform number 23 and let Revis have his old number, 24—for a reported $50,000.

CORNELIUS BENNETT ■ *Linebacker*

COLLEGE: 1983–86 . . . . **NFL:** 1987–2000, 5 Pro Bowls;
College Football HOF, Alabama Sports HOF, Rotary Lombardi Award

After starring in both college and the pros, Cornelius Bennett stays very active with work for charities and the NFL Players Association.
Credit: Paul W. Bryant Museum/
The University of Alabama

The Indianapolis Colts made Cornelius Bennett their first-round draft choice (the second pick overall) in 1987 after a senior season at Alabama that saw him win the Rotary Lombardi Award as the nation's best college lineman or linebacker. But he didn't play for the Colts until his last two National Football League seasons. Stalemated contract negotiations led the team to trade his rights to the Buffalo Bills in a 1987 midseason mega-deal that brought superstar running back Eric Dickerson to the Colts.

Because of the holdout, Bennett played only eight games. He still made an impact, recording 8.5 sacks and 69 tackles. In nine years with the Bills, Bennett was named to five Pro Bowls and reached the Super Bowl four straight years (1990–1993). After signing with the Atlanta Falcons as a free agent before the 1996 season, he also reached Super Bowl XXXIII in 1999. But his teams never won that biggest of big games.

After Super Bowl XXXIII, he signed as a free agent with the Colts for his final two seasons. He still had something left; in 1999, he recorded 72 tackles and five quarterback sacks, and forced five fumbles.

Bennett, 6-2 and 237 pounds, starred for 14 years as one of the greatest linebackers in NFL history. Since his retirement, he has lived in South Florida and devoted significant time to charitable causes, including Children's Village Inc., a group home for foster children in his hometown of Birmingham. He also chairs the NFL Players Association's Former Players Board of Directors.

"This is what I get joy from now," he told the *Birmingham News*. "I'm helping others, and I can honestly say I enjoy doing what I'm doing now more than when I was a player, because then it was only about me."

BOB BAUMHOWER ■ *Nose Tackle*

COLLEGE: 1974–76 . . . . **NFL:** 1977–84, 1986, 5 Pro Bowls; Alabama Sports HOF

Football was a lark for Bob Baumhower until Coach Bear Bryant read him the riot act at the beginning of his sophomore year. "He was right," Baumhower recalls on the website for his restaurant chain. "I'd never put my heart into football. I was just doing it for fun. He changed everything for me and made me want to be as good as I could be."

That turned out to be very good indeed. The two-time All-Southeastern Conference defensive tackle became one of the best National Football League nose tackles ever. The 6-5, 260-pound Baumhower anchored the line for the great Miami Dolphins defenses of the late 1970s and early 1980s. Along with defensive ends Doug Betters and Kim Bokamper, linebackers Bob Brudzinski and Charles Bowser, and defensive backs (and brothers) Lyle and Glenn Blackwood, he won fame as one of the team's "Killer B's."

Nose tackles take a fearsome beating. Injuries began seriously affecting Baumhower in 1984. In December, after playing in 117 consecutive games from the start of his career, he missed the second-last contest of the season. After a 38–16 Super Bowl loss to the San Francisco 49ers, he skipped the Pro Bowl in favor of knee surgery. The damage turned out to be much more extensive than the doctors had thought. Baumhower sat out the entire 1985 season, hobbled through 12 games in 1986, then retired.

Early in his pro career, he had gone into partnership with New York Jets quarterbacks Joe Namath (see page 136) and Richard Todd (see page 161)—fellow Alabama alums with whom he shared an agent—in the Bachelors III nightclub in Fort Lauderdale, Florida. A former Dolphins teammate introduced Baumhower to another restaurant that served buffalo wings. In 1981, the first Baumhower's Wings Restaurant opened in Tuscaloosa.

Today, there are nine Baumhower's Restaurants across the state of Alabama—energetic sports bars with plenty of beer, TVs, and wings. Baumhower also operates Bimini Bob's, a casual burgers-and-seafood place, in Orange Beach, Alabama, and Bob Baumhower's Compleat Angler Seafood Grill & Bar in Orange Beach and Daphne, Alabama. He lives nearby in Fairhope.

JIM BOWDOIN ■ *Guard*

COLLEGE: 1927–28 . . . . **NFL:** 1928–34

James L. "Goofy" Bowdoin, the pride of Coffee Springs, Alabama, started his college career by helping the Crimson Tide to its first national championship. As a freshman, he was a member (though he seldom played) of the 1925 team that went 10-0 and beat Washington 20-19 in the Rose Bowl (known as "The Football Game That Changed the South" for the respect it brought Southern football and the South in general).

The next year, Alabama again blitzed through a 9-0 regular season, but this time it finished the Rose Bowl in a tie, 7–7, with Stanford, splitting the national championship glory with the California school. Bowdoin again rode the bench. He earned a varsity letter in 1927 and 1928, but the team slipped to 5-4-1 and 6-3.

When Bowdoin joined the National Football League's Green Bay Packers in 1928, the league was only eight years old and just beginning to register on the nation's sporting consciousness. The 6-foot-1, 227-pound offensive and defensive guard won NFL championships in 1929, 1930, and 1931 with the Packers. He also played for the Brooklyn Dodgers, New York Giants, and Portsmouth Spartans. He died in 1969, age 65.

BRYON BRAGGS ■ *Defensive End*

COLLEGE: 1977–80 . . . . **NFL:** 1981–84

As a defensive tackle, Byron Braggs played in four straight winning bowl games for Alabama: the Sugar Bowl in 1978 (Alabama 35, Ohio State 6), 1979 (Alabama 14, Penn State 7 for a national championship), and 1980 (Alabama 24, Arkansas 9 for another national title), and the Cotton Bowl in 1981 (Alabama 30, Baylor 2).

In the National Football League, the 6-4, 290-pound Braggs moved to defensive end, spending three years with the Green Bay Packers (for whom he registered 5.5 quarterback sacks in 1983) and a final season with the Tampa Bay Buccaneers. His right knee, which required six surgeries over the years, finally knocked him out of the game.

Braggs now lives in Lansdowne, Virginia, west of Washington, D.C. He works as a criminal investigator for the U.S. Department of Homeland Security.

TOMMY BROOKER ■ *Kicker-Tight End*

COLLEGE: 1959–61 . . . . **AFL:** 1962–66, 1 All-Star Team;
Alabama Sports HOF

Tommy Brooker never missed an extra-point kick during his five-year American Football League career, going 149 for 149. Brooker had been a reliable split end as well as a kicker for Alabama teams that didn't pass much. As a pro, he caught only six passes. But in his rookie year, he kicked an overtime field goal that won the AFL championship for the Dallas Texans, who then became the Kansas City Chiefs. An injury in 1966 kept him from playing in the first-ever Super Bowl (though no last-second field goal would have prevented the Chiefs' 35–10 loss to the Green Bay Packers).

Traded to Denver, Brooker, 6-2 and 235 pounds, retired instead. He returned to Tuscaloosa and did well as an insurance and real estate broker. He is founder and president of the Alabama A-Club Educational and Charitable Foundation. In 2011, he received the Paul W. Bryant Alumni-Athlete Award for outstanding character and accomplishment.

FERNANDO BRYANT ■ *Cornerback*

COLLEGE: 1995–98 . . . . **NFL:** 1999–2008

A top cornerback and kick returner at Alabama, Fernando Bryant was never a National Football League star but always a solid starter until age and injuries finally chased him down. In 1999, the Jacksonville Jaguars made Bryant, 5-10 and 175 pounds, their first-round draft choice. He also played for the Detroit Lions and, briefly, Pittsburgh Steelers. His extensive humanitarian and charitable work has included visits with high-school athletes to counsel them about academics, peer pressure, and stress management.

BILL BUCKLER ■ *Guard*

COLLEGE: 1923–25 . . . . **NFL:** 1926–28, 1931–33

In his last collegiate game, the famous 1926 Rose Bowl in which underdog Alabama pounded out a bruising 20-19 victory over Washington, Bill Buckler provided the margin of victory. Each team scored three touchdowns. Washington made one of three extra-point kicks. Buckler, Alabama's kicker, made two of three.

Moving on to the Chicago Bears, the 6-foot, 238-pound Buckler became one of the fledgling National Football League's top lineman. The influential

Green Bay [Wisconsin] *Press-Gazette* named him to its All-Pro second team following his rookie season.

After his retirement from football, Buckler lived in Southern Illinois near St. Louis. He died in 1979, age 78.

JIM CAIN ■ *Defensive End*

COLLEGE: 1945–48 . . . . **NFL:** 1949–50, 1953–55

Jim Cain began his college career in the waning days of World War II. After he lettered for four years at Alabama as a two-way end, the Chicago Cardinals picked him in the seventh round of the 1949 National Football League draft.

Chicago head coach Buddy Parker moved to the Detroit Lions in 1950 and engineered a trade to bring Cain with him. Cain, 6-1 and 200 pounds, started at defensive end all four of his seasons with the Lions. Two years of military service during the Korean War kept him from enjoying the team's league championship in 1951, but he returned for championship and runner-up seasons in 1953 and 1954, respectively. After the Lions slipped to 3-9 in 1955, Cain retired from football. He died in 2001, four days after his 74th birthday.

ANTOINE CALDWELL ■ *Guard-Center*

COLLEGE: 2005–08 . . . . **NFL:** 2009–12

A consensus All-America center for Alabama in 2008 and a Crimson Tide co-captain in both 2007 and 2008, Antoine Caldwell went to the Houston Texans in the third round of the National Football League draft. He started part time at center and guard his first three seasons and battled an ankle injury in 2011. The 6-3, 311-pound Caldwell started the first six games of 2012 at right guard, then suffered a concussion and spent the rest of the year as a reserve. In the off-season, he signed as a free agent with the Buffalo Bills.

JAMES CARPENTER ■ *Offensive Tackle*

COLLEGE: 2009–10 . . . . **NFL:** 2011–12

Massive offensive lineman James Carpenter, 6-4 and 321 pounds, joined Alabama as a junior-college transfer in 2009. In 2010, he made some All-Southeastern Conference teams as a senior and went in the first round of the National Football League draft to the Seattle Seahawks. Midway through his rookie season, after he had established himself as the starting right tackle, he tore the anterior cruciate ligament in his left knee—during practice. He made it back for the fourth game of the 2012 season, missed two games later in the year because of a concussion, then reinjured the knee and underwent more surgery in the off-season. This is why athletes try to make as much money as they can, while they can.

PAUL OTT CARRUTH ■ *Running Back*

COLLEGE: 1981–82, 1984 . . . . **USFL:** 1985; **NFL:** 1986–89

Dependable as both a blocker and a runner, Paul Ott Carruth co-captained the Crimson Tide his senior year. After a year with the Birmingham Stallions of the United States Football League, the 6-1, 220-pound Carruth spent four years in the National Football League as an all-purpose back with the Green Bay Packers and Kansas City Chiefs. He then became an executive with McCullough Oil Company of Trussville, Alabama. In 2006, he and his wife, Lindsey, pledged $250,000 to endow an athletic scholarship at Alabama. Carruth's father, also named Paul Ott Carruth, is a singer and broadcast personality in Mississippi known professionally as Paul Ott.

BILL CHAMBERS ■ *Guard*

COLLEGE: 1942 (did not letter) . . . . **AAFC:** 1948–49

After one year of playing sparingly for Alabama, 6-2, 230-pound tackle Bill Chambers enlisted in the Navy and was sent to Georgia Tech as part of the World War II-era V-12 Navy College Training Program. While there, he played for Georgia Tech's football team in 1943 and 1944—earning induction into the Tech Athletics Hall of Fame in 1989.

His wartime teammates included additional "loaners" from Alabama, Vanderbilt, Clemson, and other schools. To this day, archrival Georgia refuses to count the 48-0 and 44-0 drubbings administered by Tech in those years, arguing that the winners weren't really Tech teams.

Chambers later attended UCLA, earning the school's "outstanding senior" award in 1947, before playing two seasons as a guard for the New York Yankees of the short-lived All-America Football Conference. The National Football League absorbed the AAFC's San Francisco 49ers, Cleveland Browns, and Baltimore Colts after the 1949 season, and the rest of the league's teams dissolved, including Chambers' Yankees.

Chambers then disappeared from public view. Not even Wikipedia seems to know what happened to him.

The Castille Connection

JEREMIAH CASTILLE ■ *Cornerback*

COLLEGE: 1979–82 . . . . **NFL:** 1983–88;
Alabama Sports HOF

TIM CASTILLE ■ *Fullback*

COLLEGE: 2003–2006 . . . . **NFL:** 2008–2010

SIMEON CASTILLE ■ *Defensive Back*

COLLEGE: 2004–07 . . . . **NFL:** 2008–09; **UFL:** 2010–11;
ArFL: 2012–13

For both Bear Bryant and Jeremiah Castille, the 1982 Liberty Bowl against Illinois was their last game at Alabama. Castille made sure the Bear went out a winner, intercepting three passes and being named the Most Valuable Player in the Crimson Tide's 21-15 victory.

Castille played cornerback in the National Football League for the Tampa Bay Buccaneers and the Denver Broncos. He peaked in 1985, starting all 16 games for the Bucs and intercepting seven passes. During the American Football Conference Championship Game after the 1987 season, the 5-10, 175-pound Castille entered Broncos lore for "The Fumble," stripping the ball from Cleveland Browns running back Earnest Byner at the two-yard line to prevent what would have been the game-tying touchdown. The Broncos won 38–33. Castille also grabbed Denver's only pass interception in the subsequent 42–10 Super Bowl loss to the Washington Redskins.

He is now an ordained minister in Birmingham, working especially with inner-city youths through his Jeremiah Castille Foundation, and has been the chaplain for the University of Alabama football team since 2001.

Two of Castille's sons also played both at Alabama and in the National Football League. Tim (5-11, 240 pounds; Arizona Cardinals, Kansas City Chiefs) was a tailback and fullback at Alabama. In the NFL, he settled in at fullback, spending most of his time blocking. He spent the 2012 season as a graduate assistant coach at Alabama.

Simeon (6-0, 190 pounds; Cincinnati Bengals, San Diego Chargers) won some All-Southeastern Conference mention at Alabama. He has also played with the Florida Tuskers and Virginia Destroyers of the United Football League and the Orlando Predators of the Arena Football League. In 2013, he became defensive coordinator for the high school football team at International Community School in Winter Park, Florida.

Alabama invited Jeremiah's youngest son, Caleb, onto the football team as a nonscholarship walk-on. After playing sparingly as a cornerback, Caleb left football after his 2012 sophomore year. He's studying communication and film at the university and works part-time as an actor and model..

THORNTON CHANDLER ■ *Tight End*

COLLEGE: 1983–85 . . . . **NFL:** 1986–89

Thornton Chandler grew up dreaming of being a deep-threat wide receiver. But then he *really* grew up, to be 6-5 and 240 pounds, and his high-school coach switched him to tight end. Chandler became a crunching blocker for Alabama and then for the Dallas Cowboys for four years in the National Football League. He's now an assistant football and basketball coach at Kingwood Park High School in Kingwood, Texas, in suburban Houston.

JACKIE CLINE ■ *Defensive End-Defensive Tackle*

COLLEGE: 1980–82 . . . . **USFL:** 1983–85; **NFL:** 1987–90

At Alabama, Jackie Cline won the Billy Neighbors Most Improved Defensive Lineman Award, given by coaches at spring practice, three years in a row, 1980–82. That could be interpreted positively (keeps improving) or negatively (keeps needing improvement). Anyway, after college he headed down Interstate 20 to play for the Birmingham Stallions of the United States Football League. He stayed with the Stallions all three years of their (and the league's) existence, compiling consecutive sack totals of 5.5, 4, and 5.

After the USFL's collapse, Cline, 6-5 and 280 pounds, caught on with the Pittsburgh Steelers for one game in 1987, then moved to the Miami Dolphins for the rest of that year plus 1988 (as a starting defensive end) and 1989. After five games with the Detroit Lions in 1990, his career ended.

Cline played at McAdory High School in McCalla, Alabama, where son Dylan was also a star lineman. Dylan is now playing at Jacksonville State University in Jacksonville, Alabama.

TERRENCE CODY ■ *Nose Tackle*

COLLEGE: 2008–09 . . . . **NFL:** 2010–12

With 6-foot-4, 350-pound (at least) Terrence Cody playing nose tackle, Alabama almost didn't need any other defensive linemen. Nor was there room for anyone else. Despite his bulk, Cody is surprisingly agile, as Tennessee discovered when he blocked two field goals during Alabama's 12-10 victory in 2008.

Conditioning issues contributed to a slow start during Cody's rookie National Football League year with the Baltimore Ravens. After the season, fun-loving "Mount Cody" got serious about workouts, slimming down to 325 pounds. In his second season, he was a full-time starter, helping the Ravens rank third in the league in total defense and second in rushing defense. Unfortunately, 2012 was a great year for the Super Bowl–winning Ravens but not for Cody, who lost his starting job and contributed only 25 tackles. Before the 2013 season, going into the last year of his $3 million contract, he had hip and elbow surgery. He also cut his trademark dreadlocks, saying, "I felt like, new year, new look."

JOHN COPELAND ■ *Defensive End*

COLLEGE: 1991–92 . . . . **NFL:** 1993–2000

After manning the defensive line on Alabama's 1992 national championship team, John Copeland was a stalwart for eight years with the Cincinnati Bengals of the National Football League. Following his playing days, big John (6-3, 285 pounds) returned to Tuscaloosa to get his degree from Alabama—and stayed. He now coaches football and other sports at the private Tuscaloosa Academy. He also does broadcast work for local media outlets, including University of Alabama television.

RUSS CRAFT ■ *Defensive Back-Halfback*

COLLEGE: 1940–42 . . . . **NFL:** 1946–54, 2 Pro Bowls

A blazing-fast halfback who could catch the ball and play defense, Russ Craft helped lead excellent Alabama teams in 1940 (7-2), 1941 (9-2; Cotton Bowl

GLEN COFFEE ■ *Running Back*

COLLEGE: 2005, 2007–08 ....**NFL:** 2009

Glen Coffee exploded for 1,383 rushing yards his junior season at Alabama, left school a year early, was drafted in the third round by the San Francisco 49ers, posted a promising National Football League rookie year as an all-purpose back—then shocked the football world by walking away from it all.

Coffee said he felt called by God to another path. He spurned a lot of money but said, "If your only focus is money, you're going to be sorely disappointed." While waiting to see where he felt called next, he worked toward his degree in consumer affairs

Glen Coffee surprised almost everyone with one of the earliest voluntary retirements in football history.

Credit: © BrokenSphere/Wikimedia Commons

at Alabama, playing semipro football (as a 6-1, 200-pound linebacker) on the side. "I want to love what I do," he said. "I don't just want to get paid." In February 2013 he enlisted in the Army with the goal of becoming a member of the Special Forces—the Green Berets. Eventually, he said, he planned to be a minister.

championship), and 1942 (8-3; Orange Bowl championship). He continued playing football during World War II for the powerful Army Doughboys team at Fort Benning, Georgia, before beginning his National Football League career with the Philadelphia Eagles in 1946.

With the 5-9, 178-pound Craft bolstering the defense, the Eagles won a division championship in 1947, their first NFL championship in 1948, and a repeat title in 1949. In 1951 and 1952, Craft was elected to the Pro Bowl. He intercepted 22 passes in his career—4 of them in one game, which tied him with several others for a still-standing NFL record.

He retired back home to West Virginia, where he ran a service station and, from 1969 until 1972, was Brooke County sheriff. He died in January 2009, age 89.

PAUL CRANE ■ *Linebacker-Center*

COLLEGE: 1963–65 . . . . **AFL:** 1966–69; **NFL:** 1970–72; Alabama Sports HOF

Tall and skinny—6-3 and barely 200 pounds—Paul Crane played for seven years as a backup linebacker and center for the New York Jets before and after the American Football League-National Football League merger. After winning national championships his last two years in college, Crane added the Super Bowl III championship in 1969, when his Jets famously upset the NFL's Baltimore Colts, 16–7.

He was an assistant coach under Bear Bryant at Alabama in 1974–77 and at the University of Mississippi in 1978–80 before returning to the Mobile area, where he grew up. He has been involved with Catholic Youth Organization sports and the Mobile Drug Education and Awareness Council. In 1991, he was inducted into the Mobile Sports Hall of Fame.

TINY CROFT ■ *Tackle*

COLLEGE: 1938 (did not letter) . . . . **NFL:** 1942–47

They called him Tiny because he wasn't. At 6-foot-3 and upward of 280 pounds, Milburn Croft was gigantic by the standards of his day and wouldn't look out of place among today's lineman—in terms of bulk if not conditioning. Croft, a Chicagoan, transferred from Alabama to Ripon College in Wisconsin. The Washington Redskins picked him in the 1942 National Football League draft, but he ended up playing with the Green Bay Packers for six seasons. He apparently stayed in Wisconsin after his playing days and died in the town of Woodruff in 1977, age 56.

HOWARD CROSS ■ *Tight End*

COLLEGE: 1985–88 . . . . **NFL:** 1989–2001; Alabama Sports HOF, Jacobs Blocking Award

Blocking was Howard Cross's specialty. At 6-5 and 270 pounds, he was good at it—good enough to win the Jacobs Award as best blocker in the Southeastern Conference during his senior year at Alabama, and good enough to knock out a 13-year National Football League career with the New York Giants. He's still second on the list of games played as a Giant, with 207.

Cross caught 201 passes for 2,194 yards and 17 touchdowns. He played in the Super Bowl in 1991, when the Giants beat the Buffalo Bills, and 2001, when they lost to the Baltimore Ravens.

Since retiring as a player, he's put together a double career. He's a television commentator for the YES Network and a sideline reporter for Giants radio broadcasts. And he's senior vice president with Cresa New York, a giant real estate company that represents commercial tenants. He also does a lot of public speaking and works with kids to encourage them to stay in school.

BRODIE CROYLE ■ *Quarterback*

COLLEGE: 2002–05 . . . . **NFL:** 2006–10

Injuries, starting with a wrecked knee his senior year in high school and continuing with major shoulder and knee damage during his sophomore and junior years at Alabama, kept Brodie Croyle from becoming one of the Crimson Tide's best-ever passing quarterbacks. Finally healthy his senior year, he showed what he could do by throwing for a then–school record 2,499 yards.

Injuries also held the 6-2, 205-pound Croyle back during his five years of part-time National Football League play with the Kansas City Chiefs. It didn't help that the Chiefs were pretty pathetic most of that time, compiling a cumulative record from 2007 through 2009 of 10-38.

In 2011, the Chiefs released him. After unsuccessful trials with other teams, he decided in 2012 to retire. He now works for a real estate and land company in Tuscaloosa. Along with former Alabama linebacker DeMeco Ryans (see page 149) and Olympics gold medal bobsledder Vonetta Flowers, he also owns D1 Birmingham sports training facility in Birmingham. Most significantly, he has become associate executive director of Big Oak Ranch, the "Christian home for children needing a chance" founded in 1974 by his father, John Croyle. John, the current executive director, said in 2013 that Brodie eventually would take over the Big Oak system, which includes boys' and girls' ranches and Westbrook Christian School. John also played for Alabama as a defensive end, lettering in 1971–73.

Super School

The Most Valuable Players in the first three Super Bowls were University of Alabama quarterbacks: Bart Starr (see page 159) in the first two and Joe Namath (see page 136) in Super Bowl III. No Crimson Tide player has won the award since.

BOB CRYDER ■ *Offensive Guard-Offensive Tackle*

COLLEGE: 1975–77 . . . . **NFL:** 1978–86

After an Alabama career that got him some Second-Team All-America mention, 6-foot-4, 275-pound Bob Cryder spent nine years in the National Football League trenches, slugging it out as an offensive tackle and guard for the New England Patriots and Seattle Seahawks. He stayed in the Seattle area after retirement and now owns L & B Equity Ventures of Redmond, Washington.

ED CULPEPPER ■ *Defensive Tackle*

COLLEGE: 1951–54 . . . . **NFL:** 1958–61; **AFL:** 1962–63

Ed Culpepper earned second-team All–Southeastern Conference mention one year at Alabama and got picked in the ninth round of the 1955 National Football League draft by the Green Bay Packers. But he didn't play in the NFL until 1958, with the Chicago Cardinals. In 1960, the 6-5, 255-pound lineman moved with the Cardinals to St. Louis.

After the season, the Minnesota Vikings plucked him in the expansion draft. He spent his only season as a full-time starter with them in 1961, then jumped to the Houston Oilers of the new American Football League in 1962. Just before the 1963 season, he left without telling anyone and drove from Houston to his home in Bradenton, Florida. "I'm not unhappy with anyone," he told a reporter. "I'm just through with football."

He wasn't, quite. He came back to play one more year with the Oilers, then quit for good and seems to have disappeared from public notice ever since.

ERIC CURRY ■ *Defensive End*

COLLEGE: 1990–92 . . . . **NFL:** 1993–99

Two decades after he left Alabama, Eric Curry still shows up on Crimson Tide top 10 lists for quarterback sacks, quarterback hurries, and tackles for loss. He and fellow hard-charging end John Copeland led a defensive line that took Alabama to the national championship in the 1992 season.

The Tampa Bay Buccaneers picked Curry, 6-5 and 270 pounds, in the first round of the National Football League draft. He played well but not brilliantly for five years with the Bucs, peaking at five sacks in his rookie year. Two years of part-time play with the Jacksonville Jaguars rounded out his career. He stayed in Jacksonville, where he's a businessman and regularly gets booked for speaking engagements. Unfortunately, he made the news in 2013 when a long-running child-support dispute with the mother of his 17-year-old daughter delayed for a time his signing a release allowing the girl to attend the U.S. Naval Academy.

MARCELL DAREUS ■ *Defensive Tackle*

COLLEGE: 2008–10 . . . . **NFL:** 2011–12

What do you do when you're named defensive Most Valuable Player in a national championship–winning game? If you're Marcell Dareus, you go pro. After playing a big role in Alabama's 37–21 thrashing of Texas for the 2009 national title, Dareus passed up his senior season and became the first-round draft choice of the Buffalo Bills—the third pick overall. He signed a four-year, $20.4 million contract.

The 6-3, 320-pound Dareus turned in a very solid rookie year, starting the entire season and leading the team with 5.5 sacks despite shoulder and hand injuries. Head coach Chan Gailey said he was "not only a great football player, but he's a great young man."

When a postseason interviewer asked whether the NFL was a big step up from college football, the affable Dareus grinned and replied, "Not from Alabama."

The 2012 season started tragically when, in early September, his younger brother Simeon Gilmore was shot and killed along with two other people in an apparent burglary. "It took a toll on me last year," Dareus said later. After struggling for a few games, he did finish strong to again total 5.5 sacks, this time second on the team. Going into the 2013 season, he was fighting for a starting job.

FRED DAVIS ■ *Tackle*

COLLEGE: 1938–40 . . . . **NFL:** 1941–42, 1945–51,
2 Pro Bowls; Alabama Sports HOF

Burly Fred Davis (6-3, 244 pounds) was voted All–Southeastern Conference his senior year. In his nine-year National Football League career—three seasons with the Washington Redskins, then six with the Chicago Bears—he played for two league champions (1942 Redskins, 1946 Bears). He also contributed to two other playoff teams and was named to the Pro Bowl in 1942 and 1950. He lost 1943, 1944, and part of 1945 to U.S. Army Air Forces service during World War II.

Davis died in 1995, age 77. Fred Davis Jr., a tackle like his father, played for Alabama in 1964.

JOHNNY DAVIS ■ *Fullback*

COLLEGE: 1975–77 . . . . **NFL:** 1978–87

A brutally effective blocker as a wishbone fullback, Johnny Davis could run too. He led Alabama in rushing all three of his varsity years. In the National Football League, the 6-1, 235-pound Davis mostly got the unglamorous job of blasting open holes for other runners—for three years with the Tampa Bay Buccaneers, a year with the San Francisco 49ers, and six years with the Cleveland Browns.

After retiring, Davis became an advertising manager for the North Jersey Media Group in Hackensack, New Jersey. He also has worked in education and does motivational speaking and charity work. And he's a skilled pianist and organist, playing jazz, blues, and gospel.

CHUCK DESHANE ■ *Quarterback (Blocking Back)-Guard-Wingback*

COLLEGE: 1940 . . . . **NFL:** 1945–49

Fans of today's National Football League may find it hard to believe that pro football spent its first few decades as a secondary sport until, in the 1960s, it started soaring to its current heights of popularity. But it's true. Consider the story of Chuck DeShane.

DeShane, then known as Charley, came from Grand Rapids, Michigan, to play quarterback at Alabama. Back then, in the single wing formation, the quarterback was mostly a blocker—and in fact the position was often called "blocking back."

After lettering for coach Frank Thomas's 7-2 Crimson Tide team in 1940, he went on to the NFL, right? Nope. First, from 1942 through 1944, he coached football at Creston High School, his alma mater, in Grand Rapids.

In 1945, DeShane finally gave the NFL a try, signing as a free agent with the Detroit Lions. He played wingback in 1945 and quarterback in 1946, plus linebacker on defense both years. In 1947, the Lions switched from the single wing to the T formation, and DeShane moved to guard. He stood 6-1 and weighed 212 pounds, so he was big for the era. But still, can you imagine Tom Brady switching in midcareer from quarterback to guard?

Unless you were a star, the NFL generally didn't pay much in those days. So DeShane worked as a railroad conductor in the off-season. After 1949, when the Lions posted their fourth straight losing record, he went back home again to Grand Rapids and built a successful career as a securities broker. He died in 2006, age 87, after a long illness.

JOE DOMNANOVICH ■ *Linebacker-Center*

COLLEGE: 1940–42 . . . . **NFL:** 1946–1951; Alabama Sports HOF, Indiana Football HOF

Joe Domnanovich, 6-1 and 215 pounds, played on Alabama's 1941 sort-of national championship team (see "National Championships," page 53) and made several All-America teams while captaining the 1942 squad. World War II service as an Army officer delayed his entry into the National Football League.

He eventually played linebacker and sometimes center for the team known variously as the Boston Yanks, New York Bulldogs, and New York Yanks. He told *The Tuscaloosa News* in 1984, "My highest contract was for $10,000, but that was real good money back in those days."

Alabama had recruited the native of South Bend, Indiana, away from Notre Dame, his hometown team. Domnanovich lived in the Birmingham area after his football days and worked as a supervisor for U.S. Steel. He died in January 2009, a couple of months short of his 90th birthday.

WALLACE GILBERRY ■ *Defensive End*

COLLEGE: 2004–07 . . . . **NFL:** 2008–12

As an undrafted free agent despite having led Alabama his junior and senior years in tackles for loss, 6-3, 267-pound Wallace Gilberry had to fight to establish a National Football League career. Signed but released before the 2008 season by the New York Giants, Gilberry caught on later that year with the Kansas City Chiefs. In 2010, he recorded 7 quarterback sacks. He slumped to 2.5 sacks in 2011 but bounced back with the Cincinnati Bengals in 2012, compiling 6.5 sacks in 14 games as a situational pass rusher. After the season, the Bengals signed him to a contract for three years and $6.75 million.

Wallace Gilberry peaked as a pro (so far) with seven sacks in 2010.
Credit: Jeffrey Beall

Goode Enough

CHRIS GOODE ■ *Cornerback*

College: 1986. . . . . NFL: 1987–93

KERRY GOODE ■ *Running Back*

College: 1983, 1986–87 . . . . NFL: 1988–89

PIERRE GOODE ■ *Wide Receiver*

College: 1987–89 . . . . NFL: none

CLYDE GOODE III ■ *Cornerback*

College: 1989–91 . . . . NFL: none

ANTONIO LANGHAM ■ *Cornerback*

College: 1990–93 . . . . NFL: 1994–2000;
Jim Thorpe Award, Jack Tatum Award

The Goode family of Town Creek, Alabama, contributed five players to the University of Alabama: four brothers and a cousin.

Chris, a 6-0, 195-pound cornerback, started his college career at Auburn, expecting a scholarship that didn't materialize. When brother Kerry, a 5-11, 200-pound running back, got a scholarship to Alabama, Chris transferred there. Chris had a seven-year National Football League career with the Indianapolis Colts and now works in Birmingham as a sports trainer. Kerry played for the NFL's Tampa Bay Buccaneers in 1988 and the Miami Dolphins in 1989. He now works in truck sales in Atlanta.

Pierre Goode, a wide receiver, and Clyde Goode III, a cornerback, also played at Alabama, but neither made it to the pros. Pierre is now the track coach at Stillman College. Clyde died in July 2012 at age 43 of leukemia.

Antonio Langham, the Goode brothers' cousin, lived with the family from about age 6. He played four years for Alabama at cornerback and won the Jim Thorpe and Jack Tatum awards in 1993 as the nation's best college defensive back. He still holds the school career record for interceptions with 19. He played for the Baltimore Ravens,

San Francisco 49ers, New England Patriots, and both versions of the Cleveland Browns in a seven-year NFL career.

Unfortunately, that's not how Crimson Tide fans remember him. He secretly signed with an agent and applied to enter the NFL draft before playing his senior year. As a result, the NCAA forced Alabama to forfeit its eight regular-season 1993 wins and a tie. He now lives in Birmingham, managing and developing real estate, and maintains close ties to the Crimson Tide. His first pro defensive coordinator, with the Cleveland Browns, was current Alabama Coach Nick Saban.

HARRY GILMER ■ *Quarterback-Halfback*

COLLEGE: 1944–47 . . . . **NFL:** 1948–52, 1954–56,
2 Pro Bowls; College Football HOF, Alabama Sports HOF

You know that cliché that goes, "He can do it all"? Well, Harry Gilmer really could. He ended his Alabama career as the school's all-time leading rusher, passer, punt returner, kickoff returner, and pass interceptor. No wonder the Washington Redskins made him the first player picked in the 1948 National Football League draft. He's still the only Alabama player drafted number one overall. (Joe Namath was the first American Football League draft pick in 1964, but he was 12th overall in that year's NFL draft.)

Gilmer became famous for his jump pass. "I didn't jump to pass except when I was running," he said years later. "I had rather stand still and throw like everybody else, but if you are chased, the fact that you don't have to stop before you throw the ball is a big body-saving asset."

In the NFL, Gilmer backed up legendary Washington Redskins quarterback Sammy Baugh for the first few years of his career. He was a true starter only one season, in 1952 as a halfback. Still, he made the Pro Bowl team in 1950 and 1952 and played eight years with the Redskins and Detroit Lions.

Gilmer stood barely 6 feet tall and weighed maybe 160 pounds. Rumors swirled in 1953 that, tired of the NFL pounding, he would quit to become an Alabama assistant coach. Gilmer had missed most of his rookie season because of a leg injury and missed the 1953 season as well.

He did go into coaching, but in the pros. He was head coach of the Lions in 1965–66 and an assistant for 25 years with four other teams. After that, he scouted for 11 years. He lives in retirement on a small farm at O'Fallon, Missouri, near St. Louis.

CORNELIUS GRIFFIN ■ *Defensive Tackle*

COLLEGE: 1998–99 . . . . **NFL:** 2000–09

A co-captain for Alabama's 1999 Southeastern Conference championship team, Cornelius Griffin spent 10 years in the National Football League trenches, four with the New York Giants and six with the Washington Redskins. In 2001, he started in Super Bowl XXXV, which the Giants lost to the Baltimore Ravens, 34–7. When the Redskins released him after the 2009 season, he decided a decade of getting beaten up by pros in the middle of the defensive line was enough. The 6-3, 300-pound Griffin retired and got into the insurance business in his hometown of Troy, Alabama. He continues a tradition he started in 2000: hosting an annual Thanksgiving dinner for several hundred elderly and ill area residents.

He also donates school supplies to the 400-plus students at Pike County Elementary School, where he was once a pupil, at the beginning of every academic year.

"If you want to effect change," he told the *Troy Messenger,* "start with the youth. They are our future. Give them an opportunity to succeed."

GEORGE GULYANICS ■ *Halfback-Punter*

COLLEGE: 1941 (did not letter) . . . . **NFL:** 1947–1952;
Indiana Football HOF

George Gulyanics, 6 feet tall and 198 pounds, briefly attended Alabama before being drafted into the Army in 1942. He served in the First Army Signal Corps during World War II and participated in the Normandy Invasion at Utah Beach in France.

After the war ended, he played football with a service team in France. Chicago Bears owner George Halas heard of his ability and offered him a tryout. Gulyanics played six years for the Bears at halfback and fullback and, for the first four years, punter. He still holds the team record for most total yards in a postseason game with 161 (94 rushing, 67 receiving) in 1950. His career average of 44.5 yards per punt ranks 18th all-time.

Gulyanics retired after the 1952 season and came home to Mishawaka, Indiana, where he had been an all-state fullback in high school and a Golden Gloves welterweight boxing champion. He was elected as Penn Township assessor in 1954 and held the position until he retired again in 1986. He died in January 1990, age 68.

LEMANSKI HALL ■ *Linebacker*

COLLEGE: 1990–93 . . . .**NFL:** 1995–2002

Alabama's leading tackler his junior and senior years (the first of those a national championship season), Lemanski Hall played sparingly for three years with the Houston Oilers-Tennessee Titans (moving with the franchise to Nashville in 1997). The compact Hall (6-0, 230 pounds) spent another year as a backup with the Chicago Bears, then one with the Dallas Cowboys. Finally, after another year as a backup with the Minnesota Vikings, he became a starter for the first time, at age 31, with the Vikings in 2001.

His playing career ended after one more part-time year at Minnesota. He is now a coach at The Ensworth School in Nashville.

JON HAND ■ *Defensive End*

COLLEGE: 1982–85 . . . .**NFL:** 1986–94

Even a body like Jon Hand's—6-7, 300 pounds—can take only so much football. Hand packed a lot of athleticism into that big body; as a sophomore, he led Alabama in passes broken up, a category usually dominated by defensive backs. In 1992, fans voted him onto the Crimson Tide's All-Century Team (see page 178).

Hand spent nine years as a defensive-line stalwart for the National Football League's Indianapolis Colts before the injuries caught up with him. He stayed in Indianapolis and successfully transitioned to the business world. In 1997, he and his wife, Tanya, established JT's Hand—A Neonatal Fund to ease the financial and emotional burden on families with babies in neonatal intensive care. Two years earlier, their own son had survived only a few days after being born prematurely.

PATRICK HAPE ■ *Tight End-Fullback*

COLLEGE: 1993–96 . . . .**NFL:** 1997–2004

Blocking was Patrick Hape's specialty. He plied that trade through four years as a tight end at Alabama and eight years at three positions in the National Football League. His first four years, he played as the second tight end and sometimes H-back (essentially a tight end who sets up a step behind the offensive line) for the Tampa Bay Buccaneers.

continued on page 108

Hulking Hannahs

HERB HANNAH ■ *Tackle*

COLLEGE: 1948–50 . . . . **NFL:** 1951

WILLIAM C. HANNAH ■ *Tackle*

COLLEGE: 1957–59 . . . . **NFL:** none

JOHN HANNAH ■ *Offensive Guard*

COLLEGE: 1970–72 . . . . **NFL:** 1973–85, 9 Pro Bowls;
Pro Football HOF, College Football HOF, Alabama Sports HOF

CHARLEY HANNAH ■ *Offensive Guard-Defensive End*

COLLEGE: 1974–76 . . . . **NFL:** 1977–88;
Alabama Sports HOF

DAVID HANNAH ■ *Offensive Tackle-Defensive End*

COLLEGE: 1975–79 . . . . **NFL:** none

While at Alabama, John Hannah played football, wrestled, and competed in the shot put and discus throw with the track and field team.

Credit: Paul W. Bryant Museum/The University of Alabama

Five members of the Hannah family have played on the offensive line for the University of Alabama. Three of them went on to National Football League careers—and *Sports Illustrated* proclaimed one of them "the best offensive lineman of all time."

Herb Hannah started it. He stood 6-3 and weighed 220 pounds. In 1951, he played a single year with the New York Giants. In 1992, fans voting for Alabama's All-Century Team put him on the second team.

Son John made the first team—and was a unanimous All-America selection in 1972. At 6-2 and 265 pounds, John was the first of three sons to follow in his father's cleat steps. In his 13 years with the New England Patriots, he was named to nine Pro Bowls. Afterward, he was inducted into both the college and pro football halls of fame—as well as placed atop the *Sports Illustrated* "best ever" pedestal.

Charley Hannah, 6-5 and 260 pounds, was primarily a defensive end at Alabama who made some All–Southeastern Conference teams his senior year. He played defensive end, offensive tackle, and offensive guard for the Tampa Bay Buccaneers and Los Angeles Raiders.

David, 6-3, 230 pounds, was, like his older brothers, an all-conference lineman at Alabama, but injuries kept him from pursuing the NFL. He played on both the offensive and defensive lines.

And William C. Hannah, brother to Herb and uncle to John, Charley, and David, manned the Alabama offensive line in the late 1950s. Like David, he didn't go on to a pro career. But he did become a coach. In 1971, he and two fellow assistants on the Cal State Fullerton staff died in a plane crash during a scouting trip. Bill was just 37. Older brother Herb coached some at the high school level and then prospered in the poultry supply business. He died in 2007, age 85, at his home in Albertville, Alabama.

As for the younger generation, Charley has been involved in real estate and construction in Tampa, Florida, since 1988. David has been a farmer and businessman and now lives in Pelham, Alabama. John has a new autobiography, *Offensive Conduct: My Life on the Line,* detailing his football career and his difficulties after retirement until he replaced his win-at-all-costs football mindset with devotion to God. He told an interviewer at WVTM-TV in Birmingham that he still loves the Crimson Tide but can't go to games because "I get so frustrated with these know-it-all fans that never played anything but peewee."

He then signed as a free agent with the Denver Broncos, who stared playing him at fullback as well as tight end. As a fullback, he didn't do much running, but at 6-4 and 260 pounds, he was a heck of a blocker.

The Broncos cut him before the 2005 season. He now sells real estate in Birmingham.

ROMAN HARPER ■ *Safety*

COLLEGE: 2002–05 . . . . **NFL:** 2006–12, 2 Pro Bowls

Ranked in the all-time Alabama top 10 list for most tackles, Roman Harper continued his hard-hitting ways in the National Football League. The only thing that significantly slowed him was a knee injury that cost him all but five games his rookie year. Otherwise, the 6-0, 195-pound Harper has been a defensive backfield stalwart for the New Orleans Saints, especially tough against the run. In 2009, he earned his first Pro Bowl berth and helped take the Saints to their first Super Bowl, a 31–17 victory over the Indianapolis Colts.

Harper was named to his second Pro Bowl in 2010. In 2012 he achieved a career high in tackles with 116, 89 of them unassisted, and intercepted two passes.

Off the field, Harper devotes considerable time, effort, and money to charitable causes, particularly through his Harper's Hope 4★1 Foundation.

DONT'A HIGHTOWER ■ *Linebacker*

COLLEGE: 2008–11 . . . . **NFL:** 2012

Despite a hamstring injury that kept him out of two games and nagged at him the second half of the season, Dont'a Hightower in 2012 put together an impressive National Football League rookie performance. As one of the NFL's new breed of massive outside linebackers (see Jarret Johnson, page 115), the 6-2, 265-pound Hightower totaled 60 tackles (43 unassisted) and four sacks for the New England Patriots. He even returned a fumble for a touchdown. The Patriots counted on him as one of their defensive stalwarts for 2013.

Considering what he accomplished at Alabama, his pro success surprised no one. During his national championship junior year in 2011, he called plays for the nation's top-ranked defense. In three-plus years as a starter (he played only four games in 2009 before a knee injury ended his season), Hightower amassed 230 tackles. The NCAA allowed him an additional year of eligibility via a medical redshirt, but he decided to forgo his senior season. The Patriots drafted him in the first round, 25th overall.

DENNIS HOMAN ■ *Wide Receiver*

COLLEGE: 1965–67 . . . . **NFL:** 1968–72; **WFL:** 1974–75;
Alabama Sports HOF

The stardom that Dennis Homan achieved in college—his 54 catches in 1967 still rank 11th all time at Alabama for a single season—remained just out of reach in the National Football League. In three years with the Dallas Cowboys and two years with the Kansas City Chiefs, he caught a total of only 37 passes—17 fewer than he'd grabbed during his All-America senior year at Alabama.

He retired, went home to Alabama, and began selling real estate with fellow ex-Crimson Tide star Tommy Brooker (see page 89). Then the new World Football League offered one last shot at glory. Homan caught 61 passes for the WFL champion Birmingham Americans during their one season before the team collapsed financially. Homan, 6 feet tall and 180 pounds, played the next year for the Birmingham Vulcans, who were leading the standings when the WFL folded before the season's end.

Homan moved back to Florence, Alabama (he grew up in nearby Muscle Shoals), and sold pharmaceuticals for 26 years before retiring in 2002.

DIXIE HOWELL ■ *Halfback*

COLLEGE: 1932–34 . . . . **NFL:** 1937;
College Football HOF, Alabama Sports HOF

In the Harper Lee novel *To Kill a Mockingbird*, Scout tries to cheer up her brother, Jem, by telling him he looks like Dixie Howell. That would have been high praise indeed in the 1930s South. Howell, Alabama's star halfback, scored two touchdowns and threw for another in Alabama's 29–13 stomping of Stanford in the 1935 Rose Bowl. One of his favorite passing targets, Don Hutson, went on to a sensational National Football League career.

Howell didn't. In the single-wing formation that Alabama used, the halfback was the passer—the equivalent of today's quarterback. In the pros, Howell, 5-11 and 175 pounds, had the misfortune to be a rookie at the same time as another man who played the same position: the legendary Slinging Sammy Baugh, one of the greatest passers in NFL history.

Howell played only one year in the NFL. He concentrated instead on his baseball career. He played in the minor leagues for eight years, 1935–42, almost everywhere on the diamond—second base, outfield, shortstop, third base, first base—but never reached the majors.

Along the way, he was head football coach at the National University of Mexico (1935), Arizona State Teachers College (now Arizona State; 1938–41), and Idaho (1947–50). In 1946, after serving in the Navy during World War II, he coached Alabama's baseball team to a 13-7 record.

He later worked in sales and public relations in the Los Angeles area. He suffered from intestinal cancer and died there in 1971, age 58.

BOBBY HUMPHREY ■ *Running Back*

COLLEGE: 1985–88 . . . .**NFL:** 1989–92, 1 Pro Bowl; Alabama Sports HOF

His football life could have been . . . well, we'll never know. Bobby Humphrey, a slashing runner at 6-1 and 201 pounds, still holds Alabama's single-season and career records for most all-purpose yards (running, receiving, returning kicks—2,016 and 4,958, respectively).

Birmingham Steeldogs coach Bobby Humphrey talks to quarterback Jeff Aaron during the 2004 season.

Credit: Birmingham Steeldogs

Humphrey gained 1,151 rushing yards his rookie year with the Denver Broncos, then 1,202 yards and a Pro Bowl berth his second year. Before his third season, he held out, wanting his contract renegotiated. The Broncos refused. He capitulated with four games to play in the season, but by then the Broncos had found another running back.

Traded to the Miami Dolphins before the 1992 season, he had a good year as an all-purpose back, gaining 471 yards rushing and another 507 yards receiving. But after the season came an arrest, revelations of drug use, a gunshot wound in the thigh while driving, and a knee injury. His football career had fizzled out. He was 26.

Humphrey's redemptive post-playing life, built on religious faith and helping others, has been more lastingly successful. He returned to his hometown of Birmingham, where he coached the Birmingham Steeldogs of the Arena Football League 2 for five years. He's had a street ministry and has focused on assisting kids. He is now a vice president at Bryant Bank, the Tuscaloosa-based community bank co-founded in 2005 by Paul Bryant Jr., son of legendary Alabama coach Paul "Bear" Bryant.

SCOTT HUNTER ■ *Quarterback*

COLLEGE: 1968–70 . . . .**NFL:** 1971–74, 1976–77, 1979;
Alabama Sports HOF

Crimson Tide fans still talk about the passing shows Scott Hunter put on during the 1969 season. On October 4, on national television, he completed 22 of 29 passes for 300 yards and a touchdown against Mississippi. The Rebels' Archie Manning (father of current National Football League star quarterbacks Peyton and Eli) outdid him, completing 33 of 52 passes for 436 yards and two touchdowns (though with one interception). Manning added 103 yards and three touchdowns on 15 rushes.

But Hunter won the game, 33–32. Afterward, Hunter said. "I was looking for Archie, and I found him. And he had tears in his eyes. I didn't even know what to say. I reached out, shook his hand, and he looked me in the eye, and I looked him in the eye. We didn't have to say a thing to each other. We just knew what we'd had, together, that night."

The Green Bay Packers selected Hunter, 6-2 and 205 pounds, in the sixth round of the NFL draft to replace another Alabama quarterback, the great Bart Starr (see page 159). In 1972, with the freshly retired Starr guiding him from the sidelines, Hunter led the Packers to their first division title since 1967—and their last until 1995.

But Hunter didn't really click in the pros. The 1974 players' strike became a turning point. Packers Coach Dan Devine wanted Hunter to play despite the strike. Hunter told the *Los Angeles Times* in 2008 that he called his old college coach, Bear Bryant, for advice. "Of course, his answer was, 'Where are the offensive linemen, Scott?' I said, 'Coach, they're out there with picket signs marching around the stadium.' And he said, 'You'd better be out there with them.'"

He did go out there with them. Devine traded Hunter to Buffalo. Hunter put in four more seasons as a backup and occasional starter before going home. He was sports director at a television station in his native Mobile, Alabama, and a college football analyst on TV, then became a financial adviser. He and his wife, a former Alabama cheerleader, live in Daphne, Alabama, and have three grown children, all Alabama graduates. Daughter Mary Scott Hunter, a lawyer who received her law degree from the university, lives in Huntsville, Alabama, and is a member of the State Board of Education.

DON HUTSON ■ *End-Defensive Back-Kicker*

COLLEGE: 1932–35 . . . . **NFL:** 1935–45, 4 Pro Bowls, 2 MVP awards; College Football HOF, Pro Football HOF, Alabama Sports HOF, Wisconsin Athletic HOF

They called Don Hutson "The Alabama Antelope." His coach at Alabama, Frank Thomas, called him "the greatest player I've ever seen." He may still be the greatest wide receiver in pro football history. Yes, even better than Jerry Rice (although Hutson himself said in 1994 that Rice was the best ever).

Hutson's 1935 Rose Bowl performance for Alabama hinted at what was to come in the pros. He caught eight passes for 164 yards and two touchdowns in the Crimson Tide's 29–13 swamping of Stanford.

In the National Football League, Hutson dominated like nobody before or since. In 1942, when he caught a then-record 74 passes, his nearest rival caught 27. That 1942 stat line, in fact, would put him among today's elite receivers: 74 catches for 1,211 yards and 17 touchdowns—and he did it in only 11 games. He led the league in touchdowns eight times; nobody else has done it more than three times. When he retired after 11 seasons, he had 488 receptions for 7,991 yards. The second-place receiver had 190 catches for 3,309 yards.

Hutson also led the league three times in kicking extra points and once in field goals—and, in those days of two-way players, once in interceptions. "In my day, we didn't have a designated kicker," Hutson told the *Los Angeles Times* in 1989. "We just got in the huddle, looked around, and asked, 'Who wants to kick this one?'

More than six decades after his retirement, Don Hutson still holds numerous NFL receiving, scoring, and kicking records.

Credit: Paul W. Bryant Museum/The University of Alabama

I only volunteered once in a while. I'd never kicked a football anywhere until I got to Green Bay."

Hutson is credited with inventing many of the pass patterns used today. At 6-1 and 180 pounds, he never suffered a major injury.

Always a sharp businessman, Hutson negotiated a rookie salary of either $175 a game (according to the Packers) or $300 (according to Hutson). Either figure would have been unheard of in those Depression days. The next year, the NFL instituted a draft to reduce players' contract-negotiating leverage. While still playing, Hutson opened a bowling alley and a car dealership in Green Bay. Later, he ran a lucrative Cadillac dealership in Racine, Wisconsin, before retiring in comfort to Rancho Mirage, California.

Hutson and his old Alabama teammate at end, Paul Bryant, remained close friends all their lives. Because of all the attention Hutson got, Bryant sarcastically referred to himself as "the other end." The Antelope outran the Bear by 14 years. Hutson died in 1997, age 84.

MARK INGRAM ■ *Running Back*

COLLEGE: 2008–10 . . . . **NFL:** 2011–12; Heisman Trophy

In 2009, Mark Ingram had about as great a season as it's possible to have. As a sophomore, he rushed for 1,658 yards and 17 touchdowns, won the Heisman Trophy (the Crimson Tide's first) as America's best college football player, and led his team to the national championship when Alabama beat Texas, 37–21, in the BCS National Championship Game.

His first National Football League season didn't go as well. Ingram, 5-9 and 215 pounds, left Alabama after his junior year and went to the New Orleans Saints in the first round of the draft (28th overall). He signed a four-year, $7.41 million contract, with a $3.89 million signing bonus, three years guaranteed, and an option for a fifth year.

Because of injuries, he played in only 10 games, and he rushed for just 474 yards. During the off-season, he rehabbed a torn tendon in a big toe and had minor surgery on a knee. After another mediocre season in 2012 (602 yards gained), Ingram embarked on a program of speed and quickness–oriented conditioning and healthy eating. He headed into 2013 free of injuries for the first time since his Alabama days. "This is the best I've felt so far, being a professional," he said. "I haven't had to deal with any off-season injuries or rehab."

Ingram's father, also named Mark, had a 10-year NFL career as a wide receiver.

KAREEM JACKSON ■ *Cornerback*

COLLEGE: 2007–09 . . . .**NFL:** 2010–12

After his junior year at Alabama, in which he led the Crimson Tide with 13 passes broken up en route to the national championship, Kareem Jackson gave up his senior year to go pro. Jackson, 5-10 and 190 pounds, signed a five-year, $13.1 million contract as the first-round draft choice of the Houston Texans. He started every game as a rookie but struggled at times during his second National Football League season, partly because of a knee injury. He rebounded in 2012 to lead the team in interceptions with four and achieve his first-ever interception runback for a touchdown.

WILBUR JACKSON ■ *Running Back*

COLLEGE: 1971–73 . . . .**NFL:** 1974–77, 1979–82;
Alabama Sports HOF

The first African-American signed as a freshman to a football scholarship at Alabama (for the 1970 season), Wilbur Jackson became a star running back out of the wishbone formation, losing only four games in the three years he played for the Crimson Tide.

The San Francisco 49ers used the 6-1, 215-pound Jackson as one of the National Football League's first all-purpose backs—half runner, half receiver. Traded to the Washington Redskins, he had an excellent season in 1980, then barely played the next two years because of knee injuries. He went out on top, retiring after the Redskins' 27–17 Super Bowl victory over the Miami Dolphins in 1983. He went back home to Ozark, Alabama, and opened a cleaning business.

CURT JARVIS ■ *Nose Tackle*

COLLEGE: 1983–86 . . . .**NFL:** 1987–90

Curt Jarvis spent a lot of time in the other team's backfield. He's still among Alabama's leaders in tackles for loss, more than two decades after his last college game. A bruised spinal cord suffered while making a tackle ended Jarvis's four-year National Football League career with the Tampa Bay Buccaneers at age 25. The 6-foot-2, 266-pound defensive lineman had been taking flying lessons, so he shifted his sights skyward. In 2000, he became one of the largest pilots in the history of Delta Airlines.

JARRET JOHNSON ■ *Linebacker-Defensive End*

COLLEGE: 1999–2002 . . . . **NFL:** 2003–12

A prolific quarterback sacker as an Alabama defensive tackle, Jarret Johnson has been more of a run-stopping specialist in the National Football League. After nine years as a defensive end and then a rather large linebacker (he's listed at 6-3 and 260 pounds) for the Baltimore Ravens, Johnson signed a four-year contract with the San Diego Chargers for a reported $19 million, $7 million of it guaranteed, starting in 2012. The Chargers' website enthused, "Johnson brought stability to the strong-side 'backer position for the Chargers, as well as a tremendous work ethic."

RASHAD JOHNSON ■ *Safety*

COLLEGE: 2005–08 . . . . **NFL:** 2009–12

It still happens every once in a while: an overlooked player from a small high school gets no major-college scholarship offers, walks on at his dream university, and becomes a star.

It happened to Rashad Johnson, from Sulligent, Alabama (population 2,151). He walked on (meaning that he tried out and made the team after enrolling in school without a scholarship) as a running back at Alabama. He eventually earned a scholarship as a defensive back and led the Crimson Tide in interceptions his junior and senior years.

Johnson went to the Arizona Cardinals in the third round of the National Football League draft. Again, he had to work his way up, playing mostly on special teams his first two years. By 2011, the 6-foot, 195-pound Johnson had earned a job as a starting safety. He became a free agent after the season, but the Cardinals re-signed him in April 2012. He played well enough in part-time duty (20 tackles, two interceptions, strong special-teams work) to earn a three-year contract in March 2013. Despite preseason knee and ankle injuries, he entered the 2013 season as the Cardinals' starting free safety.

BRUCE JONES ■ *Guard*

COLLEGE: 1923–25 . . . . **NFL:** 1927–28, 1930, 1932–34

As a senior, Bruce Jones captained Alabama's undefeated 1925 national champions. Playing in the Rose Bowl, the school's first-ever bowl game, the

Crimson Tide beat heavily favored Washington, 20–19, bringing national attention and respect to Southern football, which many sportswriters of the time considered inferior to the brand of the game being played on the East and West coasts.

Jones, 6-1 and 220 pounds, played in the National Football League for six years: two with the Green Bay Packers, one with the Newark Tornadoes, and three with the Brooklyn Dodgers. The one-year gap each time he changed teams wasn't unusual; salaries in those days usually forced players to treat the NFL as a part-time job at best.

Jones kept his ties with the Crimson Tide and was president in 1955–56 of the A-Club Alumni Association, an organization of letter-winning former student athletes. He died in 1978, age 73.

JOEY JONES ■ *Wide Receiver*

COLLEGE: 1980–83 . . . . **USFL:** 1984–85; **NFL:** 1986

Despite standing just 5-8 and weighing 165 pounds, Joey Jones led Alabama in pass receptions his sophomore, junior, and senior years.

He was a deep threat, leading the United States Football League's Birmingham Stallions in average yards per catch in 1984, finishing second in 1985, and also finishing second in touchdown catches both years. His playing career ended with a year as a seldom-used reserve with the National Football League's Atlanta Falcons in 1986.

In 1989, he turned to coaching. In his 13 years as a head coach at two Alabama high schools, his teams accumulated a 125-38 record. In 2007, he reconstituted the football program at Birmingham-Southern College after 68 years of dormancy, going 3-7 in NCAA Division III. The next year, he began creating another program from scratch, this one at the University of South Alabama, which had never offered the sport. From 2009 through 2011, the team compiled a 23-4 record as it transitioned toward NCAA Football Bowl Subdivision status. In 2012, the first year of playing a top-level schedule, the Jaguars slipped to 2-10. They achieved full FBS status and Sun Belt Conference football membership in 2013.

JULIO JONES ■ *Wide Receiver*

COLLEGE: 2008–10 . . . .**NFL:** 2011–12; 1 Pro Bowl

Julio Jones's first name is actually Quintorris.

Credit: Chris J. Nelson

Tall, strong, and fast, Julio Jones has everything you want in a wide receiver. In 2010, he set Alabama records for most catches (78) and receiving yards (1,133) in a season and rose to the occasion against top opponents. He caught 12 passes for 221 yards against Tennessee, 10 for 89 yards against LSU, and 10 more for 199 yards against Auburn.

Picked in the first round (sixth overall) of the National Football League draft by the Atlanta Falcons, Jones lost three games to a hamstring injury but still led all rookies in touchdown catches with eight. His 54 catches and 959 receiving yards ranked second among rookies to A. J. Green of the Cincinnati Bengals.

In the off-season, the 6-3, 220-pound Jones cut the dreadlocks that had been a trademark throughout his time at Alabama and in the NFL and donated them to a charity that helps children with cancer. He said he liked the new short-hair look and planned to keep it. It seemed to bring him good luck. In 2012, he was voted to his first Pro Bowl.

TERRY JONES ■ *Nose Tackle-Defensive Tackle*

COLLEGE: 1975–77 . . . .**NFL:** 1978–84

A center and nose tackle for coach Bear Bryant at Alabama, Terry Jones played nose tackle and defensive tackle for seven National Football League seasons, all with the Green Bay Packers. He eventually came back to Alabama, where he is now assistant head strength and conditioning coach. He got to coach his son Terry W. Jones Jr., a tight end who also played at Alabama and in the NFL; see next bio.

TERRY JONES JR. ■ *Tight End*

COLLEGE: 1999–2001 . . . . **NFL:** 2002–05

Terry Jones Jr., son of an Alabama player and coach (see previous bio), finished his Crimson Tide career by catching the game-winning touchdown pass in the 2001 Independence Bowl. A 6-3, 265-pound tight end, he played in the National Football League for the Baltimore Ravens and San Francisco 49ers. Beginning after his second NFL year, he and two other athletes, former Alabama safety Tony Dixon and former LSU tight end Harold Bishop, returned to West Alabama to hold a free youth football camp each summer. After retirement, he was a real estate investor and coached the defensive secondary for a time at Tucker High School in the Atlanta area.

LEE ROY JORDAN ■ *Linebacker*

COLLEGE: 1960–62 . . . . **NFL:** 1965–76, 5 Pro Bowls; College Football HOF, Alabama Sports HOF

In his college and professional careers, Lee Roy Jordan played for only two teams and two iconic coaches—both of whom were famous for their hats.

Jordan starred as a center and linebacker at Alabama for Bear Bryant—he of the houndstooth hat. Jordan then played 14 seasons for the Dallas Cowboys under Tom Landry, who always wore a fedora on the sideline.

Nobody knows how many tackles Jordan made for Alabama; teams didn't normally keep that statistic back then. We do know that Jordan made an incredible 31 tackles in Alabama's 17–0 Orange Bowl win over Oklahoma in 1963. Bryant said simply, "If they stay inside the boundaries, Lee Roy will get 'em."

The Cowboys made Jordan their first pick (sixth overall) in the National Football League draft. The Boston Patriots of the rival American Football League also drafted Jordan, but the Cowboys offered a $17,500 signing bonus and a new car, and Jordan signed with Dallas.

Though at 6-1 and 220 pounds he was small for a middle linebacker, Jordan still holds the NFL record for most consecutive starts at the position: 154 (173 including playoff games). And we do know how many tackles he made for the Cowboys' "Doomsday Defense": a team record 1,236. His Dallas teams won five conference championships, eight divisional championships, and one Super Bowl, the 1972 Super Bowl VI, 24–3, over the Miami Dolphins.

After he retired, Jordan bought a lumber company. Lee Roy Jordan Lumber Company of Dallas "leads the industry as one of the largest suppliers of redwood and other fine specialty woods in eight states," according to its website. Jordan lives near Point Clear, Alabama, about 90 miles south of Excel, where he grew up.

In 1989, Lee Roy Jordan became the seventh Dallas Cowboy inducted into the team's Ring of Honor.

Credit: Paul W. Bryant Museum/The University of Alabama

In April 2012, Jordan was the lead plaintiff among a group of 31 retired NFL players who filed a lawsuit against the league, accusing it of concealing information about the long-term effects of concussions. It was one of dozens of concussion-related lawsuits filed by a total of more than 4,500 former players and their families. A federal court consolidated the suits into one. Just before the 2013 season, the NFL and the players announced a $765 million settlement. It included $675 million for players or families of players who sustained cognitive injury, $75 million for medical exams, and $10 million for research. Payouts were capped at $5 million for men with Alzheimer's disease, $4 million for those diagnosed with chronic traumatic encephalopathy, and $3 million for those diagnosed with other forms of dementia.

The settlement did not include an admission that the NFL hid information from players. At press time, it awaited approval by a federal judge. Helmet maker Riddell, also part of the original lawsuit, did not take part in the settlement. Lawyers for former players continued legal action against Riddell.

E. J. JUNIOR ■ *Linebacker*

COLLEGE: 1977–80 . . . . **NFL:** 1981–93, 2 Pro Bowls; Alabama Sports HOF, Tennessee Sports HOF

Primarily an outside linebacker who loved to rush the quarterback, E. J. Junior was a finalist for the Rotary Lombardi Award as best college lineman or linebacker his senior year at Alabama. In the National Football League, he anchored the Cardinals' defense for eight years—their last seven years in St. Louis and their first year in Phoenix. The 6-3, 240-pound Junior then played three years with the Miami Dolphins and two more seasons split between the Tampa Bay Buccaneers and Seattle Seahawks.

After his NFL career, Junior embarked on an unusual double profession: ordained minister and football coach. He was an assistant with the Seahawks, Dolphins, Minnesota Vikings, and Jacksonville Jaguars of the NFL and the Rhein Fire of NFL Europe. Switching to the collegiate level, he was an assistant at Southwest Baptist University before becoming head coach in 2009 at Central State University in Ohio.

EMANUEL KING ■ *Linebacker*

COLLEGE: 1982–84 . . . . **NFL:** 1985–89; **WLAF:** 1992; **CFL:** 1993

After leading Alabama in both tackles and quarterback sacks his junior year, Emanuel King co-captained the Crimson Tide his senior year in 1984. A big linebacker at 6-4 and 250 pounds, he played in the National Football League for four years with the Cincinnati Bengals and one final year with the Los Angeles Raiders.

Despite injuries that, later in life, would lead to spinal surgery and daily headaches, he wasn't through with football. He came back in 1992 to play for the Montreal Machine in the World League of American Football, an NFL developmental league. In 1993, he played five games with the Sacramento Gold Miners of the Canadian Football League.

He has spent more than a decade coaching football in high school and college, most recently as an assistant coach in 2011 for UMS-Wright Preparatory School in Mobile, Alabama. He also coached linebackers for a training program called Football University.

BARRY KRAUSS ■ *Linebacker*

COLLEGE: 1976–78 . . . . **NFL:** 1979–89; Alabama Sports HOF

Some athletic heroes remain forever frozen in a defining moment. So it is with Barry Krauss, who stopped Penn State running back Mike Guman on fourth and goal at the one-foot line to win a national championship for Alabama in the 1979 Sugar Bowl.

The 6-3, 240-pound Krauss went on to an excellent National Football League career, playing 10 years for the Baltimore and Indianapolis Colts and

DRE KIRKPATRICK ■ *Cornerback*

COLLEGE: 2009–11 . . . . **NFL:** 2012

Dre Kirkpatrick came to the Crimson Tide from Gadsden, Alabama.
Credit: Navin Rajagopalan

Injuries ruined Dre Kirkpatrick's rookie National Football League season. At Alabama, he developed into a feared cornerback whom other teams threw away from. He decided to move on to the pros after his junior season, and the Cincinnati Bengals grabbed him in the first round of the NFL draft, 17th overall. But he broke a knee bone in training camp, battled tendinitis, suffered a concussion during the season, and underwent knee surgery shortly after it ended. He played in only a handful of downs across five games, making just two tackles.

For 2013, the tall, long-armed Kirkpatrick (6-1, 186 pounds) was hoping for a do-over. He went into the season as a backup, but he impressed Bengals defensive coordinator Mike Zimmer during training camp. "He's done really well," Zimmer said. "Much better than I anticipated he would."

one year for the Miami Dolphins. He amassed more than 1,000 NFL tackles before a knee injury detoured him into a new career as a sports broadcaster and motivational speaker based in the Indianapolis area.

But to many of the Crimson Tide faithful, Krauss will always be 21 years old, invincible, and adored. There are worse fates.

BILL LEE ■ *Tackle*

COLLEGE: 1932–34 . . . . **NFL:** 1935–42, 1946, 1 Pro Bowl; Alabama Sports HOF

Bill Lee captained the great 1934 Alabama team that went 10-0 and blasted Stanford 29–13 in the Rose Bowl. Coach Frank Thomas called it his best Alabama team, and Lee was a consensus All-America tackle.

He began his National Football League career with the struggling Brooklyn Dodgers. The Green Bay Packers acquired him in 1937, reuniting him with superstar end Don Hutson (see page 112), his former Alabama teammate. In 1939, the two helped lead the Packers to a 27–0 victory over the New York Giants in the NFL championship game. Each Packer received $703.97 as his share of the gate receipts—a fortune during the Depression, when players were typically paid $100 or less a game. Lee was voted to the All Pro team that year and, later, to the Pro Football Hall of Fame's 1930s All-Decade Team.

In the off-seasons, Lee, who was 6-3 and weighed 225 pounds, worked the pro wrestling circuit in California under the name Alabama Bill. World War II interrupted his Packers career one game into the 1942 season. He talked the doctors into overlooking his bad knees to allow him into the service.

Lee returned to Green Bay for four games in 1946, then went home to Eutaw, Alabama, and eventually took up the family business. Between the two of them, Lee's father and brother held the office of Greene County sheriff from 1922 until 1954. At that point, Lee won election to the job. He kept it until 1970, when changing times caught up with him. Lee, who was white, lost the election that year to Thomas Gilmore, the majority-black county's first African-American sheriff.

TOMMY LEWIS ■ *Fullback-Defensive Back*

COLLEGE: 1951–53 . . . . **CFL:** 1956–57

Fullback Tommy Lewis wishes more fans remembered his contribution to Alabama's 61–6 thrashing of Syracuse in the 1953 Orange Bowl. He scored two touchdowns and led the Crimson Tide with 77 yards rushing. But he created his legacy in the 1954 Cotton Bowl.

In the first quarter, the 6-foot, 190-pound Lewis, playing his last game for Alabama, blasted into the end zone from the one-yard line to give the Tide a 6–0 lead. But Rice running back Dicky Moegle led the Owls to a 28–6 victory, scoring three touchdowns and gaining 265 yards on only 11 carries. During what would have been a 95-yard run for the second touchdown, Lewis suddenly leaped off the bench, without a helmet, and dove onto the field, knocking Moegle's legs out from under him. The referees awarded Moegle the score anyway. Lewis tearfully apologized to Moegle at halftime and decades later still felt "devastated" about the impulsive lunge.

Two days after the game, the two players appeared on Ed Sullivan's popular TV show in New York. Sullivan asked Lewis what had happened, and Lewis replied, "Mr. Sullivan, I guess I was just so full of Alabama." Lewis later said Sullivan had scripted the line.

The Chicago Cardinals picked Lewis in the 10th round of the 1954 National Football League draft, but he never played in the NFL. Instead, two years later, he became a fullback and defensive back for the Ottawa Rough Riders, playing in a predecessor to what is now the Canadian Football League.

A knee injury prematurely ended his second season with Ottawa in 1957. Lewis, a native of Greenville, Alabama, returned to his home state and embarked on a long career as a businessman in Huntsville and a coach of high school and minor-league football. He has spent the past few years in a nursing home, suffering from Alzheimer's disease after a series of strokes.

WALTER LEWIS ■ *Quarterback*

COLLEGE: 1980–83 . . . . **USFL:** 1984–85; **CFL:** 1986

Alabama's first African-American quarterback, Walter Lewis still ranks among Alabama's career top 10 in passing yards and completion percentage, among other categories. In the pros, the 6-1, 210-pound Lewis signed with the Memphis Showboats for their second United States Football League season. He played well, and the Showboats drew excellent crowds, but the USFL collapsed around them after the 1985 season.

Lewis played for a year with the Montreal Alouettes of the Canadian Football League and had an unsuccessful tryout with the New England Patriots in 1987. Meanwhile, he had returned to Alabama to get his degree in electrical engineering. He worked in engineering and finance, spent a couple of years as an assistant football coach for the Crimson Tide and then the University of Kentucky, and returned to finance. He's now vice president for Gardnyr Michael Capital, a prominent municipal-bond underwriter in Birmingham.

ANTONIO LONDON ■ *Linebacker*

COLLEGE: 1989–92 . . . . **NFL:** 1993–98

During his junior and senior seasons, Antonio London topped the Crimson Tide in fumbles forced, demonstrating the hard hitting that earned him the nickname "Stick." For the first two of his six seasons with the National Football League's Detroit Lions, the 6-2, 238-pound London played mostly on special teams. In 1995, he recorded seven quarterback sacks, earning him a starting job in 1996 and part of 1997. After one game with the Green Bay Packers in 1998, his playing career ended. Today, he owns a facilities management services company in Alabaster, Alabama. He is also an assistant football coach in Pelham, Alabama, where one of the players was his son Antonio London Jr., now a freshman safety at the University of South Alabama.

EDDIE LOWE ■ *Linebacker*

COLLEGE: 1980–82 . . . .**CFL:** 1983–91, 1-time All-Star

At 5-8 and 195 pounds, Eddie Lowe had trouble getting coaches to take him seriously, even if he was the younger brother of College Football Hall of Fame linebacker Woodrow Lowe (see next bio). Alabama didn't offer him a scholarship, but he walked on anyway (after a year at the University of Tennessee at Chattanooga) and became a three-year letterman.

The National Football League wasn't taking 5-foot-8 linebackers seriously either, so Lowe headed north to the Canadian Football League. He played nine years for the Saskatchewan Roughriders and made a league all-star team. Running back Jonathan Lowe, Eddie's son, lettered for the Crimson Tide in 2007. In 2012, Eddie Lowe became the first African-American elected as mayor of Phenix City, Alabama, across the Chattahoochee River from his hometown of Columbus, Georgia.

WOODROW LOWE ■ *Linebacker*

COLLEGE: 1972–75 . . . .**NFL:** 1976–1986;
College Football HOF, Alabama Sports HOF

Yes, you can go home again. Ask Woodrow Lowe.

Lowe, still the Alabama record holder for tackles in a season (134 in 1973), had an 11-year National Football League career with the San Diego Chargers. He was small for a linebacker at 6-0 and 227 pounds, but he was very active, equally adept at stopping the run and the pass. He intercepted 21 NFL passes—which is a lot for a linebacker—and returned four for touchdowns. He missed only one game in those 11 seasons.

After retiring as a player, Lowe coached at Alabama high schools, then moved back to the NFL as an assistant coach with the Kansas City Chiefs and Oakland Raiders. After a five-year stint as an assistant coach at the University of Alabama at Birmingham, Lowe became head coach for Alabama's Smiths Station High School, then an assistant at Birmingham's Jackson-Olin High School.

In 2010, Lowe finally came home to his alma mater, Phenix City Central High School, as head coach. During his first two years, the Red Devils went 21-4 and reached the playoffs each season. "I'm an old, broke-down coach that doesn't have a lot left," Lowe said after the 2011 season, "but what's left will be spent here. I am a Red Devil. I began my career here, and I want to end it here."

BOBBY LUNA ■ *Punter-Safety*

COLLEGE: 1951–54 . . . . **NFL:** 1955, 1959

Alabama's career record holder for yardage on interception returns (255 on 11 interceptions), Bobby Luna also led the Crimson Tide in kickoff returns his junior year, and both punt returns and pass receptions his senior year.

After one year as a punter and defensive back for the National Football League's San Francisco 49ers, Luna tried other jobs, including defensive backfield coach at Alabama in 1958, Bear Bryant's first year as head coach. In 1959, the 5-11, 187-pound Luna returned to the NFL as a punter and defensive back for the Pittsburgh Steelers. The brand new Dallas Cowboys selected him in the expansion draft for 1960, but with a second child on the way, Luna wanted to spend more time with his family. He retired from football, returned to Alabama, and started a successful construction business. In the late 1960s, he moved to Franklin, Tennessee, where he died in 2008, age 74.

MARTY LYONS ■ *Defensive End-Defensive Tackle*

COLLEGE: 1976–78 . . . . **NFL:** 1979–89;
College Football HOF, Alabama Sports HOF

A tough guy on the field, occasionally even accused of dirty play, Marty Lyons has devoted much of his off-the-field time to helping others. He won the NFL Man of the Year Award in 1984 and The Heisman Humanitarian Award in 2011. His Marty Lyons Foundation, which he established in 1982, fulfills wishes of children who have terminal or life-threatening illnesses.

In 1978, his final year at Alabama, Lyons was defensive co-captain of a national championship squad. He led the team in tackles with 119, the most famous of which came during the legendary goal-line stand that helped beat Penn State in the 1979 Sugar Bowl.

The National Football League's New York Jets drafted him in the first round. Lyons, 6-5 and 269 pounds, played 11 years with the Jets as a defensive end and tackle, part of a ferocious defensive line nicknamed the New York Sack Exchange. In 1981, he, Mark Gastineau, Joe Klecko, and Abdul Salaam combined for 66 quarterback sacks in leading the Jets to the playoffs for the first time since 1969. Lyons and the Jets also reached the playoffs in 1982, 1985, and 1986 but never made it to the Super Bowl.

continued on next page

In 1987, his block during a fumble return on Miami Dolphins center and former Alabama teammate Dwight Stephenson (see page 160) wrecked Stephenson's knee and ended his career. Some Dolphins fans thought the hit was unnecessary because Stephenson was well behind the ball carrier—although Stephenson himself said, "I have no bitterness towards Marty Lyons. I know he didn't mean it."

In 1990, the Jets instituted an annual award for the Jets player who performs outstanding community service. The team called it the Marty Lyons Award, and Lyons was its first recipient. Lyons retired as a player after the 1989 season. Since 2002, he has been the color analyst for Jets radio broadcasts.

In 1987, Lyons missed several games after his wife was seriously injured in a late-night traffic accident in Alabama. Lyons' 5-year-old son, Rocky, coaxed and pushed his mother up an embankment to the roadside, saving her life. Inspired by the doctors who treated her, Rocky is now himself a physician with River Region Family Medicine in Wetumpka, Alabama, just north of Montgomery.

During the 1979 Sugar Bowl goal-line stand, Penn State's quarterback asked how far the ball was from the goal line. "'Bout a foot," Marty Lyons said. "You better pass."

Credit: Paul W. Bryant Museum/The University of Alabama

KEN MACAFEE ■ *End-Tight End*

COLLEGE: 1951 . . . . **NFL:** 1954–59

One spectacular game highlighted Ken MacAfee's Alabama career: six catches for 158 yards against Villanova in 1951. After two years in the Marines during the Korean War, he entered the National Football League with the New York Giants.

MacAfee, 6-2 and 212 pounds, played wide receiver and tight end, a relatively new position at the time. During his rookie year, he caught 24 passes for 438 yards and eight touchdowns. He never matched those numbers but stayed with the Giants for four more years before splitting a final season between the Washington Redskins and Philadelphia Eagles. He died on July 4, 2007, age 77, of an apparent heart attack while playing golf near his home in Brockton, Massachusetts.

His son, Ken MacAfee II, was also a tight end who earned enshrinement in the College Football Hall of Fame for his play at Notre Dame. The younger MacAfee played with the San Francisco 49ers in 1978 and 1979. When the 49ers asked him to switch to offensive guard in 1980, he quit football and enrolled in dental school. He now practices dentistry and oral surgery in Waltham, Massachusetts.

ANTHONY MADISON ■ *Cornerback*

COLLEGE: 2002–05 . . . . **NFL:** 2006–11

Anthony Madison led Alabama in interceptions and passes broken up his senior year, but that didn't impress National Football League teams, who failed to draft him. Madison caught on as a free agent with the Pittsburgh Steelers and began an NFL odyssey that has included four separate stints with the Steelers (one of which didn't involve any actual playing time) and side trips to the Tampa Bay Buccaneers (who cut him before he played a game for them), Cleveland Browns, Indianapolis Colts, and Detroit Lions. Along the way, he played for the Steelers in a winning and a losing Super Bowl (in 2009 and 2011, respectively). In 2012, the Steelers once again signed the 5-9, 180-pound Madison as a free agent, but they cut him before the season started. Madison now describes himself on his Facebook page as a "speaker, mentor, Christian." In June 2013, he put on the fourth annual Anthony Madison Football Camp at his alma mater of Thomasville (Alabama) High School.

VAUGHN MANCHA ■ *Center-Linebacker*

COLLEGE: 1944–47 . . . . **NFL:** 1948;
College Football HOF, Alabama Sports HOF

As incomprehensible as it may seem today, Vaughn Mancha preferred the job of head football coach at Livingston State Teachers College (now the University of West Alabama) in Livingston, Alabama, to a career in the National Football League.

Mancha earned enshrinement in the College Football Hall of Fame for his play at center and linebacker for Alabama. He played one NFL season for the Boston Yanks, a perennially lousy team that went 3-9 that year and then folded. Rather than catch on with another pro team, Mancha turned to Livingston. After three years and an 18-10-2 record, he moved to Florida State, coaching running backs while getting a master's degree. He followed the same plan at Columbia University in New York, earning a doctorate in education while working as an assistant football coach.

Mancha returned to Florida State in 1960 as athletics director. He greatly expanded the athletics programs at what had been a women's college as recently as 1946. In 1972, he left athletics to become a professor of media education at Florida State. He retired in 1992 and died in 2011, age 89.

JOHN MANGUM ■ *Defensive Back*

COLLEGE: 1986–89 . . . . **NFL:** 1990–98

Holder of Alabama's single-season and career records for passes broken up (24 and 47, respectively), John Mangum spent nine years in the National Football League with the Chicago Bears. Mangum, 5-10 and 187 pounds, played mostly on special teams and in passing situations as an extra defensive back. His father, John Mangum Sr., was a defensive tackle for the American

KRIS MANGUM ■ *Tight End*

COLLEGE: 1992 . . . .**NFL:** 1997–2006

Son of John Mangum Sr. and younger brother of John Mangum Jr. (see above), Kris Mangum spent his first college year at Alabama but then transferred to Mississippi. The 6-4, 250-pound tight end played for 10 years with the National Football League's Carolina Panthers, the first six as a backup to Wesley Walls. Mangum retired after the 2006 season. He coached tight ends in 2008 for Southern Mississippi, then took a job with Magnolia State Bank. He is now vice president of the bank's office in Petal, Mississippi.

Kris Mangum spent his entire 10-year pro career with one team, the Carolina Panthers.
Credit: KeithAllisonPhoto.com

Football League Boston Patriots in 1966–67. Brother Kris also played in the NFL; see the facing page.

John Jr. is now a financial adviser in Raleigh, North Carolina.

BOBBY MARLOW ■ *Running Back-Defensive Back-Linebacker*

COLLEGE: 1950–52 . . . . **CFL:** 1953–60, 5-time Divisional All-Star; Alabama Sports HOF

The New York Giants picked Bobby Marlow in the first round of the 1953 National Football League draft. The Canadian Football League offered him more money, so north he went, to the Saskatchewan Roughriders. In those days of two-way play, he racked up 4,291 yards rushing in eight seasons for the Roughriders and earned five divisional All-Star selections at defensive back (1953–55) and linebacker (1956–57).

Marlow stood 6 feet tall and weighed 195 pounds. He was both bruising and fast. He still holds the Alabama career record for most yards per rush (6.3; minimum 400 attempts) and the record for most rushing yards in an Auburn game (233 in 1951).

His parents died when he was young, and he grew up in an orphanage in Troy, Alabama. After his retirement from football, he settled in Houston, where he died of a heart attack in 1985.

EVAN MATHIS ■ *Offensive Guard*

COLLEGE: 2001–04 . . . . **NFL:** 2005–12

While at Alabama, Evan Mathis was voted onto an All–Southeastern Conference and an Academic All-SEC team. At the beginning of his pro career, the 6-5 Mathis (nephew of former Alabama star Bob Baumhower; see page 87) wandered the National Football League, spending three years with the Carolina Panthers, splitting a year between the Cincinnati Bengals and the Miami Dolphins, adding two more years with the Bengals, and then having what he called the best year of his career with the Philadelphia Eagles in 2011. It earned him a five-year, $25 million contract at season's end. He attributed his improved play to a fiendish workout routine at the Scottsdale, Arizona, fitness center he opened in December 2010.

Apparently, he continued working out. He had an even better year in 2012, muscling his way into the front ranks of NFL offensive linemen. At 290 pounds, he's relatively svelte for a guard, but he uses his strength and quickness to keep up with bigger opponents and steer them where he wants them to go.

JASON MCADDLEY ■ *Wide Receiver-Kick Returner*

COLLEGE: 1998–2001 . . . . **NFL:** 2002–05

A solid wide receiver at Alabama, where he gained 110 yards in the 1999 Arkansas game, Jason McAddley began his National Football League career as a fifth-round draft choice and part-time starter for the Arizona Cardinals. McAddley, 6-2 and 200 pounds, struggled his second year with the Cardinals, signed as a free agent with the Tennessee Titans, and reemerged as a kick returner. A final season with the San Francisco 49ers as a backup at both positions ended his career. He's now studying for a doctor of pharmacy degree at Midwestern University in Glendale, Arizona, and working as a biology and chemistry tutor at nearby Chandler-Gilbert Community College.

KEITH MCCANTS ■ *Defensive End*

COLLEGE: 1988–89 . . . . **NFL:** 1990–95

For Keith McCants, one knee made all the difference. McCants was a terror at linebacker for Alabama, big (6-3, 265 pounds), fast, and athletic. Against Auburn in 1989, he made 18 tackles, intercepted a pass, forced a fumble, and chased down Auburn receiver Shane Wasden from behind to prevent a touchdown.

After that season, he made himself eligible for the National Football League draft, forgoing his senior year. The Tampa Bay Buccaneers selected him in the first round, fourth overall. He signed a five-year, $7.4 million contract with a then-record $2.5 million signing bonus. But he had badly injured a knee. Despite surgery, his speed was gone. He switched to defensive end and turned in a couple of solid years as a starter in 1991 and 1992, recording five sacks each year. But after three years with the Bucs and three more split between the Houston Oilers and the Arizona Cardinals, he retired.

McCants was not careful with money. A sportswriter from his hometown of Mobile, Alabama, said that after signing the Bucs contract in 1990, McCants offered to buy the sportswriter a Jeep in appreciation for the coverage of the athlete's career. The sportswriter declined, but others accepted other gifts.

In 2011, McCants said in a *Tampa Tribune* interview that he was broke, in constant pain. and showing symptoms of dementia because of football injuries. He said he had used illegal drugs—he has three drug-related convictions since 2002—for pain relief but was trying to stay clean. He said he had even attempted suicide. In the past couple of years, he has been working to turn his life around. McCants, who lives in St. Petersburg, Florida, appeared in the

September 2012 ESPN documentary *Broke,* which examined the financial troubles of former NFL stars. He does frequent interviews offering himself as a cautionary tale, hoping to use his experiences to keep others from making the mistakes he did.

"This will help me not only stay clean but to educate and work with other athletes," he told blogger Dan Soden in June 2013, "and give me a purpose in life and give me motivation to keep living."

LE'RON MCCLAIN ■ *Fullback*

COLLEGE: 2003–06 . . . . **NFL:** 2007–2012, 2 Pro Bowls

Le'Ron McClain's first name is pronounced "LAY-ron."

Credit: Jeffrey Beall

Massive fullback Le'Ron McClain usually gouges out holes for other runners. That was his primary job at Alabama, where he co-captained the 2006 team, and his rookie year in the pros. In 2008, the Baltimore Ravens unleashed him as a ball carrier. The 6-0, 260-pound McClain thundered for 902 yards, caught 19 passes for 123 more yards, and earned a berth in the National Football League Pro Bowl.

Since then, he's gone back to blocking for a living. He left the Ravens for the Kansas City Chiefs in 2011, then signed a three-year contract with the San Diego Chargers in 2012. He and Rolando McClain (see next bio) are cousins.

In addition to turning in another solid year as an NFL battering ram, McClain also went back to school in 2012. He completed his University of Alabama classwork in human environmental services and received his diploma at graduation ceremonies in May.

ROLANDO MCCLAIN ■ *Linebacker*

COLLEGE: 2007–09 . . . . **NFL:** 2010–12;
Lambert Award, Butkus Award

After winning the 2009 Lambert and Butkus awards (both for top college linebacker), plus the national championship, Rolando McClain saw no further collegiate worlds to conquer. He bypassed his senior year at Alabama to join the National Football League.

McClain, cousin of Le'Ron McClain (see previous bio), stands 6-3 and weighs 255 pounds. He played solidly his rookie year, then took a step forward in 2011. Despite a nagging ankle injury, he finished second on the team in tackles with 100 and recorded five quarterback sacks.

But that season is also when McClain's life began to unravel. In November 2011, he was arrested in his hometown of Decatur, Alabama, accused of firing a gun near the ear of a childhood friend during a dispute. He was convicted in municipal court, but all charges were dropped on appeal.

In 2012, the Raiders began pulling him from the field on passing downs. He suffered a concussion early in the season. The team suspended him after a November altercation with his coach. In 2013 came a January arrest in Decatur, an April release by the Raiders, a signing later that month by the Super Bowl champion Baltimore Ravens followed almost immediately by a third arrest in Decatur, and, in May, a retirement announcement. "Quite simply, I love football, but I have decided at this time it is in my best interest to focus on getting my personal life together," McClain said in a statement. "Beyond that, I'm not sure what the future holds for me, including football."

In the summer of 2013, McClain re-enrolled at Alabama and resumed progress toward his degree. Alabama players said he occasionally worked out with the team during the off-season and gave tips to the linebackers. McClain turned 24 on July 14. The Ravens left the door open for a possible return. We can still speak of "what may be" and not "what might have been."

CURTIS MCGRIFF ■ *Defensive Tackle-Nose Tackle*

COLLEGE: 1977–79 . . . . **NFL:** 1980–85, 1987

No National Football League team drafted Curtis McGriff after he finished his Alabama career with two straight national championships. The New York Giants signed him as a free agent, and the 6-foot-5, 270-pound McGriff played for six years as a run-stopping specialist on the Giants' defensive line. A hamstring injury sidelined him for all of 1986, so he didn't get to be part of the Giants' Super Bowl win that year.

The Giants cut him after that season. The Washington Redskins used him for one game during the 1987 players' strike. Since then, McGriff has been active in charity work and has taught at a correctional school in New Jersey. He appears annually at the youth football camps the Giants run at area schools during the summer.

MARK MCMILLIAN ■ *Cornerback*

COLLEGE: 1990–91 . . . . **NFL:** 1992–99

Only 5-7 and 155 pounds, Mark McMillian nevertheless played eight years in the National Football League with the Philadelphia Eagles, New Orleans Saints, Kansas City Chiefs, Washington Redskins, and San Francisco 49ers. His big year came in 1997, when he led the league in both pass interception yards (274) and interception touchdowns (three). He grabbed eight of his 23 career interceptions that year. At Alabama, he returned an intercepted pass for a school-record 98 yards and a touchdown against Tennessee-Chattanooga in 1991.

McMillian and former Eagles linebacker Byron Evans now partner on the Internet radio program Hard Hittin Radio in Chandler, Arizona. McMillian also organizes charity events and defensive-back training camps.

DON MCNEAL ■ *Cornerback*

COLLEGE: 1976–79 . . . . **NFL:** 1980–82, 1984–89;
Alabama Sports HOF

Fans voted Don McNeal to Alabama's 1970s Team of the Decade—and a single play probably put him over the top. On third down during the 1979 Sugar Bowl goal-line stand that won Alabama a national championship, he stopped Penn State tight end Scott Fritzkee on the one-yard line.

Injuries nagged McNeal during his 10-year National Football League career with the Miami Dolphins. A broken wrist cost him three games during his 1980 rookie season. A torn Achilles tendon sidelined him for all of 1983. Knee injuries sat him several other times.

When he could play, he lived up to his status as a No. 1 draft choice. He intercepted five passes his rookie year and 18 during his career. Injuries played a part in his most-remembered play. On fourth down during the 1983 Super Bowl, the 5-11, 190-pound McNeal grabbed 6-2, 230-pound Washington Redskins running back John Riggins behind the line of scrimmage. But McNeal had two badly bruised thumbs and couldn't hang on. Riggins sprinted 43 yards for the game-winning touchdown.

McNeal stayed in the Miami area after his retirement, though he has remained part of the University of Alabama family and makes charity appearances in both South Florida and Tuscaloosa. He is counseling pastor at New Testament Baptist Church in Miami and Dade counties, working primarily with kids. He also works with the Indianapolis-based Sports World, which sends former professional athletes to speak to students around the country.

In 2007, he published his autobiography, *Home Team Advantage: From the Fields of Rural Alabama to the Pro Football Field of the Miami Dolphins*, detailing his childhood with a stern but loving father after his mother died when he was 6.

CHRIS MOHR ■ *Punter*

COLLEGE: 1985–88 . . . . **NFL:** 1989, 1991–2004; **WLAF:** 1991

Pity the poor punter: always a key player, seldom a household name. Chris Mohr was one of the best in Alabama and National Football League history, known for his exceptional hang time. He averaged 42.5 yards per punt for the Crimson Tide, fourth-best in team history. Mohr, 6-5 and 215 pounds, spent 15 years in the National Football League, with a one-season detour to the World League of American Football. He played in three straight Super Bowls with the Buffalo Bills (1992–94). He now owns a company in Thomson, Georgia, that distributes "green" cleaning products.

STEVE MOTT ■ *Center*

COLLEGE: 1980–82 . . . . **NFL:** 1983–88

After playing on Bear Bryant's last national championship team in 1979 and co-captaining Bryant's last team ever in 1982, Mott went to the National Football League's Detroit Lions. The 6-3, 266-pounder slugged it out in the middle of the offensive line for six seasons. He now lives near Birmingham, Alabama, and is chief operating officer for a company that manages hospital-based vein centers. In 2009, police returned to Mott two of his most prized possessions: stolen rings that had been given to players who participated in the national championship season in 1979 and Bryant's 315th career victory in 1981.

JOHNNY MUSSO ■ *Running Back*

COLLEGE: 1969–71 . . . . **CFL:** 1972–74; **WFL:** 1975;
NFL: 1975–77; College Football HOF, Alabama Sports HOF

Alabama fans loved the all-out running and blocking style of Johnny Musso, The Italian Stallion. After college, he spurned the National Football League's Chicago Bears and signed instead with the British Columbia Lions of the Canadian Football League. In 1973, he gained 1,029 yards and helped the Lions to a playoff berth.

Injuries sidelined him most of the next season. For 1975, the 5-11, 201-pound Musso came back home to join the Birmingham Vulcans. He had gained 681 yards when, two-thirds of the way through the schedule, the World Football League collapsed.

So Musso finally gave the Bears a chance. After three years as a backup in Chicago, he moved from football to finance. He became a commodity futures trader, then founded a private equity investment company. He and his wife, Tanner, have also long been active in a Christian youth ministry. He lives in suburban Chicago.

MICHAEL MYERS ■ *Defensive Tackle-Defensive End*

COLLEGE: 1996 . . . . **NFL:** 1998–2007

A transfer from Hinds Community College in Mississippi, Michael Myers played only one season for Alabama but was named to some All-America and All–Southeastern Conference teams. Alabama suspended Myers at the beginning of the 1997 season, saying he had accepted improper benefits from sports agents, but allowed him to keep his scholarship.

The 6-2, 300-pound Myers played 10 years with the Dallas Cowboys, Cleveland Browns, Denver Broncos, and Cincinnati Bengals in the National Football League. In 2012, he was a defensive line coach back at Hinds Community College. In February 2012, he sued the National Football League over its handling of players' head injuries, saying that concussions he suffered while playing have caused migraines, memory loss, and other medical problems. In August 2013, the NFL and former players announced a $765 million settlement; see the Lee Roy Jordan bio on page 118.

TONY NATHAN ■ *Running Back-Punt Returner-Kick Returner*

COLLEGE: 1975–78 . . . .**NFL:** 1979–87; Alabama Sports HOF

Small (6-0, 206 pounds) but elusive and sure-handed, Tony Nathan gained 3,378 all-purpose yards rushing, receiving, and running back kicks and punts for Alabama. In the National Football League, he turned in a productive nine-year career as an all-purpose back for the Miami Dolphins. He finished with 3,543 yards rushing, 3,592 receiving, and 1,617 returning punts and kicks. He then became running backs coach for the Dolphins, the Tampa Bay Buccaneers, the Baltimore Ravens, and the San Francisco 49ers of the NFL, for Florida International University, and, most recently, for Hialeah Miami Lakes High School in Florida. Nathan is now the bailiff for Dade County Court Judge Edward Newman, a former Miami Dolphins guard who was Nathan's teammate from 1979 through 1984.

JOE NAMATH ■ *Quarterback*

COLLEGE: 1962–64 . . . . **AFL:** 1965–69; **NFL:** 1970–77, 5 Pro Bowls; Pro Football HOF, Alabama Sports HOF

Joe Namath was a great quarterback. Don't let the flamboyant personality, the forays into acting and TV commercials, and the other distractions that swirled around him obscure his brilliance as a passer.

At Alabama, when Namath started at quarterback, the Crimson Tide had a record of 21-3. He chose college football over several offers from major-league baseball teams and ended up at Alabama after not quite meeting the college-board requirements for his first choice, Maryland.

Namath and his coach, Bear Bryant, admired and respected each other, even though Bryant suspended Namath for the final two games of the 1963 season, including the 1964 Sugar Bowl, for breaking training rules.

The next year, Namath's senior season, he injured his right knee against North Carolina State on October 10 and played sparingly the rest of the way. The Crimson Tide finished

After Joe Namath injured his knee in 1964, coach Bear Bryant said, "He moves like a human now. He did move like a cat."
Credit: Paul W. Bryant Museum/The University of Alabama

the regular season at 10-0, atop both major polls. Namath's knee kept him on the bench at the start of the 1965 Orange Bowl. In the second quarter, Alabama trailed, 14-0, against Texas, which had shut down the Crimson Tide running game. Namath limped onto the field and began firing passes. He completed 18 of 37 throws for 255 yards and two touchdowns, igniting a comeback that fell just short when he couldn't get across the goal line on a late-game quarterback sneak. Alabama lost, 21–17, but Namath was voted the Most Valuable Player.

Namath left Alabama with school records for passing attempts, completions, yards, and touchdowns. When he signed with the New York Jets for a then-astonishing $427,000, plus a Lincoln Continental, he instantly gave the young American Football League credibility in its battle against the established National Football League. The Jets victory he directed over the vaunted Baltimore Colts in Super Bowl III was the final step in asserting AFL-NFL parity.

A stats-oriented debate has raged in recent years over whether Namath was overrated. The newest statistical tools have looked more favorably on him. Without getting into the complexities, we offer this simple truth: Until his knees pretty much gave out around the time he hit 30, whenever Namath was able to play a full season or close to it, the Jets ranked among the league's top offensive teams. When he went down with injuries, so did the Jets' offense.

Beyond that, he was just so much fun to watch—on and off the field.

Before the injuries restricted his mobility, Namath, 6-foot-2 and 200 pounds, was a terrific all-around athlete—the greatest, said Bryant, that he ever coached. Pro Football Hall of Fame coach Bill Walsh said Namath was "the most beautiful, accurate, stylish passer with the quickest release I've ever seen." Even now, a generation and a half after his retirement following 12 years with the Jets and a final season with the Los Angeles Rams, he remains one of the most recognizable and beloved athletes in the United States. He lives in Tequesta, Florida, and keeps busy with promotional and charity work. His website (www.broadwayjoe .tv), Facebook page, and Twitter feeds overflow with both roguish charm and thoughtful insights—the latter always a part of the package but often outshone by the celebrity glow.

Namath maintains close ties with both the Jets and the Crimson Tide. In 2007, through Alabama's External Degree Program, he finally finished his schooling and received his degree in interdisciplinary studies.

BILLY NEIGHBORS ■ *Offensive Guard*

COLLEGE: 1959–61 . . . . **AFL:** 1962–69, 1 All-Star Team; College Football HOF, Alabama Sports HOF

Drafted by both the American Football League's Boston Patriots and the National Football League's Washington Redskins, Billy Neighbors presaged his successful post-football career in the financial industry by picking the Patriots' higher salary offer—$27,000.

Neighbors, not quite 6 feet tall and a muscular 250 pounds, was a member of Coach Bear Bryant's first Alabama class in 1958 and first national championship team in 1961, when the Crimson Tide went 11-0 and allowed only 25 points all year. He never won a pro championship, though he did make the 1963 AFL All-Star game. After four years with the Patriots and four with the Miami Dolphins, he retired. He had worked as a stockbroker in the off-seasons, and he continued to be a financial advisor in Huntsville, Alabama, for nearly four decades. He was also active in charitable endeavors.

Sid Neighbors, Billy's older brother, played for Alabama in 1956 and 1957. Billy's sons also lettered for Alabama, Wes as a center from 1983 through 1986 and Keith as a linebacker in 1990. And grandson Wesley (Wes's son) lettered for the Crimson Tide as a defensive back in 2010.

Neighbors, a good friend and former teammate of the late Alabama athletics director Mal Moore, maintained close ties with the Crimson Tide. He was not a "back in my day" kind of guy. He disagreed with those who ranked his 1961 Crimson Tide as the best defensive team in college football history, contending that Alabama's 2011 national champions were better.

In April 2012, he died of a heart attack. He was 72.

OZZIE NEWSOME ■ *Tight End*

COLLEGE: 1974–77 . . . . **NFL:** 1978–90, 3 Pro Bowls; Pro Football HOF, College Football HOF, Alabama Sports HOF

As great as he was on the field, Ozzie Newsome might be even better at his current job: general manager of the current Super Bowl champion Baltimore Ravens.

Newsome was a deadly wide receiver at Alabama. He finished with 2,070 receiving yards on only 102 catches for an exceptional average of 20.3 yards per grab.

In the National Football League, Newsome, along with the San Diego Chargers' Kellen Winslow, helped revolutionize the role of the tight end. It had been a blocking-oriented position. During his 13-year career with the Cleveland Browns (now the Ravens), Newsome—smaller (6-2, 230 pounds) but much faster and more athletic than the traditional tight end—ran deep pass patterns instead of hanging around the line. Defenses couldn't handle him.

Twice, he gained more than 1,000 yards in a season on pass receptions. He retired with 7,890 yards on 662 catches—more like wide receiver numbers than tight end stats.

He went directly from the locker room into the Browns' front office and moved with the team to Baltimore in 1996. In 2002, he became the NFL's first African-American general manager. Under his leadership, the team has reached the playoffs seven times, won four division championships, and claimed the 2013 Super Bowl championship.

ANTWAN ODOM ■ *Defensive End*

COLLEGE: 2000, 2002–03 . . . . **NFL:** 2004–10

A feared pass rusher at Alabama, where he's still on the career top 10 list for quarterback sacks, Antwan Odom didn't really show his college form as a pro until 2007, when he registered eight sacks in the last of his four years with the National Football League's Tennessee Titans.

The 6-4, 277-pound Odom signed a five-year, $29.5 million contract ($11.5 million of it guaranteed) with the Cincinnati Bengals as a free agent in 2008. But shoulder and foot injuries cost him playing time. He recorded eight sacks in only six games in 2009 before an Achilles tendon injury ended his season. He managed to play four games in 2010 before injuring his wrist and being suspended for violating the team's substance-abuse policy.

Odom had a bad year in 2011. In March, his Cincinnati-area house burned while he and his family were out of town. In August, a childhood friend reportedly found his girlfriend with Odom and shot Odom in the thigh with a shotgun. In December, Odom was arrested on a marijuana-possession charge.

In 2012, Odom resumed working out, hoping for a comeback. Nothing came of it, but as late as August 2013, Odom proclaimed on Twitter, "To all the teams in the NFL I can still play just need a chance I'm ready just pick up the phone. I'm sure u wont regret it."

RAY ODUMS ■ *Cornerback*

COLLEGE: 1972–74 in basketball . . **CFL:** 1975–84, 3-time All-Star; **USFL:** 1985

A basketball star at Alabama, where he led the team in assists each of his three years and still ranks in the school's career top-10 list, Ray Odums turned to football in the pros. After two Canadian Football League years split between the Winnipeg Blue Bombers and the Sasketchewan Roughriders, the 6-2, 180-pound Odums became a star in 1977 with the Calgary Stampeders. As a Stampeder, he made the CFL All-Star Team three times. He finished his career with the Memphis Showboats of the United States Football League.

Odums now works for the Parks & Recreation Department in his hometown of Birmingham.

RAY OGDEN ■ *Tight End*

COLLEGE: 1962–64 . . . .**NFL:** 1965–71

Ray Ogden was a halfback, wide receiver, and kick returner at Alabama, where he co-captained the 1964 national championship team with quarterback Joe Namath. In the National Football League, the 6-5, 225-pound Ogden played mostly tight end for the St. Louis Cardinals, Atlanta Falcons, New Orleans Saints, and Chicago Bears. He put up his best numbers for the Falcons, for whom he caught 25 passes for 452 yards in 1968.

After his career ended, he played Schmidt in the original 1974 version of the movie *The Longest Yard* (which was about a football game between prison inmates and their guards). He lives in Brunswick, Georgia, not far from his hometown of Jesup.

DAVID PALMER ■ *Punt Returner-Kick Returner-Wide Receiver*

COLLEGE: 1991–93 . . . .**NFL:** 1994–2000

One of the most sensational athletes in Alabama history, David Palmer played almost every offensive position for the Crimson Tide except lineman. Just 5-8 and 170 pounds, and quicker than a hummingbird, "The Deuce" (he wore number 2) was a threat to do something spectacular whenever he touched the ball.

Palmer returned kicks for the National Football League's Minnesota Vikings for seven years. He now coaches football and baseball—the sport he calls his first love—at Parker High School in Birmingham.

RAY PERKINS ■ *Wide Receiver*

COLLEGE: 1964–66 . . . .**NFL:** 1967–1971; Alabama head coach: 1983–86; Alabama Sports HOF, Mississippi Sports HOF

Alabama fans have mixed feelings about Ray Perkins. He was an All-America wide receiver who won national titles with the Crimson Tide in 1964 and 1965. He spent five years with the National Football League's Baltimore Colts, never a starter but peaking at 28 receptions in 1969.

The 6-3, 185-pound Perkins played in two famous Super Bowls: the Colts' shocking 1969 loss to the American Football League's New York Jets (quarterbacked by Perkins' 1964 college teammate Joe Namath) and the redemptive 1971 win over the Dallas Cowboys.

Turning to coaching, Perkins worked his way up to a four-year stint as head coach of the New York Giants. In 1983, he tried to fill the biggest shoes

CHARLIE PEPRAH ■ *Safety*

COLLEGE: 2002–05 . . . . **NFL:** 2006–12

After establishing himself quickly during his Alabama career, tying for the team lead in interceptions his freshman and sophomore years, Charlie Peprah had to learn patience as a pro. The 5-10, 200-pound defensive back played sparingly for three National Football League seasons with the Green Bay Packers. He became a free agent after a knee injury and played two games with the Atlanta Falcons in 2009. He returned to the Packers in 2010 but struggled at first with a sore quadriceps.

Then safety Morgan Burnett got hurt, and Peprah became a starter. He seized the opportunity and rode it all the way to the Super Bowl, where he led both teams in tackles (10) during the Packers' 31–25 victory over the Pittsburgh Steelers. The Packers subsequently signed him to a two-year, $2.5 million contract.

Peprah proved he belonged with 94 tackles and five interceptions in 2011, helping the Packers reach the playoffs again. Shockingly, the Packers released him on the first day of 2012 training camp after he failed his physical because of a knee injury. The Dallas Cowboys picked him up midseason, and he contributed 11 tackles and an interception in five games before a foot injury sidelined him again. Going into the 2013 season, his career seemed in doubt.

Charlie Peprah joins other Green Bay Packers riding young fans' bicycles to practice on the first day of 2011 training camp. The ride has been a Packers tradition for half a century.
Credit: Gabriel Cervantes

Peprah's mother, Elizabeth Peprah, is the daughter of Ignatius Kutu Acheampong, ruler of Ghana from 1972 to 1978. Acheampong was executed in 1979 after a coup. His daughter and her husband fled and ended up in the Dallas area, where Charlie was born and reared.

in college football, succeeding Paul Bryant as head coach at Alabama. Two Sun Bowls, an Aloha Bowl, a 2-2 record against Auburn, and the school's first losing season in 27 years (5-6 in 1984) didn't make anyone forget the Bear. After four years, Perkins left to coach the NFL's Tampa Bay Buccaneers.

That didn't work out so well either. The Bucs fired him halfway through the 1990 season. His NFL record as a head coach is 42-75. In college, including a 2-9 year with Arkansas State, it's 34-24-1—better, but still not Bearish.

After a 1999–2000 stretch as an assistant with the NFL's Cleveland Browns, Perkins went back home to Petal, Mississippi (near Hattiesburg). In December 2011, after 11 years of retirement, the 70-year-old Perkins became head coach of nearby Jones County Junior College. He explained, "I don't think you ever lose the passion for the game." In his first season, his team matched its 6-3 record of the year before.

BENNY PERRIN ■ *Free Safety*

COLLEGE: 1980–81 . . . . **NFL:** 1982–85

As a senior, Benny Perrin led Alabama with 11 passes broken up. In the National Football League, the 6-2, 180-pound Perrin quickly became the starting free safety for the St. Louis Cardinals until a knee injury ended his career midway through the 1985 season. He now owns B. B. Perrins Sports Grille, a highly regarded barbecue joint in Decatur, Alabama.

MIKE PITTS ■ *Defensive Tackle-Defensive End*

COLLEGE: 1979–82 . . . . **NFL:** 1983–94

Mike Pitts spent a lot of time in opponents' backfields. At Alabama, he led the team in tackles for loss his junior and senior seasons. In the National Football League, the 6-3, 277-pound Pitts played a dozen years as a pass-rushing defensive lineman with the Atlanta Falcons (who picked him in the first round of the 1983 draft), Philadelphia Eagles, and New England Patriots. In 1991, he and Eagles linemates Reggie White, Jerome Brown, and Clyde Simmons each recorded at least 100 tackles, combined for 39 sacks, and led a defense that ranked first in the league against both the run and the pass. Pitts now coaches defensive linemen for the Infinity Football Academy in Alpharetta, Georgia.

DANIEL POPE ■ *Punter*

COLLEGE: 1997–98 . . . . **NFL:** 1999–2001

A booming punter, Daniel Pope ranks second on Alabama's career list for average yards per punt, trailing leader Greg Gantt (1971–73) by a tenth of a yard, 43.6 to 43.5. The 5-10, 203-pound Pope played in the National Football League for the Kansas City Chiefs in 1999, Cincinnati Bengals in 2000, and, for one game, New York Jets in 2001. He now lives in Northport, Alabama, just north of Tuscaloosa. He works in medical sales and trains retriever dogs.

DERRICK POPE ■ *Linebacker*

COLLEGE: 2002–03 . . . . **NFL:** 2004–07

A transfer from Garden City Community College in Garden City, Kansas, Derrick Pope recorded 105 tackles his senior year at Alabama and was team co-captain. Not big at 6 feet tall and 232 pounds, he nevertheless managed a four-year career, mostly as a backup, with the National Football League's Miami Dolphins. In 2007, he started nine games and made 43 tackles, but the Dolphins let him go after the season. Tryouts with the NFL's Minnesota Vikings and the Canadian Football League's Hamilton Tiger-Cats came to naught.

From Southern to Westerns

The 1926 Rose Bowl made Johnny Mack Brown a movie star. Brown, a Dothan, Alabama, native known as "The Dothan Antelope," starred as a speedy halfback for Alabama in the mid-1920s. The 1926 Rose Bowl was Alabama's first bowl game, and the Crimson Tide beat heavily favored Washington 20–19. Brown scored two touchdowns and was named the game's outstanding player. "The Football Game That Changed the South" generated national respect not only for Southern football but also for the South as a region.

Brown was a handsome, engaging guy who had been involved with the drama club at Alabama. During the Rose Bowl halftime, Tide coach Wallace Wade spoke only 10 words: "And they told me boys from the South would fight." He then left the locker room. So did Brown, who strolled into the stands to chat with pretty girls.

The Rose Bowl attention got him a Hollywood contract by 1927. A starring role in 1930's *Billy the Kid* led to other major parts for "John Mack Brown." However, in 1931, his scenes in *Laughing Sinners* were reshot to substitute rising star Clark Gable, and Brown's career slipped. He turned to low-budget Westerns. Once more known as Johnny Mack Brown, he found his stride. He stood tall in the saddle for the next two decades. He did the same offscreen, playing polo with Hollywood pals.

Throughout his life, Brown remained by all accounts a gracious Southern gentleman. He died in 1974, age 70.

MIKE RAINES ■ *Defensive Tackle-Defensive End*

COLLEGE: 1972–73 . . . . **NFL:** 1974; **CFL:** 1975–82, 1-time All-Star; **USFL:** 1983–84

After starting at defensive tackle for Alabama's 1973 national championship team, Vaughn Michael Raines played in just two games the next season for the National Football League's San Francisco 49ers. He moved in 1975 to the Montreal Alouettes of the Canadian Football League, who sent him to the Ottawa Rough Riders after five games.

Suddenly the bumpy career smoothed out. Raines, 6-5 and 255 pounds, played with Ottawa for eight years. He was an East Division All-Star four times and, in 1981, a CFL All-Star. After finishing his CFL career in 1982 with seven games for the Rough Riders and one game for the Winnipeg Blue Bombers. Raines turned to the United States Football League, leading the 1983 Birmingham Stallions in sacks with eight. He finally wound down with the USFL's Jacksonville Bulls in 1984.

After football, Raines has worked in sales and technology in Jacksonville, where he still lives.

SALEEM RASHEED ■ *Linebacker*

COLLEGE: 1999–2001 . . . . **NFL:** 2002–2005; **CFL:** 2008

After leading Alabama in tackles his junior year, Saleem Rasheed skipped his senior season and entered the National Football League draft. The San Francisco 49ers signed him to a three-year contract reportedly worth $905,000 plus a $538,000 signing bonus.

But Rasheed, a smallish linebacker at 6-2 and 229 pounds, battled injuries. After four years, the 49ers let him go as a free agent. He signed with the Houston Texans but got cut before the 2006 season. In 2008, he helped the Calgary Stampeders win the Canadian Football League's Grey Cup championship despite spending nine games in the middle of the season on the injured list. He wasn't re-signed for 2009.

He returned home to the Birmingham area and worked as a high school teacher and coach. In 2012, Rasheed pleaded guilty to food stamp fraud and falsely claiming a woman as his wife on immigration forms. According to court records, he married one woman in 2005, married another in 2007 without divorcing his first wife, and eventually had two children by each woman. "He is a very devout Muslim. He believes that under Sharia law you can have more than one wife," his lawyer said. "Unfortunately, under Alabama law you cannot have more than one wife. . . . He understands that now."

In 2013, Rasheed pleaded guilty to having sex with two students at the Birmingham high school where he was teaching at the time. The students were apparently of legal age, but Alabama law prohibits teacher-student sex. Rasheed was expected to be released from prison in early 2015.

DAVID RAY ■ *Kicker*

COLLEGE: 1964–65 . . . . **CFL:** 1968; **NFL:** 1969–74

David Ray, who stood 6 feet tall and weighed 195 pounds, was a wide receiver as well as a kicker at Alabama. He led the Crimson Tide in receiving in 1964, albeit with only 19 catches for 271 yards and two touchdowns. During his junior and senior seasons, he made 44 of 46 extra-point attempts and 19 of 31 field goal tries.

In 1973, kicking for the Los Angeles Rams, Ray led the National Football League in field goals made (30) and attempted (47). The next year, he made only 9 of 16 attempts, missed a startling 6 of 31 extra-point attempts, and lost his job. What happened? In 1974, the National Football League moved the goalposts from the front of the end zone to the back. Ray couldn't handle the extra 10 yards. Here are his career success rates by field-goal distance:

Less than 40 yards: 74 percent

40 or more yards: 33 percent

Oddly, during his one year with the Montreal Alouettes of the Canadian Football League in 1968, he set a still-standing team record for longest field goal: 54 yards.

JESS RICHARDSON ■ *Defensive Tackle*

COLLEGE: 1950–52 . . . . **NFL:** 1953–61, 1 Pro Bowl;
AFL: 1962–64

Tough? Jess Richardson was tough. He refused to wear pads, believing they slowed him down, and played without a face mask—the last National Football League lineman to do so. When an errant elbow broke his nose, he'd simply step into the shower (for easier cleanup) and shove it back into place.

Richardson, 6-foot-2, ended his Alabama career on a big stage—in the first nationally televised Orange Bowl, in which Alabama routed Syracuse, 61–6. Though he began his NFL career at only 235 pounds, he used his quickness to anchor the interior of the defensive line for his hometown Philadelphia Eagles.

A knee injury sidelined him for the 1957 season. He worked hard to strengthen the knee, returned to the starting lineup in 1958, and was named to the Pro Bowl in 1959.

TRENT RICHARDSON ■ *Running Back*

COLLEGE: 2009–11 . . . . **NFL:** 2012; Doak Walker Award

Injuries to his legs and ribs slowed National Football League rookie Trent Richardson in 2012 and forced him to miss the final game of the season. Yet he still gave the Cleveland Browns 950 yards rushing plus an additional 367 yards in pass receptions. He went into 2013 lighter (a muscular 225 pounds on his 5-foot-9 frame) and healthy. But when he started slowly, the Browns pulled off a startling early-season trade and sent him to the Indianapolis Colts.

At Alabama, Richardson had to wait his turn until running back Mark Ingram decided to go pro after the 2010 season. In 2011, his junior year, Richardson actually outdid Ingram's Heisman-winning numbers from 2009, gaining 1,679 yards and scoring 21 touchdowns. (Ingram's comparable numbers were 1,658 and 17.) Another number made him especially beloved to his coaches: during his Alabama career, he touched the ball 614 times and fumbled just once.

Trent Richardson finished third in voting for the 2011 Heisman Trophy.
Credit: Erik Drost

During the 2012 NFL Draft, the Browns picked Richardson third in the first round after trading up one draft position in order to block the Tampa Bay Buccaneers, who also coveted him.

In April 2012, Richardson thrilled leukemia survivor Courtney Alvis of Hueytown, Alabama, by escorting her to her senior prom. He'd heard about her through a mutual friend of her uncle's.

The Eagles won the NFL championship in 1960, but in 1961 Richardson, then 31, started losing playing time. Before the 1962 season, the Eagles cut him. He signed with the Boston (now New England) Patriots and played three more seasons in the American Football League.

Richardson transitioned directly from playing to coaching the defensive line, first for the Patriots, then for the Eagles. He died of kidney disease in 1975 at age 44.

LARRY ROBERTS ■ *Defensive End*

COLLEGE: 1982–85 . . . . **NFL:** 1986–93

All-America and all-conference voters overlooked Larry Roberts during his college career, but National Football League scouts didn't. The San Francisco 49ers chose Roberts, 6-3 and 270 pounds, in the second round of the 1986 draft. During his eight-year NFL career, the 49ers used him mostly on passing downs. He recorded 5.5 quarterback sacks his rookie year, 6.0 in 1988, and 7.0 in 1991, and totaled 28 in his career. He now lives in the Atlanta area.

ANDRE ROYAL ■ *Linebacker*

COLLEGE: 1991–94 . . . . **NFL:** 1995–99

On the field, Andre Royal could play with anyone. Staying on the field was sometimes a problem. At Alabama, where Royal played on the 1992 national championship team, coach Gene Stallings suspended him at least four times for infractions ranging from fighting to general lack of commitment to team requirements.

In the National Football League, Royal finally achieved starter status in 1997, his third season with the Carolina Panthers. The 6-2, 232-pound linebacker registered 60 tackles and five quarterback sacks. That led to a $4.085 million guaranteed free-agent contract with the New Orleans Saints in 1998. But issues cropped up, including an arrest during a celebration of the contract, a hazing incident during which a teammate was injured, and a public argument with coach Mike Ditka. Before the season, the Saints traded Royal to the Indianapolis Colts.

In 1999, his second year with Indianapolis, the Colts mysteriously cut Royal in midseason without explanation. He never played again. He was a businessman in Charlotte, North Carolina, but moved back to Tuscaloosa in 2012. He re-enrolled at the university to finish his degree in criminal justice and signed on to coach linebackers at Tuscaloosa Academy.

DWAYNE RUDD ■ *Linebacker*

COLLEGE: 1994–96 . . . . **NFL:** 1997–2003

After leading Alabama in tackles for two straight years, Dwayne Rudd skipped his senior season and stepped up to the National Football League. The Minnesota Vikings took the 6-2, 235-pound Rudd in the first round of the draft, 20th overall. He ended up playing four years for the Vikings, two years for the Cleveland Browns, and a year for the Tampa Bay Buccaneers, starting all but the first and last seasons.

Rudd holds an odd record: most fumble return yards in a season, 157 in 1998, when he scooped up three fumbles and ran two of them back for touchdowns. He's also remembered for a mistake that cost the Browns a game. In the 2002 season opener, the Browns led the Kansas City Chiefs, 39–37, with 10 seconds left. Rudd thought he'd sacked Chiefs quarterback Trent Green as time expired and tossed his helmet in celebration, assuming the game was over. But Green had lateraled the ball to a teammate, and the play was still going on. The unsportsmanlike-conduct penalty for the helmet toss gave the Chiefs another play, and they kicked a field goal to win the game, 40–39.

Rudd now lives in Atlanta. In 2009, he pleaded guilty to failing to pay more than $540,000 in child support for his then–11-year-old daughter.

JEFF RUTLEDGE ■ *Quarterback*

COLLEGE: 1975–78 . . . . **NFL:** 1979–81, 1983–92;
Alabama Sports HOF

Backup quarterbacks can last a long time in the National Football League. Jeff Rutledge, who won a national championship as a wishbone quarterback for Alabama in 1978, played for 13 NFL seasons, starting a total of just 10 games. He reached the Super Bowl with each of his three pro teams: losing in 1980 with the Los Angeles Rams and winning in 1987 with the New York Giants and 1992 with the Washington Redskins. In the latter two games, he even got to play.

Since his retirement, Rutledge, 6-1 and 195 pounds, has coached in Montgomery, Alabama, and Henderson, Tennessee, for high schools; in college at Vanderbilt; and in the pros with the Arizona Cardinals of the NFL and the New York Sentinels of the United Football League. He is now head football coach at Valley Christian High School in Chandler, Arizona.

ROD RUTLEDGE ■ *Tight End*

COLLEGE: 1994–97 . . . . **NFL:** 1998–2002

Legendary New England Patriots quarterback Tom Brady played in only one game his rookie National Football League year. Against the Detroit Lions on Thanksgiving Day 2000, he attempted three passes and completed one. The player who caught that historic first completion was tight end Rod Rutledge.

The 6-5, 265-pound Rutledge was a co-captain his senior year on coach Mike DuBose's disappointing first Crimson Tide team, which won three of its first four games but finished with a 4-7 record. In both college and the

DeMeco Ryans still holds the Alabama record for most tackles in a nonbowl game: 25 versus Arkansas in 2003.

Credit: Christopher Brown

DEMECO RYANS ■ *Linebacker*

COLLEGE: 2002–2005
NFL: 2006–2012, 2 Pro Bowls

DeMeco Ryans blasted into the professional ranks the way he attacks offenses. Shifting from outside linebacker, where he had earned All-America honors at Alabama, to middle linebacker, he finished second in the league in tackles with 156—126 of them unassisted. He added 3.5 quarterback sacks and an interception and was named the National Football League's Defensive Rookie of the Year.

Ryans, 6-1 and 252 pounds, became a highly respected leader on and off the field for the Houston Texans, an expansion team that was only four years old when it drafted him. Fans called him "Cap'n Meco."

The Texans signed him to a six-year, $48 million contract extension in 2010. Unfortunately, a ruptured Achilles tendon sidelined him for the last 10 games of that season, and he never quite regained full speed in 2011. Before the 2012 season, the Texans traded Ryans to the Philadelphia Eagles. He rebounded in 2012, playing almost every defensive down and contributing 111 tackles, 84 of them solo. Despite being noted mostly for his run defense, he also snagged his first pass interception since 2007.

pros, Rutledge specialized in blocking; he caught only 27 passes total during his five-year NFL career.

He spent 1998 through 2001 with the Patriots, teaming with Brady that last season to win the Patriots' first Super Bowl. The Houston Texans subsequently signed Rutledge to a two-year, $1.1 million contract as a free agent. Injuries limited him to just seven games. The Texans released him after the 2002 season, and he returned to his hometown of Birmingham.

ED SALEM ■ *Halfback-Defensive Back*

COLLEGE: 1947–50 . . . . **NFL:** 1951; **CFL:** 1952;
Alabama Sports HOF

Ed Salem single-handedly demolished Auburn in 1948, the year Alabama and Auburn renewed their rivalry after a 41-year hiatus. He threw for three touchdowns, rushed for another, and kicked seven extra points in a 55–0 rout. Salem, 5-foot-11 and 190 pounds, led Alabama in passing (1948–50), rushing (1948), scoring (1948–49), and interceptions (1949) and was a first-team All-America defensive back in 1950.

He played one season with the National Football League's Washington Redskins and another with the Montreal Alouettes of the Canadian Football League, where he kicked a then–league-record 53-yard field goal.

Then Salem came home to Birmingham and became locally famous all over again. He opened several bowling alleys and a popular (though now-vanished) chain of Ed Salem's Drive In restaurants. He found another profitable venture organizing trips from Birmingham to the casinos of Atlantic City, New Jersey. Some say the taint of gambling kept him out of the Alabama Sports Hall of Fame until 2010, nine years after his death. Son Wayne now operates Salem's Diner, which features some of his father's memorabilia, in the Birmingham suburb of Homewood.

CHRIS SAMUELS ■ *Offensive Tackle*

COLLEGE: 1996–99 . . . . **NFL:** 2000–09, 6 Pro Bowls;
Outland Trophy

A scary injury in 2009 ended Chris Samuels' National Football League career. The gigantic lineman, 6-5 and 310 pounds, suffered temporary upper-body paralysis after a helmet-to-helmet hit. Doctors said the condition was related to a spinal condition he'd had since childhood. They advised him that he risked severe permanent injury if he kept playing.

Thus ended a dominant career. After winning the Outland Trophy as the best college interior lineman during his senior season at Alabama, Samuels played 10 years for the Washington Redskins. In six of those years, he was named to the Pro Bowl.

Thus also began a second career in coaching. Samuels assisted Redskins offensive line coach Chris Foerster for a year, then became offensive coordinator at Blount High School in Prichard, Alabama. In 2012, he returned to the University of Alabama to work as a student assistant coach while finishing his degree in physical education.

RANDY SCOTT ■ *Linebacker*

COLLEGE: 1978–80 . . . . **NFL:** 1981–87

After playing in 1979 for coach Bear Bryant's last national championship team at Alabama and co-captaining Bryant's 1980 team, Randy Scott got snubbed in the 1981 National Football League draft. The 6-1, 223-pound linebacker signed as a free agent with the Green Bay Packers. He became a starter the next season and kept that job for five years.

The Packers released him after the 1986 season. After two games with the Minnesota Vikings in 1987, his football career ended. Scott now lives in Atlanta and works for a company that negotiates reductions in property-tax liability for businesses and individuals.

SAM SHADE ■ *Safety*

COLLEGE: 1991–94 . . . . **NFL:** 1995–2002

Eight of the 11 defensive starters on Alabama's 1992 national championship team played in the National Football League. Then-sophomore strong safety Sam Shade, a sturdy 6-0 and 205 pounds, was one of them. First, though, in 1994, he co-captained an Alabama team that lost only one game, a 24–23 heartbreaker to Florida in the Southeastern Conference Championship.

A neck injury in 2002 hastened Shade's retirement after eight years as a National Football League strong safety with the Cincinnati Bengals and Washington Redskins. He continued his community-service work, did color commentary for a couple of years on the MBC Network cable channel, finished his bachelor's degree at Alabama, and became a financial consultant.

In 2004, Shade began working as a volunteer coach at Briarwood Christian School in Birmingham. Since 2008, he has been cornerbacks coach at Samford University in suburban Birmingham.

WILLIE SHELBY ■ *Running Back-Kick Returner-Punt Returner*

COLLEGE: 1973–75 . . . . **NFL:** 1976–78

A speedy kick and punt returner and occasional running back for Alabama's 1973 national championship team, Willie Shelby led the National Football League in kick-return yardage in 1976. That was his rookie season with the Cincinnati Bengals. The 5-11, 195-pound Shelby played one more season with the Bengals, battled some injuries, and ended his career after three games with the St. Louis Cardinals in 1978.

JUWAN SIMPSON ■ *Linebacker*

COLLEGE: 2003–06 . . . . **CFL:** 2008–13, 1 All-Star Team

After co-captaining Alabama in 2006 and tying for the team lead in tackles, Juwan Simpson went unselected in the National Football League draft. He signed with the Green Bay Packers as a free agent in 2007 but was released before the season. Simpson looked north and found a home in the Canadian Football League with the Calgary Stampeders. He was tried as an outside linebacker and a smallish (6-3, 235 pounds) defensive end before settling in at middle linebacker during an All-Star 2010 season.

In 2012, his career-high 82 tackles led the team. The Stampeders made it all the way to the Grey Cup but lost the championship game to the Toronto Argonauts, 35–22. On that same day back in Huntsville, Alabama, Simpson's first child, daughter Laila, was born. At press time, halfway through the 2013 season, Simpson remained the Stampeders' highly respected defensive captain.

ANDRE SMITH ■ *Offensive Tackle*

COLLEGE: 2006–08 . . . . **NFL:** 2009–12; Outland Trophy

After stumbling at the end of his college career and the beginning of his professional career, Andre Smith seems to have regained his footing. Smith, 6-foot-3 and 340 pounds, built a resume as a devastating run blocker at Alabama. His junior year, he won the Outland Trophy as the nation's best college lineman. But that season ended with his being suspended for the Sugar Bowl (a 31–17 Alabama loss to Utah) for unspecified violations of team rules.

Smith skipped his senior season and entered the National Football League draft. Less than optimal conditioning and an unannounced departure during the NFL scouting combine raised questions among pro teams. The Cincinnati Bengals eventually drafted him sixth overall in the first round.

JUSTIN SMILEY ■ *Offensive Guard*

COLLEGE: 2001–03 . . . . **NFL:** 2004–10

Coaches loved Justin Smiley, and then he became a coach himself. Alabama coaches voted to give Smiley, a 6-foot-3, 300-pound offensive guard, the Sylvester Croom Commitment to Excellence Award after spring practice in both 2002 and 2003, and the Mal Moore Leadership Award in 2003. Smiley played seven years in the National Football League. He spent four years with the San Francisco 49ers, then two years with the Miami Dolphins and an injury-plagued (shoulders, ankle) season with the Jacksonville Jaguars.

Justin Smiley said he was "prouder of my degree than of anything else I've ever done in my life."

Credit: Chris J. Nelson

He returned to Alabama as a student assistant coach in 2011 while working on an undergraduate degree. The end of his playing career required a surprising adjustment. "Practices and games were so structured," he told Meredith Hornsby of the *Outkick the Coverage* blog. "My life was planned for me. It was a dramatic change to be able to do things when and how I wanted. I almost didn't know what to do with myself." He figured it out, and received his bachelor's degree in December 2012. "I worked hard playing football," he said, "but I worked even harder to graduate."

A contract holdout and a fractured foot suffered during training camp ruined his first year with the Bengals. Offseason injuries and another foot fracture limited him to just seven games the next season. Finally, in 2011, a healthy, fit Smith broke through to stardom. He started 14 games and added top-notch pass protection to his run-blocking skills. "He made a transition mentally to being a pro," said Bengals coach Marvin Lewis. "He became the guy we hoped we drafted."

After a dominant 2012 season, Smith's off-season did not start well. He was arrested in January 2013 at the Atlanta airport and charged with attempting to carry a loaded gun onto a flight. Reportedly, he didn't know the gun was in his carry-on bag. In April, Smith and the Bengals said the situation was "resolved," without elaborating. The team then signed him to a new, three-year contract worth $18 million.

> ## Quarterback Connection
>
> Twice, National Football League teams have tried replacing a Hall of Fame Alabama quarterback with another Crimson Tide star. The Green Bay Packers drafted Scott Hunter (see page 111) in 1971 to succeed Bart Starr (see page 159), and the New York Jets picked Richard Todd (see page 161) in 1976 to step into Joe Namath's (see page 136) white shoes. Neither newcomer fulfilled expectations. But, really, how often does a Starr or a Namath come along?

ANTHONY SMITH ■ *Defensive End*

COLLEGE: 1985–87 (at Alabama) . . **NFL:** 1991–97

Despite considerable National Football League success, Anthony Smith has not done so well off the field. Smith, a 6-3, 265 pound defensive tackle at Alabama under coaches Ray Perkins and Bill Curry, transferred to Arizona for his final college season. The Los Angeles Raiders drafted him in the first round, 11th overall, and, after he missed his rookie year because of knee surgery, shifted him to defensive end.

Used as a pass-rushing specialist, he terrorized opposing quarterbacks, totaling 10.5, 13, and 12.5 sacks his first three years. For his fourth season, the Raiders made him a full-time starter, and his production tailed off. His last four years with the Raiders (who moved back to their original home in Oakland, California, in 1995), his sack totals were 6.0, 7.0, 2.0, and 6.5. Knee and throat injuries sidelined him for three games in 1997, his last pro season.

In 1995, he married pop singer Vanity of the 1980s group Vanity 6. She had almost died from longtime drug abuse the year before and had renounced her Vanity persona and gone back to her real name, Denise Matthews. They divorced in 1996.

In 2011, Smith and two other men were charged with murdering a man in Los Angeles County. Smith was tried in April 2012. The jury failed to reach a verdict, and the judge declared a mistrial. Prosecutors said they would retry him and added three additional murder charges. When he was arrested, he couldn't afford a lawyer and was assigned a public defender.

KENNY SMITH ■ *Defensive Tackle-Defensive End*

COLLEGE: 1997–2000 . . . . **NFL:** 2001–03, 2009

Never give up. Kenny Smith didn't, and it got him a National Football League comeback in 2009 after five years off the field. Smith, 6-4 and 295 pounds, was an excellent pass rusher at Alabama and co-captain his senior year. (He's not the Kenny Smith who triggered NCAA sanctions because of rules violations involving his recruiting.) He played three years for the New Orleans Saints, the last as a part-time starter, then spent much of the next five years on injured reserve. He joined but never played for three other teams before finally playing six games for the Kansas City Chiefs in 2009. That was probably his last hurrah. But you never know.

RILEY SMITH ■ *Blocking Back-Linebacker-Kicker*

COLLEGE: 1933–35 . . . . **NFL:** 1936–38; College Football HOF, Alabama Sports HOF, Jacobs Blocking Trophy

The first Southeastern Conference Jacobs Blocking Trophy for best blocker went in 1935 to Riley "General" Smith, Alabama's senior quarterback. (In those days of the single-wing formation, quarterback was a blocking position.)

In 1936, the 6-2, 200-pound Smith became the second man picked in the first-ever National Football League draft. He was a three-way player—blocking back, linebacker, and kicker—for the Redskins, first in Boston, then in Washington. The Redskins lost the NFL championship game his rookie year but won it in 1937. During those two seasons, he came within three minutes

The Tackle Was a Child Star

Leon Fichman had already led a pretty exciting life even before he played in the Cotton Bowl and the Orange Bowl as a tackle for Alabama after the 1941 and 1942 seasons, respectively. Growing up in Los Angeles, he was a child actor from age 2 through age 15, appearing with Mickey Rooney, Judy Garland, and Will Rogers. At age 9, he performed in three short films with baseball legend Babe Ruth.

After his college career, he served with the U.S. Army during World War II and fought in the Battle of the Bulge. Fichman, 6-1 and 215 pounds, finally began a pro career with the National Football League's Detroit Lions in 1946, but a serious knee injury knocked him out of the sport the next season after one game.

Fichman became a high-school science teacher in Glendale, California. In 1960, he moved to East Moline, Illinois, and became a youth supervisor and substitute teacher at Arrowhead Ranch, a facility for at-risk youths. He died in East Moline in 2009, age 88.

KEN STABLER ■ *Quarterback*

COLLEGE: 1965–67 . . . . **NFL:** 1970–1984, 4 Pro Bowls; Alabama Sports HOF, Bert Bell Award

Quarterback Ken Stabler (12) has a serious discussion with offensive tackle Jerry Duncan (77) during an Alabama game. Both wound up in the Alabama Sports Hall of Fame.

Credit: Paul W. Bryant Museum/ The University of Alabama

The rough and rowdy 1970s Oakland Raiders made a perfect match for Ken Stabler. Alabama coach Bear Bryant had suspended Stabler before his senior year for cutting classes, missing practice, and generally having too much fun. But that's not why he and the Raiders were a match.

The Raiders' slogan was "just win, baby." That's what Stabler did. During his 10 years with the team, his record as a starting quarterback was 69-26-1.

As an Alabama sophomore, he backed up quarterback Steve Sloan on the Crimson Tide's 1965 national champions, finishing second on the team in rushing with 328 yards. As a junior, the 6-3, 215-pound Stabler actually led the undefeated (11-0) Crimson Tide in rushing, with only 397 yards. He also passed for 956 yards that year and 1,214 the next. And after he fulfilled the terms for reinstatement after the suspension, Bryant rewarded him for buckling down by making him co-captain of the 9-2-1 1967 team.

The left-handed Stabler began his National Football League career as a scrambler and became a drop-back passer after serious knee injuries. But he never lost his deadly accurate touch. He completed 59.9 percent of his passes while in Oakland, leading the league twice in that category and twice in touchdown passes as well.

Everything came together in 1976, when Stabler led the league in pass completion percentage, touchdown passes, and game-winning drives, taking the Raiders all the way to a 32–14 Super Bowl victory over the Minnesota Vikings. He won the Bert Bell Award as the NFL's best player.

> After a contract dispute, the Raiders traded Stabler to the Houston Oilers before the 1980 season. He took the Oilers to the playoffs that year, but it was his last trip to the postseason. He signed as a free agent with the New Orleans Saints in 1982 and retired in the middle of the 1984 season.
>
> Stabler worked as a color commentator for CBS and then from 1998 through 2007 on University of Alabama radio broadcasts with play-by-play announcer Eli Gold. He took what turned out to be a permanent leave of absence in 2008 following a DUI charge of which he was later acquitted. He lives in Gulfport, Mississippi, operates the charitable XOXO Stabler Foundation, and has various business ventures, including, briefly, his own wine label. His daughter Alexa, a lawyer in New Orleans, is a graduate of Alabama and the Alabama School of Law and was the International Sweetheart of Sigma Chi (the fraternity) in 2009–11.

of playing every minute of all 26 games. Perhaps not coincidentally, an injury ended his playing career in 1938.

Smith coached at Washington and Lee University, served in the Navy during World War II, then became a real estate developer in Mobile, Alabama. He also raised money for his alma mater and for the American Heart Association. He died in 1999 at age 88.

IRVING SPIKES ■ *Kick Returner-Running Back*

COLLEGE: 1991 (at Alabama) . . . . . . **NFL:** 1994–97

Frustrated over lack of playing time at Alabama, Irving Spikes transferred to Division IAA Northeast Louisiana (now the University of Louisiana at Monroe) after his sophomore year. There, in 1993, he rushed for 1,563 yards and 14 touchdowns. In the National Football League, he did a little of everything for the Miami Dolphins. At 5-8 and 210 pounds, he was a powerful runner but fast enough to be the Dolphins' top kick returner his last two seasons. Off-the-field problems, including an arrest on charges of battery against his wife, derailed his career.

Spikes eventually pulled his life together. He moved back home to the Mississippi Gulf Coast and became a substitute teacher and volunteer football coach at Resurrection Catholic School in Pascagoula, where his son, Irving Spikes Jr., was a student and standout football player. In 2012, the younger Spikes signed to play at Southern University.

SIRAN STACY ▪ *Running Back*

COLLEGE: 1989–91 . . . .**NFL:** 1992; **WL:** 1995–07, 2000

Dreams of a Heisman Trophy collapsed along with Siran Stacy's knee in the first game of Alabama's 1990 season. After two years at Coffeyville Community College in Kansas, Stacy had made an explosive Alabama debut the year before, rushing for 1,079 yards, adding 371 yards on pass receptions, and scoring 18 touchdowns. At 5-11 and 203 pounds, he used quickness to dance through opposing defenses.

He rehabbed the knee and came back in 1991 to lead Alabama in rushing with 966 yards. The Philadelphia Eagles made him their first draft choice in 1992—in the second round of the National Football League draft because they had no first-round pick. But the Eagles gave most of the carries that year to running back Herschel Walker, signed as a free agent, relegating Stacy to special-teams duty.

Off-the-field issues ended Stacy's NFL career after that one season. He was cleared twice on charges of assaulting his girlfriend and pleaded guilty to disorderly conduct after being accused of theft at a Kmart. He went to Europe and became a star in the NFL's developmental World League. In four years with the Scottish Claymores, he set a league record for most career rushing yards, 2,362, and helped win the World Bowl in 1996.

Tragedy devastated Stacy in 2007. A pickup truck driving on the wrong side of the road ran a red light and smashed into a van Stacy was driving. The crash killed Stacy's wife and four of his children, as well as the pickup driver, who was found to have been legally intoxicated. Stacy and his 3-year-old daughter were injured but survived.

Linebacker U.?

Penn State, Southern California, Miami (Florida), Florida State, and other schools have laid claims to the unofficial title "Linebacker U." But can any of them boast a trio of linebacker alums the caliber of Derrick Thomas, Cornelius Bennett, and Lee Roy Jordan?

Any team would also love to have E. J. Junior, Barry Krauss, DeMeco Ryans, Jarret Johnson, Woodrow Lowe, Eddie Lowe, Juwan Simpson, Dont'a Hightower, Courtney Upshaw, and, going back a few years, Joe Domnanovich, Bobby Marlow, and John Wozniak—all University of Alabama products. We'll put that crew up against any other school's all-time linebacker corps.

Stacy responded by starting Siran Stacy Ministries, headquartered in the Dothan, Alabama, area. He travels extensively, speaking on behalf of the ministry, preaching a message of hope.

BART STARR ■ *Quarterback*

COLLEGE: 1952–55 . . . . **NFL:** 1956–71, 4 Pro Bowls, 2 Super Bowl MVPs; Pro Football HOF, Alabama Sports HOF, Wisconsin Athletic HOF

With freshmen newly eligible to play in the Southeastern Conference, Alabama in 1952 gave some game time to a promising new quarterback from Montgomery, Alabama, named Bryan Bartlett "Bart" Starr. In the 61–6 Orange Bowl rout of Syracuse that concluded the season, Starr took over after coach Red Drew pulled starter Clell Hobson (father of major-league baseball player Butch Hobson; see page 228). Starr completed 8 of 12 passes for 93 yards, a touchdown, and no interceptions.

As a sophomore, Starr, 6-1 and 197 pounds, started at quarterback, punter, and safety, throwing for 870 yards and eight touchdowns. But a back injury knocked him out for most of 1954. And during his senior year, new coach Ears Whitworth, displaying the judgment that led to a 4-24-2 career record, benched Starr.

Alabama basketball coach Johnny Dee saw something in the kid and recommended Starr to Green Bay Packers scout Jack Vainisi. The Packers took Starr in the 17th round of the 1956 NFL draft. He was the 200th player chosen. He signed a contract for $6,500—$1,000 up front.

Both Starr and the Packers floundered his first three years as a pro—until Vince Lombardi became the Packers' coach in 1959. The Packers went 7-5 for their first winning season since 1947. In 1960, they reached the NFL Championship game for the first time in 16 years.

They lost, 17–13, to the Philadelphia Eagles. Starr never lost another playoff game with the Packers. They, and he, won nine straight en route to NFL championships in 1961, 1962, 1965, 1966, and 1967. In that last year, Starr's one-yard quarterback sneak with 16 seconds left in the game beat the Dallas Cowboys, 21–17, in a below-zero NFL Championship game at Green Bay. The game instantly became known as the Ice Bowl.

In the first Super Bowl, in January 1967, Starr led the Packers to a 35–10 romp over the American Football League champion Kansas City Chiefs. In Super Bowl II the following January, Green Bay dismantled the AFL champion Oakland Raiders, 33–14. Starr was named Most Valuable Player of each game.

Starr retired after a 1971 season shortened by surgery on both shoulders. He had played 16 years with the Packers, appeared in four Pro Bowls, and won five NFL championships and two Super Bowls—all while calling his own plays, as all quarterbacks did at the time. A look at his statistical record reveals his precise approach to picking apart a defense. He led the league three times in completion percentage and three times in lowest percentage of passes intercepted.

After his playing days, Starr was unable to recapture the glory as an assistant coach and then head coach and general manager for the Packers. Various business ventures back in Alabama proved much more successful. He became chairman of Starr Sanders Projects, a real estate investment firm, and director of Barry, Huey, Bulek, and Cook, an advertising firm. He's still chairman of Healthcare Realty Management, successor company to Starr Sanders. He and his wife, Cherry, whom he secretly married at the end of his sophomore year at Alabama, live in Birmingham. He still gets booked regularly for speeches about business and leadership, at $10,000-plus per appearance.

Starr has financially and personally supported the Rawhide Boys Ranch, a home in Wisconsin for troubled and disadvantaged youth, since 1965.

DWIGHT STEPHENSON ■ *Center*

COLLEGE: 1977–79 . . . . **NFL:** 1980–87, 5 Pro Bowls; Pro Football HOF, Alabama Sports HOF, Virginia Sports HOF

At Alabama, Dwight Stephenson started for Bear Bryant's last two national champions in 1978 and 1979. He made Second Team All-America in 1978. The next season, he did get some first-team recognition, but he was not a consensus All-American.

In the pros, despite a slow start to his National Football League career and a premature end, Dwight Stephenson became universally regarded as the best center of the 1980s. The Miami Dolphins picked him in the second round of the 1980 draft, then stuck him on special teams until two thirds of the way through the 1981 season, when starting center Mark Dennard was injured.

Stephenson didn't relinquish the starter's position until he too was hurt. He stood 6-2, weighed 255 pounds, and possessed explosive quickness. A left knee injury—on a block by friend and former Alabama teammate Marty Lyons (see page 125)—ended his 1987 season in midyear. He tried to come back, but the explosiveness was gone.

Stephenson and his wife, Dinah, operate D. Stephenson Construction Inc. in Fort Lauderdale, Florida. Stephenson is also very active with the Dwight Stephenson Foundation, which helps charities that serve children and families.

GEORGE TEAGUE ■ *Defensive Back*

COLLEGE: 1989–1992 . . . . **NFL:** 1993–2001

Solid but not spectacular: that describes George Teague's eight-year pro career with the Green Bay Packers (who made him a first-round draft choice in 1993), Miami Dolphins, and Dallas Cowboys. His most memorable National Football League moment came with the Cowboys in 2000. Teague leveled San Francisco 49ers receiver Terrell Owens during Owens's mocking touchdown celebration on the Cowboys' midfield logo. It got Teague ejected from the game but made him a hero in Dallas. He's still in town and still a hero, working as director of athletics and physical education and head football coach at The June Shelton School and Evaluation Center, which serves students with what the school calls "learning differences."

Alabama fans revere Teague, 6-1 and 198 pounds, for one of the school's greatest defensive plays ever. During the 34-13 Sugar Bowl victory in 1993 that won the national championship for Alabama, Teague chased down Miami receiver Lamar Thomas from behind and ripped the ball out of Thomas's hands. Officially, "The Strip" never happened. The play was called back because of a penalty. But it saved what would otherwise have been a touchdown and stabbed a potential Miami comeback in the heart.

RICHARD TODD ■ *Quarterback*

COLLEGE: 1973–75 . . . . **NFL:** 1976–85; Alabama Sports HOF

Unfortunately for Richard Todd, he succeeded former Alabama star Joe Namath (see page 136) as the New York Jets' quarterback; 1976 was Todd's first and Namath's last year with the Jets. At Alabama, Todd had quarterbacked from the wishbone formation, which was geared toward the run. In his two years as a Crimson Tide starter, he threw a combined total of just 156 passes. That was about a typical month's worth of attempts for Namath. Jets fans always seemed to want more from Todd, even when he led the team in 1981 and 1982 to its first two playoff appearances since 1969.

Before the 1984 National Football League season, the 6-2, 210-pound Todd was traded to the New Orleans Saints—where he replaced another legendary ex-Alabama quarterback, Ken Stabler (see page 156). All in all, Todd put together a respectable 10-year pro career. And Crimson Tide partisans still fondly remember the quarterback who, during his three years as Alabama's starter, never lost a Southeastern Conference game. After he finally left the NFL, Todd began working for J. P. Morgan Securities in Atlanta, where he is now managing director.

DERRICK THOMAS ■ *Linebacker*

COLLEGE: 1985–88 . . . . **NFL:** 1989–99, 9 Pro Bowls;
Pro Football HOF, Alabama Sports HOF, Butkus Award

Derrick Thomas played alongside another all-time great linebacker, Cornelius Bennett, on Alabama's 1985 and 1986 teams.

Credit: Paul W. Bryant Museum/
The University of Alabama

On January 23, 2000, after finishing his 11th year as a quarterback-sacking linebacker for the Kansas City Chiefs, Derrick Thomas lost control of his Chevrolet Suburban while driving to Kansas City International Airport during a snowstorm. The vehicle flipped at least three times. Thomas, not wearing a seat belt, was thrown out and suffered a broken neck and back. The 6-3, 255-pound athlete was paralyzed from the chest down.

On February 8, a blood clot traveled to his lungs and killed him. He had turned 33 on January 1.

Thomas's brilliant career at Alabama ended with the Butkus Award as the top collegiate linebacker for his senior season in 1988. The Chiefs made him their first-round draft choice—the fourth pick overall. Thomas racked up 10 sacks in his rookie year, plus 75 tackles and the first of nine straight Pro Bowl invitations. In 1990, he led the National Football League with 20 sacks, including seven in one game, still a league record. His career total of 126.5 sacks ranks 12th all time.

Before Thomas, the Chiefs had reached the playoffs only once in 18 years. Thomas led the team to seven playoff appearances and three division titles and became an icon in Kansas City. Fans also remember his off-the-field contributions. In 1990, he founded the Third and Long Foundation to help urban children ages 9 through 13 succeed in school and life.

In 2000, the University of Alabama began annually honoring one of its football players with the Derrick Thomas Community Service Award.

KEVIN TURNER ■ *Fullback*

COLLEGE: 1988–91 . . . . **NFL:** 1992–99

As an Alabama fullback, Kevin Turner spent much of his time anonymously blocking, but he exploded for some big games. Against LSU in 1991, he gained 143 yards rushing, and he caught 10 passes for 126 yards against Mississippi in 1989.

Drafted by the New England Patriots, the 6-foot-1, 230-pound Turner played for eight years in the National Football League—three with the

Patriots, five with the Philadelphia Eagles—as an all-purpose back. He caught as many as 52 passes for 471 yards (1994), carried the ball occasionally as a battering-ram runner in short-yardage situations, and spent a lot of time knocking people out of the way to clear a path for teammates. Sometimes the linemen he blocked outweighed him by 100 pounds.

A neck injury during the 1999 season finally ended his career. He settled in the Birmingham area.

In 2010, Turner was diagnosed with amyotrophic lateral sclerosis, the muscle-weakening condition known as Lou Gehrig's disease. He participates in research about a possible link between ALS and brain damage caused by repeated blows to the head. And he's exploring new therapies and treatments. He also created the Kevin Turner Foundation (www.kevinturnerfoundation. org) to address ALS and brain trauma in athletes.

"I'm at peace," he told an interviewer in early 2012. "I don't want to die, but I'm not afraid to. I look at it as a new adventure."

Turner was one of the 4,500 plaintiffs in the giant class-action concussion-related suit by former players against the NFL. (See the Lee Roy Jordan

DESHEA TOWNSEND ■ *Cornerback*

COLLEGE: 1994–1997 . . . . **NFL:** 1998–2010

Pittsburgh Steelers defensive back Deshea Townsend (26) battles for the ball with St. Louis Rams receiver Drew Bennett as Troy Polamalu watches.
Credit: Karen Blaha

All four of his years at Alabama, Deshea Townsend led or tied for the lead in breaking up passes. But it took him a while to establish his National Football League career. At first, the Pittsburgh Steelers used the 5-10, 190-pound Townsend as a special teams player and an extra defensive back on passing downs. By 2004, his seventh season, he had finally worked his way into a starter's role. He showed his versatility that year with 56 tackles, 4 interceptions, and 4 sacks.

After a dozen years with the Steelers and two Super Bowl victories, plus a half season with the Indianapolis Colts, Townsend's playing career ended. Three months later, the Arizona Cardinals hired him as an assistant defensive backs coach. He worked under defensive coordinator Ray Horton, his old defensive backs coach with the Steelers. In 2013, he became defensive backs coach for Mississippi State University.

bio, page 118.) Chris Seeger, one of the lead attorneys for the players, told *Sports Illustrated* writer Peter King, "Nobody had a bigger impact on me in this case than Kevin did. I'd wake up at night, sometimes in a cold sweat, thinking about this man and how important it was to him that he provide for his family, that his children get the college education they deserve."

Turner will receive a maximum of $5 million from the settlement the two sides reached in August 2013. He said he was happy about the deal. "I really wasn't expecting closure of this within my lifetime, honestly."

He turned 44 on June 12, 2013.

COURTNEY UPSHAW ■ *Linebacker*

COLLEGE: 2008–11 . . . . **NFL:** 2012

What a way to start a National Football League career! Outside linebacker Courtney Upshaw played every game for the Baltimore Ravens in 2012, helping take the team all the way to the Super Bowl. Then, in the second quarter of the big game, the 6-2, 272-pound Upshaw clobbered San Francisco 49ers running back LaMichael James, forcing a fumble. The Ravens recovered and drove for a score in what ended up as a 34–31 Super Bowl victory. The pro title came one year and 25 days after Upshaw was named the Defensive Most Valuable Player in the 21–0 shutout of LSU that gave both Alabama and Upshaw their second college national championship in three years. Alabama coach Nick Saban once referred to him—admiringly—as "the meanest player I ever coached."

Upshaw, a second-round pick in the 2012 NFL draft, dominated against the running game as a rookie. Baltimore Coach John Harbaugh hopes he can hone his pass-rushing skills as well. As for a second straight Super Bowl victory, well, wherever Upshaw goes, championships seem to follow.

As a high school senior, Courtney Upshaw played both defensive end and receiver.
Credit: Thibous

MIKE WASHINGTON ■ *Cornerback*

COLLEGE: 1972–74 . . . . **NFL:** 1976–84

A national championship in 1973 and placement on some All-America teams in 1974 rewarded Mike Washington his last two years at Alabama. At first, things didn't go so well in the pros. The Baltimore Colts drafted Washington in 1975, but a pulled groin muscle sidelined him the entire season. The Colts traded him to the expansion Tampa Bay Buccaneers, who lost every game of their inaugural 1976 season. But by 1979, the Bucs' defense had become the National Football League's best, leading the team to its first playoff appearance.

Despite an intense fear of flying, Washington played nine seasons, all for Tampa Bay. Big for a cornerback at 6-2 and 197 pounds, he intercepted 28 passes—the most famous a goal-line pickoff on the final play of a 1982 Monday Night Football game against the Miami Dolphins that sealed the Bucs' 23–17 win. Coach John McKay considered him the team's best defensive back.

An elbow to the head during Washington's first play of the 1984 season led to career-ending spinal surgery. He now works as a parks and recreation supervisor in his hometown, Montgomery, Alabama, and as a field judge during Southeastern Conference football games.

JIM WHATLEY ■ *Tackle-End*

COLLEGE: 1933–35 . . . . **NFL:** 1936–38; Alabama Sports HOF, American Baseball Coaches Association HOF

Jim Whatley peaked as a pro athlete in the National Football League, but he achieved his greatest success in baseball. At Alabama, he earned 10 varsity letters in four sports. On the football field, he played tackle next to the great end Don Hutson (see page 112) for two Southeastern Conference champions and for the 1934 team that went 10-0, beat Stanford, 29–13, in the Rose Bowl, and was named national champion by some selection systems. (For details of the national championships debate, see "National Championships," page 53.)

Unfortunately, in the NFL, Whatley played for the sad-sack Brooklyn Dodgers, who compiled a record of 10-19-5 during his three-year tenure. Meanwhile, he spent the summers of 1937 and 1938 playing minor-league baseball as a first baseman. The 6-foot-5 Whatley had also been an all-Southeastern Conference basketball center in 1934 and 1936, but the National Basketball Association didn't get organized until 1946, so he couldn't try for a three-sport career.

Nicknames

- *The Alabama Antelope* (Don Hutson)
- *Bart* (Bryan Bartlett Starr)
- *Bear* (Paul Bryant)
- *The Beast* (Trent Richardson)
- *Bebes* (Gene Stallings)
- *Biscuit* (Cornelius Bennett)
- *Bo* (B'Ho Kirkland)
- *Broadway Joe, Joe Willie* (Joe Namath)
- *Buddy* (Halver Brown)
- *Bull* (Lecil Olen Wesley)
- *Butch* (Clarence Avinger, Haywood Norman, George Wilson)
- *Cap'n Meco* (DeMeco Ryans)
- *Cisco* (Vaughn Mancha)
- *Corky* (Thomas Tharp)
- *Country* (Bill Oliver—the 1920s lineman, not later Alabama player and defensive coordinator Bill "Brother" Oliver, who never went pro)
- *The Crimson Tide* (Alabama athletics teams, starting in 1907)
- *The Deuce* (David Palmer)
- *Dixie* (Millard Howell)
- *The Dothan Antelope* (Johnny Mack Brown)
- *Double* (Jarret Johnson; short for "Double J")
- *Ears* (J. B. Whitworth)
- *General* (Riley Smith)
- *The Ghost* (Shaun Alexander)
- *Goofy* (Jim Bowdoin)
- *Hawg* (John Hannah)
- *Hoss* (David Johnson)
- *Hurri* (John Cain)
- *The Italian Stallion* (Johnny Musso)
- *Jack* (Earl Jackson Gregory)
- *Julio* (Quintorris Lopez Jones)
- *Killer* (Lee Roy Jordan)
- *Mighty Mouse* (Mark McMillian)
- *Monk* (Norm Mosley)
- *Mount Cody* (Terrence Cody)
- *Pooley* (Allison Hubert)
- *Red* (Harold Drew)
- *Sackman, DT* (Derrick Thomas)
- *Sandy* (Hayward Sanford)
- *The Snake* (Ken Stabler)
- *Stick* (Antonio London)
- *Swagga* (Dre Kirkpatrick)
- *Tarzan* (Arthur White)
- *The Thin Red Line* (Alabama athletic teams until about 1907)
- *Tiny* (Milburn Russell Croft)
- *Tony* (Bernard Patrick Holm)
- *Two-Five* (Fernando Bryant, for his uniform number)
- *The Wizard of Oz* (Ozzie Newsome)
- *Woody* (Elwood Gerber)

But he did coach all three sports in college. He eventually found a home at the University of Georgia, presiding as head coach of the Bulldogs' baseball teams for 25 years (1950, 1952–75). Whatley led Georgia to Southeastern Conference championships in 1953 and 1954. He was inducted into the American Baseball Coaches Association Hall of Fame in 1987. In 2001, at age 88, he died of heart failure at his home in Athens, Georgia. At his funeral, the Georgia athletic department and everyone who had coached with him at the university acted as honorary pallbearers.

TARZAN WHITE ■ *Guard*

COLLEGE: 1934–36 . . . .**NFL:** 1937–41, 1945, 1 Pro Bowl; Alabama Sports HOF

Arthur Pershing "Tarzan" White lived an outsized life and loved to tell stories about it. Occasionally, he embellished the legend. For example, son Butch says it's not true that, while playing for the National Football League's New York Giants, his father picked up a doctorate—in math or Spanish, depending on the source—at Columbia University.

But Tarzan White was indeed a math whiz and fluent in Spanish. And he did earn membership in the exclusive academic honor society Phi Beta Kappa while playing for some great Alabama teams, including the 1934 national champions.

A stocky 5-foot-9 and 217 pounds, White got his nickname from swinging on vines over creeks as a child in Atmore, Alabama. He played in the first-ever Pro Bowl (then called the NFL All-Star Game) in 1938. That same year, his Giants beat the Green Bay Packers, 23–17, for the National Football League championship. After three seasons with the Giants and two with the Chicago Cardinals, White spent three years in the U.S. Army Air Forces during World War II, then returned for one last season with the Giants in 1945.

He wrestled professionally in the off-seasons and continued wrestling until he was 60 years old. He also coached high school football. In January 1996, after 80 fully lived years, he died.

SHERMAN WILLIAMS ■ *Running Back*

COLLEGE: 1991–94 . . . .**NFL:** 1995–99

Just 5-8 and 198 pounds, Sherman Williams nevertheless rushed for 2,486 yards (including 1,341 in 1994) and 27 touchdowns at Alabama. Fans loved his touchdown dance, the "Sherman Shake." Picked in the second round of the National Football League draft by the Dallas Cowboys, he backed up Pro Football Hall of Fame running back Emmitt Smith, which meant he didn't get a lot of playing time. His career ended after just one game of the 1999 season.

The following April, he was arrested on charges that he ran a Texas-to-Alabama marijuana distribution operation. He was convicted of three counts of conspiracy to distribute marijuana and one count of passing counterfeit money. He is scheduled to be released from prison in 2014.

In a 2012 letter to the *Tuscaloosa News*, Williams blamed himself for "wrong decisions" and said, "Thanks to the teaching of Christ, I do feel that my future is much brighter than my past." On his release, he and former Alabama teammate David Palmer (see page 140), a close friend, plan to start a nonprofit organization, the Palmer-Williams Group, to help disadvantaged youth.

"I think it has taken a toll on him," Palmer told Tommy Deas of the *News*, "but he's been doing a lot of studying and reading to get himself on the right path. He has put a lot of time into getting his mind right."

BUTCH WILSON ■ *Tight End*

COLLEGE: 1960–62 . . . . **NFL:** 1963–69

Primarily a halfback and defensive back at Alabama, Butch Wilson, 6-2 and 228 pounds, played tight end in the National Football League. He did a lot of blocking. During his seven-year career—five seasons with the Baltimore Colts, then two with the New York Giants—he caught a total of only 25 passes for 317 yards and three touchdowns. He now owns Butch Wilson Sporting Goods in Bessemer, Alabama, near Birmingham.

RICH WINGO ■ *Linebacker*

COLLEGE: 1976–78 . . . . **NFL:** 1979–84

Alabama's 1978 national championship team was so deep at linebacker that Rich Wingo, who went on to play five seasons in the National Football League, didn't start. He did make a major contribution, though; he helped stuff Penn State during the legendary goal-line stand that preserved Alabama's 14-7 national championship–winning Sugar Bowl victory at the end of that season.

The following year, despite being 6-1 and a relatively light 230 pounds, he started at middle linebacker for the National Football League's Green Bay Packers. He missed 1980 after back surgery, but started for three more seasons, then finished his pro career as a backup for the Packers in 1984.

The Alabama Informals

MITCH OLENSKI ■ *Tackle*

COLLEGE: 1942 and, unofficially, 1943
AAFC: 1946; **NFL:** 1947

Officially, Alabama didn't field a football team in 1943. Military trainees weren't permitted to compete intercollegiately, and that left only two players available on the squad. Unofficially, the "Alabama Informals" posted a 2-1 record and almost played a fourth game—against inmates from Draper Correctional Facility.

Tackle Mitch Olenski, 6-3 and 220 pounds, captained the Informals. He had been a backup for the 1941 team that went 9-2 and won the Cotton Bowl. As a junior, he lettered for the 8-3 1942 squad that won the Orange Bowl. The Informals squad consisted of 17-year-olds (too young for military service) and older players with draft deferments. The team was permitted to use the university's equipment and facilities.

The Informals opened with a 42–6 drubbing in Denny Stadium at the hands of Birmingham's Howard College (now Samford University). Howard's players were members of a Navy training program. Most of the gate receipts went to war-related charities.

The Informals regrouped by sweeping a home-and-home series against Marion Military Institute of Marion, Alabama. They planned to finish the season in late November against inmates from Draper, a state prison in Elmore, Alabama. University officials canceled the game, saying students needed to concentrate on their final exams. One suspects the administration had other reasons for saying no.

Olenski later went into the Army and played service football with the Fort Warren Broncos of Cheyenne, Wyoming. After the war, he played a year apiece with the Miami Seahawks of the All-America Football Conference and the Detroit Lions of the National Football League. He died in 2000, age 79.

Wingo spent 1987–89 as strength coach for Alabama football and still lives in Tuscaloosa. He was the longtime president of AIG Baker Real Estate, a shopping center developer, and is chief operating officer for United American Assurance, a health insurance company. He also co-owns a residential construction company. Son Luke worked his way into a starting role during his 2012 freshman season as a quarterback at the University of North Alabama.

In June 2013, Wingo announced that he planned to run as a Republican candidate for the Alabama House of Representatives in 2014.

JOHN WOZNIAK ■ *Guard-Linebacker*

COLLEGE: 1944–47 . . . . **AAFC:** 1948–49; **NFL:** 1950–52, 1 Pro Bowl; **CFL:** 1953–56

Military service during World War II delayed John Wozniak's college career. In his senior year, 1947, he captained Alabama's 9-2 team. Drafted by the Pittsburgh Steelers of the National Football League, Wozniak instead signed with the Brooklyn Dodgers of the short-lived All-America Football Conference. He stayed with the team for five years through name changes (Brooklyn-New York Yankees, New York Yanks, Dallas Texans) and a merger with the NFL, making the Pro Bowl in his last season. He then played four years in the Canadian Football League with the Saskatchewan Roughriders, achieving induction into their Plaza of Honor.

Wozniak, a 6-foot, 218-pound native of Pennsylvania, returned to Tuscaloosa in the off-seasons and earned a master's degree in education. He joined a Tuscaloosa chemical company in 1950 and rose through its sales executive ranks. He died of a heart attack in 1982, age 61.

STEVE WRIGHT ■ *Offensive Tackle*

COLLEGE: 1962–63 . . . . **NFL:** 1964–72; **WFL:** 1974

Steve Wright was a character. He was also a pretty good blocker. During the Green Bay Packers' National Football League glory years in the mid-1960s, the 6-foot-6, 250-pound Wright helped protect Bart Starr (see page 159).

After the Packers won Super Bowl II, legendary coach Vince Lombardi left the sideline for the general manager's office. Wright requested a trade and was swapped to the New York Giants before the 1968 season, receiving a substantial raise—from $14,500 a year to $20,000. After two years, he moved to the Washington Redskins, then the Chicago Bears, then the St. Louis Cardinals, seldom a starter but always a useful reserve. After a year out of football, he played for the Chicago Fire of the World Football League, only to retire during the middle of the increasingly chaotic season. He joked that he had been offered a million-dollar contract: "a dollar a year for a million years."

That was in 1974, the year his book came out. *I'd Rather Be Wright: Memoirs of an Itinerant Tackle* is self-indulgent but scathingly funny—and a window into a time before the National Football League became a polished corporate behemoth. Despite his habitual irreverence, Wright became the model for the NFL's Walter Payton Man of the Year trophy when artist Daniel Bennett Schwartz sculpted it in 1969. The NFL office told the Giants to send a player to Schwartz's studio in Manhattan. For reasons that Wright doesn't remember, they picked him.

He now lives with his wife, Sandy, in Augusta, Georgia, retired after a successful career as a salesman of veterinary pharmaceuticals and insurance. He collects cowboy boots and antique furniture and claims to remember his football career fondly but not sentimentally. In 2011, he briefly made headlines when he auctioned his ring from the first Super Bowl for $73,409.

But he still has the ring from Super Bowl II.

BILL YOUNG ■ *Tackle*

COLLEGE: 1936 . . . . **NFL:** 1937–42, 1946, 1 All-Star Game

As a sophomore, big Bill Young (6-1, 247 pounds) played on Alabama's 1934 national championship team with Bear Bryant, Don Hutson (see page 112), and Dixie Howell (see page 109). In the pros, after five seasons of part-time play for the Washington Redskins, Young had a breakout year in 1942. He made the All-Star Game, and the Redskins won the National Football League championship. But World War II was raging, and Young enlisted in the Navy. He spent part of the next three years playing for service teams. He returned to the Redskins for eight final games in 1946. From 1950 through 1954, he was head coach at Furman. He died in 1994, age 79.

SID YOUNGELMAN ■ *Defensive Tackle-Defensive End*

COLLEGE: 1952–54 . . . . **NFL:** 1955–1959; **AFL:** 1960–1963

A big, brash Jewish kid from Brooklyn named Sid Youngelman came to Tuscaloosa, Alabama, in the early 1950s—and got along just fine. In fact, he captained the Crimson Tide squad his senior year.

In the National Football League, he played for the San Francisco 49ers, Philadelphia Eagles, and Cleveland Browns. After he got into a dispute with an assistant coach, the Browns released him following the 1959 season. Youngelman jumped to the new American Football League, playing two years apiece for the New York Titans and Buffalo Bills. He supplemented his football income by working as a professional wrestler and, believe it or not, a schoolteacher.

He had a reputation as a tough, even dirty player. Off the field, he was intelligent and charming. He stood 6-foot-3 and weighed 255 pounds— somewhat more near the end of his career. He died in 1991 a few days after his 60th birthday.

Alabama Single-Game Records

Yards Rushing

291 Shaun Alexander at LSU, 1996	**220** Bobby Humphrey at Penn State, 1987
284 Bobby Humphrey at Mississippi State, 1986	**218** Glen Coffee versus Kentucky, 2008
246 Mark Ingram versus South Carolina, 2009	**217** Bobby Humphrey at Tennessee, 1986
233 Bobby Marlow versus Auburn, 1951	**216** Harry Gilmer at Kentucky (in only six attempts), 1945
221 Johnny Musso versus Auburn, 1970	**214** Shaun Alexander at Mississippi, 1999

Yards Passing

484 Scott Hunter versus Auburn, 1969	**363** Gary Hollingsworth at Mississippi, 1989
396 Jay Barker versus Georgia, 1994	**363** John Parker Wilson versus Tennessee, 2007
379 Gary Hollingsworth versus Tennessee, 1989	**340** Gary Hollingsworth at Auburn, 1989
377 Greg McElroy versus Auburn, 2010	**336** Walter Lewis at Penn State, 1983
367 Mike Shula at Memphis State, 1985	**336** Andrew Zow versus Florida, 1999

Pass Receptions

13 DJ Hall versus Tennessee, 2007	**11** DJ Hall at Mississippi, 2007
12 David Bailey versus Tennessee, 1969	**10** Kevin Turner at Mississippi, 1989
12 David Bailey at Tennessee, 1970	**10** Freddie Milons versus Florida, 1999
12 Julio Jones at Tennessee, 2010	**10** DJ Hall versus Tennessee, 2005
11 Dennis Homan versus Southern Mississippi, 1967	**10** DJ Hall versus Mississippi State, 2006
11 Quincy Jackson versus Brigham Young, 1998	**10** Julio Jones at LSU, 2010
11 DJ Hall versus Utah State, 2005	**10** Julio Jones versus Auburn, 2010

Yards Receiving

221	Julio Jones at Tennessee, 2010	**173**	Toderick Malone versus Georgia, 1994
217	David Palmer at Vanderbilt, 1993	**171**	David Palmer versus Mississippi State, 1993
199	Julio Jones versus Auburn, 2010		
187	David Bailey versus Auburn, 1969	**162**	Amari Cooper versus Tennessee, 2012
185	DJ Hall versus Tennessee, 2007	**159**	Dennis Homan versus Florida State, 1967

Alabama Season Records

Total Touchdowns (Rushing, receiving, and passing)

31	A. J. McCarron, 2012	**20**	Mark Ingram, 2009
24	Shaun Alexander, 1999	**19**	Walter Lewis, 1983
24	Trent Richardson, 2011	**19**	Eddie Lacy, 2012
22	Harry Gilmer, 1945	**18**	Siran Stacy, 1989
22	John Parker Wilson, 2007	**18**	A. J. McCarron, 2011

Touchdowns Scored

24	Shaun Alexander, 1999	**17**	Shaun Alexander, 1998
24	Trent Richardson, 2011	**16**	Johnny Musso, 1971
20	Mark Ingram, 2009	**16**	Shaud Williams, 2003
19	Eddie Lacy, 2012	**15**	Cotton Clark, 1962
18	Siran Stacy, 1989	**15**	Tony Nathan, 1977
17	Bobby Humphrey, 1986		

Touchdown Passes

30	A. J. McCarron, 2012	**16**	A. J. McCarron, 2011
20	Greg McElroy, 2010	**14**	Brodie Croyle, 2004
18	John Parker Wilson, 2007	**14**	Walter Lewis, 1983
17	John Parker Wilson, 2006	**14**	Gary Hollingsworth, 1989
17	Greg McElroy, 2009	**14**	Jay Barker, 1994
16	Mike Shula, 1985	**14**	Freddie Kitchens, 1996
16	Brodie Croyle, 2005		

Remembering John Forney

Alabama Sports Hall of Fame broadcaster John Forney began his radio career in 1943 in Tuscaloosa while in high school. Forney went on to call both Alabama and Auburn basketball games while attending Alabama. In 1953, he became the color commentator for Alabama football radio broadcasts. In 1964, he graduated to the top spot: play-by-play man, which he held for 19 years.

In those days, when radio was still king, Forney truly was the voice of the Crimson Tide. His excited calls thrilled Alabama fans. But Forney suffered a stroke in 1982, and for the 1983 season new Alabama Coach Ray Perkins (see page 114) wanted Paul Kennedy instead. Forney returned for one year, in 1988, then gave way to the current play-by-play announcer, Eli Gold.

Forney still did pre- and postgame radio coverage. He also hosted the weekly television shows for Alabama coaches Bear Bryant and Gene Stallings, and worked in advertising in Birmingham. He died of heart failure in 1997, age 70, stricken during the annual Southeastern Conference preseason meeting between coaches and the media.

Yards Rushing

1,679	Trent Richardson, 2011	**1,367**	Shaud Williams, 2003
1,658	Mark Ingram, 2009	**1,360**	Eddie Lacy, 2012
1,471	Bobby Humphrey, 1986	**1,341**	Sherman Williams, 1994
1,383	Shaun Alexander, 1999	**1,255**	Bobby Humphrey, 1987
1,383	Glen Coffee, 2008	**1,242**	Kenneth Darby, 2005

Yards Passing

2,987	Greg McElroy, 2010	**2,508**	Greg McElroy, 2009
2,933	A. J. McCarron, 2012	**2,499**	Brodie Croyle, 2005
2,846	John Parker Wilson, 2007	**2,379**	Gary Hollingsworth, 1989
2,707	John Parker Wilson, 2006	**2,303**	Brodie Croyle, 2003
2,634	A. J. McCarron, 2011	**2,273**	John Parker Wilson, 2008

Pass Receptions

78	Julio Jones, 2010	**59**	Amari Cooper, 2012
67	DJ Hall, 2007	**58**	Julio Jones, 2008
65	Freddie Milons, 1999	**56**	David Bailey, 1969
62	DJ Hall, 2006	**56**	Marquis Maze, 2011
61	David Palmer, 1993	**55**	David Bailey, 1970

Yards Receiving

1,133	Julio Jones, 2010	**924**	Julio Jones, 2008
1,056	DJ Hall, 2006	**820**	Dennis Homan, 1967
1,005	DJ Hall, 2007	**804**	Ozzie Newsome, 1977
1,000	David Palmer, 1993	**790**	David Bailey, 1970
1,000	Amari Cooper, 2012	**781**	David Bailey, 1969

Touchdown Catches

11	Amari Cooper, 2012	**7**	Julio Jones, 2010
10	Al Lary, 1950	**6**	David Bailey, 1970
9	Dennis Homan, 1967	**6**	Ozzie Newsome, 1976
8	Al Bell, 1985	**6**	Joey Jones, 1982
7	Ray Perkins, 1966	**6**	Curtis Brown, 1994
7	Wayne Wheeler, 1972	**6**	Michael Vaughn, 1996
7	David Palmer, 1993	**6**	DJ Hall, 2007

Alabama Career Records

Total Touchdowns (Rushing, receiving, and passing)

52	Harry Gilmer, 1944–47	**42**	Walter Lewis, 1980–83
52	A. J. McCarron, 2010–12	**41**	Jeff Rutledge, 1975–78
50	Shaun Alexander, 1996–99	**40**	Joe Namath, 1962–64
46	Mark Ingram, 2008–10	**40**	Johnny Musso, 1969–71
43	John Parker Wilson, 2005–07	**40**	Bobby Humphrey, 1985–88
43	Trent Richardson, 2009–11		

Touchdowns Scored

50	Shaun Alexander, 1996–99	**32**	Eddie Lacy, 2010–12
46	Mark Ingram, 2008–10	**30**	Bobby Marlow, 1950–52
43	Trent Richardson, 2009–11	**29**	Tony Nathan, 1975–78
40	Bobby Humphrey, 1985–88	**27**	Siran Stacy, 1989–91
38	Johnny Musso, 1969–71	**23**	Harry Gilmer, 1944–47

Touchdown Passes

49	A. J. McCarron, 2010–12	**35**	Andrew Zow, 1998–2001
47	John Parker Wilson, 2005–08	**30**	Jeff Rutledge, 1975–78
41	Brodie Croyle, 2002–05	**30**	Freddie Kitchens, 1993–97
39	Greg McElroy, 2007–10	**29**	Harry Gilmer 1944–47
35	Mike Shula, 1983–86	**29**	Walter Lewis, 1980–83

Most Wins as a Starting Quarterback

35	Jay Barker, 1991–94	**22**	Joe Namath, 1962–64
25	John Parker Wilson, 2006–08	**22**	Mike Shula, 1984–86
25	A. J. McCarron, 2011–12	**21**	Terry Davis, 1971–72
24	Jeff Rutledge, 1976–78	**18**	Ken Stabler, 1966–67
24	Greg McElroy, 2007–10	**18**	Richard Todd, 1974-75
23	Pat Trammell, 1959–61	**18**	Andrew Zow, 1998–2001

Yards Rushing

3,565	Shaun Alexander, 1996–99	**2,741**	Johnny Musso, 1969–71
3,420	Bobby Humphrey, 1985–88	**2,645**	Dennis Riddle, 1994–97
3,324	Kenneth Darby, 2003–06	**2,560**	Bobby Marlow, 1950–52
3,261	Mark Ingram, 2008–10	**2,519**	Johnny Davis, 1974–77
3,130	Trent Richardson, 2009–11	**2,486**	Sherman Williams, 1991–94

Iron Men

Before 1941, college football rules allowed only limited substitutions (except for an 1897–1904 period of unlimited substitution). So most athletes played both offense and defense. Usually, receivers doubled as defensive backs, running backs and quarterbacks played defensive back or linebacker, centers played middle linebacker, and other linemen stayed where they were.

Starting in 1941, because the World War II–related military buildup was creating a shortage of players, the NCAA greatly relaxed the substitution rule. Further changes in 1947 and 1948 removed virtually all restrictions. Starting in 1954, however, the NCAA switched to allowing only one player to be substituted between plays. The primary reason was financial. With fewer substitutes permitted, you need fewer players and therefore can offer fewer scholarships. Expenses for equipment and travel also decrease.

In 1965, the NCAA again tossed out substitution restrictions, giving us the specialist-oriented game we have today.

The National Football League at first followed college rules. In 1943, it began allowing free substitution because of wartime player shortages. With the war's end, the rule changed in 1946 to permit no more than three substitutions at a time. In 1950, free substitution returned.

Because colleges were still turning out some players skilled and experienced at both offense and defense, the NFL still featured a few full-time two-way players through the 1950s. The last and most famous was the ferocious Philadelphia Eagles center and middle linebacker Chuck Bednarik (1949–62). Since then, with occasional part-time exceptions such as defensive back and sometime running back and wide receiver Deion Sanders (1989–2000, 2004–05), specialists have ruled.

Yards Passing

7,924 John Parker Wilson, 2005–08	**5,689** Jay Barker, 1991–94
6,382 Brodie Croyle, 2002–05	**4,899** Scott Hunter, 1968–70
5,983 Andrew Zow, 1998–2001	**4,668** Freddie Kitchens, 1993–97
5,959 A. J. McCarron, 2010–12	**4,257** Walter Lewis, 1980–83
5,691 Greg McElroy, 2007–10	**4,069** Mike Shula, 1983–86

Pass Receptions

194	DJ Hall, 2004–07	**108**	Lamonde Russell, 1987–90
179	Julio Jones, 2008–10	**106**	Curtis Brown, 1991–95
152	Freddie Milons, 1998–2001	**106**	Antonio Carter, 1999–2004
136	Marquis Maze, 2008–11	**102**	Ozzie Newsome, 1974–77
132	David Bailey, 1969–71	**102**	David Palmer, 1991–93
117	Keith Brown, 2004–07		

Yards Receiving

2,923	DJ Hall, 2004–07	**1,857**	David Bailey, 1969–71
2,653	Julio Jones, 2008–10	**1,844**	Marquis Maze, 2008–11
2,070	Ozzie Newsome, 1974–77	**1,611**	David Palmer, 1991–93
1,859	Freddie Milons, 1998–2001	**1,568**	Curtis Brown, 1991–95
1,863	Keith Brown, 2004–07		

Touchdown Catches

18	Dennis Homan, 1965–67	**11**	Wayne Wheeler, 1971–73
17	DJ Hall, 2004–07	**11**	Jesse Bendross, 1980–83
16	Ozzie Newsome, 1974–77	**11**	Al Bell, 1985–86
15	Joey Jones, 1980–83	**11**	David Palmer, 1991–93
15	Julio Jones, 2008–10	**11**	Curtis Brown, 1991–95
14	Al Lary, 1948–50	**11**	Toderick Malone, 1993–95
13	David Bailey, 1969–71	**11**	Amari Cooper, 2012
13	Keith Brown, 2004–07		

All-Century Team

(Selected by fan ballot in 1992)

- **Quarterback:** Joe Namath, 1962–64; Ken Stabler, 1965–67
- **Running back:** Bobby Marlow, 1950–52; Johnny Musso, 1969–71; Bobby Humphrey, 1985–88
- **End:** Don Hutson, 1932–34; Ozzie Newsome, 1974–77
- **Offensive tackle:** Fred Sington, 1928–30; Billy Neighbors, 1959–61
- **Offensive guard:** John Hannah, 1970–72

- **Center:** Vaughn Mancha, 1944–47; Dwight Stephenson, 1977–79
- **Kicker:** Van Tiffin, 1983–86
- **Defensive line:** Bob Baumhower, 1974–76; Marty Lyons, 1976–78; Jon Hand, 1982–85
- **Linebacker:** Cornelius Bennett, 1983–86; Derrick Thomas, 1985–88; Lee Roy Jordan, 1960–62; Barry Krauss, 1976–78
- **Defensive back:** Harry Gilmer, 1944–47; Don McNeal, 1976–79; Jeremiah Castille, 1979–82; Tommy Wilcox, 1979–82
- **Punter:** Johnny Cain, 1930–32
- **Coach:** Bear Bryant, 1958–82

Alabama Hall of Famers

College Football Hall of Fame Players and Coaches

- **Cornelius Bennett,** linebacker
- **Johnny Mack Brown,** halfback
- **Paul "Bear" Bryant,** coach (played for Alabama 1933–35)
- **John "Hurri" Cain,** quarterback-fullback
- **Harry Gilmer,** halfback
- **John Hannah,** offensive guard-offensive tackle
- **Frank Howard,** coach (inducted for his coaching career at Clemson; played for Alabama 1928–30)
- **Millard "Dixie" Howell,** halfback
- **Pooley Hubert,** fullback
- **Don Hutson,** end
- **Lee Roy Jordan,** center-linebacker
- **Woodrow Lowe,** linebacker
- **Marty Lyons,** defensive tackle
- **Vaughn Mancha,** center-linebacker
- **Johnny Musso,** halfback
- **Billy Neighbors,** tackle
- **Ozzie Newsome,** wide receiver
- **Fred Sington,** tackle
- **Riley Smith,** quarterback
- **Gene Stallings,** coach
- **Frank Thomas,** coach
- **Wallace Wade,** coach
- **Don Whitmire,** tackle

Pro Football Hall of Fame Players

- **John Hannah,** offensive guard
- **Don Hutson,** end
- **Joe Namath,** quarterback
- **Ozzie Newsome,** tight end
- **Bart Starr,** quarterback
- **Dwight Stephenson,** center
- **Derrick Thomas,** linebacker

Top 10 Colleges by Pro Football Hall of Fame Inductees

- Southern California 11
- Notre Dame 10
- Ohio State 9
- Michigan 8
- Pittsburgh 8
- **Alabama 7**
- Syracuse 7
- Illinois 6
- Miami (Florida) 6
- Minnesota 6
- Oregon 6

Starr, Stabler, or Namath?

Who was Alabama's best pro quarterback? Everyone agrees on the nominees: Bart Starr, Joe Namath, and Ken Stabler. Beyond that:

Starr and Namath are in the Pro Football Hall of Fame; Stabler is not, although his qualifications have been hotly debated.

Each quarterback went undefeated in Super Bowls—Starr in two and Namath and Stabler in one each. Starr also won three National Football League championships in pre–Super Bowl days.

Namath played in five Pro Bowls. Starr and Stabler played in four each.

Their records as starting quarterbacks, with winning percentages, were: Stabler 96-49-1, 66.2 percent; Starr 94-57-6, 62.2 percent; Namath 62-63-4, 49.6 percent.

Starr's career started slowly, then hit a sustained peak in the 1960s. Same with Stabler in the 1970s. Namath began more spectacularly but flamed out more quickly.

Starr avoided major injuries until late in his career; Namath and Stabler hobbled on increasingly rickety knees.

Starr and Stabler played high-percentage passing games, trying to avoid mistakes. Namath liked to go for broke.

All three quarterbacks called their own plays, although Namath's and Stabler's careers lasted into the era when coaches began assuming that responsibility.

We picked Starr as our all-star quarterback, but it was a tough decision.

Other Alabama Athletes Who Went Pro

Pro Career Started in the 1920s

NAME	POSITION	COLLEGE	PRO	TEAMS
Ben Hunt	*Tackle*	1920–22	NFL 1923	Toledo Maroons
Bill Oliver	*Guard*	1922–23, 1925	NFL 1927	New York Yankees
Claude Perry	*Tackle-Guard-End*	1925	NFL 1927–35	Green Bay Packers, Brooklyn Dodgers
Bull Wesley	*Center-Guard-Tackle-Fullback*	1922–23	NFL 1926–28, 1930	Providence Steam Roller, New York Giants, Portsmouth Spartans

Pro Career Started in the 1930s

NAME	POSITION	COLLEGE	PRO	TEAMS
Lew Bostick	*Guard-Tackle*	1936–38	NFL 1938, 1942	Cleveland Rams
Jess Eberdt	*Center*	1929–30	NFL 1932	Brooklyn Dodgers
Tony Holm	*Fullback*	1927–29	NFL 1930–33	Providence Steam Roller, Portsmouth Spartans, Chicago Cardinals, Pittsburgh Pirates
Tom Hupke	*Guard-Tackle*	1931–33	NFL 1934–39	Detroit Lions, Cleveland Rams
Bo Kirkland	*Guard*	1931–33	NFL 1935–36	Brooklyn Dodgers
Ben Smith	*End-Blocking Back-Defensive End*	1929–31	NFL 1933–37	Green Bay Packers, Pittsburgh Pirates, Washington Redskins

Pro Career Started in the 1940s

NAME	POSITION	COLLEGE	PRO	TEAMS
Don Avery	*Tackle*	1941; did not letter	NFL 1946–47, AAFC 1948	Washington Redskins, Los Angeles Dons
Dave Brown	*Wingback-Fullback-Halfback*	1940–42	NFL 1943, 1946–47	New York Giants
Mike Cassidy	*Tackle-Guard-Nose Tackle*	1944–47	CFL 1948–55	Saskatchewan Roughriders

NAME	POSITION	COLLEGE	PRO	TEAMS
Ted Cook	*End-Defensive Back*	1942–46	NFL 1947–50	Detroit Lions, Green Bay Packers
Leon Fichman	*Tackle*	1941–42	NFL 1946–47	Detroit Lions
Woody Gerber	*Guard*	1940	NFL 1941–42	Philadelphia Eagles
Fred Grant	*Running Back*	1944–46	CFL 1947	Saskatchewan Roughriders
Jack Gregory	*Guard*	1936; did not letter	NFL 1941	Cleveland Rams
George Hecht	*Guard*	1940–42	NFL 1947	Chicago Rockets
Ralph Jones	*End-Defensive End*	1944	NFL 1946, AAFC 1947	Detroit Lions, Baltimore Colts
Mike Katrishen	*Guard*	1941; did not letter	NFL 1948–49	Washington Redskins
Larry Knorr	*End*	1936; did not letter	NFL 1942, 1945	Detroit Lions
Butch Lee	*End*	1947; did not letter	CFL 1948	Saskatchewan Roughriders
Tony Leon	*Guard-Linebacker*	1941–42	NFL 1943–46	Washington Redskins, Brooklyn Tigers, Yanks (Boston Yanks-Brooklyn Tigers), Boston Yanks
Frank Martin	*Halfback*	1941; did not letter	NFL 1943–45	Brooklyn Dodgers, Brooklyn Tigers, New York Giants, Yanks (Boston Yanks-Brooklyn Tigers)
Joel McCoy	*Tailback*	1941; did not letter	NFL 1946	Detroit Lions
Charlie McGibbony	*Tailback*	1938; did not letter	NFL 1944	Brooklyn Tigers
Walt Merrill	*Tackle*	1937–39	NFL 1940–42	Brooklyn Dodgers
Norm Mosley	*Tailback*	1942, 1946–47	NFL 1948	Pittsburgh Steelers
Russ Mosley	*Halfback*	1941–42	NFL 1945–46	Green Bay Packers
Jimmy Nelson	*Halfback*	1939–41	AAFC 1946	Miami Seahawks
Norm Olsen	*Tackle*	1939; did not letter	NFL 1944	Cleveland Rams

NAME	POSITION	COLLEGE	PRO	TEAMS
Ken Reese	*Halfback-Quarterback*	1942	NFL 1947	Detroit Lions
Ray Richeson	*Guard*	1946–48	AAFC 1949	Chicago Hornets
Hosea Rodgers	*Fullback*	1942; did not letter	AAFC 1949	Los Angeles Dons
Sandy Sanford	*End*	1936–37	NFL 1940	Washington Redskins
Vaughn Stewart	*Center*	1941	NFL 1943–44	Chicago Cardinals, Brooklyn Dodgers
Lowell Tew	*Fullback*	1944–47	AAFC 1948–49	New York Yankees
Bob Trocolor	*Quarterback-Halfback*	1940; did not letter	NFL 1942–44	New York Giants, Brooklyn Tigers
George Weeks	*Defensive End*	1940–42	NFL 1944	Brooklyn Tigers
Bobby Wood	*Tackle*	1937–38	NFL 1940	Chicago Cardinals, Green Bay Packers
John Wyhonic	*Guard*	1939–41	NFL 1946–49	Philadelphia Eagles, Buffalo Bills

Bearing Down

Bob Baumhower's father was certainly not overprotective. Baumhower (see page 65) starred as a defensive lineman for the University of Alabama and Miami Dolphins. The website of his Baumhower's Restaurant chain says that when Baumhower was a high school junior, his father talked him into wrestling a 450-pound bear at a boat show. "Baumhower tried to take the bear down low," the website says, "and the animal knocked him across the ring. He then went high, and for a triumphant moment held the bear in a hammerlock. An instant later the bear was sitting on top of Baumhower, licking him with its long tongue."

Obviously, Bob "Bear" Baumhower was destined to play for Paul "Bear" Bryant (whose own bear-wrestling episode took place at age 13 in Fordyce, Arkansas).

Pro Career Started in the 1950s

NAME	POSITION	COLLEGE	PRO	TEAMS
Butch Avinger	*Fullback*	1948–50	CFL 1952, NFL 1953	Saskatchewan Roughriders, New York Giants
Tom Calvin	*Halfback*	1948–50	NFL 1952–55	Pittsburgh Steelers
Larry Lauer	*Center*	1948–50	NFL 1956–57	Green Bay Packers
Harry Lee	*Guard*	1951–54	CFL 1957	Hamilton Tiger-Cats
Billy Shipp	*Tackle*	1949, 1952–53	NFL 1954, CFL 1955–65	New York Giants, Montreal Alouettes, Toronto Argonauts
Rebel Steiner	*Defensive Back*	1945, 1947–49	NFL 1950–51	Green Bay Packers
Jerry Watford	*Guard-End-Defensive End*	1950–52	NFL 1953–54	Chicago Cardinals

Pro Career Started in the 1960s

NAME	POSITION	COLLEGE	PRO	TEAMS
Steve Bowman	*Halfback*	1963–65	NFL 1966	New York Giants
Bobby G. Jackson	*Defensive Back*	1957–58	NFL 1960–61	Philadelphia Eagles, Chicago Bears
Les Kelley	*Linebacker*	1964–66	NFL 1967–69	New Orleans Saints
Benny Nelson	*Defensive Back*	1961–63	AFL 1964	Houston Oilers
Charlie Rieves	*Linebacker*	1958; did not letter	AFL 1962–65	Oakland Raiders, Houston Oilers
Steve Sloan	*Quarterback*	1963–65	NFL 1966–67	Atlanta Falcons
Corky Tharp	*Defensive Back*	1951–54	CFL 1955, 1957–59, AFL 1960	Toronto Argonauts, New York Titans
Tommy Tolleson	*Wide Receiver*	1963–65	NFL 1966	Atlanta Falcons
Wayne Trimble	*Defensive Back*	1964–66	NFL 1967	San Francisco 49ers
Ed Versprille	*Defensive Back*	1961–63	CFL 1964	Hamilton Tiger-Cats

Pro Career Started in the 1970s

NAME	POSITION	COLLEGE	PRO	TEAMS
David Bailey	*Wide Receiver*	1969–71	CFL 1974	Winnipeg Blue Bombers
Buddy Brown	*Guard*	1971–73	CFL 1975–78	Winnipeg Blue Bombers
Sylvester Croom	*Center*	1972–74	NFL 1975	New Orleans Saints
Calvin Culliver	*Running Back*	1973–76	CFL 1978	British Columbia Lions
Ricky Davis	*Defensive Back*	1973–74	NFL 1975–77	Cincinnati Bengals, Tampa Bay Buccaneers, Kansas City Chiefs
Jim Duke	*Defensive End*	1967–69	CFL 1970-75	Saskatchewan Roughriders, British Columbia Lions, Winnpieg Blue Bombers
Greg Gantt	*Punter*	1971–73	NFL 1974–75	New York Jets
Paul Harris	*Linebacker*	1974–76	NFL 1977–78	Tampa Bay Buccaneers, Minnesota Vikings
Mike Kramer	*Defensive Back*	1975–77	CFL 1979	Toronto Argonauts
Jim Krapf	*Guard*	1970–72	CFL 1973	British Columbia Lions
Willie McCray	*Defensive End*	1974; did not letter	NFL 1978	San Francisco 49ers
Butch Norman	*Offensive Tackle*	1973	CFL 1974–80	Winnipeg Blue Bombers
Chuck Strickland	*Linebacker*	1971–73	CFL 1974	Winnipeg Blue Bombers
Tom Surlas	*Linebacker*	1970–71	CFL 1973	Toronto Argonauts
Wayne Wheeler	*Wide Receiver*	1971–73	NFL 1974	Chicago Bears

Pro Career Started in the 1980s

NAME	POSITION	COLLEGE	PRO	TEAMS
Buddy Aydelette	*Offensive Tackle*	1977–79	NFL 1980, 1987, USFL 1983–85	Green Bay Packers, Pittsburgh Steelers, Birmingham Stallions
Albert Bell	*Wide Receiver*	1985–86	NFL 1988	Green Bay Packers
Jesse Bendross	*Wide Receiver*	1980–83	NFL 1984–85, 1987	San Diego Chargers, Philadelphia Eagles

NAME	POSITION	COLLEGE	PRO	TEAMS
George Bethune	*Linebacker-Defensive End-Defensive Tackle*	1986–88	NFL 1989–90, WLAF 1992, CFL 1993–95	Los Angeles Rams, Sacramento Surge, Winnipeg Blue Bombers, Sacramento Gold Miners, San Antonio Texans
Thomas Boyd	*Linebacker*	1978–81	USFL 1984, NFL 1987	Birmingham Stallions, Detroit Lions
Joe Carter	*Running Back*	1980–83	NFL 1984–86	Miami Dolphins
Wayne C. Davis	*Linebacker*	1983–86	NFL 1987–88	St Louis-Phoenix Cardinals
Randy Edwards	*Defensive End-Nose Tackle*	1980–83	NFL 1984–87	Seattle Seahawks
Preston Gothard	*Tight End*	1983–84	NFL 1985–88	Pittsburgh Steelers
Billy Jackson	*Running Back*	1978–80	NFL 1981–84	Kansas City Chiefs
Hoss Johnson	*Offensive Tackle*	1984–86	NFL 1987	Tampa Bay Buccaneers
Robbie Jones	*Linebacker*	1979–82	NFL 1984–87	New York Giants
Ricky Moore	*Running Back*	1981–84	NFL 1986–88	Buffalo Bills, Houston Oilers, Phoenix Cardinals
Greg Richardson	*Wide Receiver*	1983–86	NFL 1987–88	Minnesota Vikings, Tampa Bay Buccaneers
Freddie Robinson	*Safety*	1983–86	NFL 1987–88	Indianapolis Colts
Mike Rodriguez	*Linebacker*	1981–83	NFL 1987	Los Angeles Raiders
Willard Scissum	*Tackle-Guard*	1981–84	NFL 1987	Washington Redskins
Bill Searcey	*Offensive Guard*	1978–80	USFL 1983–84, NFL 1985	Birmingham Stallions, Houston Gamblers, San Diego Chargers
Ricky Thomas	*Defensive Back*	1983–86	NFL 1987	Seattle Seahawks
Van Tiffin	*Kicker*	1983–86	NFL 1987	Miami Dolphins, Tampa Bay Buccaneers
Paul Tripoli	*Defensive Back*	1983–84	CFL 1986–87, NFL 1987	Toronto Argonauts, Tampa Bay Buccaneers

Pro Career Started in the 1990s

NAME	POSITION	COLLEGE	PRO	TEAMS
Jay Barker	*Quarterback*	1991–94	CFL 1998–2000	Toronto Argonauts
Kendrick Burton	*Defensive End*	1993–95	NFL 1996	Houston Oilers
Brad Ford	*Cornerback*	1994–95	NFL 1996	Detroit Lions
Dameian Jeffries	*Defensive End*	1991–94	NFL 1995	New Orleans Saints
Gene Jelks	*Wide Receiver*	1985–89	CFL 1991	Saskatchewan Roughriders
Tommy Johnson	*Defensive Back*	1991–94	NFL 1995, ArFL 1998–2000	Jacksonville Jaguars, Albany Firebirds, Carolina Cobras
Tony Johnson	*Tight End*	1992–95	NFL 1996–98	New Orleans Saints
Derrick Lassic	*Running Back*	1989–92	NFL 1993	Dallas Cowboys
Kevin Lee	*Wide Receiver*	1990–93	NFL 1995–96	New England Patriots, San Francisco 49ers
Jeremy Nunley	*Defensive End*	1990–93	NFL 1994	Houston Oilers
Derrick Oden	*Linebacker*	1989–92	NFL 1993–95	Philadelphia Eagles
Roosevelt Patterson	*Offensive Tackle*	1991–93	CFL 1995–97	Birmingham Barracudas, Hamilton Tiger-Cats, Toronto Argonauts, Montreal Alouettes
Thomas Rayam	*Offensive Guard-Defensive Tackle-Offensive Tackle*	1987–88,	NFL 1992–93, CFL 1995–2002	Cincinnati Bengals, Birmingham Barracudas, Edmonton Eskimos
Trevis Smith	*Linebacker*	1995–98	CFL 1999–2005	Saskatchewan Roughriders
Ralph Staten	*Defensive Back*	1993–96	NFL 1997–98, CFL 2000–02	Baltimore Ravens, Edmonton Eskimos, Ottawa Renegades
John Sullins	*Linebacker*	1988–91	NFL 1992	Denver Broncos
George Thornton	*Defensive Tackle-Defensive End-Nose Tackle*	1988–90	NFL 1991–93	San Diego Chargers, New York Giants
Prince Wimbley	*Wide Receiver-Slotback*	1988–89, 1991–92	CFL 1994–95, 1997	Las Vegas Posse, Birmingham Barracudas, Saskatchewan Roughriders, Hamilton Tiger-Cats
Willie Wyatt	*Nose Tackle*	1986–89	NFL 1990	Tampa Bay Buccaneers

Pro Career Started in the 2000s

NAME	POSITION	COLLEGE	PRO	TEAMS
Curtis Alexander	*Running Back*	1994–97	CFL 2002	Hamilton Tiger-Cats
Waine Bacon	*Defensive Back*	2001–02	NFL 2004	Indianapolis Colts
Kecalf Bailey	*Cornerback*	1997–2000	CFL 2001	Montreal Alouettes
Wesley Britt	*Offensive Tackle*	2001–04	NFL 2006–08	New England Patriots
Anthony Bryant	*Defensive Tackle*	2001, 2003–04	NFL 2005–07, 2010	Tampa Bay Buccaneers, Detroit Lions
Travis Carroll	*Linebacker*	1997–98	NFL 2002–03	New Orleans Saints, Houston Texans
Jeremy Clark	*Defensive Tackle*	2003–06	NFL 2008, 2010	New York Giants, Philadelphia Eagles, Dallas Cowboys
Kenneth Darby	*Running Back*	2003–06	NFL 2007–10	Tampa Bay Buccaneers, St. Louis Rams
Brandon Deaderick	*Defensive End*	2006–09	NFL 2010–12	New England Patriots
Gerald Dixon	*Linebacker-Defensive Back*	1999–2002	CFL 2005–06	Edmonton Eskimos
Tony Dixon	*Safety*	1997–2000	NFL 2001–04	Dallas Cowboys
Dante Ellington	*Offensive Tackle*	1999–2001	NFL 2005	Arizona Cardinals
Alonzo Ephraim	*Center*	2000–02	NFL 2003–05, ArFL 2007–08	Philadelphia Eagles, Miami Dolphins, New York Dragons
Terry Grant	*Running Back*	2007–09	CFL 2011	Hamilton Tiger-Cats
Reggie Grimes	*Defensive End*	1996–99	NFL 2000	New England Patriots
Quincy Jackson	*Wide Receiver*	1997–98	CFL 2001–03	Edmonton Eskimos, Saskatchewan Roughriders
Marquis Johnson	*Cornerback*	2006–09	NFL 2010–11	St. Louis Rams
Kenny King	*Defensive End*	1999–2002	NFL 2003	Arizona Cardinals
Milo Lewis	*Defensive Back*	1999–2000	CFL 2002–04	Winnipeg Blue Bombers, Calgary Stampeders
Triandos Luke	*Wide Receiver*	2000–03	NFL 2004	Denver Broncos
Greg McElroy	*Quarterback*	2008–10	NFL 2012	New York Jets

NAME	POSITION	COLLEGE	PRO	TEAMS
Nautyn Mc-Kay-Loescher	*Defensive End*	2001–03	CFL 2004–09	British Columbia Lions, Hamilton Tiger-Cats
Brandon Miree	*Running Back*	2000	NFL 2006	Green Bay Packers
Aries Monroe	*Linebacker*	2000–01	CFL 2003	Calgary Stampeders
Michael Moore	*Offensive Guard*	1996–97	NFL 2000, 2003–04	Washington Redskins, Atlanta Falcons
Kindal Moorehead	*Defensive Tackle*	1998–99, 2001–02	NFL 2003–08	Carolina Panthers, Atlanta Falcons
Reggie Myles	*Defensive Back*	1998–2001	NFL 2002–05, CFL 2008	Cincinnati Bengals, British Columbia Lions
Marico Portis	*Offensive Guard*	1999, 2001–02	NFL 2004	Tennessee Titans
Ramzee Robinson	*Defensive Back*	2003–06	NFL 2007–09	Detroit Lions, Philadelphia Eagles, Cleveland Browns
Brad Smelley	*Tight End*	2008–11	NFL 2012	Cleveland Browns
Marcus Spencer	*Defensive Back*	1997–2000	CFL 2002–04	Hamilton Tiger-Cats
Chavis Williams	*Linebacker*	2007–10	NFL 2011	Baltimore Ravens
Shaud Williams	*Running Back*	2002–03	NFL 2004–06, UFL 2009–11	Buffalo Bills, Florida Tuskers, Omaha Nighthawks
Cornelius Wortham	*Linebacker*	2000–04	NFL 2005	Seattle Seahawks

BASEBALL SOFTBALL

BASEBALL

By any measure, the University of Alabama has presented one of the most successful collegiate baseball programs in history. Through 2013, Alabama ranks 15th all time among NCAA Division I schools in victories and 27th in winning percentage. Among Southeastern Conference teams, the Crimson Tide is third to Texas A&M and Mississippi State in all-time victories, and second to Louisiana State University in conference championships. In the conference, Alabama also trails only LSU in the number of major-league players produced. In pre-SEC days, the Tide won two Southeastern Conference championships and seven Southern Intercollegiate Athletic Association titles.

Five times, Alabama has reached the College World Series. The Tide made it to the championship game in 1983 (losing to Texas, 4–2) and 1997 (losing to LSU, 13–6).

Alabama won the first baseball game it ever played, defeating Sewanee (formally known as The University of the South), 6-3, at Lakeview Park in Birmingham on July 1, 1892. That was apparently Alabama's first intercollegiate athletic competition. It preceded Alabama's first football game (played at the same location) by four months and 10 days.

Top 30 All-Time College Teams

(Ranked by wins through 2013)

RECORD	TEAM	WINNING %	SEASONS PLAYED
4,342-2,197-48	Fordham	.663	153
3,303-1,179-31	Texas	.735	117
2,741-1,550-28	Southern California	.638	119
2,732-1,589-36	Michigan	.631	140
2,727-1,714-35	Stanford	.613	120
2,709-1,311-8	Arizona State	.674	102
2,665-983-11	Florida State	.730	66
2,655-1,408-23	Arizona	.653	108
2,641-1,466-30	Clemson	.642	116
2,635-1,543-37	North Carolina	.630	124
2,587-1,621-6	Washington State	.615	118
2,479-1,404-42	Texas A&M	.637	111
2,467-1,512-25	Minnesota	.619	125
2,460-1,438-27	Mississippi State	.630	124
2,459-1,491-23	**Alabama**	**.622**	**121**
2,450-1,847-21	California	.570	122
2,441-1,586-38	Illinois	.605	134
2,434-1,677-35	Harvard	.591	146
2,432-1,431-8	Fresno State	.629	85
2,427-1,228-4	Oklahoma State	.664	102
2,420-1,572-40	Ohio State	.605	130
2,412-1,385-11	Oklahoma	.635	108
2,412-1,445-17	South Carolina	.625	121
2,392-981-18	Miami (Florida)	.708	69
2,358-1,443-21	Notre Dame	.620	121
2,353-1,499-6	LSU	.612	118
2,325-1,923-23	UCLA	.547	94

RECORD	TEAM	WINNING %	SEASONS PLAYED
2,305-1,480-24	Florida	.608	99
2,301-1,538-38	San Diego State	.598	81
2,285-2,052-41	Yale	.527	149

Note: These are NCAA records. They don't match Alabama's school records because the latter include games against professional minor-league teams and other noncollegiate opponents.

(Ranked by winning percentage through 2013; a tie counts as half a win, half a loss per NCAA practice)

WINNING %	TEAM	RECORD
.735	Texas	3,303-1,179-31
.730	Florida State	2,665-983-11
.708	Miami (Florida)	2,392-981-18
.682	Wichita State	2,113-985-8
.674	Arizona State	2,709-1,311-8
.664	Oklahoma State	2,427-1,228-4
.663	Fordham	4,342-2,197-48
.661	Southern	1,459-746-4
.658	Grambling	1,729-898-3
.658	Oral Roberts	1,716-893-3
.655	Cal State Fullerton	1,900-997-14
.653	St. John's (New York)	1,940-1,030-0
.653	Arizona	2,655-1,408-23
.652	Coastal Carolina	1,380-736-0
.650	East Carolina	1,722-925-11
.642	Clemson	2,641-1,466-30
.641	South Alabama	1,687-946-3
.638	Southern California	2,741-1,550-28
.637	Texas A&M	2,479-1,404-42
.635	Oklahoma	2,412-1,385-11
.631	Michigan	2,732-1,589-36
.630	Mississippi State	2,460-1,438-27

WINNING %	TEAM	RECORD
.630	North Carolina	2,635-1,543-37
.629	Fresno State	2,432-1,431-8
.625	South Carolina	2,412-1,445-17
.624	Florida International	1,497-900-1
.622	**Alabama**	**2,459-1,491-23**
.621	North Carolina State	2,166-1,318-27
.620	Notre Dame	2,358-1,443-21
.619	Minnesota	2,467-1,512-25

Note: These are NCAA records. They don't match Alabama's school records because the latter include games against professional minor-league teams and other noncollegiate opponents.

Alabama in the College World Series

1950 fifth of eight teams
1983 second
1996 fifth
1997 second
1999 fourth

College World Series Appearances

(Through 2013; includes teams with 5 or more appearances)

34 Texas, 6 championships	**16** Cal State Fullerton, 4	**10** Oklahoma, 2
23 Miami (Florida), 4	**16** LSU, 6	**9** Mississippi State, 0
22 Arizona State, 5	**16** Stanford, 2	**8** Florida, 0
21 Florida State, 0	**12** Clemson, 0	**7** Arkansas, 0
21 Southern California, 12	**11** South Carolina, 2	**7** Maine, 0
19 Oklahoma State, 1	**10** North Carolina, 0	**7** Michigan, 2
16 Arizona, 4	**10** Northern Colorado, 0	**7** Rice, 1

College World Series Appearances *(continued)*

7 Wichita State, 1	**6** Western Michigan, 0	**5** Penn State, 0
6 California, 2	**5** **Alabama, 0**	**5** Southern Illinois, 0
6 Georgia, 1	**5** Connecticut, 0	**5** Texas A&M, 0
6 Missouri, 1	**5** Minnesota, 3	**5** UCLA, 1
6 St. John's (New York), 0	**5** Oregon State, 2	

College World Series Championships

(Through 2013)

12 Southern California	**2** Michigan	**1** Ohio State
6 LSU	**2** Oklahoma	**1** Oklahoma State
6 Texas	**2** Oregon State	**1** Pepperdine
5 Arizona State	**2** South Carolina	**1** Rice
4 Arizona	**2** Stanford	**1** UCLA
4 Cal State Fullerton	**1** Fresno State	**1** Wake Forest
4 Miami (Florida)	**1** Georgia	**1** Wichita State
3 Minnesota	**1** Holy Cross	
2 California	**1** Missouri	

Southeastern Conference Championships

(Regular season through 2013)

16 LSU	**6** Mississippi	**2** Arkansas
14 **Alabama**	**5** Auburn	**1** Georgia Tech
12 Florida	**5** Vanderbilt	**1** Kentucky
7 Mississippi State	**4** South Carolina	
6 Georgia	**3** Tennessee	

(Tournament through 2013)

10 LSU	6 Florida	2 Mississippi
7 Alabama	3 Auburn	2 Vanderbilt
7 Mississippi State	3 Tennessee	1 South Carolina

2013 Division I College Baseball Home Attendance Leaders

TEAM	AVERAGE PER GAME ATTENDANCE	TOTAL SEASON ATTENDANCE
LSU	11,006	473,298
Arkansas	8,335	250,055
Mississippi	7,996	239,909
Mississippi State	7,617	281,840
South Carolina	7,445	260,605
Texas	5,793	185,400
Clemson	4,751	147,296
Florida State	4,594	183,770
Texas A&M	4,523	149,263
Creighton	4,041	88,916
Texas Christian	3,570	107,117
Florida	3,511	126,421
Hawaii	3,357	97,355
Alabama	**3,262**	**101,137**
Rice	3,252	97,582

HEAD COACHES

From 1892, Alabama's first baseball season, through 1900, the team had a different coach each year. Most successful was the marvelously named Kid Peeples, who led the 1897 squad to a 10-0 record. William "Kid" Peeples, a light-hitting shortstop, played from 1886 through 1903 for 19 minor-league teams in 10 leagues and 10 states. His stops included the Montgomery, Alabama, team of the old Southern Association in 1895 and 1896, so a coaching stint up the road in Tuscaloosa after the 1896 season made sense.

Thomas C. Stouch arrived in 1901, age 31, and stayed five seasons. His teams posted a combined record of 49-25-1, including a 9-4 victory over the minor-league Birmingham Barons in 1903. Stouch was another longtime minor leaguer, a second baseman who hit .313 during his lone major league stint: four games with the Louisville Colonels, a predecessor to today's Pittsburgh Pirates, in 1898. Among his teammates was Hall of Fame shortstop Honus Wagner.

During his Alabama coaching years, Stouch played minor-league ball in Selma, Alabama (1901), Atlanta (1902), and Decatur, Alabama (1904). He coached the University of Georgia in 1906 and 1907, going 12-9, before resuming his minor-league career. In 1908, as player-manager for the Greenville (South Carolina) Spinners, he signed a rookie out of the South Carolina mill leagues: future major league star "Shoeless" Joe Jackson.

By 1912, Alabama had established a full athletics department. Coaches began wearing more than one hat, or cap. From 1912 through 1979, only three head baseball coaches (Gordon Lewis in 1920, Sam Hinton in 1931–32, and Joe Sewell in 1964–69) concentrated on that sport without other major responsibilities. Here are Alabama's other head baseball coaches during that time, with their full portfolios:

1912–15: D. V. Graves, 66-30-1; *also head football coach, 1911–14, and head basketball coach, 1912–15*

1916–19: B. J. "Loonie" Noojin, 55-18; *also football assistant, 1915–16, athletics director, 1916-20, and head basketball coach, 1917–18*

1921–23: Charles Bernier, 28-35-4; *also football assistant, 1920, and athletics director and head basketball coach, 1920–23*

1924–27: Wallace Wade, 61-32-2; *also head football coach and athletics director, 1923–30*

1928: Hank Crisp, 12-7-2; *also football assistant, 1921–42 and 1950–57, head track coach, 1921–27, head basketball coach, 1923–42 and 1945–46, and athletics director, 1930–40 and 1954–57*

1929–30: Jess Neely, 26-15-2; *also football assistant, 1928–30*

1933–34: J. B. Whitworth, 21-11; *also football assistant, 1932–34, and head football coach, 1955–57*

1935–42, 1947–63: Tilden Campbell, 355-168-4; *also football assistant, 1935–41 and 1947–55*

1943: Paul Burnham, 12-6; *also football assistant, 1930–42, and head basketball coach, 1942–43*

1946: Dixie Howell, 13-7; *also football assistant, 1946*

1970–79: Hayden Riley, 236-206-1; *also football assistant, 1958–69, and head basketball coach, 1960–68*

Here's a closer look at Campbell, Alabama's first great baseball coach:

The Tilden Campbell Era

Like two other pivotal coaches at Alabama, Bear Bryant (see page 37) and Ears Whitworth (see page 42), Tilden "Happy" Campbell hailed from Arkansas—in his case, Pine Bluff. Campbell lettered as a backup quarterback (then mostly a blocking position) for Alabama's football team in 1934 and 1935. The 1935 team went 10-0 and shared unofficial NCAA national championship recognition with 8-0 Minnesota; Bryant was one of his teammates.

Campbell also played baseball for the Crimson Tide from 1933 through 1935, but never earned a letter. After graduation, he stayed at Alabama as head baseball coach and football backfield coach, beginning in 1935. He would keep both positions for the next two decades, except for three years in the Navy during World War II and one year (1946) as a football backfield coach at the University of Mississippi.

Though some of his predecessors had good runs, none stayed for more than five years. Campbell coached for 24 years, compiling an exceptional record of 344-158-4. (That's his real record, but it's not his official record; see below.) He never had a losing season, and only once did his team finish at .500 (10-10 in 1939). His teams won nine Southeastern Conference championships, played in four NCAA regional tournaments, and once (1950) reached the College World Series, finishing fifth.

After 1955, Campbell dropped his football duties, but he remained baseball coach until he died of a heart attack on February 23, 1963, less than three weeks before the beginning of the season. He was 54 years old. Bryant, Alabama's athletic director, appointed Sam Bailey, an assistant football coach, and Hayden Riley, head basketball coach and also a football assistant, as co-head coaches for the rest of that season, but Alabama still officially credits that 11-10 season to Campbell.

The Joe Sewell Era

Joe Sewell (see page 239), the only Baseball Hall of Fame inductee from the University of Alabama, came back to his alma mater as head baseball coach in 1964 and stayed through 1969, leaving only after he had reached the mandatory retirement age of 70. Sewell had stayed active in baseball as a coach and a scout after his playing career ended in 1933. His Hall of Fame induction would not come until 1977, but he was highly respected as a person and a baseball man.

Alabama's baseball fortunes had slipped a bit. The team had posted losing Southeastern Conference records in two of the previous three years. Sewell started slowly, with .500 records his first two years. In 1968, however, his team went 24-14, won the conference championship, and reached the NCAA district playoffs. Overall, his teams went 106-79.

In 1978, Alabama rechristened its baseball park. What had been known as Thomas Stadium became Sewell-Thomas Stadium. Locals call it "The Joe."

The Hayden Riley Era

Riley, a longtime member of the Alabama athletics staff, got his shot at leading the baseball program in 1970. Riley had lettered for Alabama in baseball (1946) and basketball (1947 and 1948) after World War II interrupted his college education. He was the Crimson Tide's head basketball coach from 1960 through 1968, finishing with a record of 102-104. He was also a football assistant from 1958, when Bear Bryant hired him as recruiting coordinator, through 1969.

In 10 years as head baseball coach, Riley managed an overall record of 236-206-1 with two Southeastern Conference divisional titles but no conference championships. He stepped down because of health problems in 1979 but stayed with the athletic department as director of corporate relations. In 1982, he left for a two-year stint as commissioner of the Gulf South Conference before finally retiring. He died of a heart attack in 1995, age 73.

The Barry Shollenberger Era

In 1962, Barry Shollenberger, a 21-year-old pitcher out of Moravian College in Bethlehem, Pennsylvania, posted a 16-5 record and a 2.14 earned run average with the Waterloo Hawks of the Midwest League, a Boston Red Sox farm club. Then came the injuries. The following year, his record was 1-10. After 1965, his playing career was over.

He turned to coaching. From 1977 through 1979, he had a record of 77-64-3 at Western Kentucky University. Alabama hired him, and from 1980 through 1994, his teams went 487-334-1. In 1983, Dr. Shollenberger (he picked up a doctorate in social psychology at Alabama) took the Crimson Tide and their star first baseman, Dave Magadan (see page 232), to a regular-season Southeastern Conference championship and all the way to the title game of the College World Series. Alabama lost to Texas, 4–3, but it was a great year.

Shollenberger had some more good years but never matched that peak. He retired in 1994 and began an entirely new career. At Alabama, he had become associate director of distance education and president of the State of Alabama Distance Learning Association. After leaving the university, he moved into the world of private, for-profit universities and became a teacher of American history. He is provost emeritus at Virginia College in Birmingham, Alabama. Since 1997, he has taught at the American Public University System, an online-learning institution.

The Jim Wells Era

Jim Wells, Alabama's greatest baseball coach, succeeded Shollenberger. In 15 years, from 1995 until he retired in 2009, Wells became the Crimson Tide's all-time winningest coach by a wide margin, with a record of 625-322. His teams won two Southeastern Conference regular-season championships and five SEC Tournament championships, and reached the College World Series three times in four years (1996–97, 1999). Twelve of his 15 teams reached NCAA postseason play.

Wells came to Alabama after putting up a record of 192-89 in five years at his alma mater, little Northwestern State in Natchitoches, Louisiana. He left Alabama in 2009 under slightly mysterious circumstances. He had "retired" for a few days in 2007 but changed his mind,

Jim Wells
Credit: EMCC Athletics

and he was only 54 when he quit the second time. A few weeks after his departure, he told an interviewer only, "It's time to move on."

After taking some time off, he spent 2012 as an assistant coach at East Mississippi Community College in Scooba. In 2013, he was a volunteer assistant coach, focusing on pitchers, at Northridge High School in Tuscaloosa, where he still lives. He worked under head coach Travis Garner, who had played for Wells at Alabama as an outfielder on Southeastern Conference championship teams in 2002 and 2003.

"Travis gave me an opportunity to come over here, which I'm grateful for because I was driving back and forth to Mississippi," Wells told the *Tuscaloosa News*. "When he called and said there might be an opportunity to come over here, I jumped on it because my son is on the middle-school team. I get to see him and be around him every day. These are good kids, and it's fun to teach baseball again."

Dorsett Vandeventer Graves

A century ago at Alabama, Dorsett Vandeventer Graves was head coach of three major sports simultaneously—a common practice at the time. In fall, he coached football (going 21-12-3 in 1911–14); in winter, basketball (20-12, 1912–15); and in spring, baseball (66-30-1, 1912–15).

Graves went by "D. V.," although everybody called him "Tubby" because he weighed 200 pounds as a youth. He played football and baseball at Missouri, lettering as a tackle (1906–08) and first baseman (1909). He was also senior class president and a member of the Quo Vadis Club, which the *Kansas City Journal* newspaper described as "an organization of student hoboes."

A minor-league baseball career fizzled, so Graves began coaching at Alabama. He moved on to Texas A&M and what is now Montana State before settling at Washington. From 1923 through 1946, he coached the Huskies' baseball teams to a 234-166-4 record, winning seven Pacific Coast Conference and PCC North titles. He was also an assistant football coach. Washington named its athletics offices building and its former baseball field for him and inducted him into the Husky Hall of Fame. Graves died in Seattle in 1960, age 73.

The Mitch Gaspard Era

Four years after his elevation from assistant coach and ace recruiter to the top job, Mitch Gaspard already ranks fifth all time in victories (133) among Alabama head coaches. Nonetheless, the Crimson Tide faithful have hesitated to embrace him. After all, Gaspard's predecessor and former boss, Jim Wells, took teams to the College World Series twice during his first four seasons. Gaspard has yet to reach the CWS. And in 2012, he presided over Alabama's first losing team since 1994.

Gaspard did rebound in 2013 with a 35-28 mark and a berth in the NCAA Regional. Unfortunately, two losses to in-state rival Troy bounced the Tide out of the postseason. And Gaspard has never achieved a winning Southeastern Conference record, coming closest with a 15-15 mark in his rookie season, 2010.

The 2013 team was young, with five freshmen among the top 10 nonpitchers in terms of games started. With 12 saves, freshman closer Ray Castillo tied for the third-best single-season mark in Alabama history. If Gaspard's kids blossom, he could win over the doubters.

Head Coaching Records
(In chronological order)

YEARS	COACH	RECORD	WINNING %
1892	Shelby Fletcher	1-0	1.000
1893	W. M. Walker	4-6-1	.409
1894	J. H. Lyons	10-3	.769
1895	J. F. Jenkins	9-3	.750
1896	Eli Abbott	5-5	.500
1897	Kid Peeples	10-0	1.000
1898	Joseph Black	2-3	.400
1899	F. C. Owen	3-6	.333
1900	Ardis Smith	9-3	.750
1901–05	Thomas Stouch	49-25-1	.660
1906	Schwartz (first name not recorded)	4-16-1	.214
1907–10	J. W. H. Pollard	66-22-1	.747

YEARS	COACH	RECORD	WINNING %
1911	Guy S. Lowman	12-5	.706
1912–15	D. V. Graves	66-30-1	.686
1916–19	Loonie Noojin	55-18	.753
1920	Gordon Lewis	15-2	.882
1921–23	Charles Bernier	28-35-4	.448
1924–27	Wallace Wade	61-32-2	.653
1928	Hank Crisp	12-7-2	.619
1929–30	Jess Neely	28-15-2	.644
1931–32	Sam Hinton	23-7-2	.750
1933–34	J. B. Whitworth	21-11	.656
1935–42, 1947–63	Tilden Campbell	355-168-4	.677
1943	Paul Burnham	12-6	.667
1944–45	no team (World War II)		
1946	Dixie Howell	13-7	.650
1947–63	Campbell; see above		
1964–69	Joe Sewell	106-79	.573
1970–79	Hayden Riley	236-206-1	.533
1980–94	Barry Shollenberger	487-334-1	.593
1995–2009	Jim Wells	625-322	.656
2010–13	Mitch Gaspard	133-115	.536

Note: Some of these coaching records include games against professional minor-league teams and other noncollegiate opponents, so they don't match official NCAA records.

(Ranked by victories)

RECORD	COACH	YEARS COACHED
625-322	Jim Wells	1995–2009
487-334-1	Barry Shollenberger	1980–94
355-168-4	Tilden Campbell	1935–42, 1947–63
236-206-1	Hayden Riley	1970–79
133-115	Mitch Gaspard	2010–13
106-79	Joe Sewell	1964–69
66-22-1	J. W. H. Pollard	1907–10

RECORD	COACH	YEARS COACHED
66-30-1	D. V. Graves	1912–15
61-32-2	Wallace Wade	1924–27
55-18	Loonie Noojin	1916–19
49-25-1	Thomas Stouch	1901–05
28-15-2	Jess Neely	1929–30
28-35-4	Charles Bernier	1921–23
23-7-2	Sam Hinton	1931–32
21-11	J. B. Whitworth	1933–34
15-2	Gordon Lewis	1920
13-7	Dixie Howell	1946
12-5	Guy S. Lowman	1911
12-6	Paul Burnham	1943
12-7-2	Hank Crisp	1928
10-0	Kid Peeples	1897
10-3	J. H. Lyons	1894
9-3	J. F. Jenkins	1895
9-3	Ardis Smith	1900
5-5	Eli Abbott	1896
4-6-1	W. M. Walker	1893
4-16-1	Schwartz	1906
3-6	F. C. Owen	1899
2-3	Joseph Black	1898
1-0	Shelby Fletcher	1892

Note: Some of these coaching records include games against professional minor-league teams and other noncollegiate opponents, so they don't match official NCAA records.

(Ranked by winning percentage; a tie counts as half a win, half a loss, per NCAA practice)

WINNING %	RECORD	COACH	YEARS COACHED
1.000	10-0	Kid Peeples	1897
1.000	1-0	Shelby Fletcher	1892
.882	15-2	Gordon Lewis	1920
.769	10-3	J. H. Lyons	1894

WINNING %	RECORD	COACH	YEARS COACHED
.753	55-18	Loonie Noojin	1916–19
.750	23-7-2	Sam Hinton	1931–32
.750	9-3	J. F. Jenkins	1895
.750	9-3	Ardis Smith	1900
.747	66-22-1	J. W. H. Pollard	1907–10
.706	12-5	Guy S. Lowman	1911
.686	66-30-1	D. V. Graves	1912–15
.660	49-25-1	Thomas Stouch	1901–05
.677	355-168-4	Tilden Campbell	1935–42, 1947–63
.667	12-6	Paul Burnham	1943
.656	625-322	Jim Wells	1995–2009
.656	21-11	J. B. Whitworth	1933–34
.653	61-32-2	Wallace Wade	1924–27
.650	13-7	Dixie Howell	1946
.644	28-15-2	Jess Neely	1929–30
.619	12-7-2	Hank Crisp	1928
.593	487-334-1	Barry Shollenberger	1980–94
.573	106-79	Joe Sewell	1964–69
.536	133-115	Mitch Gaspard	2010–13
.533	236-206-1	Hayden Riley	1970–79
.500	5-5	Eli Abbott	1896
.448	28-35-4	Charles Bernier	1921–23
.409	4-6-1	W. M. Walker	1893
.400	2-3	Joseph Black	1898
.333	3-6	F. C. Owen	1899
.214	4-16-1	Schwartz	1906

Note: Some of these coaching records include games against professional minor-league teams and other noncollegiate opponents, so they don't match official NCAA records.

MAJOR LEAGUE PLAYERS

Alabama's best major league players have been Joe Sewell (see page 239), a shortstop and third baseman of the 1920s and '30s, who is the Crimson Tide's only representative in the Baseball Hall of Fame, and starting pitcher Frank Lary (see page 231), whose 1962 arm injury short-circuited what otherwise might have been a Hall of Fame career.

The defensive skills of catcher Luke Sewell earned him a 20-year American League career in the 1920s and '30s. The now-forgotten Del Pratt, the first Alabama player to make the majors, was one of baseball's top second basemen in the 1910s and '20s. Riggs Stephenson, an outfielder who was a contemporary and friend of the Sewell brothers, compiled a .336 lifetime batting average.

From 1964 through 1968, Al Worthington of the Minnesota Twins reigned as baseball's finest closer—though the term hadn't yet been invented. He was one of the first relief pitchers regularly brought in to shut down the other team at the end of a close game. Every big-league team has a closer today, but the position wasn't conclusively defined until the late 1980s, when Oakland A's manager Tony LaRussa began using Dennis Eckersley almost exclusively to pitch the last inning of games the A's were leading.

Ike Boone was probably the finest hitter the University of Alabama has produced, though he did his best work in the minor leagues at a time when minor-league teams enjoyed far greater independence than they do now.

Two current players have embarked on promising careers. The Detroit Tigers' Alex Avila (see page 220), who reached the major leagues in 2009, two years later played in the All-Star Game and won the Silver Slugger Award as the league's best hitter at his position. He and his team reached the playoffs in 2011 and went all the way to the World Series in 2012 (although the Tigers lost to the San Francisco Giants). New York Yankees relief pitcher David Robertson (see page 237), called up to the majors in 2008, also has been an All-Star. When Yankees closer Mariano Rivera suffered a knee injury in May 2012, Robertson had the opportunity to move into that role—until he himself went on the disabled list 12 days later with a strained muscle in his ribcage. He returned after a month but had an inconsistent season by his standards, although he still struck out nearly a third of the batters he faced.

Through the 2012 season, 63 former Alabama players have made it to the majors. The most recent Tide big leaguer, Josh Rutledge (see page 238), was called up to the Colorado Rockies in 2012 and has played shortstop (filling in for the often-injured Troy Tulowitzki) and second base. From 1927 through 1934, seven Alabama players made their major league debuts with the Washington Senators, the most notable being Jackie Hayes (see page 226). The Birmingham Barons minor-league team, just down the road from Tuscaloosa, had connections to the Senators and was the conduit for most of the signings. That was in the freewheeling days before Major League Baseball instituted a draft of free-agent players in 1965.

Since the draft began, Alabama has had four players picked in the first round: Joe Vitiello (see page 250) in 1991, Jeremy Brown (see page 223) in 2002, Taylor Tankersley (see page 250) in 2004, and Tommy Hunter (see page 229) in 2007. Vitiello, taken seventh overall by the Kansas City Royals, went the highest. The 6-2, 215-pound, right-handed outfielder, first baseman, and designated hitter played parts of five seasons with the Royals, plus a partial season apiece with the San Diego Padres and Montreal Expos. He hit for decent power and drew some walks, but he struck out a lot—165 times in only 791 plate appearances—and managed a career batting average of only .248.

Major League Players by School

Top 25 Colleges (Through 2012)

106 Southern California	**67** LSU	**56** Oklahoma State
101 Arizona State	**63** **Alabama**	**56** Santa Clara
101 Texas	**63** Oklahoma	**54** Florida
83 Stanford	**61** Florida State	**53** Pennsylvania
77 Michigan	**60** Notre Dame	**52** Ohio State
76 Holy Cross	**58** Saint Mary's of California	**51** Cal State Fullerton
71 Illinois	**57** California	**51** Texas A&M
69 Arizona	**56** Fordham	
69 UCLA	**56** North Carolina	

■ *Southeastern Conference (Through 2012)*

67	LSU	42	Arkansas
63	**Alabama**	42	Tennessee
54	Florida	39	Mississippi
51	Texas A&M	37	Missouri
46	Auburn	34	Georgia
45	Mississippi State	27	Kentucky
43	South Carolina	25	Vanderbilt

MAJOR LEAGUE MANAGERS

Only three University of Alabama alumni have managed in the major leagues. That includes Andy Cohen (see page 224), who logged all of one game with the Philadelphia Phillies in 1960 after Eddie Sawyer unexpectedly resigned in midseason. Cohen, a Phillies coach, was interim manager until Gene Mauch, who had been managing the minor-league Minneapolis Millers, could join the team. The Phillies won the game.

Luke Sewell remains the sole ex-Alabama player to win a pennant as a major-league manager. He led the St. Louis Browns to the only World Series in their history in 1944. The Browns lost the series, four games to two, to the St. Louis Cardinals, with whom they shared Sportsman's Park. In 1954, the Browns became the Baltimore Orioles. They have had considerably more success in Baltimore than they had in St. Louis.

Butch Hobson (see page 228) managed the Boston Red Sox for three sub-.500 years in the 1990s.

You'd think that Joe Birmingham should be on this list, given his last name. But Birmingham, who managed the Cleveland team in the American League for part of 1912, all of 1913 and 1914, and part of 1915, was born in Elmira, New York, and attended Cornell University.

Major League Managers Who Attended Alabama

NAME	RECORD	WINNING %	YEARS	TEAMS
Andy Cohen	1-0	1.000	1960	Philadelphia Phillies
Luke Sewell	606-644	.485	1941–46, 1949–52	St. Louis Browns, Cincinnati Reds
Butch Hobson	207-232	.472	1992–94	Boston Red Sox

The Hall of Famers Who Got Away

Of the 11 Hall of Fame baseball players born in Alabama, shortstop and third baseman Joe Sewell (see page 239) is the only one who attended Alabama. Only one other, shortstop Ozzie Smith, attended college anywhere (Cal Poly, San Luis Obispo). The rest began their pro careers right out of high school: outfielders Henry Aaron, Monte Irvin, Heinie Manush, Willie Mays, and Billy Williams, first baseman Willie McCovey, and pitchers Satchel Paige, Don Sutton, and Early Wynn.

SOFTBALL

A funny thing happened to softball coach Patrick Murphy on his way to Louisiana State University. He won a national championship at Alabama.

Alabama softball's first national championship was also the Crimson Tide's fourth in a remarkable 2012 that saw the football, gymnastics, and women's golf squads also gaining the right to chant "we're number one!"

The softball team earned the title on a rainy June night in Oklahoma City. In the third and deciding game of the championship round of the Women's College World Series, Alabama beat Oklahoma, 5-4.

Sophomore pitcher Jackie Traina, a 5-11 right-hander, set a school record with 42 wins. Her game-ending strikeout of Oklahoma pitcher and slugger Keilani Ricketts (the Collegiate Women Sports Awards national player of the year) was Traina's 361st of the year, also a school record.

A year previously, almost to the day, Murphy had announced that he was leaving his job as Alabama's softball coach and would move to Southeastern Conference rival LSU. He changed his mind and returned three days later—after Alabama agreed to bump his compensation up from $140,000 to the $225,000 that LSU had offered.

Excellent choice, as it turned out.

Alabama came late to women's fast-pitch college softball. But it has emphatically made up for lost time, thanks largely to Murphy. In just a decade and a half, the Crimson Tide team became an NCAA power and perennial Women's College World Series competitor. In fact, Patrick Murphy has more wins—789 through 2013—than any other Alabama coach in any sport, ever.

The NCAA held its first Women's College World Series in 1982. Before the NCAA got involved with women's sports, the Association for Intercollegiate Athletics for Women had administered a Women's College World Series from 1973 through 1982 (overlapping with the NCAA its final year). And even before that, an AIAW predecessor organization called the Division for Girls' and Women's Sports put on a women's college softball championship from 1969 through 1972.

The Crimson Tide didn't field its first team until 1997. But the program was sensationally successful almost from the beginning. Alabama softball has never had a losing season. The closest it came was in the first year, when coach Kalum Haack's squad went 29-29—but 16-14 in the Southeastern Conference.

Haack had been a successful coach at the University of Kansas, posting a 283-158-2 record from 1988 through 1995, before Alabama hired him to launch its softball program. He lasted a second season with the Tide, achieving a 49-18 record and an SEC championship, before resigning after the 1998 season. He is now the softball coach at Katy High School in Katy, Texas. One of his star players there was his daughter, Matte, who hit .326 with 13 home runs in 2013 as a senior first baseman at the University of Louisiana at Lafayette.

Haack built a good program from scratch. Murphy took over as head coach in 1999 and made it great. Murphy had also been with Alabama since the beginning, arriving as an assistant coach after one year as a college head coach at Northwest Missouri State. There, his team went 28-20 in 1995.

Softball coach Patrick Murphy leads what the National Fastpitch Coaches Association named the Division I National Coaching Staff of the Year in 2012.

Through 2013, Murphy had led Alabama to four regular-season SEC championships, five SEC tournament championships, eight Women's College World Series appearances, and NCAA regional tournament appearances in all 15 years of his tenure.

Plus a national championship. Of course, that meant the 2013 team, which earned a 45-15 record and won its NCAA Regional Tournament before faltering in the Super Regional, qualified as a mild disappointment. Welcome to life at the top, coach. Despite the pressure, it's a good place to be. Just ask Nick Saban.

Head Coaching Records

(In chronological order)

YEARS	COACH	RECORD	WINNING %
1997–1998	Kalum Haack	78-47	.624
1999–2013	Patrick Murphy	789-213	.787

(Ranked by victories)

RECORD	COACH	YEARS
789-213	Patrick Murphy	1999–2013
78-47	Kalum Haack	1997–1998

(Ranked by winning percentage)

WINNING %	RECORD	COACH	YEARS
.787	789-213	Patrick Murphy	1999–2013
.624	78-47	Kalum Haack	1997–1998

Alabama in the Women's College World Series

1999 tied for fifth of eight teams		**2008** tied for third	
2003 tied for seventh		**2009** tied for third	
2005 tied for fifth		**2011** tied for third	
2006 tied for seventh		**2012** first	

Women's College World Series Appearances

(Through 2013)

25	UCLA, 12 championships*	**3**	Nevada-Las Vegas, 0
22	Arizona, 8	**3**	South Carolina, 0
12	California, 1	**3**	Utah, 0
12	Fresno State, 1	**2**	Adelphi, 0
11	Arizona State, 2	**2**	Baylor, 0
11	Washington, 1	**2**	Cal State Northridge, 0
10	Michigan, 1	**2**	Creighton, 0
8	**Alabama, 1**	**2**	Georgia, 0
8	Nebraska, 0**	**2**	Indiana, 0
8	Oklahoma, 2	**2**	Oregon, 0
7	Florida State, 0	**2**	Princeton, 0
7	Oklahoma State, 0	**2**	Southern Mississippi, 0
7	Texas A&M, 2	**2**	Stanford, 0
6	Cal State Fullerton, 1	**1**	Central Michigan, 0
6	Missouri, 0	**1**	Connecticut, 0
6	Tennessee, 0	**1**	Hawaii, 0
5	Florida, 0	**1**	Illinois-Chicago, 0
5	Long Beach State, 0	**1**	Kansas, 0
5	Northwestern, 0	**1**	Kent State, 0
5	Southwestern Louisiana/ Louisiana-Lafayette, 0	**1**	Northern Illinois, 0
		1	Oregon State, 0
5	Texas, 0	**1**	Pacific, 0
4	Cal Poly Pomona, 0	**1**	South Florida, 0
4	DePaul, 0	**1**	Toledo, 0
4	Iowa, 0	**1**	Utah State, 0
3	LSU, 0	**1**	Virginia Tech, 0
3	Louisiana Tech, 0	**1**	Western Michigan, 0
3	Massachusetts, 0		

*Includes the 1995 title, which the NCAA vacated because of scholarship violations
**Includes Nebraska's 1985 runner-up finish, which the NCAA vacated because it ruled that two of Nebraska's players were ineligible*

Women's College World Series Championships

(Through 2013)

UCLA, 12*	Texas A&M, 2	Fresno State, 1
Arizona, 8	**Alabama, 1**	Michigan, 1
Arizona State, 2	California, 1	Washington, 1
Oklahoma, 2	Cal State Fullerton, 1	

Includes the 1995 title, which the NCAA vacated because of scholarship violations

ATTENDANCE

Alabama broke its own national college softball home attendance records in 2013. The Crimson Tide drew 93,332 to Rhoads Stadium, an average of 2,916 per game. That eclipsed the previous highs of 91,541 and 2,619, which Alabama set in 2012 and 2011 respectively.

Arizona finished second with a total 2013 attendance of 57,615 and an average of 2,134. Since 2006, Alabama and Arizona have battled for the NCAA softball attendance crown every year. Alabama finished first in total attendance in 2008–10 and 2012–13, and second in 2006–07 and 2011. The Crimson Tide led in average attendance in 2008 and 2011–13, while Arizona was first in 2006–07 and 2009–10.

Rhoads Stadium, built in 2000, has already been expanded three times, most recently after the 2011 season. Its official capacity is now 3,940.

College Softball Top Two in Home Attendance

RANK	TEAM	AVERAGE PER GAME ATTENDANCE	TOTAL SEASON ATTENDANCE
2013			
1	Alabama	2,916	93,332
2	Arizona	2,134	57,615

RANK	TEAM	AVERAGE PER GAME ATTENDANCE	TOTAL SEASON ATTENDANCE
2012			
1	Alabama	2,474	91,541
2	Arizona	2,328	55,882
2011			
1	Alabama	2,619	68,119
2	Arizona	2,370	77,129
2010			
1	Arizona	2,266	52,125
2	Alabama	2,260	63,271
2009			
1	Arizona	2,434	46,249
2	Alabama	2,090	48,066
2008			
1	Alabama	1,890	51,024
2	Arizona	1,878	39,435
2007			
1	Arizona	1,589	44,487
2	Alabama	1,417	36,841

PRO LEAGUES

Women's professional softball had a couple of false starts. The International Women's Professional Softball Association began ambitiously in 1976 with 10 teams from across the country, each playing a 120-game schedule consisting of 60 doubleheaders. It ran out of money after four seasons.

The current National Pro Fastpitch league has its roots in Women's Pro Fastpitch, which began league play in 1997. Former Utah State University softball player Jane Cowles and her college coach, John Horan, planned the league. Cowles's parents, Sage and John Cowles Jr., owners of the Cowles Media Company, provided financial backing.

Women's Pro Fastpitch started with six teams in the eastern half of the country. It changed its name to the Women's Professional Softball League for the 1999 season, contracted to four teams in 2000, tried an 11-city "Tour of Fastpitch Champions" in 2001, and suspended play in 2002.

The league relaunched itself as National Pro Fastpitch in 2004, with six teams spread across the country. After many franchise moves, additions, and subtractions, it continues today with four teams: USSSA Pride of Kissimmee, Florida, the Akron (Ohio) Racers, the Chicago Bandits, and the NY/NJ Comets, who play home games in Pomona, New York; Montclair and Bridgewater, New Jersey; and Allentown, Pennsylvania.

Of the 10 Alabama softball players who have gone pro, the best by far has been right fielder Kelly Kretschman (see page 230). In seven years with National Pro Fastpitch, she has hit .336 with a slugging percentage of .519 and a superb on-base percentage of .468. And that doesn't count her fine play in the 2004 and 2008 Olympics. As the starting right fielder, she helped Team USA to a gold and a silver medal, respectively, hitting for a combined batting average of .341, on-base percentage of .400, and slugging percentage of .591.

Women's Professional Softball Champions

International Women's Professional Softball Association

1976	Connecticut Falcons
1977	Connecticut Falcons
1978	Connecticut Falcons
1979	St. Louis Hummers

Women's Pro Fastpitch

1997	Orlando Wahoos
1998	Orlando Wahoos

Women's Professional Softball League

1999	Tampa Bay FireStix
2000	Florida Wahoos

National Pro Fastpitch

2004	New York/New Jersey Juggernaut	**2009**	Rockford Thunder
2005	Akron Racers	**2010**	USSSA Pride
2006	New England Riptide	**2011**	Chicago Bandits
2007	Washington Glory	**2012**	USSSA Pride (regular season; Championship Series rained out)
2008	Chicago Bandits		

Nicknames

> *Big Jim* (James Sheehan)

> *Bruce* (Broadus Milburn Connatser)

> *Butch* (Clell Hobson)

> *Buck, Lefty* (Lee Rogers)

> *Dan* (James Albert Boone)

> *Del* (Derrill Burnham Pratt)

> *Football Freddy* (Fred Sington)

> *Happy* (Coach Tilden Campbell)

> *Houdini* (David Robertson)

> *Jackie* (Minter Carney Hayes)

> *Jim* (Ernest James Wingard)

> *Lena* (William Styles)

> *Loonie* (Coach B. L. Noojin)

> *Lovely* (Emile Barnes, who was more commonly known as *Red*)

> *Luke* (James Luther Sewell)

> *Mo* (Meredith Sanford)

> *Moose* (Guy Morton Jr.)

> *Old Hoss* (Jackson Riggs Stephenson)

> *Rawhide* (Jim Tabor)

> *Red* (Emile Barnes, Al Worthington)

> *Skeeter* (Frank Scalzi)

> *Trackhorse* (Frank Pratt)

> *The Tuscaloosa Terror* (Andy Cohen)

> *Whitey* (Walter Hilcher)

> *The Yankee Killer, Mule, Taters* (Frank Lary)

> *Ziggy* (Ken Sears)

OUR ALABAMA ALL-STARS: BASEBALL

(based on their pro careers)

Starting Pitcher: **FRANK LARY**

Relief Pitcher: **AL WORTHINGTON**

Catcher: **LUKE SEWELL**

First Base: **DAVE MAGADAN**

Second Base: **DEL PRATT**

Shortstop: **JOE SEWELL**

Third Base: **JIM TABOR**

Left Field: **RIGGS STEPHENSON**

Center Field: **DUSTAN MOHR**

Right Field: **IKE BOONE**

Best player: Gotta be **JOE SEWELL,** the only University of Alabama player in the Hall of Fame. A good defensive shortstop who hits .312 lifetime and is a threat to both score and drive in 100 runs a year can play on our team anytime.

PLAYER BIOS

College years are years receiving a varsity letter.

Pro years are years actually played through 2012.

Statistics are career totals through the 2012 season:

Pitchers: win-loss record, earned run average, saves

Nonpitchers: batting average/on-base percentage/slugging percentage

---

MLB: Major League Baseball

NPF: National Pro Fastpitch, a women's professional softball league

HOF: Hall of Fame

ALEX AVILA ■ *Catcher*

COLLEGE: 2006–08 . . . . **MLB:** 2009–12, .261/.359/.432, 1 All-Star Team

In 2007, Alex Avila was a sophomore at Alabama, playing first base, third base, and designated hitter. Four years later, as a catcher, he started in the Major League All-Star Game, helped the Detroit Tigers to a division championship, and won the Silver Slugger Award as the league's best hitter at his position.

Alex Avila's godfather is former Los Angeles Dodgers manager Tommy Lasorda, a longtime family friend.
Credit: KeithAllisonPhoto.com

It's not surprising that Alabama Coach Jim Wells converted Avila to catcher in 2008, Avila's last season at Alabama before the Tigers drafted him that summer. His strong arm and sturdy physique (5-11, 210 pounds) are perfect for the position. And, though like all catchers he throws right-handed, he bats left-handed, giving him the platoon advantage against the more numerous right-handed pitchers.

Avila's father, Al, a longtime baseball executive, is assistant general manager for the Tigers. Grandfather Ralph was an international scout for the Los Angeles Dodgers. Alex said he spent his childhood "shagging balls and hanging out at the ballpark."

At Alabama, Avila was known for his hitting. In 2007 and 2008, he led the team in both runs batted in (61 and 62, respectively) and home runs (14 and 17). But after just five years as a catcher, he draws raves from his Tigers teammates for his defensive ability. Detroit pitcher Justin Verlander told ESPN: "I think most people saw that Alex was going to hit, but I don't think they saw him becoming this good a catcher this quickly. He's fantastic at taking constructive criticism. Sometimes he's not happy to hear some things, but he immediately works on it and gets better at it."

RED BARNES ■ *Center Field*

COLLEGE: 1925–26 . . . . **MLB:** 1927–30, .269/.317/.357

Alabama's 1926 team managed a record of only 10-12-1, but four of its players made the majors. Red Barnes was the most successful—meaning that the other three, Bruce Connatser, Verdo Elmore, and Grant Gillis, didn't make much of a splash at all.

Barnes, 5-10 and 158 pounds, also started at halfback for Alabama's great 1925 (10-0) and 1926 (9-0-1) football teams, both of which laid claims to national championships. He captained the 1926 squad.

In 1927, he played minor-league baseball with his home-state Birmingham Barons, hitting .293 with 13 home runs. The Washington Senators brought him to the big leagues for three games at the end of that season, then made him their regular center fielder in 1928. Barnes, who threw right-handed but batted left-handed, hit .305, with an excellent .391 on-base percentage, 22 doubles, and 15 triples. The next year, his batting average collapsed to .200. The Senators traded him to the Chicago White Sox during the 1930 season, but he hit only .248 that year and never played in the majors again.

He did keep playing in the minor leagues until he was 40, almost always averaging better than .300 at the plate. During his last seven seasons, he doubled as his team's manager. He finally went back home to Suggsville, Alabama, where he operated a small store and post office. He died of lymphoma in 1959, age 55.

Best Tide Team Ever?

The 1919 Alabama baseball team featured seven future major leaguers, including Hall of Famer Joe Sewell (see page 239) and longtime big-league stars Riggs Stephenson (see page 244) and Luke Sewell, Joe's brother (see page 236). The other four were brothers Dan and Ike Boone (see page 222), a pitcher and outfielder, respectively, plus catcher-first baseman Lena Styles and outfielder Frank Pratt. In 1920, the team lost Dan Boone and Styles but added eventual major-league pitcher Ernie Wingard (see page 246). Alabama went 16-2 in 1919 and 15-2 in 1920, winning the Southern Intercollegiate Athletic Association championship each year.

Alabama's 2006 Southeastern Conference champion (44-21) may eclipse those early 20th-century squads in terms of big-league talent. The 2006 team has so far graduated five players to the majors: pitcher David Robertson (see page 237) and catcher Alex Avila (see page 220), both all-stars, plus pitchers Tommy Hunter (see page 229) and Wade LeBlanc (see page 231) and infielder Matt Downs (see page 226).

IKE BOONE ■ *Right Field*

COLLEGE: 1919–20 . . . . **MLB:** 1922–25, 1927, 1930–32, .321/.394/.475; International League HOF, Pacific Coast League HOF

Five batting titles, single-season batting averages of .407 and .402, 55 home runs one year—Ike Boone was one heck of a hitter. In fact, his bat earned him recognition in two halls of fame.

So why has he been forgotten? Because he accomplished most of his feats in the minor leagues, where he compiled an incredible .370 lifetime batting average in 14 seasons (better than Ty Cobb's major league record of .366). In 1929, he had a season for the ages with Mission in the Pacific Coast League, winning the league triple crown with a .407 batting average, 55 home runs, and 218 runs batted in. He played in 198 games (the PCL featured very long seasons), but those were still astonishing numbers.

Boone, 6 feet tall and a muscular 195 pounds, threw right-handed but batted left-handed. He starred for the 1919 and 1920 Alabama teams that went a combined 31-4 (two of those losses coming against the Birmingham Barons professional minor-league team) and won two Southern Intercollegiate Athletic Association championships. He did pretty well in the majors, too. He hit .337 in 1924 and .330 in 1925 for the Boston Red Sox—good for at least one Most Valuable Player vote each year.

But the Red Sox didn't like Boone's fielding or his slowness afoot. And in those days, the minor leagues were independent entities, not controlled by big-league teams. With the majors extending only as far west as St. Louis and as far south as Washington, DC, huge swaths of the country embraced local minor-league heroes every bit as much as, and often more than, they followed the far-off big-league exploits of Rogers Hornsby and Babe Ruth. Minor-league stars might even make more money than they could have in the National or American League.

Ike Boone was definitely a star. Brendan Macgranachan, writing for the baseball website *Seamheads,* called him "the best pure hitter in minor league baseball history." Boone won five batting titles in four different minor leagues. The last came in 1934 when, at age 37, he hit .372 for the Toronto Maple Leafs, was named the International League's most valuable player, and managed the team to the league championship.

If you add all of his professional numbers, Boone compiled 2,893 hits and a .363 batting average over 17 seasons. One heck of a hitter, indeed. He died in 1958, age 61.

The *Moneyball* Man

JEREMY BROWN ■ *Catcher*

COLLEGE: 1999–2002 . . . . **MLB:** 2006, .300/.364/.500 (5 games)

For a guy who played only five games in the major leagues, Jeremy Brown sure received a lot of attention. He got caught in the crossfire between baseball's tobacco-spitting traditionalists and its numbers-crunching computer nerds—which probably cost him a much longer big-league career.

Brown came from Hueytown, Alabama, to star for the Crimson Tide, winning the 2002 Johnny Bench Award as the nation's best college catcher. A right-handed hitter and thrower, he still (through 2012) holds a bunch of school records, including career marks for most games played, most runs scored and batted in, and most walks.

A best-selling book made Jeremy Brown famous, unfortunately for him.
Credit: Justin Lafferty

The latter statistic helped make him famous. The best-selling book *Moneyball* chronicled the 2002 amateur player draft of the Oakland A's and their maverick general manager, Billy Beane. Beane placed more faith in a player's statistics than in the observation-based projections of his scouts. Over the scouts' strenuous objections, he made Brown a first-round draft choice.

Beane loved Brown's willingness to take a walk, which gave him a high on-base percentage. The scouts hated the catcher's less-than-sculpted body (he stood 5-10 and weighed 226 pounds), to which Beane famously replied, "We're not selling jeans here."

So the battle lines were drawn, and poor Jeremy Brown—by all accounts a quiet guy who just wanted to play baseball—drew intense

continued on next page

scrutiny from both sides. Stat geeks cheered him and old-school scouts jeered him, both hoping Brown's success or failure would vindicate their side of the argument.

Brown reached the majors with the A's late in 2006, hitting well in five games. He spent 2007 at the highest level of the minor leagues, bopping 14 home runs and compiling a .276 batting average, a .364 on-base percentage, and a .469 slugging percentage. For a catcher, that's excellent hitting. But Brown received no repeat call-up to the A's.

Eventually, he probably could have returned to the majors and played a few years as an offense-oriented backup catcher. Instead, at age 27, he went home to Hueytown and disappeared from the public spotlight.

The 2011 movie version of *Moneyball* barely mentioned Brown. No doubt he was grateful.

ANDY COHEN ■ *Second Base-Shortstop*

COLLEGE: 1923–25 . . . . **MLB:** 1926, 1928–29, .281/.317/.392

New York fans carried second baseman Andy Cohen off the field on their shoulders after the Giants' 5-2 opening-day win over the Boston Braves in 1928. Superstar second baseman Rogers Hornsby had been traded in the off-season to those very Braves. But Cohen, his replacement, had smacked two singles and a double, scored two runs, and driven in two more. Hornsby had managed merely a harmless single. Who needed him?

Cohen had starred for some good Alabama teams from 1923 through 1925, including the 1924 Southern Conference champions. (Syd Cohen, his brother, pitched for Alabama from 1925 through 1927; see page 248.) Andy Cohen had hit .312 in the Texas League and, after a brief 1926 trial with the Giants, .353 in the International League.

And, not incidentally, he was Jewish. Giants manager John McGraw, battling the star power of the rival New York Yankees' Babe Ruth, hyped Cohen shamelessly, hoping to lure fans from New York's substantial Jewish population. Even vendors got into the act, rechristening their frozen treats as "ice cream Cohens."

The 5-8, 155-pound Cohen—a right-handed batter and thrower—turned in a solid year. He played good defense and hit .274, scoring 64 runs, driving in 59, and launching nine home runs. Hornsby, however, led the league at .387, scored 99 runs, drove in 94, and hit 21 homers. The Giants did win 92 games, one more than they had in 1927. They finished second. (Hornsby's Braves finished seventh.)

Cohen and Giants catcher Shanty Hogan put together a vaudeville act after the season, telling stories and singing parody songs. "If we didn't kill vaudeville, we sure helped," he told a reporter years later. Still, the duo commanded $1,800 a week (more than $24,000 in today's dollars).

In 1929, Cohen improved his batting average to .294 but hit for even less power. It was to be his last year in the big leagues. He was 24.

After playing and managing in the minor leagues, fighting in World War II, and coaching for the Philadelphia Phillies in 1960, Cohen went back to El Paso, Texas, where he had grown up. He started the baseball program at The University of Texas at El Paso and coached there from 1963 through 1978, the first 12 years without pay. Cohen Stadium, home to the El Paso Diablos of the American Association of Independent Professional Baseball, is named for Andy and Syd.

Andy Cohen died in 1988, four days after his 84th birthday.

LANCE CORMIER ■ *Relief Pitcher*

COLLEGE: 1999–2002 . . . .
MLB: 2004–2011, 24-28, 5.07, 3 saves

At first a workhorse reliever, then a workhorse starter at Alabama, the 6-1, 200-pound Lance Cormier pitched mostly out of the bullpen in the major leagues. His career typified the life of a right-handed middle reliever: eight major-league seasons, five major-league teams, 10 minor-league teams (four of them more than once) in eight different leagues, one trade, four free-agent signings, and a peak salary of $1.2 million. Cormier, who was a first-team Academic All-America selection in Alabama in 2002 and graduated with a degree in finance, can especially appreciate that last part. Between seasons and after his career ended in May 2011, he has lived quietly with his family in Tuscaloosa.

Lance Cormier recorded two of his three major-league saves for the Tampa Bay Rays, one of five teams he played for.
Credit: Wikimedia Commons

MATT DOWNS ■ *Infield*

COLLEGE: 2004–06 . . . . **MLB:** 2009–12, .230/.296/.406

At Alabama, Matt Downs had to wait till his senior year for a chance to play. He made the most of it, hitting .298 with 62 runs batted in and 52 runs scored in 2006. With a strong offensive year for the Houston Astros in 2011 (a .276 batting average, a .347 on-base percentage, a .518 slugging percentage, and 10 home runs in only 199 at bats), the right-handed Downs scrapped his way into an "I'll play anywhere" utility role. He manned every infield position plus left and right field. Unfortunately, after a 2012 batting average of.202, the 6-1, 190-pound Downs began 2013 in the Miami Marlins' minor-league system, still hustling in hopes of another chance.

JACKIE HAYES ■ *Second Base*

COLLEGE: 1926–27 . . . . **MLB:** 1927–40, .265/.318/.344; Alabama Sports HOF

At spring training in 1940, Jackie Hayes's right eye began bothering him. Hayes, a 33-year-old second baseman for the Chicago White Sox, was entering his 14th major-league season. After two years playing for average Alabama teams (a combined 23-20-2 record), he had left college early to sign a minor-league contract with the Birmingham Barons in 1927. Before he could play a professional game, the Barons had sold him to the Washington Senators for the then-princely sum of $25,000. By August of that year, he had reached the big leagues with the Senators.

The White Sox had picked him up in 1932. Never much of a hitter, the 5-10, 165-pound Hayes, a right-handed batter and thrower, shone on defense, especially when turning the double play.

But you can't play baseball if you can't see. The eye deteriorated quickly. Hayes hit .195 in 18 games in 1940 before giving up. By August, his right eye was blind. He returned home to Clanton, Alabama. Three years later, he lost the vision in his left eye as well. Nevertheless, he was elected tax collector for Chilton County and, with his wife's help, ran the office for 12 years.

In an interview years later, he said he had no regrets. "I loved baseball," he said. "My daddy wanted me to follow in his shoes and be a doctor, but when I was in the laboratory working on an experiment, and the soft spring breezes drifted through the window, and the crack of ball against bat could be distinctly heard in the distance, I knew I had to be a ballplayer."

He died in 1983, age 76.

How About That!

Southern boy and University of Alabama graduate Mel Allen achieved his greatest fame as a Yankee. Allen announced New York Yankees baseball games on radio almost every year from 1939 through 1964. He also did play-by-play for 22 World Series, 24 All-Star Games, numerous college bowl games, and three National Football League teams, becoming a national celebrity for his exuberant drawl and such catch phrases as "How about that!" He won a whole new generation of fans as host of the syndicated television show *This Week in Baseball* from 1977 until his death of heart failure at age 83 in 1996.

Allen entered the University of Alabama at age 15 and earned an undergraduate degree and then a law degree. He was student manager of the football team and public-address announcer for home games. In 1935, he began doing radio broadcasts of both Alabama and Auburn University football games while still in law school.

Mel Allen makes a point while announcing a 1955 New York Yankees game for WPIX TV in New York.
Credit: Library of Congress, Prints & Photographs Division, NYWT&S Collection

During a 1936 Christmas vacation in New York, he auditioned at CBS, more or less on a whim. The network hired him the next year as a $45-a-week news and sports announcer. In 1978, Allen became one of the first two members of the National Baseball Hall of Fame broadcasters' wing, along with a former colleague and rival, Yankees and Brooklyn Dodgers announcer Red Barber.

GREG HIBBARD ■ *Pitcher*

COLLEGE: 1985–86 . . . .**MLB:** 1989–94, 57-50, 4.05, 1 save

A *"finesse" left-hander,* 6-0, 180-pound Greg Hibbard didn't throw hard. But he didn't walk many batters, and he kept the ball down, inducing ground balls while minimizing line drives. He was a relief pitcher at Alabama and still holds the Crimson Tide's single-season record for most appearances, 29 in 1986.

In the major leagues he thrived as a starter. In 1993, he went 15-11 with a 3.96 earned run average for the Chicago Cubs. That netted him a three-year, $6.75 million free-agent contract from the Seattle Mariners—big money at the time. Unfortunately, Hibbard suffered a torn rotator cuff in his pitching shoulder, struggled to a 1-5 record in half a season, and never pitched again. He has spent the past decade as a pitching coach in the Cleveland Indians' minor-league system.

BUTCH HOBSON ■ *Third Base*

COLLEGE: 1970, 1972–73 . . . .**MLB:** 1975–1982, .248/.297/.423

Clell "Butch" Hobson, 6-foot-1 and 193 pounds, played baseball the way he played football for Bear Bryant at Alabamaa. Fans loved his all-out style, but it took a toll on his body.

Hobson, a backup quarterback, got a chance to shine in the 1972 Orange Bowl. Nebraska beat Alabama, 38–6, to win the national championship, but Hobson, substituting in the fourth quarter for the injured Terry Davis, ran for 59 yards on 15 carries out of the wishbone formation.

The next year, his senior season, Hobson dropped football to concentrate on baseball. Hobson later told *Baseball Digest,* "I told coach Bryant my decision, and he told me, 'Well, Butch, from what I've seen of you on the baseball field, you'll be playing football for me next year.'"

For once, Bryant was wrong. Hobson, who both threw and batted right-handed, led Alabama in hits (38), home runs (13), and runs batted in (37), and tied for the lead in runs (20). The Boston Red Sox picked him in the eighth round of the 1973 draft.

In 1977, his first full big-league season, Hobson hit .265 with 30 home runs and 112 runs batted in as the Red Sox third baseman. The next season, bone chips sometimes made his right elbow lock up as he threw. Hobson committed 43 errors and had a fielding percentage of .899, the first sub-.900 fielding percentage for a big-league regular since 1916. He also hit .250 with only 17 homers and 80 RBI.

After elbow surgery, Hobson rebounded in 1979 to hit .261 with 28 homers and 93 RBI (and commit only 25 errors). It was his last good year. Injuries and, he later admitted, substance abuse, cut his career short.

In 1987, he turned to managing. Again, he achieved early success. *Baseball America* named him its Minor League Manager of the Year in 1991. But in three years managing the Red Sox (1992–94), he never finished above .500. A return to managing in the minors was interrupted in 1996 by a charge of cocaine possession.

Hobson entered a first-offender program, rebuilt his life, and found a niche in baseball's independent minor leagues. Through the 2013 season, he had managed for 14 straight years in the Atlantic League and Canadian-American Association, most recently for the Lancaster (Pennsylvania) Barnstormers of the Atlantic League.

TOMMY HUNTER ■ *Pitcher*

COLLEGE: 2006–07 . . . . **MLB:** 2008–12, 33-24, 4.77

A durable college starter who topped 100 innings both of his seasons at Alabama, Tommy Hunter seemed on his way to big things in 2010.

But after spring-training injuries kept him off the opening-day roster for three straight years, the Texas Rangers, who had taken him as a first-round draft choice in 2007, traded him to the Baltimore Orioles in 2011. Still mostly a starting pitcher, Hunter continued to flounder until the Orioles made him a full-time reliever in 2013. Suddenly, nobody could hit him.

What made the difference? Learning to pitch, not just throw, Hunter said. The massive right-hander (6-3, 280 pounds) with the impish personality (his Twitter handle is @TommyGoesBoom) said he finally started planning pitch sequences instead of just rearing back and trying to throw the ball as hard as he can. "Set guys up, throw the right pitch with confidence," he said. "All I know is, I've got a pretty good game plan right now."

Tommy Hunter was a two-time Junior Olympics gold medalist in judo.

Credit: KeithAllisonPhoto.com

The Hobson family has now sent three generations into pro baseball. Butch's dad, Clell Lavern Hobson Sr., a football and baseball star at Alabama, was a minor-league second baseman from 1953 through 1957. K. C. Hobson is a first baseman in the Toronto Blue Jays' minor-league system.

KELLY KRETSCHMAN ■ *Right Field*

COLLEGE: 1998–2001 . . . . **OLYMPICS:** 2004, 1 gold medal; 2008, 1 silver medal; **NPF:** 2005–2007, 2009–2012, .336/.468/.519, 4 All-Star Teams

Kelly Kretschman has played for USA Softball, the American national team, as well as in the National Pro Fastpitch league.

Credit: USSA Media

Slugging right fielder Kelly Kretschman, a right-handed thrower but left-handed batter, played on her fourth National Pro Fastpitch championship team in 2012 and made her fourth all-star team. Over the equivalent of a little more than one major-league baseball season (spread across seven pro years with the USSSA Pride of Kissimmee, Florida, the Washington Glory, the Connecticut Brakettes, and the Akron Racers), she has batted .336, hit 23 home runs, scored 123 runs, driven in 111, and walked an amazing 148 times.

The 5-foot-5 Kretschman won a gold medal with the U.S. Olympic team in 2004 and a silver in 2008. That followed an Alabama career during which she was a four-time National Fastpitch Coaches Association All-America pick. She led the NCAA in home runs with 25 as a freshman shortstop and still holds Alabama career records for most walks (161), runs (288), and home runs (60).

After coaching during the off-season at Kentucky and Maryland, Kretschman has joined fellow softball pros Caitlin Lowe and Monica Abbott to put on softball clinics under the name Triple Threat Camps.

FRANK LARY ■ *Pitcher*

COLLEGE: 1949–50 . . . . **MLB:** 1954–65, 128-116, 3.49, 11 saves, 3 All-Star Teams; 1 Gold Glove; Alabama Sports HOF

"The Yankee Killer." That's what they called Frank Lary in the 1950s, when the lordly New York Yankees ruled the American League and Lary's Detroit Tigers finished either fourth or fifth for six straight years. Lary, a fun-loving, guitar-playing Southerner from Northport, Alabama, had a lifetime record against the Yankees of 28-13.

The 5-11, 175-pound Lary beat lots of other teams, too. In fact, he might have reached the Hall of Fame if an arm injury hadn't robbed him of his fastball in 1962. Through 1961, at age 31, he had a 117-93 win-loss record with two 20-win seasons and a 3.33 earned-run average in eight big-league years. At the same age, Hall of Famer and fellow right-hander Jim Bunning, Lary's longtime teammate, was 118-87 with one 20-win season and a 3.45 ERA in nine years. After the injury, Lary managed a record of only 11-23 in four years before retiring.

After his playing career, Lary did a little coaching and scouting before going back home to Northport, just a few miles from where he had starred for Alabama, and getting into auto sales. He had turned pro after his sophomore

WADE LEBLANC ■ *Pitcher*

COLLEGE: 2004–06 . . . .
MLB: 2008–12, 19-27, 4.38

Wade LeBlanc won a fistful of awards at Alabama, including a spot on *Collegiate Baseball* newspaper's All-America team in 2006. Just two years later, the 6-foot-2, 215-pound left-hander reached the majors with the San Diego Padres. He never quite established himself in four years with the Padres and a year-plus with the Miami Marlins, mostly as a starter. A June 2013 trade gave him a fresh start in the bullpen of the Houston Astros.

Wade LeBlanc holds Alabama's single-season and career strikeout records.

Credit: Wikimedia Commons

DAVE MAGADAN ■ *Third Base-First Base*

COLLEGE: 1981–83 . . . . **MLB:** 1986–2001, .288/.390/.377; College Baseball HOF

Dave Magadan (left) laughs with slugger David Ortiz in the Boston Red Sox dugout.

Credit: Photo by Cyn Donnelly/www.toeingtherubber.com

Dave Magadan, a brilliant college player for Alabama, just didn't fit in the majors. In 1983, his last year at Alabama, he won the Golden Spikes Award as the player of the year, thanks to one of the most awesome seasons in college baseball history: a .525 batting average, 67 runs scored, and an incredible 95 runs batted in in 56 games.

In the pros, Magadan, a 6-3, 190-pound right-handed thrower and left-handed batter, delivered decent defense at third and first base. Offensively, he excelled at getting on base, by hit or walk. He's one of the few recent players with more career walks, 718, than strikeouts, 546. He almost never pulled the ball, instead lashing line drives to the opposite field, often slicing them down the left field line.

But he had no power (42 career home runs in 16 seasons) and even less speed (11 stolen bases), so managers didn't know where to put him in the batting order. His career tailed off in a succession of years as a fill-in starter and pinch hitter.

After he stopped playing, Magadan found his calling. Following three and a half years as hitting coach with the San Diego Padres, he took the same position with the Boston Red Sox in 2007—and that year finally got a World Series championship ring.

The Red Sox finished among the American League's top three teams in runs scored in five of Magadan's six years in Boston. For 2013, the Texas Rangers gave him a big raise to move west and work his magic with their hitters. If only he could have had himself as hitting coach.

year at Alabama, when he won 10 games and helped pitch the Crimson Tide into the College World Series.

Four of his six brothers—Al, Ed, Gene, and Joe—also lettered in baseball for the Crimson Tide. In fact, after Frank led Alabama in pitching wins with 10 in 1950, Al (better known as a star end for the football team) led with 6 in 1951, and brother Gene led with 5 in 1952 and 8 in 1955. Al also pitched briefly in the major leagues; see page 249.

FRANK MENECHINO ■ *Infield*

COLLEGE: 1992–93 . . . . **MLB:** 1999–2005, .240/.358/.383

At Alabama, right-handed second baseman Frank Menechino hit for a nice average (.349 in 1992) with some triples, some stolen bases, and good defense. That got him drafted by the Chicago White Sox—in the 43rd round, as the 1,261st player chosen overall. In late 1999, after six years in the minor leagues, Menechino, age 28, finally reached the majors with the Oakland A's. He spent most of the next six seasons with the A's and the Toronto Blue Jays, occasionally as a starting second baseman but primarily as a utility infielder.

The 5-9, 175-pound Menechino, not really expected to make the big leagues, hustled and scrapped his way to a seven-year American League career. His reported major-league salaries totaled $2,305,500. He missed out on some of that because of occasional demotions to the minors, during which he didn't receive big-league pay. But still, not bad. He's now back in the minors, coaching in the New York Yankees' system.

DUSTAN MOHR ■ *Outfield*

COLLEGE: 1995–97 . . . . **MLB:** 2001–2007, .249/.322/.422

A slugging outfielder who bashed 25 home runs his last season at Alabama, the 6-foot, 210-pound Dustan Mohr began his major-league career solidly. In 2002, his first full season, he hit .269 for the Minnesota Twins with 12 home runs and finished eighth in Rookie of the Year voting. But he never matched that performance and slipped out of the majors after seven games with Tampa Bay in 2007. Mohr, a right-handed hitter and thrower, hung on through 2010 in the minors, finishing with the Long Island Ducks of the independent Atlantic League.

KELLEY MONTALVO ■ *Third Base*

COLLEGE: 2006–09 . . . . **NPF:** 2010–12, .177/.342/.264

Always known for her glove, Kelley Montalvo was the National Pro Fastpitch co-defensive player of the year in 2012. But Montalvo contributed with the bat that year as well. In her third season with the Akron Racers, she posted career highs in batting average (.202), on-base percentage (.374), slugging percentage (.393), hits (17), runs (14), runs batted in (7), doubles (5), home runs (3), and games played (44).

Montalvo, a right-handed thrower and batter, stands just 4-11 but blasted 30 home runs and hit .333 during her four-year career at Alabama. After college, she delayed her pro career a year to care for her mother, who was ill. In 2013, Montalvo took an off-season job as an assistant softball coach at Middle Tennessee State University, but her ultimate goal lies farther west. She's writing a movie script and wants to work in Hollywood.

CHARLOTTE MORGAN ■ *First Base*

COLLEGE: 2007–10 . . . . **NPF:** 2010–2012, .255/.350/.454

A top National Pro Fastpitch slugger her first two years with the USSSA Pride of Kissimmee, Florida, Charlotte Morgan slumped to a .174 batting average in 2012, although she did bash a career-high six home runs. The 5-foot-10 Morgan, a rare left-handed thrower but right-handed batter, was the Southeastern Conference Player of the Year in both her junior and senior seasons at Alabama. She reached double figures in home runs all four of her years with the Crimson Tide and added 51 wins (against 12 losses) as a pitcher. The Pride made her the league's first overall draft choice in 2010, and she won the NPF home run derby that year.

In the off-season, she has been the pitching coach for the University of Maryland and an instructor at softball camps. The Akron Racers signed her for 2013, reuniting her with former Alabama teammate Kelley Montalvo (see previous bio).

ANDY PHILLIPS ■ *First Base-Third Base*

COLLEGE: 1996–99 . . . . **MLB:** 2004–08, .250/.294/.384

After setting school records as a shortstop for Alabama (he's still the all-time leader in home runs and total bases), spending parts of four seasons with the New York Yankees, and playing for two years in Japan, Andy Phillips came

The Greatest Player You've Never Heard Of

DEL PRATT ■ *Second Base*

COLLEGE: 1908–09 . . . . **MLB:** 1912–1924, .292/.345/.403; Alabama Sports HOF

The first Alabama player to make it to the major leagues, Del Pratt was one of the elite second base-man of his time. But he never played on a pennant-winning team. Baseball's 1920s offen-sive explosion came too late in his career to boost his numbers much. And his argumentative nature (after playing as an under-grad at Georgia Tech, he studied law at Alabama, though he didn't get a law degree) got him traded from the New York Yankees just as Babe Ruth was beginning to take the team to glory. So the fiery player described as a "high-strung Southern gentleman" by Branch Rickey, one of his manag-ers, has been forgotten.

Del Pratt poses for a 1913 photo. Because of the era's slow film speeds, photographers generally created staged shots instead of trying to capture game action.

Credit: George Grantham Bain Collection/Library of Congress

He certainly kicked up a ruckus in his day. Pratt, a right-hander, was big for the era at 5-11 and 175 pounds and a fine fielder. He had been shortstop and team captain both of his years at Alabama for squads with a cumulative record of 33-7. In the majors, he finished among the league's top 10 twice in runs, five times in runs batted in (leading the league with 103 in 1916), eight times in doubles, three times in home runs, and twice in slugging percentage.

continued on next page

He always seemed to be embroiled in controversy. Once, he sued his team's owner, Phil Ball of the St. Louis Browns, for libel after Ball accused unspecified players of "laying down" (i.e., not trying their hardest). Pratt frequently held out for a larger salary, threatening to take offers to coach football at Alabama, Michigan, and other schools. (As a running back and dropkicker, he had starred in football as well as baseball at Alabama, and he was an assistant football coach for the Crimson Tide in 1912.)

Pratt spent his first six major-league seasons with the Browns. He also played for the Yankees (who traded him for being too open about his ambition to manage the Yankees in place of the incumbent, Miller Huggins), Boston Red Sox, and Detroit Tigers. After the 1924 season, the Tigers released him, though he had hit better than .300 for five straight years. Pratt headed south and spent several years as a player-manager in the Texas League. In 1927, at age 39, he won the league triple crown with a .386 batting average, 32 home runs, and 140 runs batted in for the Waco Cubs.

Pratt lived in Texas the rest of his life, running a gas station in Galveston for many years. When he was inducted into the Alabama Sports Hall of Fame in 1972, he told the Galveston *Daily News*, "I've got a pretty good record. But I don't talk about it much." He died in 1977, age 89.

home in 2011. The 6-foot, 205-pound Tuscaloosa native, a right-handed hitter known as one of the nicest guys in baseball, is a hitting and infield coach at his alma mater. His wife is Christian singer-songwriter Bethany Barr Phillips. His cousin Paul Phillips (see page 249), a catcher, played in the major leagues for parts of seven years in the 2000s.

LUKE SEWELL ■ *Catcher*

COLLEGE: 1919–21 . . . . **MLB:** 1921–39, 1942, .259/.323/.341, 1 All-Star Team; Alabama Sports HOF

Luke Sewell always was a fast learner. As a child in a one-room schoolhouse, he kept pace with older brother Joe so well that the two eventually enrolled at the University of Alabama together when Luke was only 15. He thus got to join Joe on the great 1919 and 1920 Alabama teams that won consecutive Southern Intercollegiate Athletic Association championships.

DAVID ROBERTSON ■ *Relief Pitcher*

COLLEGE: 2005–06 . . . .
MLB: 2008–12, 16-13, 2.95,
5 saves, 1 All-Star Team

A closer at Alabama, in his hometown of Tuscaloosa, David Robertson didn't draw much big-league interest despite impressive strikeout rates (12.8 per nine innings as a freshman in 2005). Scouts thought him a bit small (he's generously listed at 5-11 and 195 pounds). The New York Yankees finally drafted him in the 17th round. In 2008, he reached the big leagues as a middle reliever.

In 2011, his fourth year with the Yankees, everything came together. Robertson's strikeout rate soared to an incredible 13.5 batters per nine innings. He pitched in the All-Star Game (his catcher was former Crimson Tide teammate Alex Avila) and received votes for both the Cy Young and the Most Valuable Player awards.

Robertson, a right-hander, can throw 95 mph, and he's developed a hard cut fastball that moves in on the hands of left-handed batters. He became the Yankees' eighth-inning setup man—and, when the legendary Mariano Rivera suffered a knee injury early in 2012, the team's closer. Unfortunately, Robertson himself went on the disabled list a few days later with a strained muscle in his rib cage and never quite got back to his usual dominating self all season.

Teammate Joba Chamberlain nicknamed Robertson "Houdini" because of his propensity for getting himself into jams with walks and then escaping without giving up a run. Fans love his old-school high-socks look—and all those strikeouts.

David Robertson and his wife, Erin, started a foundation called High Socks for Hope to help 2011 Tuscaloosa tornado victims.
Credit: KeithAllisonPhoto.com

JOSH RUTLEDGE ■ *Shortstop–Second Base*

COLLEGE: 2008–10 . . . .
MLB: 2012, .274/.306/.469

After batting .347 during his three-year Alabama career and setting team single-season records for most hits (107) and runs batted in (69) by a shortstop, Josh Rutledge made it to the major leagues in 2012. The Colorado Rockies called him up to replace injured shortstop Troy Tulowitzki. Rutledge made an excellent first impression, batting .274 with 20 doubles and eight home runs in 73 games.

He won the Rockies' starting second baseman job in 2013. However, Rutledge, a 6-1, 190-pound right-handed hitter and thrower, struggled to control the strike zone, and his defense drew mixed reviews. But with Tulowitzki having lost significant time to injuries in half of his eight seasons so far, Rutledge will likely get several chances to prove himself.

Josh Rutledge was the Colorado Rockies' third-round draft choice in 2010.
Credit: David B. King

After graduating, Luke played just 17 minor-league games before being called up to join Joe again, this time with the Cleveland Indians. Luke stayed in the majors for 20 seasons. His 5-9, 160-pound body withstood the rigors of catching so well that he still ranks 26th in career games at the position (1,562).

Sewell, a right-handed batter and thrower, was, frankly, a lousy hitter. But pitchers loved having him behind the plate (he caught three no-hitters). Opposing would-be base stealers hated it. Sewell led the league in assists by a catcher four years, including three years in a row (1926–28).

In 1933, the Indians traded Sewell to the Washington Senators. Player-manager Joe Cronin, the Senators' shortstop, put Sewell in charge of the pitching staff. The Senators won their first pennant since 1925, and Sewell got to play in his only World Series, which the Senators lost to the Giants.

JOE SEWELL ■ *Shortstop-Third Base*

COLLEGE: 1918–20; coach 1964–69 . . . .
MLB: 1920–33, .312/.391/.413; Baseball HOF, College Baseball HOF, Alabama Sports HOF

At Alabama, Joe Sewell played second base. His 1918–20 teams went 44-8 and won three straight Southern Intercollegiate Athletic Association championships. Just five months after leaving the campus, he was a world champion.

Late in the 1920 season, the Cleveland Indians' shortstop, Ray Chapman, was struck in the head and killed by a pitch. To replace him, the Indians plucked the little man with the big ears from the minor-league New Orleans Pelicans.

Sewell, 5-foot-6 and 155 pounds, was uncharacteristically shaky in the field, but he hit .329 in 22 games. The Indians won the pennant and then the World Series, beating the Brooklyn Dodgers in seven games.

Sewell is remembered today mostly for one thing: he rarely

Joe Sewell shows off his "Worlds Champions" uniform after his Cleveland Indians won the World Series in his rookie year.
Credit: George Grantham Bain Collection/Library of Congress

struck out. In his 11 years with the Indians, he struck out only 99 times total. He also hit .320, and his 654 walks helped give him a superb .398 on-base percentage. From 1922 into 1930, he played in 1,103 consecutive games, still the seventh-longest streak in major-league history.

The Indians released him after the 1930 season. The New York Yankees snapped him up and made him their third baseman for three years. Sewell, a right-handed thrower, batted left-handed, so he could reach the shallow right-field fence in Yankee Stadium if he pulled the ball down the right-field line. In

continued on next page

1932, he hit 11 home runs, almost a quarter of his career total of 49—all 11 at Yankee Stadium.

In both of his World Series, Sewell witnessed the improbable. In 1920, his second-base partner, Bill Wambsganss, made the only unassisted triple play in World Series history. In 1932, when Sewell helped the Yankees sweep the Chicago Cubs in four games, Yankees slugger Babe Ruth allegedly "called his shot" before blasting a home run against Cubs pitcher Charlie Root. Ruth did make some sort of gesture. People still argue over whether he meant to signal a homer. "I don't care what anybody says," Sewell insisted. "He did it."

Sewell coached with the Yankees in 1934 and 1935 and later scouted for other teams. Back in Alabama, he opened a hardware store and worked for a dairy in Tuscaloosa. In 1964, he returned to his alma mater as baseball coach. In six seasons, until he reached the mandatory retirement age of 70, his teams posted a 106-79 record. His 1968 squad took the Southeastern Conference championship. One of his pitchers, a 1966 10th-round draft choice of the New York Yankees, was a lefty named Ken Stabler, who decided that he preferred football (see page 156).

In 1978, the university renamed its baseball stadium Sewell-Thomas Stadium in Sewell's honor. Today, most people call it "The Joe."

Sewell built a reputation as a kind man. During the Depression, he brought bats, balls, and gloves to children in his native Elmore County, Alabama. His marriage to the former Willie Veal produced three children and lasted 63 years, until her death in 1984.

Sewell died on March 6, 1990, in Mobile, Alabama. He was 91 years old.

His success as the Senators' de facto pitching coach presaged his greatest post-playing feat. He took over as manager of the woeful St. Louis Browns in 1941. Three years later, he led them to their only American League championship. Looking at the roster, it's hard to see how. Most fans today wouldn't recognize a single name. The star was shortstop Vern Stephens (.293, 20 home runs, a league-leading 109 runs batted in), the only player on the team with more than 83 RBI or 11 homers. Again, Sewell's team lost the World Series, this time to the cross-town St. Louis Cardinals.

After several other managing and coaching jobs, Sewell left baseball in the mid-1950s and became owner of a bronze castings company. He retired in 1970, played a lot of golf, and died of colon cancer in 1987, age 86.

FRED SINGTON ■ *Outfield*

COLLEGE: 1928–30 . . . . **MLB:** 1934–39, .271/.382/.401;
College Football HOF, Alabama Sports HOF

At Alabama, Fred Sington earned All-America honors in both football and baseball. He finished his college football career with a 10-0 season that included a 24–0 thrashing of Washington State in the Rose Bowl, in which he starred as a tackle and linebacker. He was such a hero that singer Rudy Vallee dedicated his version of the 1930 hit song "Football Freddy" to Sington. Here are, in their entirety, the lyrics:

Fred Sington spent his last two years in baseball with the Brooklyn Dodgers, hitting a combined .307.

Credit: Courtesy of Fred Sington's family

> *Football Freddy, rugged and tan;*
> *Football Freddy, my collegiate man.*
> *When he huddles, he's dynamite;*
> *How he cuddles on a Saturday night.*
> *He can't speak Latin or Greek;*
> *He's not too good at school,*
> *But when he kisses your cheek,*
> *He knocks you for a ghoul.*
> *Rough and ready, no one can tan*
> *Football Freddy, my collegiate man.*

Check out the snappy version by the Six Jumping Jacks on YouTube. "Knock you for a ghoul," incidentally, was a 1920s variation of "knock you for a loop." We have no idea how it originated, and we're not sure we want to know. Anyway, Football Freddy starred off the field as well. He was accepted into the Phi Beta Kappa academic honor society and won the Pan Hellenic Award for best student. He even played saxophone in the band.

The square-jawed, strapping Sington—6-2, 215 pounds, and the Crimson Tide's second-fastest player—received post-college offers from professional football, baseball, and wrestling, plus a Hollywood movie studio.

Why did he choose baseball? Probably because the National Football League, just 10 years old at the time, got about as much public attention as the Arena Football League does today. Baseball, college football, even boxing and horse racing enjoyed considerably more popularity—and baseball offered significantly more financial potential as well.

continued on next page

Sington played for parts of six years as a major-league outfielder, never as a regular. The Washington Senators had him for four years before trading him to the Brooklyn Dodgers for the final two seasons of his career. Sington was probably better than his teams realized. His ability to work pitchers for walks, an underappreciated skill at the time, gave him an excellent career on-base percentage of .382. He had been a pitcher as well as an outfielder at Alabama, and he threw out eight base runners in only 141 games in the big leagues.

His minor-league power (he hit 29 home runs at the top level of the minors in 1934) didn't translate to the big leagues, where he totaled only seven home runs in 516 at bats. However, Sington was right-handed, and Griffith Stadium, the Senators' home park, was death to right-handed sluggers. The left-field fence was more than 400 feet away at the foul line; the longest comparable distance at any current major-league stadium is 355 feet.

Sington spent five years in the Navy during World War II, then came home to Birmingham and became a star in the business world. He started a successful chain of sporting goods stores. He also worked as a football official in the Southeastern Conference and the NFL, and became a member of practically every civic and charitable organization in town. His sons, Fred Sington Jr. and Dave Sington, both tackles like their father (Fred Jr. was also a kicker), lettered at Alabama in the late 1950s. Grandson Fred Sington III was an offensive lineman and punter at Troy State (now Troy University) in the late 1980s and is a sportswriter in Gadsden, Alabama.

Even today, more than a decade after Sington's death in 1998 at age 88, mention of his name in Birmingham makes faces light up in fond remembrance. Football Freddy may have been only an OK pro baseball player, but he was a great man.

CRAIG SHIPLEY ■ *Infield*

COLLEGE: 1982–84 . . . . **MLB:** 1986–87, 1989, 1991-98, .271/.302/.371

Hailing from way *down south* (Australia), Craig Shipley hit a home run in his first at-bat for Alabama, started at shortstop for two years, then carved out an 11-year major-league career with five teams as a light-hitting but defensively versatile right-handed utility infielder. From 2006 until 2011, the 6-1, 175-pound Shipley led the international scouting department of the Boston Red Sox. In 2012, the Arizona Diamondbacks named him an assistant to general manager Kevin Towers, with responsibilities that included international scouting and evaluation of the team's farm system.

JIM TABOR ■ *Third Base*

COLLEGE: 1935–36 . . . .**MLB:** 1938–47, .270/.322/.418

Considered a budding star his first few years with the Boston Red Sox, Jim "Rawhide" Tabor burned out quickly. Tabor had played for Tilden "Happy" Campbell's first two Alabama teams, both Southeastern Conference champions. Big for the time at 6-2 and 175 pounds, he achieved major-league career peaks of 21 home runs (1940) and 101 runs batted (1941). A right-handed batter and thrower, he drew raves for his defense and possessed maybe the league's most powerful infield arm.

But Tabor was prone to injuries (partly because of his hard-nosed, sometimes hotheaded playing style) and he had a reputation as a drinking man. He entered the Army after the 1944 season. When he returned to baseball in 1946 after World War II's end, it was with the Philadelphia Phillies, to whom the Red Sox had sold him. He struggled to a .235 batting average with only four home runs in 1947, and that ended his major-league career. He was not yet 31. He continued playing in the minor leagues until 1952. Tabor died of heart failure in 1953, just 36 years old.

Jim Tabor tries to avoid the catcher's tag as he slides home.
Credit: Wikimedia Commons

RIGGS STEPHENSON ■ *Left Field-Second Base*

COLLEGE: 1919–20 . . . . **MLB:** 1921–34, .336/.407/.473;
Alabama Sports HOF

From 1921 through 1925, the Cleveland Indians somehow couldn't find a regular spot in their lineup for a second baseman whose yearly batting averages were .330, .339, .319, .371, and .296. So they traded Jackson Riggs "Old Hoss" Stephenson to the Chicago Cubs, who had correctly diagnosed the problem: Stephenson couldn't really play second base.

His football days at Alabama had damaged Old Hoss's right shoulder— his throwing shoulder. (He also batted right-handed.) The Cubs put him in left field, where his weak arm posed less of a problem. In 1927, Stephenson, at age 29, blossomed into a star, hitting .344 with 101 runs scored, 82 runs batted in, and a league-leading 46 doubles. He wasn't big (5-10, 185 pounds) and didn't hit a lot of home runs. But over the next six years, he posted batting averages ranging from .319 to .367. He received Most Valuable Player votes in three separate years.

In the 1932 World Series, Stephenson witnessed one of the most controversial plays in baseball history: New York Yankees slugger Babe Ruth's "called shot" home run in the third game, played at the Cubs' Wrigley Field. Did Ruth really gesture in advance that he was going to hit the homer? Years later, Stephenson said he wasn't sure. But he added:

"I can tell you this. That was the only ball in the nine years that I was there that was hit over the stands in center field. There never was a ball hit near that far while I was there. Babe was unusual. He was just out of the ordinary. He was a fellow that didn't take good care of himself, but he could rise to the occasion."

Could modern shoulder surgery have given Stephenson a Hall of Fame career? Probably. Except for throwing, he was apparently a good-fielding second baseman. In fact, he played the more demanding position of shortstop at Alabama, relegating Joe Sewell (see page 239), later a star major-league shortstop, to second base. In 1952, *Newsweek* named Stephenson to its all-time college baseball team.

Stephenson compiled an excellent .336 lifetime batting average. More playing time during his Indians years would have put him over the 1,000 mark in both runs scored and runs batted in (he finished at 714 and 773, respectively). That's Hall of Fame territory for a middle infielder.

Stephenson went directly to the Indians from college, leaving before the end of the spring semester to replace injured second baseman Bill Wambsganss. There he also joined his old Crimson Tide teammate and lifelong friend Sewell.

Brother Acts

Four sets of brothers played baseball at Alabama and in the major leagues. Hall of Famer Joe Sewell (see page 239) and his brother Luke (see page 236) starred for many years in the American League. Their younger brother Tommy played for the Crimson Tide in 1926 and 1927 and made one pinch-hitting appearance for the Chicago Cubs in 1927. He had a five-year minor-league career (1927–31) as a light-hitting infielder.

A Sewell cousin, Truett "Rip" Sewell, a year younger than Tommy, attended Vanderbilt and pitched in 13 major-league seasons (1932 and 1938-49), winning 143 games. He famously employed a high-arcing blooper pitch nicknamed the "eephus pitch." Joe, Luke, and Rip have all been inducted into the Alabama Sports Hall of Fame.

Ike and Dan Boone were definitely heavy hitters, though it took Dan a while to get there. Dan (whose real name was James Albert Boone) played baseball for Alabama in 1918–19 and Ike (see page 222) in 1919–20. Dan began as a pitcher but had only middling success in either the major (an 8-13 cumulative win-loss record in 1919 and 1921–23) or minor leagues (a 72-64 record in six seasons).

During the 1925 season, at age 30, he moved to the outfield. Starting in 1926, he ripped off season batting averages of .399, .342, .419, .372, .395, .372, .349, and .307, and home run totals of 28, 12, 38, 46, 25, 23, 17, and 14, all in the lower levels of the minor leagues.

In 1929, the Boones combined to hit 101 home runs: 55 by Ike for Mission in the Pacific Coast League, and 46 by Dan for High Point in the Piedmont League. Each total was a career high.

Andy Cohen was, briefly, the toast of New York (see page 224). Younger brother Syd, a pitcher, compiled a 3-7 record with a 4.54 earned run average in 1934, 1936, and 1937 with the Washington Senators. He bounced around the minor leagues until he was 49, stringing together a bunch of unexciting years (13-10, 11-10, 16-6, 7-8, 8-9, 8-6, 11-16, etc.) and finishing with a 133-157 minor-league record.

The Detroit Tigers' Frank Lary (see page 231) was one of the American League's top starting pitchers in the 1950s. Older brother Al, a star football receiver at Alabama who also played baseball and basketball, pitched in a total of 16 games for the Chicago Cubs in 1954 and 1962, going 0-1. In the minor leagues from 1951 through 1964 (except for 1953–54, when he was an Army officer who earned a bronze star in Korea), he won 103 games and lost 100.

After Stephenson's baseball days ended, he opened a lumberyard in his hometown of Akron, Alabama, then had an automobile dealership in Tuscaloosa before retiring. He died in Tuscaloosa in 1985, at age 87.

ERNIE WINGARD ■ *Pitcher-First Base*

COLLEGE: 1920–21 . . . .**MLB:** 1924–27, 29-43, 4.64, 4 saves

Connoisseurs of oddball statistics love Ernie Wingard, one of six future major leaguers on the 15-2 Alabama team of 1920. Wingard's 13 victories for the St. Louis Browns in 1924 are the most rookie-year victories by anyone whose first professional season came in the major leagues. He hit three home runs in 1927, which ties for the second-most by a pitcher in his last major-league season. The 6-2, 175-pound left-hander struck out only 101 batters in $688^1/_3$ career innings.

In 1927, when Babe Ruth hit a record 60 home runs, Wingard gave up No. 42. It was his last major-league season; he posted a 2-13 record with a 6.56 earned run average.

In 1928, Wingard rebounded to 24-10 with a 3.27 ERA for the minor-league Milwaukee Brewers. The Philadelphia Athletics reportedly paid $20,000 for Wingard's 1929 contract but offered to return him to Milwaukee, subject to possible recall. Baseball Commissioner Kenesaw Mountain Landis voided the deal, ruling that the A's and Brewers had conspired to circumvent a draft of minor-league players.

While playing semipro ball after college, Wingard had befriended former star outfielder Shoeless Joe Jackson, whom Landis had banned from organized baseball for involvement in the fixing of the 1919 World Series. During Wingard's first year with the Browns, Jackson traveled with the rookie to help him adjust to the big leagues. Did the imperious Landis block Wingard from the big leagues in 1929 as a warning that he should choose his friends more carefully?

We'll never know. We do know that the A's that year won the first of three straight American League pennants—while Wingard pitched in the minor leagues for Toledo.

Unfortunately, he pitched badly (10-15, 5.03 ERA), then became primarily a first baseman for the rest of his career, all of it spent in the minor leagues. He batted and threw left-handed, and he could hit: .342 with 24 homers in 1930, .343 in 1932, and .353 in 1941, his last year, as a 40-year-old player-manager in the low-level minors.

In 1977, at age 76, Wingard died in the town where he had been born, Prattville, Alabama.

AL WORTHINGTON ■ *Pitcher*

COLLEGE: 1949–51 . . . .**MLB:** 1953–54, 1956–60, 1963–69, 75-82, 3.39, 110 saves; Alabama Sports HOF, Liberty University Athletics HOF

Cheating has always been part of baseball, but Al Worthington still didn't think it was right. He became a devout Christian after attending two Billy Graham rallies in 1958. In 1959, while pitching for the San Francisco Giants, he stopped a plot to steal the opposing catcher's signs by using a spy with a telescope in the scoreboard. Traded to the Chicago White Sox the next year, he quit the team rather than tolerate a similar scheme there. He spent most of that year and all of the next two years pitching in the minor leagues.

"Red" Worthington, solidly built at 6-2 and 195 pounds, led Alabama in innings pitched (65) and strikeouts (55) as a starter in 1951. In the majors, perhaps because of his principles or because his teams kept switching him between starting and relieving, consistent success eluded him until it was almost too late. In 1964, the Cincinnati Reds sold him to the Minnesota Twins. Suddenly, Worthington, age 35, became a star.

The Twins used him for just an inning or two at the end of a game to lock down a lead or keep the score close. Today, we'd call him a closer, but the role was novel back then. For six years, Worthington thrived, compiling 88 saves and a 2.62 earned run average. He helped carry the Twins to the American League pennant in 1965, when he won 10 games and posted a career-high 21 saves. In the World Series loss to the Los Angeles Dodgers, he allowed only one run, unearned, in two relief appearances.

Worthington owed part of his Minnesota success to his development of a sidearm curveball. According to *Cool of the Evening,* a book about the 1965 Twins, the right-hander threw mostly sidearm early in the season during his Minnesota years, gradually switching to a more overhand delivery as the season progressed.

After his playing career, he became baseball coach (1974–86) and athletics director (1983–89) at what is now Liberty University. In 1986, Liberty named its baseball field after him. Worthington now lives in retirement in Sterrett, Alabama, near Birmingham. He still proclaims—and lives—his faith, and he has a reputation for dealing kindly with fans who contact him for autographs or information.

Others in the Majors

NAME	POSITION	COLLEGE	MLB	STATS	TEAMS
John Baum-gartner	*Third Base*	1950 (did not letter)	1953	.185/.185/.185	Detroit Tigers
Jack Bolling	*First Base*	1936–39	1939, 1944	.313/.361/.427	Philadelphia Phillies, Brooklyn Dodgers
Dan Boone	*Pitcher*	1918–19	1919, 1921–23	8-13, 5.10, 1 save	Philadelphia Athletics, Detroit Tigers, Cleveland Indians
Vic Bradford	*Left Field*	1938–39	1943	.200/.333/.200	New York Giants
John Campbell	*Pitcher*	1925–27	1933	0-0, 0.00	Washington Senators
Syd Cohen	*Pitcher*	1925–27	1934, 1936–37	3-7, 4.54, 5 saves	Washington Senators
Bruce Connatser	*First Base*	1925–26	1931–32	.257/.302/.330	Cleveland Indians
Jim Dunn	*Pitcher*	1951–52	1952	0-0, 3.38	Pittsburgh Pirates
Verdo Elmore	*Right Field*	1925–26	1924	.176/.222/.353	St. Louis Browns
Hersh Freeman	*Pitcher*	1947	1952–53, 1955–58	30-16, 3.74, 37 saves	Boston Red Sox, Cincinnati Reds, Chicago Cubs
Grant Gillis	*Second Base, Shortstop, Third Base*	1925–26	1927–29	.245/.299/.327	Washington Senators, Boston Red Sox
Whitey Hilcher	*Pitcher*	1929–30	1932–32, 1935–36	3-6, 5.29	Cincinnati Reds

NAME	POSITION	COLLEGE	MLB	STATS	TEAMS
Randy Hunt	*Catcher*	1981	1985–86	.194/.250/.284	St. Louis Cardinals, Montreal Expos
Bryan Kelly	*Pitcher*	1981	1986–87	1-3, 4.70	Detroit Tigers
Jack Kubiszyn	*Shortstop, Third Base*	1956–58	1961–62	.188/.239/.238	Cleveland Indians
Doc Land	*Center Field*	1923–24	1929	.000/.250/.000	Washington Senators
Al Lary	*Pitcher*	1950–51	1954, 1962	0-1, .6.53	Chicago Cubs
Moose Morton	*Catcher*	1949 (did not letter)	1954	.000/.000/.000	Boston Red Sox
Ray Pepper	*Outfield*	1926–27	1932–36	.281/.321/.387	St. Louis Cardinals, St. Louis Browns
Paul Phillips	*Catcher-First Base*	1998	2004–10	.262/.298/.357	Kansas City Royals, Chicago White Sox, Colorado Rockies
Frank Pratt	*Outfield*	1917–20	1921	.000/.000/.000	Chicago White Sox
Lee Rogers	*Pitcher*	1934–35	1938	1-3, 6.14	Boston Red Sox, Brooklyn Dodgers
Max Rosenfeld	*Outfield*	1922–24	1931–33	.298/.322/.474	Brooklyn Dodgers
Mo Sanford	*Pitcher*	1985–88	1991, 1993, 1995	2-4, .4.81	Cincinnati Reds, Colorado Rockies, Minnesota Twins

NAME	POSITION	COLLEGE	MLB	STATS	TEAMS
Skeeter Scalzi	*Shortstop, Third Base*	1935–36	1939	.333/.429/.333	New York Giants
LeGrant Scott	*Right Field*	1933–34	1939	.280/.343/.366	Philadelphia Phillies
Ken Sears	*Catcher*	1936–37	1943, 1946	.282/.338/.347	New York Yankees, St. Louis Browns
Tommy Sewell	*Second Base, Shortstop, Third Base*	1926–27	1927	.000/.000/.000	Chicago Cubs
Jim Sheehan	*Catcher*	1934	1936	.000/.000/.000	New York Giants
Bobby Sprowl	*Pitcher*	1975–77	1978–81	0-3, 5.44	Boston Red Sox, Houston Astros
Lena Styles	*Catcher-First Base*	1917–19	1919–21, 1930–31	.250/.320/.313	Philadelphia Athletics, Cincinnati Reds
Taylor Tankersley	*Pitcher*	2002–04	2006–08	8-3, 4.58, 4 saves	Florida Marlins
Joe Vitiello	*Designated Hitter, First Base*	1989–91	1995–2000, 2003	.248/.335/.415	Kansas City Royals, San Diego Padres, Montreal Expos
Ed White	*Right Field*	1948–50	1955	.500/.600/.500	Chicago White Sox
Tim Young	*Pitcher*	1995–96	1998, 2000	0-0, 6.23	Montreal Expos, Boston Red Sox

Others in Pro Softball

NAME	POSITION	COLLEGE	NPF	STATS	TEAMS
Ashley Courtney	Catcher-Outfield	2002–05	2005	.314/.402/.392	New England Riptide
Kelsi Dunne	Pitcher	2008–11	2011	0-4, 7.20	NPF Diamonds
Ashley Holcombe	Catcher	2006–09	2009–10	.127/.250/.182	Rockford Thunder, Chicago Bandits
Ginger Jones-Powers	First Base	1998–2001	2004	.218/.342/.297	Texas Thunder
Whitney Larsen	Infield	2008–12	2012	.193/.220/.281	Chicago Bandits
Amanda Locke	First Base	2008–12	2012	.200/.333/.327	Carolina Diamonds
Jazlyn Lunceford	Outfield	2009–12	2012	.074/.219/.074	Carolina Diamonds
Staci Ramsey	Infield	2003–06	2007	.235/.316/.294	Akron Racers
Stephanie VanBrakle	Pitcher	2003–06	2006	5-9, 3.25	Philadelphia Force
Kasey Whitehead	Pitcher	1999 (at Alabama)	2004	0-2, 3.08	Akron Racers

Alabama Season Baseball Records (Through 2013)

Batting Average (Minimum 100 at bats)

.525 Dave Magadan, 1B, 1983	**.396** Andy Phillips, SS, 1999
.411 Peter Stonard, 2B-OF, 2002	**.395** Joe Vitiello, RF, 1991
.405 Chris Glass, 2B, 1982	**.395** Taylor Dugas, CF, 2010
.405 Chris Moller, 1B, 1995	**.395** Dave Magadan, 3B, 1982
.400 Roberto Vaz, OF-DH, 1997	**.395** G. W. Keller, OF, 1999
.399 Mike Twardoski, RF, 1986	

Runs

88	Bret Elbin, 3B, 1983	**76**	Joe Caruso, 2B, 1996
87	Roberto Vaz, OF-DH, 1997	**74**	Brent Boyd, 3B, 2000
86	David Tidwell, OF, 1997	**73**	Ted McClendon, 3B, 1983
85	G. W. Keller, OF, 1999	**73**	Mike Twardoski, RF, 1986
77	Jeremy Brown, 1B, 1999	**71**	Andy Phillips, SS, 1999

Runs Batted In

95	Dave Magadan, 1B, 1983	**81**	Kent Matthes, RF, 2009
83	Sam Bozanich, 2B, 2000	**79**	Dustan Mohr, RF, 1997
82	Doug Duke, C, 1986	**76**	Joe Caruso, 2B, 1997
82	Beau Hearod, RF, 2003	**74**	Roberto Vaz, OF-DH, 1997
81	Andy Phillips, 3B, 1998	**72**	G. W. Keller, OF, 1999

Home Runs

28	Kent Matthes, RF, 2009	**21**	G. W. Keller, OF-DH, 1997
27	Doug Duke, C, 1986	**21**	Andy Phillips, 3B, 1998
25	Dustan Mohr, RF, 1997	**20**	Mike Pitisci, 1B, 1984
22	Doug Duke, C, 1985	**20**	Robbie Tucker, 1B, 1997
22	Roberto Vaz, OF-DH, 1997	**20**	Aaron Clark, 1B, 2001
22	Matt Frick, C, 1998	**20**	Beau Hearod, RF, 2003
22	Andy Phillips, SS, 1999		

Walks

69	Jeremy Brown, C, 2002	**49**	G. W. Keller, OF, 1999
66	Bret Elbin, 3B, 1983	**48**	Jeremy Brown, 1B, 2000
59	Taylor Dugas, CF, 2010	**47**	Bret Elbin, SS, 1982
57	Jeremy Brown, C, 1999	**46**	Joe Vitiello, LF, 1990
51	Mike Twardoski, RF, 1986	**46**	Brent Reese, 1B, 1989
51	Evan Bush, 3B, 2005		

Stolen Bases

50 David Fowke, OF, 1981	**33** Robert Fletcher, 2B, 1988
44 Ted Williams, CF, 1985	**32** Chris Glass, 2B, 1981
42 G. W. Keller, OF, 1999	**30** Omar Fernandez, CF, 1987
36 Emeel Salem, OF, 2006	**29** Chris Arago, SS, 1977
35 David Tidwell, OF, 1997	**29** Sam Bozanich, 2B, 2000
33 Ralph Lusian, 2B, 1987	

Wins

13 Heath Henderson, 1997	**10** Jeff Oyster, 1984
12 Frank Roland, 1956	**10** Pete Roberts, 1986
11 Rick Browne, 1983	**10** Joel Colgrove, 1996
11 Dean Hayes, 1983	**10** Pete Fisher, 1997
11 Dennis Walsh, 1991	**10** Jarrod Kingrey, 1997
11 Tim Young, 1996	**10** Jonathan Blankenship, 1999
11 Lance Cormier, 2002	**10** Manny Torres, 1999
10 Frank Lary, 1950	**10** Brent Carter, 2003
10 Vince Barrentine, 1981	

Saves

14 Ben Short, 1991	**11** Skip Ames, 1996
13 Jarrod Kingrey, 1998	**11** Lance Cormier, 1999
12 Troy Brauchle, 1983	**11** Jonathan Smart, 2011
12 Brian Reed, 2003	**10** Greg Hibbard, 1986
12 Ray Castillo, 2013	**10** David Robertson, 2006

Pitching Strikeouts

128 Wade LeBlanc, 2006	**104** Joel Colgrove, 1996
118 Bobby Sprowl, 1977	**104** Heath Henderson, 1997
108 Wade LeBlanc, 2005	**103** Manny Torres, 1999
105 Brent Carter, 2003	**101** Al Drumheller, 1992
105 David Robertson, 2005	**100** Justin Smith, 1999

Alabama Career Baseball Records

Games Played

251 Jeremy Brown, 1B-C, 1999–2002	**226** Allen Rice, IF, 2002–05
244 Andy Phillips, 3B-SS, 1996–99	**223** Evan Bush, IF, 2003–06
242 Joe Caruso, 2B, 1994–97	**222** Emeel Salem, CF, 2004–07
242 Brent Boyd, IF, 1999–2002	**216** Brett Taft, SS, 1993–96
241 Taylor Dugas, CF, 2009–12	**216** Jake Smith, IF-P, 2007–10
227 Scott McClanahan, OF, 1999–2002	**216** Brett Booth, C-3B-LF, 2010–13

Batting Average (Minimum 400 at bats)

.439 Dave Magadan, 1B-3B, 1981–83	**.366** Mike Twardoski, RF, 1985–86
.381 G. W. Keller, OF, 1997–99	**.360** Taylor Dugas, CF, 2009–12
.375 Chris Moller, 1B, 1995–96	**.356** Andy Phillips, 3B-SS, 1996–99
.375 Joe Vitiello, OF-DH, 1989–91	**.349** Ted McClendon, 3B, 1983–85
.370 Peter Stonard, 2B-OF, 2001–02	**.347** Josh Rutledge, SS, 2008–10

Runs

244 Jeremy Brown, 1B-C, 1999–2002	**206** Joe Caruso, 2B, 1994–97
233 Brent Boyd, IF, 1999–2002	**191** Josh Rutledge, SS, 2008–10
232 Taylor Dugas, CF, 2009–12	**188** Scott McClanahan, OF, 1999–2002
222 Andy Phillips, 3B-SS, 1996–99	**177** Sam Bozanich, 2B, 1998–2000
214 G. W. Keller, OF, 1997–99	**176** Ted McClendon, 3B, 1983–85

Runs Batted In

230 Jeremy Brown, 1B-C, 1999–2002	**190** Allan Stallings, CF, 1982–85
224 Andy Phillips, 3B-SS, 1996–99	**188** Dave Magadan, 1B-3B, 1981–83
203 G. W. Keller, OF, 1997–99	**186** Kent Matthes, RF, 2006–09
195 Brent Boyd, IF, 1999–2002	**181** Joe Caruso, 2B, 1994–97
191 Beau Hearod, RF, 2001–03	**178** Dustan Mohr, RF, 1995–97

Home Runs

61	Andy Phillips, 3B-OF, 1996–99	**47**	Jake Smith, 3B, 2007–10
50	Doug Duke, C, 1984–86	**46**	Jeremy Brown, 1B-C, 1999–2002
50	G. W. Keller, OF, 1997–99	**40**	Beau Hearod, RF, 2001–03
48	Kent Matthes, RF, 2006–09	**38**	Matt Frick, C, 1997–98
47	Dustan Mohr, RF, 1995–97	**38**	Brent Boyd, IF, 1999–2002

Walks

207	Jeremy Brown, 1B-C, 1999–2002	**109**	Brent Boyd, IF, 1999–2002
151	Taylor Dugas, CF, 2009–12	**102**	Joe Vitiello, OF-DH, 1989–91
132	Evan Bush, IF, 2002–06	**101**	Alex Avila, C, 2006–08
125	Bret Elbin, 3B, 1981–83	**97**	Dave Magadan, 1B-3B, 1981–83
117	Ted McClendon, 3B, 1983–85	**96**	Ross Wilson, 2B, 2008–10

Stolen Bases

77	Emeel Salem, CF, 2004–07	**55**	Ted Williams, CF, 1985–86
68	David Fowke, LF, 1980–81	**54**	Mick Kerns, OF, 1989–92
62	David Tidwell, OF, 1996–97	**53**	Chris Arago, 2B, 1977–78
56	Chris Glass, 2B, 1981–82	**53**	G. W. Keller, 1997–99
56	Scott McClanahan, OF, 1999–2002	**51**	Robert Fletcher, 2B, 1987–88

Wins

31	Lance Cormier, 1999–2002	**22**	Mike Sodders, 1985–88
25	Brent Carter, 2002–05	**22**	Al Drumheller, 1991–93
24	Wade LeBlanc, 2004–06	**21**	John Paul Anderson, 1952–55
23	Jonathan Blankenship, 1998–2000	**21**	Gene Lary, 1952–55
23	Nathan Kilcrease, 2008–11	**21**	Frank Roland, 1956–57
22	Mike Innes, 1968–71	**21**	Manny Torres, 1996–99

Saves

21	Brian Reed, 2002–03	**18**	David Robertson, 2005–06
19	Troy Brauchle, 1983–84	**17**	Jimbo Lindsay, 1974–76
19	Greg Hibbard, 1985–86	**17**	Jarrod Kingrey, 1997–98

Saves (continued)

17	Lance Cormier, 1999–2002	**11**	Skip Ames, 1996
16	Ben Short, 1991–92	**11**	Taylor Tankersley, 2002–04
12	Ray Castillo, 2013	**11**	Jonathan Smart, 2010–11

Pitching Strikeouts

334	Wade LeBlanc, 2004–06	**240**	Nathan Kilcrease, 2008–11
307	Brent Carter, 2002–05	**237**	Joel Colgrove, 1993–96
289	Lance Cormier, 1999–2002	**237**	Chris Eilers, 1994–97
274	Mike Sodders, 1985–88	**232**	Taylor Tankersley, 2002–04
262	Al Drumheller, 1991–93	**228**	Jackie Glover, 1967–69

Alabama Season Softball Records (Through 2013)

Batting Average (Minimum 135 at bats)

.505	Kayla Braud, 2B, 2010	**.452**	Brittany Rogers, CF, 2008
.471	Kayla Braud, LF, 2013	**.451**	Kelly Kretschman, CF, 2001
.467	Kelly Kretschman, SS, 1998	**.436**	Kelly Kretschman, CF, 2000
.465	Haylie McCleney, CF, 2013	**.436**	Kayla Braud, LF, 2011
.457	Lauren Parker, 2B-SS, 2007	**.427**	Brittany Rogers, CF, 2006

DP stands for designated player, a designated hitter who can also play defense.

Runs

94	Kelly Kretschman, SS, 1998	**68**	Kaylie McCleney, CF, 2013
83	Kelly Kretschman, CF, 2000	**66**	Jennifer Fenton, CF, 2012
79	Brittany Rogers, CF, 2008	**65**	Kayla Braud, LF, 2013
75	Kayla Braud, 2B, 2010	**60**	Brittany Rogers, CF, 2006
71	Kayla Braud, LF, 2011	**60**	Kayla Braud, LF, 2012
68	Brittany Rogers, CF, 2007		

Runs Batted In

79	Charlotte Morgan, DP*-P-1B, 2008	**64**	Whitney Larsen, SS, 2011
77	Kaila Hunt, SS, 2012	**62**	Carrie Moreman, C, 1998
74	Charlotte Morgan, 1B-P, 2010	**60**	Kaila Hunt, 2B, 2013
69	Ginger Jones, 1B, 2000	**59**	Jackie McClain, RF, 2001
64	Kelly Kretschman, SS, 1998	**59**	Charlotte Morgan, DP*-P-1B, 2009

**DP stands for designated player, a designated hitter who can also play defense.*

Home Runs

25	Kelly Kretschman, SS, 1998	**17**	Amanda Locke, DP*-1B-P, 2010
21	Kaila Hunt, SS, 2012	**17**	Charlotte Morgan, 1B-P, 2010
19	Charlotte Morgan, DP*-P-1B, 2008	**15**	Carrie Moreman, C, 1998
18	Amanda Locke, DP*-P, 2012	**15**	Whitney Larsen, SS, 2010
17	Ginger Jones, 1B, 2000	**15**	Kaila Hunt, 2B, 2013

**DP stands for designated player, a designated hitter who can also play defense.*

Walks

66	Cassie Reilly-Boccia, RF, 2010	**46**	Stephanie VanBrakle, P-DH, 2005
52	Kelley Montalvo, 3B, 2009	**45**	Kelly Kretschman, CF, 2001
51	Kelly Kretschman, CF, 2000	**41**	Stephanie VanBrakle, P-DH, 2006
47	Jackie McClain, 1B, 2004	**41**	Dani Woods, OF-1B, 2008
47	Cassie Reilly-Boccia, 1B, 2012	**40**	Cassie Reilly-Boccia, OF-1B, 2009

Stolen Bases

60	Brittany Rogers, CF, 2008	**43**	Kelly Kretschman, CF, 2000
58	Kayla Braud, LF, 2011	**41**	Kayla Braud, LF, 2012
52	Brittany Rogers, CF, 2009	**40**	Kelly Kretschman, SS, 1998
48	Brittany Rogers, CF, 2007	**38**	Brittany Rogers, CF, 2006
45	Kayla Braud, 2B, 2010	**38**	Kayla Braud, LF, 2013
44	Jennifer Fenton, CF, 2012		

Wins

42	Jackie Traina, 2012	**32**	Shelley Laird, 2001
38	Shelley Laird, 2000	**30**	Kelsi Dunne, 2010
34	Stephanie VanBrakle, 2005	**29**	Kelsi Dunne, 2011

Wins (continued)

28	Stephanie VanBrakle, 2006	**24**	Penny Cope, 1998
28	Kelsi Dunne, 2009	**24**	Shelley Laird, 2002
26	Kelsi Dunne, 2008	**24**	Chrissy Owens, 2007

Saves

11	Chrissy Owens, 2005	**4**	Jackie Traina, 2011
5	Shelley Laird, 2000	**3**	Shelley Laird, 1999
5	Shelley Laird, 2002	**3**	Shelley Laird, 2001
5	Chrissy Owens, 2008	**3**	Jennifer Wright, 2002
4	Stephanie VanBrakle, 2004	**3**	Chrissy Owens, 2006
4	Kelsi Dunne, 2008		

Pitching Strikeouts

361	Jackie Traina, 2012	**310**	Shelley Laird, 2000
355	Kelsi Dunne, 2010	**282**	Shelley Laird, 2002
345	Stephanie VanBrakle, 2006	**275**	Kelsi Dunne, 2008
341	Stephanie VanBrakle, 2005	**258**	Kelsi Dunne, 2009
331	Kelsi Dunne, 2011	**242**	Shelley Laird, 2001

Alabama Career Softball Records

Games Played

277	Jackie Wilkins, CF, 2002–05	**269**	Staci Ramsey, 3B, 2003–06
274	Ashley Courtney, OF-C, 2002–05	**266**	Christy Kyle, RF-3B-LF, 1997–2000
273	Kelly Kretschman, SS-CF, 1998–2001	**263**	Lacy Prejean, C-DH, 2000–03
270	Jennifer Reach, SS, 2000–03	**263**	Jackie McClain, 1B-RF, 2001–04
269	Dominique Accetturo, 2B-SS, 2003–06	**262**	Jordan Praytor, OF-DP*, 2005–08

DP stands for designated player, a designated hitter who can also play defense.

Batting Average (Minimum 300 at bats)

.438	Kayla Braud, LF-2B, 2010–13	**.387**	Charlotte Morgan, DP*-P-1B, 2007–2010
.437	Kelly Kretschman, SS-CF, 1998–2001	**.387**	Jackie McClain, 1B-RF, 2001–04
.417	Brittany Rogers, CF, 2006–09	**.368**	Lauren Parker, 2B-SS, 2007–09

Batting Average (continued)

.365 Ashley Courtney, OF-C, 2002–05	**.356** Jordan Praytor, OF-DP*, 2005–08
.361 Jennifer Fenton, CF, 2009–12	**.335** Jackie Traina, P-DH, 2011–13

DP stands for designated player, a designated hitter who can also play defense.

Runs

288 Kelly Kretschman, SS-CF, 1998–2001	**202** Jennifer Fenton, CF, 2009–12
271 Kayla Braud, LF-2B, 2010–13	**176** Whitney Larsen, SS, 2008–11
256 Brittany Rogers, CF, 2006–09	**174** Kelley Montalvo, 3B, 2006–09
207 Ashley Courtney, OF-C, 2002–05	**171** Jackie Wilkins, CF, 2002–05
202 Jordan Praytor, OF-DP*, 2005–08	**157** Charlotte Morgan, DP*-P-1B, 2007–2010

DP stands for designated player, a designated hitter who can also play defense.

Runs Batted In

264 Charlotte Morgan, DP*-P-1B, 2007–2010	**174** Dani Woods, OF-1B, 2005–08
195 Whitney Larsen, SS, 2008–11	**173** Kaila Hunt, SS-2B-3B, 2011–13
191 Kelly Kretschman, SS-CF, 1998–2001	**172** Cassie Reilly-Boccia, OF-1B, 2009–12
181 Jackie McClain, 1B-RF, 2001–04	**168** Christy Kyle, RF-3B-LF, 1997–2000
175 Staci Ramsey, 3B, 2003–06	**161** Amanda Locke, DP*-1B-P, 2009–12

DP stands for designated player, a designated hitter who can also play defense.

Home Runs

60 Kelly Kretschman, SS-CF, 1998–2001	**40** Stephanie VanBrakle, P-DH, 2003–06
58 Charlotte Morgan, DP*-P-1B, 2007–2010	**39** Ginger Jones, 1B, 1998–2001
54 Amanda Locke, DP*-1B-P, 2009–12	**36** Jackie Traina, P-DH, 2011–13
48 Whitney Larsen, SS, 2008–11	**32** Staci Ramsey, 3B, 2003–06
46 Kaila Hunt, SS-2B-3B, 2011–13	**32** Cassie Reilly-Boccia, OF-1B, 2009–12

DP stands for designated player, a designated hitter who can also play defense.

Walks

180 Cassie Reilly-Boccia, OF-1B, 2009–12	**131** Kelley Montalvo, 3B, 2006–09
161 Kelly Kretschman, SS-CF, 1998–2001	**113** Kayla Braud, LF-2B, 2010–13
151 Stephanie VanBrakle, P-DH, 2003–06	**111** Dani Woods, OF-1B, 2005–08
139 Jackie McClain, 1B-RF, 2001–04	**110** Jordan Praytor, OF-DP*, 2005–08
134 Charlotte Morgan, DP*-P-1B, 2007–2010	**95** Kelley Askew, C-DH, 1998–2001

DP stands for designated player, a designated hitter who can also play defense.

Stolen Bases

198	Brittany Rogers, CF, 2006–09	**71**	Ashley Courtney, OF-C, 2002–05
182	Kayla Braud, LF-2B, 2010–13	**61**	Mandy Burford, LF-RF, 2004–07
133	Kelly Kretschman, SS-CF, 1998–2001	**57**	Kelley Montalvo, 3B, 2006–09
133	Jennifer Fenton, CF, 2009–12	**55**	Keima Davis, RF, 2010–13
102	Jordan Praytor, OF-DP*, 2005–08	**53**	Suzanne Olcott, 2B, 1999–2002

DP stands for designated player, a designated hitter who can also play defense.

Wins

115	Shelley Laird, 1999–2002	**62**	Erin Wright, 2001–04
113	Kelsi Dunne, 2008–11	**52**	Jennifer Wright, 2002–05
97	Stephanie VanBrakle, 2003–06	**51**	Charlotte Morgan, 2007–10
80	Jackie Traina, 2011–13	**37**	Penny Cope, 1998–99
67	Chrissy Owens, 2005–08	**31**	Christy Caccavo, 1997–98

Saves

21	Chrissy Owens, 2005–08	**3**	Amy Bernard, 1998–99
16	Shelley Laird, 1999–2002	**2**	Christy Caccavo, 1997–98
9	Stephanie VanBrakle, 2003–06	**2**	Penny Cope, 1998–99
8	Kelsi Dunne, 2008–11	**2**	Blair Potter, 2006–07
7	Jackie Traina, 2011–13	**2**	Charlotte Morgan, 2007–10
4	Erin Wright, 2001–04	**2**	Lauren Sewell, 2010–12
4	Jennifer Wright, 2002–05	**2**	Leslie Jury, 2012–13

Pitching Strikeouts

1,219	Kelsi Dunne, 2008–11	**558**	Erin Wright, 2001–04
1,113	Stephanie VanBrakle, 2003–06	**379**	Jennifer Wright, 2002–05
1,045	Shelley Laird, 1999–2002	**294**	Charlotte Morgan, 2007–10
765	Jackie Traina, 2011–13	**268**	Penny Cope, 1998–99
576	Chrissy Owens, 2005–08	**235**	Christy Caccavo, 1997–98

BASKETBALL

MEN

Among Southeastern Conference schools, Alabama ranks second only to Kentucky in all-time men's basketball wins. Alabama's 1,568 victories (in 100 seasons) stand 31st among Division I schools. The Crimson Tide's all-time winning percentage of .623 ranks 29th in Division I and third in the SEC behind Kentucky and Arkansas. And the fans supply plenty of support; Alabama ranks 31st in Division I per-game attendance at 11,159.

So how come nobody thinks of Alabama as a basketball school? The Tide has more victories and a better winning percentage than Missouri, Kansas State, Ohio State, Michigan, Michigan State, Tennessee, Marquette, Southern California, Arizona State, DePaul, Florida State, Georgia Tech, Iowa, Iowa State, Maryland, South Carolina, Stanford, Virginia, Wisconsin, or Wake Forest. Why isn't Alabama at least thought of as a Michigan or an Ohio State—a school with a storied football program but also a perennially strong basketball team?

Alabama has achieved flashes of glory—the "Rocket 8" teams of the mid-1950s, the three straight Southeastern Conference championships in the mid-1970s, the Associated Press number one ranking for a couple of weeks in 2002–03—as well as long stretches of consistent basketball excellence. Since 1975, the Crimson Tide has reached the NCAA tournament 20 times, including six years in a row from 1982 through 1987, six of seven seasons from 1989 through 1995, and five seasons in a row from 2002 through 2006. With six SEC tournament championships, the Tide trails only Kentucky (28). Alabama's eight SEC regular-season titles tie for third (with Tennessee) behind Kentucky (45) and LSU (11).

But Alabama has never won a national championship. It has never reached an NCAA Final Four and only once has gotten as far as the Elite Eight (the quarterfinals). It can boast no college or pro hall of fame players.

The Crimson Tide just hasn't produced the kinds of exclamation-point feats or players that put a program in the national spotlight.

Still, many major schools can only dream of the kind of success that Alabama has sustained in the past four decades. Since 1971-72, Alabama has played in 32 postseason tournaments, finished in the top 25 of the final Associated Press poll 14 times, hit the 20-win threshold 25 times, and suffered only three losing seasons.

C. M. Newton, who arrived as head coach in 1968, led Alabama to its first six postseason tournaments and earned enshrinement in the National Collegiate Basketball and Naismith Memorial Basketball halls of fame. But he began his Alabama career with three straight losing seasons. It's a testament to how far the program has come to realize that no Alabama coach today could keep his job after such a slow start.

Top 35 All-Time Division I College Teams

(Ranked by wins through the 2012–13 season)

RECORD	TEAM	WINNING %	SEASONS
2,111-661-1	Kentucky	.761	110
2,101-812-0	Kansas	.721	115
2,090-745-0	North Carolina	.737	103
2,001-840-0	Duke	.704	108
1,874-832	Syracuse	.693	112
1,814-992-0	Temple	.646	117
1,754-931-0	St. John's (New York)	.653	106
1,753-779-0	UCLA	.692	94
1,748-949-1	Notre Dame	.648	108
1,719-966-0	Indiana	.640	113
1,706-1,020-2	Pennsylvania	.626	113
1,697-869-0	Louisville	.661	99
1,690-910-0	Illinois	.650	108

RECORD	TEAM	WINNING %	SEASONS
1,690-1,026-0	Brigham Young	.622	111
1,685-936-0	Utah	.643	105
1,683-1,095-0	Washington	.606	111
1,675-844-0	Western Kentucky	.665	94
1,675-994-0	Texas	.628	107
1,658-9-072-0	Purdue	.569	115
1,654-1,251	Oregon State	.571	112
1,646-963-0	Cincinnati	.631	112
1,645-900-1	Arizona	.646	108
1,636-1,025-0	Princeton	.615	113
1,634-1,024-0	West Virginia	.615	104
1,617-980-0	North Carolina State	.623	101
1,590-1,083-0	Bradley	.595	109
1,589-888-0	Connecticut	.642	10
1,584-903-0	Villanova	.637	93
1,575-892-0	Missouri State	.638	101
1,569-962-0	Georgetown	.620	105
1,568-949-1	**Alabama**	**.623**	**100**
1,558-1,009-0	Ohio State	.607	112
1,558-1,080-0	Oklahoma State	.591	104
1,556-880-0	Arkansas	.639	90
1,553-1,054-0	Missouri	.596	107

Official NCAA records, adjusted for vacated and forfeited games; includes only schools with at least 25 years in Division I

(Ranked by winning percentage through the 2012–13 season)

WINNING %	TEAM	RECORD
.761	Kentucky	2,111-661-1
.737	North Carolina	2,090-745-0
.721	Kansas	2,101-812-0
.713	Nevada–Las Vegas	1,158-466-0
.704	Duke	2,001--840-0

WINNING %	TEAM	RECORD
.693	Syracuse	1,874-832-0
.692	UCLA	1,753-779-0
.665	Western Kentucky	1,675-844-0
.661	Louisville	1,697-869-0
.653	St. John's (New York)	1,754-931-0
.650	Illinois	1,690-910-0
.648	Notre Dame	1,748-949-1
.646	Temple	1,814-992-0
.646	Arizona	1,645-900-1
.643	Utah	1,685-936-0
.643	Virginia Commonwealth	818-455-0
.643	Murray State	1,501-835-0
.642	Connecticut	1,589-888-0
.640	Indiana	1,719-966-0
.639	Arkansas	1,556-880-0
.639	Weber State	945-535-0
.638	Missouri State	1,575-892-0
.637	Villanova	1,584-903-0
.632	Memphis	1,441-838-1
.631	Cincinnati	1,646-963-0
.630	Purdue	1,658-972-0
.628	Texas	1,675-944-0
.626	Pennsylvania	1,706-1,020-2
.624	Alabama-Birmingham	695-418-0
.623	**Alabama**	**1,568-949-1**
.623	North Carolina State	1,617-980-0
.622	Marquette	1,520-922-0
.622	Brigham Young	1,690-1,026-0
.620	Georgetown	1,569-962-0
.615	Princeton	1,636-1,025-0

Official NCAA records, adjusted for vacated and forfeited games; includes only schools with at least 25 years in Division I

Southeastern Conference Teams

■ *(Ranked by wins through the 2012–13 season)*

RECORD	TEAM	WINNING %	SEASONS
2,111-661-1	Kentucky	.761	110
1,568-949-1	**Alabama**	**.623**	**100**
1,556-880-0	Arkansas	.639	90
1,553-1,054-0	Missouri	.596	107
1,528-972-2	Tennessee	.611	104
1,511-1,063-0	Vanderbilt	.587	111
1,445-1,104-0	LSU	.567	105
1,320-1,104-0	Mississippi State	.545	101
1,312-1,220-0	Georgia	.518	108
1,311-1,167-0	South Carolina	.529	105
1,307-1,190-0	Texas A&M	.523	101
1,295-1,047-0	Florida	.553	94
1,250-1,115-1	Auburn	.529	107
1,199-1,229-0	Mississippi	.494	103

Official NCAA records, adjusted for vacated and forfeited games

■ *(Ranked by winning percentage through the 2012–13 season)*

WINNING %	TEAM	RECORD
.761	Kentucky	2,111-661-1
.639	Arkansas	1,556-880-0
.623	**Alabama**	**1,568-949-1**
.611	Tennessee	1,528-972-2
.596	Missouri	1,553-1,054-0
.587	Vanderbilt	1,511-1,063-0
.567	LSU	1,445-1,104-0
.553	Florida	1,295-1,047-0
.545	Mississippi State	1,320-1,104-0
.529	South Carolina	1,311-1,167-0
.529	Auburn	1,250-1,115-1

WINNING %	TEAM	RECORD
.523	Texas A&M	1,307-1,190-0
.518	Georgia	1,312-1,220-0
.494	Mississippi	1,199-1,229-0

Official NCAA records, adjusted for vacated and forfeited games

Southeastern Conference Championships

(Regular season, through 2013)

45 Kentucky	6 Mississippi State	1 Georgia
11 LSU	3 Vanderbilt	1 South Carolina
8 **Alabama**	2 Arkansas	1 Tulane
8 Tennessee	2 Auburn	
6 Florida	2 Georgia Tech	

(Tournament, through 2013)

28 Kentucky	3 Mississippi State	1 Arkansas
6 **Alabama**	2 Georgia	1 Auburn
4 Tennessee	2 Mississippi	1 Georgia Tech
3 Florida	2 Vanderbilt	1 LSU

Nicknames

> *Big Shot Rob* (Robert Horry)

> *Buck* (Alfonso Johnson Jr.)

> *Crash* (Gerald Wallace)

> *Dice* or *Dice Man* (Antonio McDyess)

> *Heavy D* (Derrick McKey)

> *Hollywood* (James Robinson)

> *Mo* (Maurice Williams)

> *Moose* (Jerrry Harper)

> *Nique* (Dominique Canty)

> *Mule* (Reggie King)

> *Shay* (Shalonda Enis)

> *Spree* (Latrell Sprewell)

> *Wimp* (Winfrey Sanderson)

Top 35 Division I Home Attendance 2012–13

TEAM	AVERAGE PER GAME ATTENDANCE	TOTAL SEASON ATTENDANCE
Kentucky	23,099	415,775
Syracuse	22,439	426,347
Louisville	21,571	345,129
North Carolina	19,350	309,603
Indiana	17,412	330,832
Creighton	17,155	291,643
Wisconsin	16,843	303,172
Tennessee	16,635	282,794
Ohio State	16,524	297,428
Kansas	16,438	295,889
Memphis	16,336	294,044
North Carolina State	16,299	277,087
Brigham Young	15,986	287,750
Nevada–Las Vegas	15,196	334,320
Marquette	15,033	240,530
New Mexico	15,022	240,351
Illinois	14,817	237,077
Michigan State	14,341	258,138
Arizona	14,157	226,505
Arkansas	13,750	261,242
Iowa	13,625	272,496
Iowa State	13,393	227,683
Minnesota	12,580	213,865
Kansas State	12,528	225,503
Maryland	12,439	261,211
Dayton	12,438	211,446
San Diego State	12,414	186,210
Michigan	12,138	261,211
Missouri	11,996	203,929
Purdue	11,857	225,286
Alabama	**11,159**	**223,171**

TEAM	AVERAGE PER GAME ATTENDANCE	TOTAL SEASON ATTENDANCE
Texas	10,945	175,116
Georgetown	10,911	185,490
Connecticut	10,728	171,644
Florida	10,677	160,160

Southeastern Conference Home Attendance 2012–13

TEAM	AVERAGE PER GAME ATTENDANCE	TOTAL SEASON ATTENDANCE
Kentucky	23,099	415,775
Tennessee	16,635	282,794
Arkansas	13,750	261,242
Missouri	11,996	203,929
Alabama	**11,159**	**223,171**
Florida	10,677	160,160
Vanderbilt	10,637	159,557
South Carolina	8,603	154,858
LSU	7,653	130,105
Mississippi State	6,721	94,092
Texas A&M	6,331	113,950
Auburn	6,257	106,375
Georgia	6,198	111,571
Mississippi	6,067	103,142

NCAA VERSUS NIT

The NCAA Division I men's basketball tournament—March Madness, the Big Dance—has become such a huge event, with television coverage of each game and millions of Americans filling out brackets for office pools, that the poor National Invitation Tournament has become an afterthought. The introduction of the Preseason NIT in 1985 (now known as the NIT Season Tip-Off) further diluted the NIT brand.

Once, however, the postseason NIT was not a bittersweet consolation prize for teams not good enough to qualify for the NCAA's main event. It's actually older, having been founded in 1938—a year before the NCAA tournament. Originally, it carried equal or greater prestige, partly because all games were played in the media showcase of Madison Square Garden in New York. Some teams played in both tournaments. In 1950, City College of New York won both.

By the late 1960s, the NCAA had become dominant. The NIT was a sort of cottage industry, founded by the Metropolitan Basketball Writers Association in New York and carried on by its successor organization, the Metropolitan Intercollegiate Basketball Association.

The MIBA eventually consisted of five New York-area colleges and universities: Fordham, Manhattan, St. John's, Wagner, and New York University. Against the NCAA's wealth and marketing muscle, it stood no chance. Since 1951, the NCAA tournament had invited more teams than the NIT. More teams and more games meant more TV and other media exposure. In 2005, the NCAA bought the NIT, permanently ensuring the latter's secondary status.

Tallstop, Shortstop

Derrick McKey (see page 307) played shortstop on his high school baseball team in Meridian, Mississippi. He was 6 feet 9 inches tall.

Jack Kubiszyn, who was 5-11 and weighed 170 pounds, played shortstop for the Cleveland Indians in the American League. In 1961 and 1962, he appeared in a total of 50 games, hitting .188 with one home run. Kubiszyn lettered for Alabama in both baseball (1956–58) and basketball (1955–58). A guard, he still has the Crimson Tide's top two single-season scoring averages, 24.6 points per game in 1956–57 and 23.3 in 1957–58. He scored more than 40 points in three different games, peaking at 47 against Mississippi College in 1957. That's the Crimson Tide's second-highest single-game point total, behind Mike Nordholz's 50 in 1967.

Kubiszyn was, to say the least, not afraid to shoot. He also still holds Alabama records for most field goal attempts in a game (39) and season (557). His career shooting percentage was only .374.

An injury ended his baseball career after the 1962 season. Kubiszyn came back to Tuscaloosa and built a long, prosperous career at the Jack Kubiszyn Insurance Agency, which he had founded during the off-season in 1960.

Alabama has made 20 NCAA tournament appearances, the first in 1975. The 2004 team advanced the furthest: to the quarterfinals before losing, 87–71, to eventual national champion Connecticut.

Alabama made the first of its 12 NIT appearances in 1973, reaching the Final Four. Twice, in 2001 and 2011, the Crimson Tide has been the NIT runner-up.

Alabama in the NCAA Tournament

(Through 2013; includes furthest round achieved)

1975 First Round	***1987** Sweet 16	**2002** Second Round
1976 Sweet 16	**1989** First Round	**2003** First Round
1982 Sweet 16	**1990** Sweet 16	**2004** Elite Eight
1983 First Round	**1991** Sweet 16	**2005** First Round
1984 First Round	**1992** Second Round	**2006** Second Round
1985 Sweet 16	**1994** Second Round	**2012** First Round
1986 Sweet 16	**1995** Second Round	

Vacated by the NCAA because Alabama player Derrick McKey had improperly signed with an agent during the season
The tournament included 32 teams in 1975–78, 40 teams in 1979, 48 teams in 1980–84, 64 teams in 1985–2000, 65 teams in 2001–10, and 68 teams 2011–present.

Alabama in the NIT

(Postseason NIT only; through 2013; includes furthest round achieved)

1973 Final Four	**1993** First Round	**2007** First Round
1977 Final Four	**1996** Final Four	**2011** Championship (lost, 66–57, to Wichita State)
1979 Final Four	**1999** First Round	
1980 Sweet 16	**2001** Championship (lost, 79–66, to Tulsa)	**2013** Elite Eight
1981 Sweet 16		

The tournament included 16 teams in 1968–78, 24 teams in 1979, 32 teams in 1980–2001 and 2007–2013, and 40 teams in 2002–2006. The field is now set again at 32 teams.

NCAA Championships

(Through 2013)

11 UCLA	**2** Oklahoma State	**1** Michigan
8 Kentucky	**2** San Francisco	**1** Nevada–Las Vegas
5 Indiana	**1** Arizona	**1** Ohio State
5 North Carolina	**1** Arkansas	**1** Oregon
4 Duke	**1** California	**1** Stanford
3 Connecticut	**1** CCNY	**1** Syracuse
3 Kansas	**1** Georgetown	**1** Texas–El Paso
3 Louisville	**1** Holy Cross	(then Texas Western)
2 Cincinnati	**1** La Salle	**1** Utah
2 Florida	**1** Loyola (Illinois)	**1** Villanova
2 Michigan State	**1** Marquette	**1** Wisconsin
2 North Carolina State	**1** Maryland	**1** Wyoming

NIT Championships

(Postseason NIT only; through 2013)

***6** St. John's (New York)	**2** Temple	**1** Holy Cross	**1** Southern Illinois
	2 Tulsa	**1** Indiana	**1** Southern Mississippi
4 Bradley	**2** Virginia	**1** LaSalle	**1** San Francisco
3 Dayton	**2** Virginia Tech	**1** Louisville	**1** St. Bonaventure
****3** Michigan	**2** West Virginia	**1** Marquette	**1** St. Louis
2 Brigham Young	**1** Baylor	**1** Maryland	**1** Texas
2 Kentucky	**1** California	**1** Memphis	**1** UCLA
2 Long Island	**1** CCNY	**1** Nebraska	**1** Utah
*****2** Minnesota	**1** Colorado	**1** North Carolina	**1** Vanderbilt
2 Ohio State	**1** Connecticut	**1** Penn State	**1** Villanova
2 Providence	**1** DePaul	**1** Princeton	**1** Wake Forest
2 South Carolina	**1** Duquesne	**1** Purdue	**1** Wichita State
2 Stanford	**1** Fresno State	**1** Seton Hall	**1** Xavier

**Includes the 2003 title, which the NCAA vacated because of an ineligible player*
***Includes the 1997 title, which the NCAA vacated because of ineligible players*
****Includes the 1998 title, which the NCAA vacated because of academic fraud*

NCAA Tournament Field

1939–50 8 teams		**1979** 40 teams	
1951–52 16 teams		**1980–82** 48 teams	
1953, 1966 22 teams		**1983** 52 teams	
1954–55, 1958, 1961 24 teams		**1984** 53 teams	
1956, 1960, 1962–64, 1969–74 25 teams		**1985–2000** 64 teams	
1957, 1959, 1965, 1967–68 23 teams		**2001–10** 65 teams	
1975–78 32 teams		**2011–13** 68 teams	

Postseason NIT Field

1938–40 6 teams		**1968–78** 16 teams	
1941–48 8 teams		**1979** 24 teams	
1949–64 12 teams		**1980–2001, 2007–13** 32 teams	
1965–67 14 teams		**2002–06** 40 teams	

HEAD COACHES

The first basketball game ever was played in 1892; Alabama took up the sport 31 years later. The Crimson Tide lost its first game, played in Bessemer, Alabama, against the Bessemer Athletic Club in 1913. The score was 22-20.

In fact, Alabama lost its first four games before closing out the season with seven straight wins to finish 7-4. Records are sketchy, but the season apparently ended in February or early March. Head coach D. V. Graves also coached the baseball team, so he would have shifted his attention to the diamond when the weather warmed.

Coaches often undertook such double or even triple duties throughout much of the 20th century. Here's a list of Alabama head basketball coaches who also had other major athletics responsibilities:

1912–15: D. V. Graves, 20-12; *also head football coach, 1911–14, and head baseball coach, 1912–15*

1917–18: B. J. "Loonie" Noojin, 2-5; *also football assistant, 1915–16, head baseball coach, 1916–19, and athletics director, 1916–20*

1920–23: Charles Bernier, 47-19; *also football assistant, 1920, athletics director, 1920–23, and head baseball coach, 1921–23*

1923–42, 1945–46: Hank Crisp, 264-133; *also football assistant, 1921–42 and 1950–57, head track coach, 1921–27, head baseball coach, 1928, and athletics director, 1930–40 and 1954–57*

1942–43: Paul Burnham, 10-10; *also football assistant, 1930–42, and head baseball coach, 1943*

1944–45: Malcolm Laney, 10-5; *also football assistant, 1944–57*

1952–56: Johnny Dee, 68-25; *also football assistant, 1952*

1960–68: Hayden Riley, 236-206-1; *also football assistant, 1958–69, and head baseball coach, 1970–79*

Until 1923, basketball coaches lasted a season or two, maybe three, before moving on. That changed when Hank Crisp took over.

The Hank Crisp Era

Henry Gorham Crisp had already achieved remarkable things by the time he arrived at Alabama in 1921, age 24. When he was 13, he lost his right hand in a farm accident. Nevertheless, he lettered in football (as a tackle and fullback), basketball, and track in college, first at Hampden-Sydney College and then at Virginia Polytechnic Institute (today commonly known as Virginia Tech).

He followed football coach Charles Bernier from Hampden-Sydney to VPI and then, after finishing his collegiate playing career, to Alabama, where Bernier had become basketball coach and athletics director in 1920. Crisp stayed at Alabama for much of the next five decades.

In 1923, he succeeded his mentor as basketball coach, and built on Bernier's success. In three years, Bernier's teams had posted a cumulative 47-19 record. In 20 seasons, Crisp's teams went 264-133. His victory total remains second only to Wimp Sanderson's among Alabama coaches.

Crisp brought Alabama a Southern Conference championship and the school's only undefeated season (20-0), both in 1929–30, plus Southeastern Conference championships in 1938–39 and 1939–40, and an SEC Tournament championship in 1934.

Meanwhile, he put in two long stints as a football assistant, mostly coaching the line (1921–42 and 1950–57), and also spent two terms as athletics director (1930–40 and 1954–57). During World War II, he was a civilian physical training instructor for the U.S. Navy preflight school at the University of Georgia. He resumed his career as a football line coach with the Miami

Seahawks of the All-America Football Conference in 1946 and then Tulane (1947–49) before returning to Alabama.

Crisp retired as football assistant and athletics director in 1957, after the debacle of the Ears Whitworth era in football. He stayed at the university and directed intramural athletics until 1967.

In 1970, the Alabama Sports Hall of Fame inducted Crisp. He died the day before the induction after suffering a heart attack at the Hall of Fame banquet on January 23, 1970. Alabama's Hank Crisp Indoor Facility, an indoor practice facility for football, soccer, baseball, and softball, was renamed for him in 1991.

The Johnny Dee Era

Johnny Dee flashed across the Alabama basketball scene like, appropriately, a rocket. He arrived in 1952, captivated the state with a hustling, high-scoring team nicknamed the Rocket 8, then left in a huff after only four years.

Alabama hired the 28-year-old Dee away from Notre Dame, where he had been an assistant coach and had earned a law degree. At the time, he was the youngest basketball coach in NCAA history. Back then, colleges could try out players before awarding scholarships. When Dee came to Tuscaloosa, he brought along five freshmen who had failed their Notre Dame tryouts. They formed the starting five for all four of his Crimson Tide teams (see "The Rocket 8 Take Off," page 285).

Dee's teams went 12-9, 16-8, 19-5, and 21-3. Dee called his 1955–56 squad "the greatest in collegiate history." It ranked fifth in the final Associated Press poll and went 14-0 in the Southeastern Conference, earning the conference's automatic berth in the NCAA tournament.

It would have been the Crimson Tide's first-ever postseason tournament. But the NCAA banned anyone who had played as a freshman. That knocked out all of Alabama's starters. Dee wanted to take the rest of the team anyway, but the university overruled him. So Dee quit. He moved to Denver, where he worked as a lawyer, focusing on the oil and gas industry, and coached the Denver-Chicago Truckers, an Amateur Athletic Union team (see "Couldn't Stop the Moose," page 283).

Dee returned to Notre Dame in 1964 for his only other college coaching stint. In seven seasons, his teams put up a record of 116-80. They won 20 games in each of his last four years—the first 20-win seasons in team history.

Dee left coaching after the 1970–71 season and returned to Denver. There, he practiced law, managed the city's parks and recreation department, and became city auditor. He died of cancer in 1999, age 75.

Dee's .731 winning percentage at Alabama is the highest of any coach who stayed more than one season. At a Rocket 8 reunion at Tuscaloosa in 1981, he mused about what might have been had he not left: "Maybe, given proper breaks along the way, we could have had some NCAA championship teams at Alabama by now."

Perhaps. Here's something we know for sure: every player Dee recruited at both Alabama and Notre Dame received his undergraduate degree.

The C. M. Newton Era

Charles Martin "C. M." Newton played, albeit sparingly, for the 1950–51 University of Kentucky team that went 32-2 and won the national championship. His coach, the legendary Adolph Rupp, later recommended Newton for his first two head coaching jobs. Newton left Kentucky in 1951, after his junior season, when the New York Yankees signed him to a pro baseball contract. Newton was a 6-foot-3, 190-pound right-handed pitcher. He had good stuff but lousy control. Pitching for the Norfolk Tars in the Piedmont League in 1952, mostly in relief, he allowed only 60 hits in 84 innings but walked 75 batters.

At the same time, starting in 1951, he began his basketball coaching career at Transylvania University in Lexington, Kentucky. His first two teams went 1-15 and 6-12. After a two-year break to serve in the Air Force during the Korean War, he turned in one last undistinguished minor-league season in baseball but hit his stride in basketball. Despite that 7-27 start at Transylvania, Newton put together a 176-165 overall record in 14 seasons. In 1963, he took the Pioneers to the second round of the National Association of Intercollegiate Athletics tournament.

In the 12 years after Johnny Dee left, Alabama basketball muddled to a cumulative 151-153 record. Athletics director Bear Bryant, on Rupp's recommendation, hired Newton to reinvigorate the program. Again, Newton started slowly. His first three teams went a combined 22-54. Then came nine straight winning seasons, Alabama's first postseason appearances (the National Invitation Tournament in 1973, 1977, 1979, and 1980, the NCAA tournament in 1975 and 1976), and three straight Southeastern Conference championships, starting in 1973–74.

In 1969, Newton recruited Alabama's first African-American scholarship player, Wendell Hudson, now Alabama's women's basketball coach. In 1965, he had similarly integrated Transylvania's team.

After the 1979–80 season, Newton left Alabama to become assistant commissioner of the Southeastern Conference. A year later, Vanderbilt lured him back into coaching. In eight seasons, his Vanderbilt teams went 129-115. In 1989, Newton returned to his alma mater, Kentucky, as athletics director. There, he hired the school's first African-American women's and men's basketball coaches, Bernadette Mattox in 1995 and Tubby Smith in 1997.

Newton retired from Kentucky in 2000. He now lives in Tuscaloosa and is a consultant to the Southeastern Conference commissioner. He has been inducted into the National Collegiate Basketball Hall of Fame, the Naismith Memorial Basketball Hall of Fame, and the Alabama Sports Hall of Fame.

The Wimp Sanderson Era

What do Michael Ansley, Keith Askins, David Benoit, Jason Caffey, Jim Farmer, Robert Horry, Buck Johnson, Derrick McKey, Eddie Phillips, James Robinson, Latrell Sprewell, Marcus Webb, and Ennis Whatley have in common? They all played basketball at Alabama and in the National Basketball Association. And their college coach was Wimp Sanderson.

Wynfrey Sanderson joined the Crimson Tide basketball program as a graduate assistant for the 1960–61 season under Hayden Riley, his coach when Sanderson played at Coffee High School in Florence, Alabama. Sanderson became a full assistant coach the following year and kept that job until 1980, when he was named head coach after C. M. Newton's departure.

Sanderson was famous, or infamous, for his plaid sport coats and his scowl. In 12 seasons as Alabama's head coach, 1980–81 through 1991–92, he compiled a 267-119 record and a .692 winning percentage. Nine times his team won 20 games; only once did it have a losing season. Under his leadership, the Crimson Tide won five Southeastern Conference tournaments and played in 10 NCAA tournaments (though the NCAA wiped out the 1987 Sweet 16 finish because Crimson Tide star Derrick McKey had improperly signed with an agent during the season). In 1990, he was inducted into the Alabama Sports Hall of Fame.

Sanderson coached 13 of the 25 Alabama players who went on to NBA careers. In the pros, most had reputations as fundamentally sound, well-rounded athletes. "There are three characteristics you could say about our teams back then," Sanderson once told an interviewer. "We had good players, we played good defense, and we played hard."

Sanderson was forced to leave Alabama in 1992 after an administrative assistant filed a sexual-discrimination claim against him. Sanderson

Wimp Sanderson cuts down the net after winning one of his five Southeastern Conference tournament championships.
Courtesy of Wimp Sanderson

denied the accusation; a subsequent lawsuit was settled out of court. He compiled an 85-58 record in five years as head coach at Arkansas-Little Rock before retiring after the 1998–99 season.

He and an old colleague, former Auburn basketball coach Sonny Smith, did a free-wheeling radio show for a few years, offering their deep-fried Southern takes on basketball and everything else. Sanderson still does regular commentary on several radio stations in Alabama and Florida, and has published an autobiography, *Plaid and Parquet*. He lives in Birmingham.

The man had no fashion sense, but he sure could coach.

The Mark Gottfried Era

Just as assistant coach Wimp Sanderson had succeeded C. M. Newton, assistant coach David Hobbs succeeded Sanderson. But Hobbs didn't have Sanderson's colorful personality nor, despite 20-victory seasons in 1993–94 and 1994–95, his success. During what would turn out to be a 15-16 campaign in 1996–97, Hobbs was informed he would be fired at season's end.

Alabama turned to Mark Gottfried, who had played guard for Sanderson on three straight NCAA tournament teams in the mid-1980s. Gottfried was head coach at Murray State, coming off three impressive years that featured a 68-24 record and three Ohio Valley Conference championships.

Gottfried took the Crimson Tide to five straight NCAA tournament appearances from 2002 through 2006. His teams achieved Alabama's first appearance in the NCAA quarterfinals (2004), and, for two weeks in 2002–03, the Crimson Tide's first-ever number one ranking in the Associated Press poll.

But injuries and early defections of players to the pros took a toll. Gottfried's tenure ended with three straight years of losing records against Southeastern Conference teams. He resigned during the 2008–09 season.

Gottfried became coach at North Carolina State before the 2011–12 season. His first two teams each won 24 games and competed in the NCAA tournament, reaching the Sweet Sixteen in 2012 and the second round in 2013.

Mark Gottfried (with ball) demonstrates a basketball drill during a 2006 tournament for U.S. military teams in Kuwait.
Credit: Sergeant Robert Adams/U.S. Army

The Anthony Grant Era

To replace Mark Gottfried, Alabama chose Anthony Grant, another hotshot young coach whose Virginia Commonwealth teams had gone 76-25 over three years. In his second season, Grant took the Crimson Tide to the championship game of the National Invitation Tournament (losing to Wichita State, 66–57). In his third, Alabama made the NCAA Tournament for the first time since 2006 (losing in the first round to Creighton, 58–57).

In 2013, Grant's fourth season, Alabama put together another good year, going 23-13 (12-6 in the Southeastern Conference) and reaching the NIT quarterfinals. But is "good" enough for the fans—or new athletics director Bill Battle? Alabama hasn't won a Southeastern Conference regular-season championship since 2002 or an SEC tournament since 1991. Adding one or the other to the resume might improve job security.

Anthony Grant arrives in Tuscaloosa in 2009 after accepting the job as Alabama's head basketball coach.
Credit: Wikimedia Commons

Men's Head Coaching Records

(In chronological order, including record and winning percentage)

YEAR	COACH	RECORD	WINNING %
1912–15	D. V. Graves	20-12	.625
1915–16	Griff Harsh	13-4	.765
1916–17	Thomas Kelly	6-8	.429
1917–18	B. L. Noojin	2-5	.286
1918–19	Yancey Goodall	3-3	.500

YEAR	COACH	RECORD	WINNING %
1919–20	Bill Moore	5-7	.417
1920–23	Charles Bernier	47-19	.712
1923–42, 1945–46	Hank Crisp	264-133	.665
1942–43	Paul Burnham	10-10	.500
1944–45	Malcolm Laney	10-5	.667
1946–52	Floyd Burdette	81-59	.579
1952–56	Johnny Dee	68-25	.731
1956–60	Eugene Lambert	49-49	.500
1960–68	Hayden Riley	102-104	.495
1968–80	C. M. Newton	211-123	.632
1980–92	Wimp Sanderson	267-119	.692
1992–98	David Hobbs	110-76	.591
1998–2009	Mark Gottfried	216-138	.610
2009–13	Anthony Grant	86-52	.623

(Ranked by victories)

RECORD	COACH	YEARS
267-119	Wimp Sanderson	1980–92
264-133	Hank Crisp	1923–42, 1945–46
216-138	Mark Gottfried	1998–2009
211-123	C. M. Newton	1968–80
110-76	David Hobbs	1992–98
102-104	Hayden Riley	1960–68
86-52	Anthony Grant	2009–13
81-59	Floyd Burdette	1946–52
68-25	Johnny Dee	1952–56
49-49	Eugene Lambert	1956–60
47-19	Charles Bernier	1920–23
20-12	D. V. Graves	1912–15
13-4	Griff Harsh	1915–16
10-5	Malcolm Laney	1944–45
10-10	Paul Burnham	1942–43

RECORD	COACH	YEARS
6-8	Thomas Kelly	1916–17
5-7	Bill Moore	1919–20
3-3	Yancey Goodall	1918–19
2-5	B. L. Noojin	1917–18

(Ranked by winning percentage)

WINNING %	RECORD	COACH	YEARS
.765	13-4	Griff Harsh	1915–16
.731	68-25	Johnny Dee	1952–56
.712	47-19	Charles Bernier	1920–23
.692	267-119	Wimp Sanderson	1980–92
.667	10-5	Malcolm Laney	1944–45
.665	264-133	Hank Crisp	1923–42, 1945–46
.632	211-123	C. M. Newton	1968–80
.625	20-12	D. V. Graves	1912–15
.623	86-52	Anthony Grant	2009–13
.610	216-138	Mark Gottfried	1998–2009
.591	110-76	David Hobbs	1992–98
.579	81-59	Floyd Burdette	1946–52
.500	49-49	Eugene Lambert	1956–60
.500	10-10	Paul Burnham	1942–43
.500	3-3	Yancey Goodall	1918–19
.495	102-104	Hayden Riley	1960–68
.429	6-8	Thomas Kelly	1916–17
.417	5-7	Bill Moore	1919–20
.286	2-5	B. L. Noojin	1917–18

PRO PLAYERS

Most sports evolve from other games or sports without any one single moment of creation. Sorry, baseball fans, but the whole Abner Doubleday story is a fabrication; the sport developed organically from the English game of rounders and similar children's pastimes.

Basketball, on the other hand, was invented by a specific person at a specific time and place. In December 1891, James Naismith, a Canadian

Couldn't Stop the Moose

More than half a century after he set them, every meaningful Alabama rebounding record still belongs to Jerry "Moose" Harper. The 6-foot-8, 215-pound Harper played center for Alabama's "Rocket 8" teams of the mid-1950s (see "The Rocket 8 Take Off," page 285). His Crimson Tide records include 33 rebounds in a game, 517 in a season, and 1,688 in his four-year career (1952–53 through 1955–56). He has seven of Alabama's top ten single-game rebounding totals. He averaged a staggering 21.5 rebounds per game in 1955–56 and 18.2 in his career.

For good measure, he also holds the Alabama record for career scoring average: 20.0 points per game.

Harper was from Louisville, Kentucky, and studied engineering at Alabama. The New York Knicks drafted him in 1956, but he spurned the National Basketball Association for the Amateur Athletic Union. That sounds crazy in today's world of multimillion-dollar NBA salaries, but it was a savvy financial move at the time.

According to the Association for Professional Basketball Research, the average NBA salary in 1956 was $6,000. The corporations that sponsored AAU teams offered better financial security and sometimes even better pay. Their top players' jobs might or might not include significant business responsibilities but definitely included basketball duties.

Harper played for the Houston Ada Oilers and Phillips 66ers. Injury shortened his basketball career, but he continued working for Phillips Petroleum, then moved to Montgomery, Alabama, and built a successful business career. He died in September 2001, age 67. He was inducted into Alabama Sports Hall of Fame in February of that year, but was too ill to attend the ceremony.

physical-education instructor at the International YMCA Training School in Springfield, Massachusetts, began drawing up rules for an indoor game. He based it vaguely on ancient ball sports such as those played by the Olmec, Mayan, and Aztec cultures of Mexico and Central America.

On January 20, 1892, the first game of basketball was played. Players tried to toss a soccer ball into one of two peach baskets attached to the wall.

By the 1920s, hundreds of men's professional teams had formed. Barnstorming teams such as the Original Celtics, the New York Renaissance ("Rens"), and the Harlem Globetrotters crisscrossed the country. Some pro leagues formed, but they dissolved almost as quickly. The American Basketball League, loosely affiliated with the then-nascent National Football League, lasted longer than most: six seasons, from 1925–26 through 1930–31.

Finally, in 1946, a league with staying power came together: the Basketball Association of America. Three of its original 11 franchises remain active in the National Basketball Association: the Philadelphia (now Golden State) Warriors, New York Knickerbockers (Knicks), and Boston Celtics.

In the 1949–50 season, the National Basketball Association formed from a merger of the BAA with the older but much less organized National Basketball League, which began in 1937. NBL teams still in the NBA are the Buffalo Bisons/Tri-Cities Blackhawks (the team moved during its first season from Buffalo to the Tri-Cities area of Rock Island and Moline, Illinois, and Davenport, Iowa; it's now the Atlanta Hawks), Detroit Gems (Los Angeles Lakers), Fort Wayne Zollner (now Detroit) Pistons, Rochester Royals (Sacramento Kings), and Syracuse Nationals (Philadelphia 76ers).

The NBA traces its official founding to the BAA's formation in 1946. But not until the Boston Celtics' string of championships in the late 1950s and 1960s (every year from 1957 through 1969 except 1958 and 1967) did the NBA truly draw national attention. Until the Lakers moved from Minneapolis to Los Angeles before the 1960–61 season, the league had no teams outside the Northeast and Midwest—except, in 1949–50, the original Denver Nuggets.

To get an idea of the NBA's status a decade after its formation, consider the case of star Alabama center Jerry Harper (see "Couldn't Stop the Moose," page 283). In 1956, the New York Knicks picked Harper in the third round of the NBA draft. He elected to play for the semipro Houston Ada Oilers instead.

In 1967, the American Basketball Association formed, challenging the older league with such flashy innovations as three-point shots (later adopted by the NBA) and a red, white, and blue ball (not). When the two leagues finally merged after the 1975–76 season, the NBA absorbed four ABA teams: the New York (now Brooklyn) Nets, Denver Nuggets, Indiana Pacers, and San Antonio Spurs.

Alabama has produced 25 National Basketball Association players (counting Keith McCord, who played three years with Alabama, transferred to Alabama-Birmingham for his final year, and had a two-game NBA career). Carl Shaeffer (see page 311) was the first. The best? See "Our Alabama All-Stars," page 299.

The Rocket 8 Take Off

Alabama has Notre Dame to thank for what may still be its most famous basketball teams: the "Rocket 8" squads that went 19-5 in 1954–55 and 21-3 (with a 14-0 Southeastern Conference record) in 1955–56. Five members of the team had tried out with the Fighting Irish but didn't get scholarship offers. Shortly after the tryout, Notre Dame assistant coach Johnny Dee (see page 275) took the head-coaching job at Alabama and lured the quintet south to Tuscaloosa.

Dee molded the Fighting Irish rejects into a hustling group of five starters that played together from 1952–53 though 1955–56: center Jerry Harper, point guard Leon Marlaire, forwards Dennis O'Shea and George Linn, and

Johnny Dee (right) used guard Dale Shuman (left) as one of his top substitutes on the 1955–56 "Rocket 8" team. Other subs included (starting second from left) Tom Crosby, Roy Forbus, Kevin Barry, and Jim Bogan.

Credit: Paul W. Bryant Museum/The University of Alabama

continued on next page

guard Dennis Gunder. As for the rest of the "8," Dee used a regular rotation of three top substitutes—usually forward Billy Crews, center-forward Dick Wise, and guard Jim Bratton in 1954–55, and center-forward Jim Fulmer, guard Dale Shuman, and guard Jack Kubiszyn the next year.

Alabama sports information director Finus Gaston Sr. came up with the Rocket 8 name during the 1954–55 season. It derived from the name of the Oldsmobile Rocket 88, introduced in 1949 and a top winner on the NASCAR stock-car circuit into the early 1950s. The car inspired a 1951 rhythm-and-blues song called "Rocket 88," recorded by Ike Turner and His Kings of Rhythm (under the name Jackie Brenston and His Delta Cats).

Alabama's 1955–56 basketball squad really did rocket through its schedule. It averaged 87.9 points per game—in an era with no three-point shot, dunk, shot clock, or clock stoppage when the ball went out of bounds. On February 25, in the Garrett Coliseum in Montgomery, Alabama, the Crimson Tide beat Kentucky 101-77, becoming the first team to top 100 points against the Wildcats.

But the Rocket 8, despite a final ranking of fifth in the Associated Press poll, never got to show what they could do on the biggest national stage. At the time, the NCAA had a rule against freshman participation. The starting five had all played as freshmen, so they were ineligible for the NCAA postseason tournament.

Dee wanted to take his second-team players anyway. All five starters were graduating, so he figured it would be great experience for the following season. But the athletics department said no. Alabama turned down the SEC's automatic tournament bid, which went to Kentucky instead. Dee, angry about the decision, left for a job in Denver. The run of the Rocket 8 had ended. But it was quite a ride while it lasted.

NBA, ABA, and BAA Players by School

Top 75 Colleges (Through 2013)

94	Kentucky	83	UCLA	57	Duke
83	North Carolina	62	Kansas	54	Indiana

52	Notre Dame	32	Cincinnati	24	San Francisco
49	Louisville	32	Washington	24	South Carolina
49	St. John's (New York)	32	Western Kentucky	24	Wisconsin
47	Illinois	31	Florida State	22	Kansas State
46	Minnesota	30	Tennessee	22	La Salle
43	Arizona	29	California	22	Oklahoma
43	Michigan	29	Houston	22	Vanderbilt
43	North Carolina State	29	Iowa	21	Bradley
43	Ohio State	29	Texas	21	Colorado
41	Villanova	29	Wake Forest	21	Detroit Mercy
40	Syracuse	28	Arkansas	21	Duquesne
39	Georgetown	27	Missouri	21	NYU
39	Southern California	27	Stanford	21	Oregon
38	Maryland	27	Utah	20	Auburn
38	Michigan State	26	Arizona State	20	Brigham Young
36	Georgia Tech	26	Boston College	20	Cal State Long Beach
36	Nevada–Las Vegas	26	Long Island	20	Fresno State
35	LSU	26	Providence	20	Iowa State
34	Connecticut	26	Seton Hall	20	Virginia
34	Marquette	**25**	**Alabama**	19	Dayton
34	Purdue	25	Florida	19	Pepperdine
34	Temple	25	Oklahoma State	18	Pittsburgh*
33	DePaul	25	Oregon State	18	St. Joseph's
33	Memphis	25	Wyoming		

Includes Thomas Hamilton, who attended Pittsburgh but did not play basketball there

Southeastern Conference

94	Kentucky	**25**	**Alabama**	17	Georgia
35	LSU	25	Florida	15	Mississippi State
30	Tennessee	24	South Carolina	12	Texas A&M
28	Arkansas	22	Vanderbilt	8	Mississippi
27	Missouri	20	Auburn		

WOMEN

Ah, the '90s, when Nirvana vied with Pearl Jam for grunge-rock supremacy, *Seinfeld* and *Friends* ruled Thursday-night television, and the Alabama women's basketball team took up regular residence in the Associated Press top 25 poll and the NCAA postseason tournament.

Alabama began playing women's basketball in 1974. The program has never won a national championship, but it came tantalizingly close in 1994, reaching the NCAA Final Four before losing, 69–66, to Louisiana Tech. That came during a stretch of eight straight NCAA appearances. Alabama hasn't won a Southeastern Conference championship or SEC tournament either. To be fair, it hasn't had many chances; the SEC didn't officially acknowledge women's basketball until the 1982–83 season.

The Crimson Tide did finish second in the SEC regular season in 1996–97, when the team had a 25-7 overall record and ranked as high as second in the Associated Press sportswriters poll and *USA Today*/ESPN coaches poll. (The AP poll began ranking women's college basketball in 1976–77; the coaches began their rankings in 1984–85.) Alabama reached the SEC championship game in 1996 and 1998, losing each time.

Altogether, Alabama has appeared in the NCAA tournament 10 times and the Women's National Invitation Tournament five times.

Over the years, the Crimson Tide women have played most of their home games in cavernous Coleman Coliseum. In January 2011, the team moved into the renovated, and far cozier, Foster Auditorium (see page 9), a white-columned National Historic Landmark built in 1939.

Southeastern Conference Teams

(Ranked by wins through the 2012–2013 season)

RECORD	TEAM	WINNING %	SEASONS PLAYED
1,213-273	Tennessee	.816	39
860-360	Georgia	.705	40
828-393	Auburn	.678	42
819-381	LSU	.683	38
753-440	Mississippi	.631	39
722-331	Vanderbilt	.686	33
663-530	Texas A&M	.556	39
651-497	Florida	.567	39
650-489	Missouri	.571	38
616-368	Arkansas	.626	32
597-449	**Alabama**	**.571**	**35**
578-416	Kentucky	.581	33
542-576	Mississippi State	.485	39
522-399	South Carolina	.567	31

(Ranked by winning percentage through the 2012–2013 season)

WINNING %	TEAM	RECORD
.816	Tennessee	1,213-273
.705	Georgia	860-360
.686	Vanderbilt	722-331
.683	LSU	819-381
.678	Auburn	828-393
.631	Mississippi	753-440
.626	Arkansas	616-368
.581	Kentucky	578-416
.571	**Alabama**	**597-449**

WINNING %	TEAM	RECORD
.571	Missouri	650-489
.567	Florida	651-497
.567	South Carolina	522-399
.556	Texas A&M	663-530
.485	Mississippi State	542-576

2012–13 Southeastern Conference Home Attendance

TEAM	AVERAGE PER GAME ATTENDANCE	TOTAL SEASON ATTENDANCE
Tennessee	11,390	205,027
Kentucky	6,144	104,447
Texas A&M	5,556	105,556
Vanderbilt	4,022	56,309
South Carolina	3,952	63,224
LSU	3,846	65,383
Georgia	3,131	50,091
Auburn	2,098	39,867
Arkansas	1,933	34,794
Missouri	1,536	29,193
Mississippi State	1,317	22,384
Florida	1,190	19,035
Alabama	**1,145**	**17,178**
Mississippi	903	13,546

NCAA VERSUS WNIT VERSUS AIAW

For most of its existence since its founding in 1906, the National Collegiate Athletic Association has been, in effect, the National Collegiate Athletic Association for Men. Two things changed that: Title IX and money.

In 1972, Congress passed Title IX of the Educational Amendments of 1972 (see "Title IX and Women's Sports," page 27). Its effect was to require colleges to provide equal sports opportunities for both sexes. The number of women's collegiate athletic teams exploded.

The first women's college basketball games took place in 1896. As early as the 1940s, national groups had begun trying to oversee women's intercollegiate sports. The most prominent emerged in 1966 as the Commission on Intercollegiate Sports for Women, renamed the Commission on Intercollegiate Athletics for Women in 1967 and succeeded by the Association for Intercollegiate Athletics for Women in 1971. The AIAW put together postseason championship tournaments in many sports, most prominently softball and basketball.

The CIAW and AIAW disapproved of what they saw as the NCAA's commercialism and divergence from the ideal of the student-athlete. Initially, they banned scholarships and off-campus recruiting. The scholarship ban ended in 1973 after a lawsuit by players and coaches. The idealism eroded as some of the AIAW's postseason tournaments, including the basketball championship, began to become popular and profitable, attracting corporate sponsorship and TV coverage—in other words, money.

The money also drew the attention of the NCAA. The AIAW had almost 1,000 member schools at its peak, but when the NCAA decided to muscle in on women's championship tournaments, the AIAW had no chance. The NCAA approved championships for Divisions II and III in 1980 and Division I in 1981.

For the 1981–82 season, schools could choose between AIAW and NCAA tournaments. Some schools in some sports competed in both. But 17 of the top 20 basketball schools switched to the NCAA tournament. The AIAW lost its TV contract. It ceased operations in mid-1982, failed in an antitrust lawsuit against the NCAA, and went out of business in 1983.

Independently, the Women's National Invitation Tournament (originally the National Women's Invitation Tournament) has operated since 1969 (except for 1997). It began as an eight-team tournament and now invites 64 non-NCAA tournament teams. Like the men's NIT, with which it's not affiliated, it's considered respectable but second-tier.

Also like the men's NIT, it offers preseason and postseason tournaments, with the postseason version being the one fans care about.

Since 2010, teams not asked to the NCAA or WNIT events have had a third option: the 16-team Women's Basketball Invitational.

Alabama has played in 10 NCAA tournaments and five postseason WNITs.

Alabama Women in the Postseason (Through 2013)

Women's NIT (Postseason only; includes record or furthest round achieved)

1977	0-3	**2002**	Elite Eight
2000	First Round	**2011**	Sweet 16
2001	Second Round		

The tournament included 8 teams in 1969–1997, 16 teams in 1998, 32 teams in 1998–2005, 40 teams in 2006, 48 teams in 2007–09, and 64 teams in 2010–12.

Women's NCAA Tournament (Includes furthest round achieved)

1984	Second Round	**1996**	Sweet 16
1988	First Round	**1997**	Sweet 16
1992	Second Round	**1998**	Sweet 16
1994	Final Four	**1999**	Second Round
1995	Sweet 16		

The tournament included 32 teams in 1982–85, 40 teams in 1986–88, 48 teams in 1989–93, and 64 teams in 1994–2012.

Women's Postseason Championships (Through 2013)

CIAW Tournament (1969–71)

1	Cal State Fullerton
1	Mississippi State College for Women (now Mississippi University for Women)
1	West Chester State

AIAW Tournament (1972–82)

3 Delta State		**1** Louisiana Tech
3 Immaculata		**1** Rutgers
2 Old Dominion		**1** UCLA

Women's NIT (1969–2013) (Postseason)

9 Wayland Baptist	**1** Georgia	**1** Old Dominion
2 Arkansas	**1** Georgia Tech	**1** Penn State
2 Oregon	**1** Idaho	**1** Santa Clara
2 Oregon State	**1** Kansas State	**1** South Carolina
1 Arizona	**1** Kentucky	**1** South Florida
1 Arkansas State	**1** LSU	**1** Missouri State
1 Auburn	**1** Marquette	**1** Texas A&M
1 California	**1** New Orleans	**1** Toledo
1 Creighton	**1** Ohio State	**1** Vanderbilt
1 DePaul	**1** Oklahoma	**1** Wisconsin
1 Drexel	**1** Oklahoma State	**1** Wyoming

Women's NCAA Tournament (1982–2013)

8 Connecticut	**2** Stanford	**1** Purdue
8 Tennessee	**1** Maryland	**1** Texas
2 Baylor	**1** North Carolina	**1** Texas A&M
2 Louisiana Tech	**1** Notre Dame	**1** Texas Tech
2 Southern California	**1** Old Dominion	

Women's Basketball Invitational (2010–13)

1 Alabama-Birmingham	**1** Minnesota
1 Appalachian State	
1 Detroit	

HEAD COACHES

Rick Moody dominates the list of Alabama women's basketball coaches. With 311 victories in 16 seasons, he has almost as many wins as the other seven coaches combined (who have totaled 346 in 39 years). He also has more victories than any Crimson Tide men's basketball coach. We'd call him the Bear Bryant of Alabama women's basketball except that, for all his success, he never quite managed to win something that the Bear collected routinely: a championship.

Moody came to Alabama for the 1989–90 season. Starting in 1991–92, his teams turned in eight straight 20-win seasons. In each of those years, the Crimson Tide reached the NCAA tournament and finished in the top 25 of the coaches poll. In 1994, the Tide made it to the NCAA Final Four. In 1996–97, the team finished second in the Southeastern Conference regular-season standings, and in 1996 and 1998, it finished second in the SEC tournament.

Then the magic dimmed. Alabama slipped to 15-14 in 1999–2000. Moody's teams made three more postseason appearances, all in the Women's National Invitation Tournament. But they never again had a winning record in the SEC or reached the 20-victory mark. After three straight losing seasons, Moody retired in 2005.

In 2007, he came out of retirement to become an assistant coach for the Syracuse women's team under head coach Quentin Hillsman, who was an assistant under Moody at Alabama in 2004–05. After the 2010–11 season, Moody retired again.

Son Ben Moody competed on the Alabama golf team in the late 2000s. Ben's mother, Sandra, was his high-school coach. The school had no golf team, so she volunteered to coach if the school would start one. Ben now works for Golf for Goodness Sake, an Atlanta-based organization that raises money for charities via golf tournaments. Among his fellow staffers is David Hobbs, former Alabama men's basketball coach.

Former Alabama star Wendell Hudson was reassigned within the athletics department in April 2013 after coaching the women's team to a 68-87 record in five seasons. Hudson played for the Tide from 1970 through 1973. He ranks third all time at Alabama in career points per game at 19.2 and second in career rebounds per game at 11.9. But his skills didn't translate to coaching.

Hudson represents new athletics director Bill Battle's first coaching change. In May 2013, Battle hired Kristy Curry away from Texas Tech, where she had compiled a 130-98 record in seven years as head coach. *AL.com* reported that she would be paid $400,000, the most of any women's team coach at Alabama.

Women's Head Coaching Records

(In chronological order)

YEARS	COACH	RECORD	WINNING %
1974–77	Stephanie Schleuder	39-36	.520
1977–80	Ed Nixon	46-38	.548
1980–81	Ann Cronic	21-12	.636
1981–85	Ken Weeks	74-43	.632
1985–89	Lois Myers	71-44	.617
1989–2005	Rick Moody	311-176	.653
2005–08	Stephany Smith	27-61	.307
2008–13	Wendell Hudson	68-87	.439

(Ranked by victories)

RECORD	COACH	YEARS
311-176	Rick Moody	1989–2005
74-43	Ken Weeks	1981–82
71-44	Lois Myers	1985–86
68-87	Wendell Hudson	2008–13
46-38	Ed Nixon	1977–80
39-36	Stephanie Schleuder	1974–77
27-61	Stephany Smith	2005–08
21-12	Ann Cronic	1980–81

(Ranked by winning percentage)

WINNING %	RECORD	COACH	YEARS
.653	311-176	Rick Moody	1989–2005
.636	21-12	Ann Cronic	1980–81
.632	74-43	Ken Weeks	1981–82
.617	71-44	Lois Myers	1985–86
.548	46-38	Ed Nixon	1977–80
.520	39-36	Stephanie Schleuder	1974–77
.439	68-87	Wendell Hudson	2008–13
.307	27-61	Stephany Smith	2005–08

PRO LEAGUES

Women's professional basketball began with the Women's Professional Basketball League, which operated for three seasons, 1978–79 through 1980–81, collapsing under $14 million in cumulative losses. It had 8 teams its first season, 13 its second (until the Philadelphia and Washington teams disbanded in midseason), and 9 in the third (losing the New England franchise in midseason).

In 1980, the Ladies Professional Basketball League competed with the WPBL, briefly. It folded seven games into the season.

Next came the Women's American Basketball Association, which lasted just a couple of months in the fall of 1984. The league announced nine teams, started play with six, and crumbled quickly. In a hastily arranged championship game, the Dallas Diamonds defeated the Chicago Spirit.

The Women's Basketball Association tried something new: playing in the summer, during the National Basketball Association's off-season, instead of trying to compete directly with the pro men. This was the most stable women's league to that point, making it through the 1993 season with six teams, then the 1994 and 1995 seasons with eight teams. Liberty Sports of Dallas broadcast the games. When Fox Sports bought both Liberty Sports and the WBA, it dissolved the league.

The American Basketball League went up against the NBA. It lasted two and a half seasons. The ABL was formed as the NBA was putting together the Women's National Basketball Association. The WNBA plays during the summer; the ABL played a fall-winter schedule. It had eight teams in its first two seasons, 1996–97 and 1997–98, and nine during the partly completed 1998–99 season.

Finally, starting in 1997, the NBA brought deep pockets and marketing clout to the women's game. Most WNBA teams play in the same arenas used by NBA counterparts. At first, the NBA owned all teams, but the league is transitioning toward a broader base of financial support. Currently, the Connecticut, Seattle, Tulsa, Chicago, Atlanta, and Los Angeles franchises are independently owned. League size has varied from 8 teams to the current 12. National WNBA telecasts on ESPN draw more viewers than Major League Soccer or the National Hockey League.

Meanwhile, an amateur association called the National Women's Basketball League added a pro league in 2001. It played during the WNBA off-seasons, and some WNBA stars competed in both leagues. It began with four teams, added a team a year to reach seven in 2004, then dropped to six in 2005 and five in 2006, its final season.

In 2002, a second Women's American Basketball Association formed with five teams in Pennsylvania and one in Delaware. It lasted a season.

Alabama has sent seven players to the WNBA, including at least one active player in each of the league's first 16 years of existence. By far the best has been Dominique Canty (see page 301), the league's last Tide player, at least for a while. Her stellar 14-year career career ended in 2012.

Women's Professional Basketball Champions

Women's Professional Basketball League

1978–79	Houston Angels
1979–80	New York Stars
1980–81	Nebraska Wranglers

Women's American Basketball Association

1984	Dallas Diamonds

Women's Basketball Association

1993	Kansas Crusaders
1994	Nebraska Express
1995	Chicago Twisters

American Basketball League

1996–97	Columbus Quest
1997–98	Columbus Quest
1998–99	Columbus Quest had best record when league dissolved

◼ Women's National Basketball Association

1997	Houston Comets	**2005**	Sacramento Monarchs
1998	Houston Comets	**2006**	Detroit Shock
1999	Houston Comets	**2007**	Phoenix Mercury
2000	Houston Comets	**2008**	Detroit Shock
2001	Los Angeles Sparks	**2009**	Phoenix Mercury
2002	Los Angeles Sparks	**2010**	Seattle Storm
2003	Detroit Shock	**2011**	Minnesota Lynx
2004	Seattle Storm	**2012**	Indiana Fever

◼ National Women's Basketball League

2001	Atlanta Justice	**2004**	Dallas Fury
2002	Houston Stealth	**2005**	Colorado Chill
2003	Houston Stealth	**2006**	Colorado Chill

◼ Women's American Basketball Association II

2002	York City Noise

PLAYER BIOS

College years are years receiving a varsity letter unless otherwise noted.

Pro years are years actually played through 2012–13.

Statistics are career averages through the 2012–13 season: points per game/rebounds per game/assists per game.

ABL: American Basketball League
NBA: National Basketball Association
WNBA: Women's National Basketball Association
NWBL: National Women's Basketball League
HOF: Hall of Fame

OUR ALABAMA ALL-STARS: BASKETBALL

Men

Point Guard: **MO WILLIAMS**

Shooting Guard: **LATRELL SPREWELL**

Small Forward: **ROBERT HORRY**

Power Forward: **GERALD WALLACE**

Center: **ANTONIO MCDYESS**

Best Player: For all-around skills and endless hustle, we'll take **GERALD WALLACE.** Though if Antonio McDyess's knees had held up ...

Women

Point Guard: **NIESA JOHNSON**

Shooting Guard: **DOMINIQUE CANTY**

Small Forward: **LINDA BURGESS**

Power Forward: **SHALONDA ENIS**

Center: **TAUSHA MILLS**

Best Player: **DOMINIQUE CANTY,** without a doubt

KEITH ASKINS ■ *Guard-Forward*

COLLEGE: 1986–90 . . . . **NBA:** 1990–99, 3.8/2.9/0.8

Both at Alabama and in the National Basketball Association, Keith Askins did whatever his team needed him to do. Standing 6-7 and weighing 197 pounds, he played guard, forward, and center for the Crimson Tide, starting as a junior, coming off the bench his other three years.

As a pro, he spent nine years with the Miami Heat as a versatile reserve, three-point shooter, and defensive specialist—exactly what he had contributed to the Crimson Tide. In his best year, 1995-96, Askins averaged 6.1 points, 4.3 rebounds, and 1.6 assists per game. He has stayed with the Heat as an assistant coach, working primarily with forwards.

DAVID BENOIT ■ *Forward*

COLLEGE: 1988–90 . . . . **NBA:** 1991–96, 1997–98, 2000–01, 7.0/4.0/0.6

For an undrafted free agent, David Benoit did pretty well. He was a 6-foot-8, 220-pound center at Alabama, starting for two years and averaging 10.8 and 10.5 points per game.

Benoit played for seven years in the National Basketball Association, primarily for the Utah Jazz but also with the New Jersey Nets and Orlando Magic. He finished fourth in the 1993 NBA Slam Dunk Contest. His pro resume also includes teams in Spain, Israel, China, and Japan. Since the end of his playing career, he has been a head coach in Japan's top professional league, in Qatar and in Taiwan.

LINDA BURGESS ■ *Forward*

COLLEGE: 1990–92 . . . . **WNBA:** 1997–2000, 5.8/3.7/0.5

After starring for two years at Calhoun Community College in Decatur, Alabama, where she also set school hitting records in softball, Linda Burgess became a prolific scorer and rebounder for the Crimson Tide. In 1991–92, her senior season, the 6-1 forward averaged 20.3 points and 8.2 rebounds per game.

Burgess continued her basketball career with professional teams in Switzerland, Israel, and France—coming back to Alabama to complete her bachelor's degree in education in 1993. Finally, in 1997, she got an opportunity in her home country. She played for the Los Angeles Sparks in the first-ever Women's National Basketball Association game on June 21, 1997. (The Sparks lost to the New York Liberty, 67–57.)

Burgess played one year for the Sparks and three years for the Sacramento Monarchs. Her first year with the Monarchs, 1998, was her best as a pro. She averaged 7.5 points, 4.9 rebounds, and 1.4 steals per game.

Burgess has been an assistant coach at the University of West Alabama and head coach for a year at Stillman College in Tuscaloosa. Her nephew Fernandez Lockett is a professional basketball player in Australia.

DOMINIQUE CANTY ■ *Guard*

COLLEGE: 1996–99 . . . . **WNBA:** 1999–2012, 7.3/2.5/2.8; **NWBL:** 2003, 15.4/5.8/3.3; Illinois High School Basketball HOF

The Women's National Basketball Association career of Dominique Canty ended quietly when the Washington Mystics released her six games into the 2012 season. She had played sparingly and averaged just 2.8 points a game. Thus ended a sterling 14-year run as a point guard, shooting guard, and small forward for the Detroit Shock, the Houston Comets, her hometown Chicago Sky, and the Mystics (plus a season in 2003 with the Chicago Blaze of the National Women's Basketball League).

Canty still holds the Alabama career scoring record, male or female, with 2,294 points. (Reggie King—see page 307—has the men's record with 2,168.) As a 5-9, 166-pound guard, she did much of that shooting from long range and still compiled a field goal percentage of .509. She also specialized in slashing drives to the basket, which is why she's also Alabama's career women's leader in free throws attempted (875) and made (628). She averaged 7.2 rebounds and 3.6 assists per game.

Dominique Canty spent five WNBA seasons with her hometown Chicago Sky.
Credit: KeithAllisonPhoto.com

In the WNBA, she finished with 2,779 points, 966 rebounds, 1,051 assists, 358 steals, and near-universal respect from teammates and opponents alike. In the off-seasons (the WNBA plays during the summer), she worked in public relations with the Shock and the Dallas Mavericks of the National Basketball Association, was an assistant coach at Chicago State University, and played professionally in Israel, Poland, and Turkey. She's now in Houston pursuing another longtime interest: selling real estate.

JASON CAFFEY ■ *Forward*

COLLEGE: 1991–95 . . . . NBA: 1995–2003, 7.3/4.4/0.9

Bruising power forward Jason Caffey went to a postseason tournament all four of his years at Alabama. He was a solid scorer, averaging 14.5, 12.8, and 12.1 points per game his last three years, and reliable rebounder, twice averaging eight or more per game.

Big and strong he may be—6-8 and a chiseled 255 pounds during his National Basketball Association days—but Caffey has also battled a much tougher foe: depression.

He won NBA championship rings with the Chicago Bulls his first two seasons and later had some promising years with the Golden State Warriors and Milwaukee Bucks, peaking at 12 points and 6.8 rebounds per game with the Warriors in 1999–2000. But depression, injuries, and other personal problems led the Bucks to buy out the remaining two seasons of his contract for $11.8 million after the 2002–03 season.

Caffey faced post-career financial difficulties, partly because of child support owed for 10 children he fathered with eight different women. He was named coach of his hometown Mobile Bay Hurricanes in the semipro American Basketball Association in 2010 but was replaced during the season. He has worked with troubled youths in Mobile.

LEON DOUGLAS ■ *Center-Forward*

COLLEGE: 1972–76 . . . . NBA: 1976–83, 7.9/6.5/1.1;
Alabama Sports HOF

At Alabama, Leon Douglas anchored the middle for teams that won three straight Southeastern Conference championships, finished 14th, 10th, and 6th in the final Associated Press polls, and appeared in two NCAA tournaments and one National Invitation Tournament. Three and a half decades later, he remains seventh in career scoring average (17.2 points per game) and third in rebounding average (11.5 per game).

The Detroit Pistons picked him fourth overall in the 1976 National Basketball Association draft, making him the first Crimson Tide player to be drafted in the first round. But Douglas never quite found fulfillment as a pro until after his NBA career.

With the Pistons, he backed up star center Bob Lanier and had to endure a chaotic atmosphere—four coaches in his four years. Traded to the Kansas

City Kings, the 6-foot-10, 220-pounder again backed up an established veteran, Sam Lacey. When he left the NBA to play for nearly a decade in France and Italy, "It became a game again after being a business for a long time," he told interviewer Jon Teitel at CollegeHoops.net. In Europe, he played for "the John Wooden of Yugoslavian basketball," Aca Nickolić. (Wooden coached UCLA to 10 national championships in 12 seasons during the 1960s and '70s.) "Playing for him rejuvenated my game," Douglas said, "and some of the conditioning drills I use as a coach today I learned from him."

Douglas, who got his degree in social work at Alabama in three and a half years, has coached for Stillman College in Tuscaloosa and, since 2006, Tuskegee University in Tuskegee, Alabama. He has won a Southern Intercollegiate Athletic Conference championship at each school.

T. R. DUNN ■ *Guard-Forward*

COLLEGE: 1973–77 . . . . **NBA:** 1977–91, 5.1/4.4/1.6;
Alabama Sports HOF

For a little guy—6-4, 192 pounds, which qualifies as little in basketball—T. R. Dunn could rebound. He grabbed 20 rebounds in a 1974 game against Auburn and averaged 6.7 per game over his four-year Alabama career.

In the National Basketball Association, he was even better. His per-game averages for the three years starting in 1981–82 were 6.8, 7.5, and 7.2, respectively.

His other specialty was defense. Those two skills gave him a 14-year NBA career with the Portland Trail Blazers (three seasons) and Denver Nuggets.

Since retiring as a player, Dunn has been an assistant coach for the Charlotte Hornets, Sacramento Kings, Houston Rockets, and, most recently, Minnesota Timberwolves. He was also an assistant briefly at Alabama and coached the Charlotte Sting of the Women's National Basketball Association.

SHALONDA ENIS ■ *Forward-Center*

COLLEGE: 1995–97 . . . . **ABL:** 1997–98, 16.8/7.7/1.6;
WNBA: 1999–2003, 7.7/4.2/0.8

Recruited from Trinity Valley Community College in Athens, Texas, Shalonda Enis led Alabama in scoring and rebounding each of her two seasons in Tuscaloosa. She holds the Crimson Tide records for best scoring average in a single season (23.9 points per game in 1995–96) and a career (20.5), and she's second in career rebounds-per-game average at 9.2.

The 6-1, 185-pound Enis began her pro career with the Seattle Reign of the short-lived American Basketball League in 1997–98. She was named rookie of the year and most valuable player of the all-star game. But the league collapsed halfway through the next season, and she moved on to the Women's National Basketball Association.

After a year with the Washington Mystics, she was traded to the Charlotte Sting and had her best WNBA year, averaging 11.6 points and 3.8 rebounds per game. She also played overseas during the WNBA off-season, including in Korea in 2004–05. She is now leadership coordinator for The North Texas Job Corps Center in McKinney, Texas.

JIM FARMER ■ *Guard*

COLLEGE: 1983–87 . . . . **NBA:** 1987–91, 1993–94, 5.3/1.4/0.8

After a versatile career as a guard and forward for four Alabama NCAA tournament teams, Jim Farmer bounced around the National Basketball Association for parts of five seasons. He played for the Dallas Mavericks (who drafted him in the first round), Utah Jazz, Seattle SuperSonics, Philadelphia 76ers, and Denver Nuggets.

Between and after his NBA stints, the 6-4, 190-pound Farmer played for several Continental Basketball Association minor-league teams, an Italian team, and an all-star team put together by NBA legend-turned-businessman Magic Johnson. Farmer also coached the Birmingham Magicians during their one season (2005–06) in the semipro version of the American Basketball Association.

On the side, he began modeling. Eventually, he settled on a full-time second career: country music. A 2002 diagnosis of colon cancer, successfully treated with surgery and chemotherapy, slowed him only briefly. At last report, he was still singing and writing songs in Nashville, and frequently playing in charity basketball games.

ALONZO GEE ■ *Guard-Forward*

COLLEGE: 2005–09 . . . . **NBA:** 2009–13, 9.1/4.0/1.4

Always a solid but not spectacular scorer at Alabama (he led the team his senior year with an average of 15 points per game), Alonzo Gee had to kick his game up a notch for the pros. Undrafted after college, the 6-6, 220-pound Gee signed with the Austin Toros of the National Basketball Association Developmental League and averaged 21 points and 6.6 rebounds a game.

ROBERT HORRY ■ *Forward*

COLLEGE: 1988–92 . . . . **NBA:** 1992–2008, 7.0/4.8/2.1; Alabama Sports HOF

Even in college, Robert Horry was the ultimate complementary player—never the flashiest guy, but always contributing in ways big and small. He played for four years and ranks 13th all-time at Alabama in career points, but he never led any of his teams in scoring. He also ranks third in career steals (168) and first in career blocked shots (286). In his senior year, he even topped Alabama in assists and made the Southeastern Conference Academic Honor Roll.

Clutch shooting in the National Basketball Association playoffs earned Horry the nickname "Big Shot Rob." He won seven NBA championships: two with the Houston Rockets (1994–95), three straight with the Los Angeles Lakers (2000–02), and two with the San Antonio Spurs (2005, 2007). He played only half a season with the Phoenix Suns, so he didn't have time to bring them a title, too.

Horry's playoff heroics—hitting all seven of his three-point shots for the Lakers in 1997, hitting shots within the last minute to win or clinch seven different playoff games, setting an NBA Finals record with seven steals in one game in 1995—distort the memory of his skills. With a top points-per-game average of 12.0 in 1995–96, he was never a big pro scorer. But Horry, a long, lean 6-foot-9 and 220 pounds, could do everything well: shoot from any range, play defense, grab rebounds (7.5 per game in 1997–98), pass (4.0 assists per game in 1995–96), and block shots (1.5 per game in 1995–96).

Horry (rhymes with "glory"; the "H" is silent) now works as a commentator for Time Warner Cable SportsNet and is a partner in Ajuúa! Mexican Bar & Grill in

Whether taking a key shot or taking interview questions, Robert Horry always stays cool.
Credit: Jeff Kern

continued on next page

> San Antonio. As part of another partnership, he owns the Robert Horry Center for Sports & Physical Rehabilitation in Sugar Land, Texas, near Houston.
>
> In June 2011, Horry's 17-year-old daughter, Ashlyn, died. She had suffered from a rare genetic condition that caused health and developmental problems her entire life. Horry and his wife, Keva, created The Ashlyn Horry Foundation to help other youths with disabilities and their caretakers.

That earned him a few appearances with the NBA Washington Wizards at the end of the 2009–10 season and stints the following year with the San Antonio Spurs, the Wizards, and the Cleveland Cavaliers.

During the 2011 NBA lockout, Gee played in Poland. When the NBA came back, so did he. He started every game at small forward with Cleveland in 2012–13, averaging 10.3 points and 3.9 rebounds per game.

BUCK JOHNSON ■ *Forward*

COLLEGE: 1982–86 . . . . **NBA:** 1986–93, 9.1/3.5/1.7; Alabama Sports HOF

Buck Johnson played well if not spectacularly in the late 1980s and early 1990s for a series of good but not great Houston Rockets teams.

Johnson, 6-7 and 190 pounds, was one of the most celebrated high school and college players ever in Alabama. (He attended the now-closed Hayes High School in Birmingham.) He's still fourth in career points for the Crimson Tide (1,869) and averaged 20.7 points per game his senior year.

For the Rockets, he averaged 14.8 points per game in 1989–90 and 13.6 the following year, but he was let go after slipping to 8.6 the next season. After one last National Basketball Association year with the Washington Bullets, he dropped to the Wichita Falls Texans of the minor-league Continental Basketball Association in 1993.

A decade overseas followed—Turkey, Israel, Greece, Spain—and then one last season back home with the Birmingham Magicians of the semipro American Basketball Association in 2005–06.

Johnson now lives in Harvest, Alabama, near Huntsville. He and his wife have an engineering services company called Recast, Inc. He has been a volunteer basketball coach in Madison, Alabama, at James Clemens High School, where son Alfonso Jr. played until he graduated in 2013. Johnson also coaches his two younger children in recreational leagues.

REGGIE KING ■ *Forward*

COLLEGE: 1975–79 . . . . **NBA:** 1979–85, 8.9/6.2/1.6;
Alabama Sports HOF

Still the holder of the Alabama men's career scoring record with 2,168 points, Reggie King was drafted by, appropriately, the Kansas City Kings. At 6-6 and 225 pounds, he was a powerful rebounder (10.7 rebounds per game in college, fourth on Alabama's all-time list) as well as a shooter.

King averaged career highs of 14.9 points and 9.7 rebounds per game during his second National Basketball Association season, when Kansas City acquired his old Alabama teammate Leon Douglas. The Kings, 40–42 in the regular season, got hot in the playoffs and made it all the way to the conference final before losing, four games to one, to the Houston Rockets.

After another good year, King started to battle injuries. Kansas City traded him to the Seattle SuperSonics for his last two seasons. A shoulder injury finally forced him into retirement.

In 2001, King and his wife, Erieka, started Best Choice Home Health, a home health care company, in Kansas City, Kansas. He also developed The Villas Ridge Pointe, an independent senior community.

DERRICK MCKEY ■ *Forward-Center*

COLLEGE: 1984–87 . . . . **NBA:** 1987–2002, 11.0/4.7/2.4

Scandal prematurely ended Derrick McKey's Alabama career. During his junior year, the 6-9, 205-pound McKey averaged 18.6 points and 7.5 rebounds per game in leading the Crimson Tide to a 28-5 record that included two victories in the NCAA tournament.

But he was one of 58 football and basketball players who, while still in college, signed falsely postdated representation agreements with agents Norby Walters and Lloyd Bloom. That violated NCAA rules. The NCAA voided Alabama's tournament games and made McKey ineligible to play his senior year, forcing him to declare for the National Basketball Association draft.

Walters and Bloom were convicted of various federal charges, but the convictions were overturned on appeal. Walters went back to his main business, entertainment. He now lives in semiretirement in Los Angeles and produces the annual Night of 100 Stars gala at the Beverly Hills Hotel on Academy Awards night. Bloom was found shot to death in his Malibu, California, home in 1993, at age 36.

ANTONIO MCDYESS ■ *Forward-Center*

COLLEGE: 1993–95 . . . . **NBA:** 1995–2002, 2003–11, 12.0/7.5/1.3, 1 All-Star Team; **OLYMPICS:** 2000, 1 gold medal

After a devastating knee injury, Antonio McDyess remade his game with the Detroit Pistons.

Credit: KeithAllisonPhoto.com

At Alabama, Antonio McDyess was just beginning to show what he could do when he went pro after his sophomore season. He led the Crimson Tide in scoring that year, though with a modest 13.9 points per game, and he averaged 10.2 rebounds and 2.0 blocked shots. But in his last two games, in the first two rounds of the NCAA tournament, he exploded for 39 points and 19 rebounds against Pennsylvania and 22 points and 17 rebounds in a losing effort against Oklahoma State.

During his first six years in the National Basketball Association (five with the Denver Nuggets and one with the Phoenix Suns), McDyess averaged 17.7 points, 8.8 rebounds, and 1.7 blocked shots per game. He also earned a gold medal playing for the U.S. team in the 2000 Olympics.

McDyess was 6-foot-9 and 220 pounds, an explosive leaper and thunderous dunker who was strong enough to hold his own among the big bodies under the basket. He played suffocating defense. He worked hard in the off-seasons. He had become the quiet leader for the Nuggets, a team seemingly on the rise. He was 27 years old as the 2001–02 season began.

Ten games into the season, he injured his left knee. Badly. He didn't play the rest of the year. Or the following year. He hobbled through 2003–04 with the New York Knicks and then the Suns.

For 2004–05, he signed with the Detroit Pistons. His knee was finally strong. He settled into a supporting role for five seasons, first as a top reserve and then as the starting power forward, contributing eight to 10 points and six to 10 rebounds a game. The spring had left his legs, but he rebuilt his game around deadly midrange shooting and smart positioning.

After two final seasons with the San Antonio Spurs, he waited until the week before the lockout-delayed 2011–12 season started in December before deciding to forgo the last year of his contract and retire. At the beginning of the 2012–13 season he talked about coming back to the NBA, but nothing came of it.

He never won an NBA championship. The Hall of Fame berth that once seemed realistic now appears unlikely. But McDyess played his heart out every game and earned nearly universal respect both on and off the court. No athlete has better represented the tradition and ideals of the Crimson Tide.

McKey put his mistake behind him and concentrated on basketball. Like most Alabama players of the 1980s and '90s, he played a complete game. He could score (he averaged 15.9 points per game in 1988–89, the first of eight straight seasons in double figures), rebound, pass, and play strong defense.

That team-oriented approach gave him a 15-year NBA career with the Seattle SuperSonics, the Indiana Pacers, and, for one final season, the Philadelphia 76ers.

McKey lives in the Indianapolis area, where he is still popular from his eight years with the Pacers. He participates in charity events, holds basketball camps in his native Meridian, Mississippi, and spends time with his four children. He told an interviewer in 2012, "I was smart with my money."

JAMES ROBINSON ■ *Guard*

COLLEGE: 1990–93 . . . . **NBA:** 1993–99, 2000–01, 7.6/1.7/1.9

As a pro shooting guard, James Robinson showed flashes of the scoring ability that had allowed him to average 20.6 points per game his junior year at Alabama (after which he entered the National Basketball Association draft). Playing for the Portland Trail Blazers, for example, he scored 23 points in 10 minutes in a 1996 game against the Cleveland Cavaliers.

After three years with the Trail Blazers, the 6-2, 180-pound Robinson split three seasons between the Minnesota Timberwolves and Los Angeles Clippers, then spent several years playing in Greece, Russia, and Italy, punctuated by a brief NBA return with the Orlando Magic in 2000–01. His playing career ended with the Las Vegas Rattlers of the semipro American Basketball Association in 2004. After his NBA days, he started a little-noticed record label, Da Dirty South Records, and reportedly owned a lingerie shop in Las Vegas.

LATRELL SPREWELL ■ *Guard-Forward*

COLLEGE: 1990–92 . . . . **NBA:** 1992–2005, 18.3/4.1/4.0,
4 All-Star Teams

Even in a game full of passionate personalities, Latrell Sprewell stood out. Recruited as a defensive specialist out of a Missouri junior college by coach Wimp Sanderson, Sprewell elevated his game so much in just two years at Alabama that he finished second on the team in scoring, at 17.8 points per game, his senior year. His teammates included three other future pro players, James Robinson, Jason Caffey, and Robert Horry.

Sprewell made more National Basketball Association All-Star teams (four) than all other former Alabama players combined (Antonio McDyess, Gerald Wallace, and Mo Williams played in one each). At 6-5 and 190 pounds, he could light up the scoreboard playing point guard, shooting guard, or small forward, and he remained a tenacious defender. Seven times in his 13-year career, his scoring average topped 18 points per game.

In 1996–97, his fifth season with the Golden State Warriors, he averaged 24.2 points (his career high), 4.6 rebounds, 6.3 assists (also his career high), and 1.7 steals per game, and made the All-Star Team for the third time.

But the intensity that drove him to greatness sometimes bedeviled him as well. He was suspended for most of the 1997–98 season after a physical altercation with his coach. He came back to star for the New York Knicks for five years. Traded to the Minnesota Timberwolves, he combined with Kevin Garnett and Sam Cassell to form the league's highest-scoring trio of teammates in 2003–04.

Before the 2004–05 season, Minnesota offered Sprewell a three-year, $21 million contract extension. He was due to make $14.63 million that season alone in the final year of his previous contract. He rejected the offer, saying, "I've got a family to feed." He later downplayed that choice of words, saying he was simply trying to negotiate the best deal for himself and his

Alabama's First Pro

CARL SHAEFFER ■ *Forward-Guard*

COLLEGE: 1945–49 ....
NBA: 1949–51, 3.1/1.0 (statistics incomplete)/0.9

Carl Shaeffer met his future pro coach, Cliff Barker, when both were inmates in a German World War II prison camp. They were Indiana boys, Shaeffer from Delhi and Barker from Yorktown. After the war, both became college basketball stars, Shaeffer at Alabama and Barker as one of the "Fabulous Five," the core of Kentucky's 1947–48 national championship team and of the gold medal–winning 1948 U.S. Olympics basketball team.

In 1949, the Indianapolis Olympians joined the newly created National Basketball Association, with four of the Fabulous Five as players and part owners: center Alex Groza, guard Ralph Beard, forward Wallace "Wah Wah" Jones, and guard-coach Barker.

Barker brought in his old friend Shaeffer, 6-3 and 185 pounds, the first Alabama player ever drafted by the pros. Shaeffer had led Alabama in scoring as a freshman and had been runner-up the next three years. He averaged 3.5 points in 43 games in 1949–50, when Indianapolis won a division championship, then 1.5 points in 10 games the next season, when the team slipped to 31-37.

That ended Shaeffer's NBA career. The Olympians didn't last much longer. After the 1950–51 season, Groza and Beard admitted having been paid by gamblers to influence the scores of games while at Kentucky. The NBA banned them for life. Two seasons later, the team dissolved.

Shaeffer became a businessman in Indianapolis. He died on October 25, 1974, his 50th birthday.

family. He decided to play out the last year of his contract and become a free agent.

Sprewell was 34. He had his worst NBA season. Afterward, he got a few contract feelers, but nothing he decided to accept. In the years since, he has been in the news for a series of financial setbacks.

He does have a non-basketball legacy. The type of wheel covers that keep

GERALD WALLACE ■ *Forward*

COLLEGE: 2000–01 . . . . **NBA:** 2001–13, 12.9/6.2/2.1, 1 All-Star Team

Gerald Wallace joined the New Jersey Nets late in the 2011–12 season, just before the team's move to Brooklyn.

Credit: Wikimedia Commons

After only one year of college, during which he averaged 9.8 points and 6.0 rebounds per game, 6-foot-7, 215-pound Gerald Wallace left for the National Basketball Association. He spent the next three years sitting on the Sacramento Kings' bench, earning (a total of $2.5 million) and learning. In 2004, the new Charlotte Bobcats took him in the expansion draft, and he immediately became a starter. In 2005–06, he led the league in steals per game (2.5) and became only the third player (after David Robinson and Hakeem Olajuwon) to average more than two steals and two blocked shots per game for a season.

In 2009–10, Wallace made the All-Star Team and the NBA All-Defensive Team, and the Bobcats made the play-offs for the first time. Wallace averaged 18.2 points and 10.0 rebounds a game.

The only flaw in his game stems from one of his strengths. His hustling, diving style of play—earning him the nickname "Crash"—takes a toll on his body. Wallace estimated during the 2009–10 season that he had suffered at least five concussions during his career. Bernie Bickerstaff, Wallace's head coach in Charlotte for three years, told *The Oregonian* newspaper of Portland, "They used to put a sign in his locker saying, 'Don't dive.'"

During the 2010–11 season, the Bobcats traded Wallace to the Portland Trail Blazers. The following season, the Blazers traded him to the New Jersey (now Brooklyn) Nets. The Nets had a great year, reaching the playoffs for the first time in six years. Wallace didn't. He signed a new contract worth a reported $40 million over four years and then, pestered by injuries, averaged only 7.7 points per game. In a blockbuster postseason trade that brought stars Paul Pierce and Kevin Garnett to Brooklyn, Wallace moved to the Boston Celtics.

> While in Charlotte, Wallace created The Gerald Wallace Foundation to help underserved children and their families, both in his team's city and in Childersburg, Alabama, his hometown. The foundation focuses on recreational activities.

spinning when the car stops are nicknamed "sprewells." Sprewell promoted them through his high-performance car shop, Sprewell Motorsports (now SWR Motorsports), of Alhambra, California.

ENNIS WHATLEY ■ *Point Guard*

COLLEGE: 1981–83 . . . . **NBA:** 1983–89, 1991–92, 1993–95, 1996–97, 5.6/1.8/4.6

Basketball fans in Birmingham still talk about the astonishing ball-handling and no-look passes of Phillips High School's Ennis (rhymes with "Venus") Whatley. Whatley spent two years at Alabama, leading the Crimson Tide to the NCAA tournament both years and establishing the school career record for assists per game (6.3), then went into the National Basketball Association draft. The Kansas City Kings picked him in the first round and immediately traded him to the Chicago Bulls.

Whatley played well, starting 73 games. He averaged 8.4 points, but as a classic point guard—6-3, 177 pounds, and quick—he was always more interested in setting up scores for others. His 8.3 assists per game ranked eighth in the NBA. Twice, he dished out 22 assists in a game. He was 21 years old and holding his own among the best players in the world. Life was good.

Too good. Whatley, he later admitted, partied. In 1984–85, his scoring and assists averages slipped to 5.0 and 5.4, respectively. The Bulls traded him to the Cleveland Cavaliers, who waived him, at age 23, during the middle of the following season. He played for five more teams (Washington Bullets, San Antonio Spurs, Atlanta Hawks, Los Angeles Clippers, Portland Trail Blazers) and seven more seasons in the NBA, only once as a starter. He also played in the minor-league Continental Basketball Association, and in Lithuania and the Philippines.

Now an ordained minister and motivational speaker, Whatley lives in Maryland. His wife, Ritza, is recording secretary and chaplain for Behind the Bench, the National Basketball Wives Association, which consists of wives and life partners of current and retired NBA players. Ennis Whatley Jr. just finished his senior season as a starting forward for Vanguard University in Costa Mesa, California.

MO WILLIAMS ■ *Guard*

COLLEGE: 2001–03 . . . .**NBA:** 2003–13, 13.8/2.9/5.0, 1 All-Star Team

The Utah Jazz played Mo Williams sparingly his rookie National Basketball Association year, then released him. The 6-1, 185-pound point guard had been drafted in the second round after leaving Alabama two years early. With the Crimson Tide, he had averaged 16.4 points, 3.9 rebounds, and 3.9 assists per game his second and final season—solid but not spectacular for a point guard.

In 2011–12, Mo Williams helped lead the Los Angeles Clippers to their first playoff appearance in six years.

Credit: KeithAllisonPhoto.com

The Milwaukee Bucks picked him up, and he blossomed. He averaged more than six assists a game in three of his four years with the Bucks and began a streak of three straight years of scoring 17-plus points per game. A free agent after the 2006–07 season, he stayed with the Bucks and signed a six-year, $52 million contract.

Traded to the Cleveland Cavaliers in 2008, Williams got to play for two years with LeBron James and scored 12 points in the 2009 All-Star Game.

Before the 2010–11 season, James famously took his talents to South Beach (the Miami Heat) as a free agent. The Cavaliers' record crashed from 61-21 to 19–63. Still, Williams begged via Twitter not to be traded.

Nevertheless, he was—in midseason to the perennially woeful Los Angeles Clippers. In 2011–12, however, the Clippers became formidable. Playing behind newly acquired point guard Chris Paul, Williams became a key weapon off the bench, inserted to give the team a scoring spark and getting as many minutes as most of the starters. For 2012–13, Williams was traded back to the Jazz. Despite a thumb injury that limited him to 46 games, he turned in another reliable season as the starting point guard, averaging 12.9 points and 6.2 assists per game. Wherever he turns up next, he'll be an asset.

Others in the NBA

NAME	POSITION	COL-LEGE	NBA	STATS	TEAMS
Michael Ansley	*Forward*	1985–89	1989–92	6.9/4.2/0.4	Orlando Magic, Philadelphia 76ers, Charlotte Hornets
Jermareo Davidson	*Forward*	2003–07	2007–09	3.1/1.8/0.3	Charlotte Bobcats, Golden State Warriors
Keith McCord	*Guard*	1975–78, 1979–80	1980–81	0.0/1.0/0.5	Washington Bullets
Eddie Phillips	*Forward*	1978–82	1982–83	3.2/1.6/0.6	New Jersey Nets
Roy Rogers	*Forward*	1992–96	1996–98, 1999–2000	4.8/3.5/0.4	Vancouver Grizzlies, Boston Celtics, Toronto Raptors, Denver Nuggets
Eric Washington	*Guard*	1993–97	1997–99	6.9/2.1/1.0	Denver Nuggets
Marcus Webb	*Forward-Center*	1988–91	1992–93	4.3/1.1/0.2	Boston Celtics

Others in the WNBA

NAME	POSITION	COL-LEGE	WNBA	STATS	TEAMS
Cassandra Crumpton-Moorer	*Forward*	1983–84	1997	1.0/1/0/0.5	New York Liberty

NAME	POSITION	COLLEGE	WNBA	STATS	TEAMS
Neisa Johnson	*Guard*	1992–95	1999–2000	2.0/0.6/1.5	Charlotte Sting
Tausha Mills	*Center*	1997–98	2000–2003, 2007	2.7/2.6/0.2	Washington Mystics, San Antonio Silver Stars, Detroit Shock
Navonda Moore	*Guard*	2004–07	2007–2008	2.0/0.9/0.3	Minnesota Lynx

Alabama Men's Basketball Records

Single-Game Points

50	Mike Nordholz, 1967	**41**	Jack Kubiszyn, 1958
47	Jack Kubiszyn, 1957	**39**	Antonio McDyess, 1995
46	Bob Andrews, 1965	**38**	George Linn, 1955
45	Jack Kubiszyn, 1956	**38**	Jerry Harper, 1956
43	Jerry Harper, 1956	**38**	Jack Kubiszyn, 1958
43	Reggie King, 1978	**38**	Reggie King, 1979
41	Jerry Harper, 1956		

Single-Game Rebounds

33	Jerry Harper, 1956	**25**	Jerry Harper, 1955
28	Jerry Harper, 1956	**25**	Leon Douglas, 1975
28	Jerry Harper, 1956	**24**	Jerry Harper, 1953
28	Jerry Harper, 1956	**23**	Reggie King, 1976
28	Harry Hammonds, 1965	**23**	Richard Hendrix, 2007
27	Jerry Harper, 1955		

Season Points

747	Reggie King 1978–79	**615**	Derrick McKey, 1986–87
661	James Robinson, 1991–92	**611**	Rod Grizzard, 2000–01
630	Michael Ansley, 1988–89	**599**	Buck Johnson, 1985–86
623	Latrell Sprewell, 1991–92	**598**	James Robinson, 1992–93
620	Wendell Hudson, 1972–73	**596**	Eric Washington, 1995–96

Season Rebounds

517	Jerry Harper, 1955–56	**359**	Reggie King, 1977–78
456	Jerry Harper, 1954–55	**358**	Jerry Harper, 1952–53
383	Jim Fulmer, 1956–57	**357**	Jerry Harper, 1953–54
362	Wendell Hudson, 1972–73	**353**	Leon Douglas, 1974–75
361	Erwin Dudley, 2000–01	**348**	Leon Douglas, 1975–76

Season Scoring Average

24.6	Jack Kubiszyn, 1956–57	**21.2**	Reggie King, 1977–78
23.3	Jack Kubiszyn, 1957–58	**21.0**	Jerry Harper, 1954–55
23.2	Jerry Harper, 1955–56	**21.0**	Mike Nordholz, 1966–67
22.6	Reggie King, 1978–79	**20.7**	Buck Johnson, 1985–86
22.2	George Linn, 1955–56	**20.7**	Leon Douglas, 1974–75
21.4	Jim Fulmer, 1956–57		

Season Rebounding Average

21.5	Jerry Harper, 1955–56	**13.3**	Reggie King, 1977–78
19.0	Jerry Harper, 1954–55	**13.1**	Wendell Hudson, 1971–72
17.0	Jerry Harper, 1952–53	**13.1**	Leon Douglas, 1974–75
14.9	Jerry Harper, 1953–54	**12.4**	Leon Douglas, 1975–76
14.7	Jim Fulmer, 1956–57	**12.1**	Wendell Hudson, 1972–73

Career Points

2,168 Reggie King, 1975–79	**1,813** James Robinson, 1990–92
1,937 Eddie Phillips, 1978–82	**1,775** Erwin Dudley, 1999–2003
1,909 Leon Douglas, 1972–76	**1,759** Brian Williams, 1995–99
1,869 Buck Johnson, 1982–86	**1,749** Michael Ansley, 1985–89
1,861 Jerry Harper, 1952–56	**1,697** Bobby Lee Hurt, 1981–85

Career Scoring Average

20.0 Jerry Harper, 1952–56	**18.3** Jack Kubiszyn, 1955–58
19.9 Mike Nordholz, 1965–68	**17.3** Brian Williams, 1995–99
19.2 Wendell Hudson, 1970–73	**17.2** Leon Douglas, 1972–76
18.9 James Robinson, 1990–93	**16.5** Bob Andrews, 1962–65
18.4 Reggie King, 1975–79	**16.2** Kennedy Winston, 2002–05

Career Rebounding Average

18.2 Jerry Harper, 1952–56	**9.4** Jim Fulmer, 1955–58
11.9 Wendell Hudson, 1970–73	**9.3** Eddie Phillips, 1978–82
11.5 Leon Douglas, 1972–76	**9.3** Antonio McDyess, 1993–95
10.7 Reggie King, 1975–79	**9.2** Rich Deppe, 1966–69
10.3 Alan House, 1969–72	**9.2** Erwin Dudley, 1999–2003

Alabama Women's Basketball Records

Single-Game Points

38 Amy Lannon, 1992	**33** Carol Smith, 1985
37 Linda Burgess, 1991	**33** Niesa Johnson, 1995
35 Shalonda Enis, 1995	**33** Yolanda Watkins, 1995
34 Cassandra Crumpton, 1983	**33** Shalonda Enis, 1996
34 Linda Burgess, 1991	**33** Dominique Canty, 1999
34 Shalonda Enis, 1995	**33** LaToya Thomas, 2002
33 Terri Hillard, 1982	**33** Varisia Raffington, 2009

Single-Game Rebounds

27 Tierney Jenkins, 2009

24 Leslie Payne, 1979

22 Carol Smith, 1986

21 Laura Heard, 1989

21 Michelle Smith, 1990

20 Carol Smith, 1982

19 Carol Smith, 1986

19 Monique Bivins, 2004

18 Carol Smith, 1984

18 Carol Smith, 1984

18 Laura Heard, 1989

18 Michelle Smith, 1991

18 Erin Hogue, 2011

Season Points

766 Shalonda Enis, 1995–96

732 Dominique Canty, 1997–98

653 Niesa Johnson, 1994–95

612 Dominique Canty, 1998–99

610 Linda Burgess, 1991–92

569 Terri Hillard, 1981–82

564 Carol Smith, 1985–86

559 Cassandra Crumpton, 1983–84

543 Shalonda Enis, 1996–97

532 Cassandra Crumpton, 1982–83

Season Rebounds

350 Tierney Jenkins, 2010–11

320 Yolanda Watkins, 1993–94

309 Carol Smith, 1985–86

305 Shalonda Enis, 1995–96

291 Sandra Murray, 1977–78

284 Shalonda Enis, 1996–97

270 Laura Heard, 1988–89

267 Yolanda Watkins, 1992–93

264 Sylvia Akers, 1981–82

264 Tierney Jenkins, 2009–10

Season Scoring Average

23.9 Shalonda Enis, 1995–96

21.5 Dominique Canty, 1997–98

21.1 Niesa Johnson, 1994–95

20.3 Linda Burgess, 1991–92

20.3 Terri Hillard, 1981–82

19.7 Dominique Canty, 1998–99

19.6 Julie Ellis, 1974–75

19.4 Carol Smith, 1985–86

18.3 Cassandra Crumpton, 1982–83

17.5 Cassandra Crumpton, 1983–84

Season Rebounding Average

10.7 Carol Smith, 1985–86	**9.8** Yolanda Watkins, 1993–94
10.6 Tierney Jenkins, 2010–11	**9.7** Julie Ellis, 1974–75
10.1 Carol Smith, 1984–85	**9.5** Shalonda Enis, 1995–96
10.0 Laura Heard, 1988–89	**9.4** Sylvia Akers, 1981–82
9.9 Mary Hudgins, 1975–76	**9.4** Sandra Murray, 1977–78

Career Points

2,294 Dominique Canty, 1996–99	**1,535** Tierney Jenkins, 2008–11
2,134 Niesa Johnson, 1992–95	**1,519** Betsy Harris, 1990–94
2,018 Carol Smith, 1982–86	**1,411** Shondra Johnson, 1998–2002
1,778 Yolanda Watkins, 1993–97	**1,309** Shalonda Enis, 1995–97
1,606 Terri Hillard, 1980–84	**1,299** Leslie Payne, 1977–81

Career Scoring Average

20.5 Shalonda Enis, 1995–97	**17.1** Niesa Johnson, 1992–95
18.2 Cassandra Crumpton, 1982–84	**14.2** Yolanda Watkins, 1993–97
18.1 Linda Burgess, 1990–92	**13.4** Terri Hillard, 1980–84
18.1 Dominique Canty, 1995–99	**12.6** Tierney Jenkins, 2008–11
17.3 Carol Smith, 1982–86	**12.6** Tracey Rutledge, 1985–88

Career Rebounding Average

9.3 Carol Smith, 1982–86	**8.1** Linda Burgess, 1990–92
9.2 Shalonda Enis, 1995–97	**7.2** Leslie Payne, 1977–81
8.7 Yolanda Watkins, 1992–97	**7.2** Dominique Canty, 1995–99
8.5 Tierney Jenkins, 2008–11	**7.0** Laura Heard, 1986–90
8.2 Justina Smith, 1983–84	**6.9** Terri Hillard, 1980–84

Selected NCAA Individual Records Men

Blocked Shots in a Game

16	Mickell Gladness, Alabama A&M, 2007	**14**	Loren Woods, Arizona, 2000
14	David Robinson, Navy, 1986	**14**	Darrius Garrett, Richmond, 2010
14	Shawn Bradley, Brigham Young, 1990	**13**	tie among 12 players
14 Roy Rogers, Alabama, 1996			

Rebounds in a Career

2,201	Tom Gola, La Salle, 1951–55	**1,802**	Dickie Hemric, Wake Forest, 1951–55
2,030	Joe Holup, George Washington, 1952–56	**1,751**	Paul Silas, Creighton, 1961–64
1,916	Charlie Slack, Marshall, 1952–56	**1,716**	Art Quimby, Connecticut, 1951–55
1,884	Ed Conlin, Fordham, 1951–55	**1,688 Jerry Harper, Alabama, 1952–56**	
***1,820**	Robert Parish, Centenary, 1972–76	**1,679**	Jeff Cohen, William & Mary, 1957–61

**Not recognized by the NCAA because of sanctions over Parish's eligibility*

GOLF

MEN

It's official: Alabama is now a golf powerhouse. After coming within one hole of winning its first national title in 2012, the Alabama men's team took the crown decisively in 2013. The Crimson Tide beat Illinois, 4 matches to 1, in the NCAA Championships.

The men's team has now reached the finals in seven of the past nine seasons and has won the past two Southeastern Conference championships. Alabama's top male three golfers, Cory Whitsett, Justin Thomas, and Bobby Wyatt, all return next season. All three finished under par overall for 2012–13. Meanwhile, the women's team (see page 331) won its first national championship in 2012 and finished seventh nationally in 2013, extending its string of consecutive NCAA Championships appearances to eight.

Alabama launched its golf program auspiciously in 1951–52. The Crimson Tide's Bobby Hill won the Southeastern Conference individual championship. But Alabama didn't become consistently successful for two more decades, until Conrad Rehling became the first full-time golf coach in 1971–72. Jay Seawell arrived in 2002–03 and elevated men's golf even further. Now, opponents speak of it in the same way that they speak of Alabama football: as an annual threat to win it all.

Alabama NCAA Finals Appearances

1973 17th		**1992** 11th		**2008** 13th	
1974 14th		**1993** 29th		**2009** 15th	
1975 tied for 3rd		**1996** 28th		**2011** 14th	
1981 17th		**2005** 28th		**2012** 2nd	
1983 17th		**2007** 6th		**2013** 1st	

Southeastern Conference

Team Championships

28	Georgia	3	Auburn	1	Georgia Tech
15	Florida	3	Tennessee	1	Kentucky
15	LSU	2	Mississippi State	1	Mississippi
4	**Alabama**	1	Arkansas		

Individual Champions

22	Florida	4	Tennessee	1	Mississippi State
16	LSU	***3**	**Alabama**	1	South Carolina
15	Georgia	2	Arkansas	1	Tulane
4	Auburn	1	Georgia Tech		
4	Mississippi	1	Kentucky		

Bobby Hill, 1952; Michael Thompson, 2008; Justin Thomas, 2012

HEAD COACHES

During golf's first couple of decades at Alabama, the athletics department treated it as a distinctly minor sport. Coaches were part time—usually either assistant football coaches (Malcolm Laney, Bubber Nesbit, Gene Stallings, Steve Sloan) or local club pros (Jackie Maness, Ronnie Laffoon).

Finally, in 1971, athletics director Bear Bryant hired the school's first full-time golf mentor, former University of Florida coach Conrad Rehling.

> ## Not Really His Sport
>
> Gene Stallings, who later became one of Alabama's most successful football head coaches (see page 45), also coached the golf team from 1957–58 through 1959–60, when he was an assistant football coach for Bear Bryant. In matches, Stallings' golf teams went 4-4, 3-4, and 4-5. His football teams of the 1990s did considerably better.

The Conrad Rehling Era

Conrad Rehling played basketball at Taylor University, an evangelical Christian college in Indiana, but he made his mark as a golf coach, first at Florida (1956–63) and then at Alabama from 1971–72 through 1987–88. He took the Crimson Tide to its first Southeastern Conference championship in 1979 and to NCAA finals appearances in 1973, 1974, 1975 (when Alabama tied for third), 1981, and 1983.

Rehling helped found the women's golf program at Alabama and coached the women's team in 1977–78 and 1978–79. His prize pupil, male or female, was Jerry Pate (see page 342), who came to Alabama at the same time that Rehling did. "He had a remarkable ability to mold kids, to make winners out of them," Pate said years later.

"It was more than helping them win golf championships. He really turned my life around. I had bumps along the way when I was in my middle 30s, and he guided me through the Fellowship of Christian Athletes Golf Ministry to lead a better path."

Rehling also coached several other golfers at Alabama who reached the PGA or LPGA Tour: Steve Lowery, Spike McRoy, Tom Garner, Barry Harwell, Tony Hollifield, Tab Hudson, Gordon Johnson, Alan Pate (no relation to Jerry), Lee Rinker, Gary Trivisonno, and Peggy Kirsch.

After retiring from Alabama in 1988, Rehling turned his considerable charm, energy, and skill toward teaching golf to the physically challenged. He won The PGA of America's Horton Smith Award in 1992 for his educational efforts in general and a Lifetime Achievement Award in 2005 for his work on golf in the Special Olympics. The PGA also established the Conrad Rehling Award for contributions to Special Olympics golf.

Rehling is enshrined in the Golf Coaches Association of America Hall of Fame and the Alabama Sports Hall of Fame. He died of congestive heart failure in 2007. He was 87.

The Jay Seawell Era

Dick Spybey came to Alabama as a graduate assistant to Conrad Rehling in 1984. He continued as a men's assistant coach while also coaching the Alabama women's team. In 1988, he succeeded his boss as head men's coach.

Spybey took Alabama to the NCAA finals in 1992, 1993, and 1996 and coached future PGA Tour pros Spike McRoy, Dicky Pride, David Kirkpatrick, and Mårten Olander. He left Alabama in 2002 in favor of high school teaching and coaching. He is now athletics director and middle school principal at Westminster Christian Academy in Huntsville, Alabama.

To succeed Spybey, Alabama hired Jay Seawell, who has a degree in hotel and restaurant management from South Carolina and was coaching, quite successfully, at Augusta State University in Augusta, Georgia. In this case, the cliché applies: Seawell really has taken Alabama to the next level.

Under Seawell, the Crimson Tide has become a perennial national power. His teams have reached the NCAA finals in 2005, 2007–09, and 2011–13. Alabama won the Southeastern Conference title in 2008, 2012, and 2013, and freshman Justin Thomas won the SEC individual title in 2012 as well. Youngsters Bud Cauley, Michael Thompson, and Hunter Hamrick, all of whom Seawell coached at Alabama, have already made impressions on the PGA Tour.

List of Head Coaches

Golf coaches are sometimes ranked by total matches won and lost and sometimes by tournaments entered and won. Neither method is exceptionally precise, and complete records for some of Alabama's coaches are not available. So we're simply listing the Crimson Tide's golf coaches in chronological order:

1951–54 Malcolm Laney	**1968–70** Steve Sloan
1954–57 Bubber Nesbit	**1970–71** Ronnie Laffoon
1957–60 Gene Stallings	**1971–88** Conrad Rehling
1960–64 Dick Pride	**1988–2002** Dick Spybey
1964–68 Jackie Maness	**2002–13** Jay Seawell

JERRY PATE NATIONAL INTERCOLLEGIATE

College golf's top early-season tournament happens in Alabama every October: the Jerry Pate National Intercollegiate. The 12-team tournament, begun in 1986, represents a partnership between the University of Alabama and its greatest pro golfer alum, Jerry Pate (see page 342). Pate does more than lend his name. He plays an active role in everything from selecting teams to presenting trophies.

The tournament began in Pate's hometown of Pensacola, Florida. He moved it to Birmingham's Shoal Creek course in 1992. Since 1997, the tournament has taken place at the Old Overton Club in the Birmingham suburb of Vestavia Hills.

The selection committee, which has included such marquee pros as Arnold Palmer and Ben Crenshaw, tries to invite the strongest field possible. In recent years, the host team has added to that strength. Alabama won four years in a row, 2006 through 2009. Alabama golfers posted the top individual score in 1991 (David Kirkpatrick, 221 over 72 holes), 2006 (Joseph Sykora, 199), 2007 (Mark Harrell, who tied with East Tennessee State's Seamus Power at 198), 2009 (Hunter Hamrick, 65 in a rain-shortened tournament), and 2012 (Justin Thomas, 208).

The medalist in 1994, with a score of 206, was a member of the winning Stanford team, Tiger Woods. You may have heard of him.

The 2011 tournament presaged the NCAA championship eight months later. Texas won; Alabama finished in a second-place tie with Clemson. Texas and Alabama also finished first and second, respectively, at the NCAA championships in June 2012. Alabama won both the Pate Intercollegiate title and the national championship during the 2012–13 season, but Florida, which finished second in the Pate, trailed in 25th place at the NCAA Championships. National runner-up Illinois wasn't invited to the Pate.

YEAR	WINNING TEAM	MEDALIST
1986	Columbus College	Peter Dyson, West Florida
1987	South Alabama	Nolan Henke, Florida State
1988	LSU	David Toms, LSU
1989	Florida State	Mike Hemen, Southwest Louisiana
1990	Miami	Steve Pope, Mississippi State
1991	North Florida	**David Kirkpatrick, Alabama**
1992	Oklahoma State	David Berganio, Arizona

YEAR	WINNING TEAM	MEDALIST
1993	Wake Forest	Ron Whittaker, Wake Forest
1994	Stanford	Tiger Woods, Stanford
1995	Arizona State	Rob Bradley, North Carolina
1996	Oklahoma State	Edward Loar, Oklahoma State
1997	Clemson	Rory Sabbatini, Arizona
1998	Clemson	Jeremy Anderson, Nevada-Las Vegas
1999	Clemson	B. J. Schlagenhauf, UCLA
2000	Clemson	Bryce Molder, Georgia Tech
2001	Oklahoma State	tie, D. J. Trahan, Clemson
		tie, Hunter Mahan, Oklahoma State
2002	Clemson	Chris Nallen, Arizona
2003	Oklahoma State	Bill Haas, Wake Forest
2004	Augusta State	Kalle Edberg, Augusta State
2005	Georgia Tech	Garratt Osborn, Alabama-Birmingham
2006	**Alabama**	**Joseph Sykora, Alabama**
2007	**Alabama**	tie, **Mark Harrell, Alabama**
		tie, Seamus Power, East Tennessee State
2008	**Alabama**	Kelly Kraft, SMU
2009	**Alabama**	**Hunter Hamrick, Alabama**
2010	Auburn	Niclas Carlsson, Auburn
2011	Texas	Corbin Mills, Clemson
2012	**Alabama**	**Justin Thomas, Alabama**

PRO PLAYERS

Professional golf tournaments date back to the 19th century. The Western Open (now the BMW Championship) was first played in 1899. Even before that, 10 pro golfers and one amateur played in the first U.S. Open in 1895. Starting as early as the 1910s, such legendary pro golfers as Walter Hagen, Gene Sarazen, Byron Nelson, Ben Hogan, and Sam Snead caught the public's attention.

The Professional Golfers' Association of America was formed in 1916, though the membership consisted chiefly of club rather than touring pros. By the early 1920s, a winter series of tournaments had been organized that began on the West Coast. Golfers played their way east through Texas and Florida and finished at Pinehurst, North Carolina in the spring. The PGA Tournament Bureau began in 1930, and the first organization of "playing pros" came together in 1932.

Two things catapulted the professional golf tour into the sports mainstream in the late 1950s: television and Arnold Palmer. TV brought the game into millions of living rooms, and the big-hitting, affable Palmer specialized in come-from-behind finishes and wasn't afraid to show the ecstasy and agony of every great shot and missed putt.

In 1968, what's now called the PGA Tour spun off from the PGA, which remained an organization of club pros. (Officially, it's the PGA TOUR, but the all-capitals look is a bit much on the printed page, so we're toning it down a bit.)

The PGA Tour currently operates three tours. The top circuit, the PGA Tour itself, consists of tournaments run by the PGA as well as several organized by outside entities. The four "major" tournaments—the Masters Tournament, U.S. Open, British Open, and PGA Championship—all fall into the "outside" category.

Not just anybody gets to play in the PGA Tour. Golfers have to earn their way to the top, usually through a qualifying tournament or finishing among the top 25 money winners in the Web.com Tour, a developmental circuit. (Essentially, it's tournament golf's minor league.) Founded in 1990, the junior tour also has been known as the Ben Hogan Tour, the Nike Tour, the Buy.com Tour, and the Nationwide Tour.

The Champions Tour, founded in 1980 as the Senior PGA Tour, is for golfers age 50 or older.

Among the Crimson Tide golfers who have played on the PGA Tour, two stand out: Gardner Dickinson (see page 338) and Jerry Pate (see page 342).

Dickinson, a native of Dothan, Alabama, starred on the LSU golf team in the late 1940s. He attended graduate school at Alabama in 1950–51, but the university didn't have a golf team until 1952. He won seven PGA Tour events.

Pate did him one better, winning eight PGA tournaments, including the 1976 U.S. Open.

Several young players out of Alabama, including Bud Cauley (see page 338), Hunter Hamrick (see page 341), and Michael Thompson (see page 344), may challenge those legacies. And a number of current Tide players also seem poised for PGA Tour careers. If you like golf, it's a good time to be an Alabama fan.

WOMEN

As good as the Alabama men's golf team has been in recent years, the women have been even better. Since Mic Potter became coach in 2005–06, his teams have reached the NCAA Championships every single year. In 2012, the women gave Alabama its first national title in a sport other than football or gymnastics. The golfers beat the softball team to that distinction by 13 days—and beat their male golfing counterparts to a national championship by one year.

In 2013, the Tide women entered the NCAA Championships ranked second nationally but finished seventh. Alabama did win the Southeastern Conference title, its second (with the other one coming in 2010). Stephanie Meadow became Alabama's first female individual SEC champion, shooting an even-par 216 in cold and rainy conditions.

Meadow, a native of Northern Ireland, won the British Ladies Amateur Golf Championship in 2012 and had the NCAA's best scoring average in 2012–13 at 71.24. She returns for 2013–14, as do three more of Alabama's five leading scorers. Before Potter's arrival, the Crimson Tide had only one other NCAA Championships appearance, in 1987.

In the early days, the Tide did have a string of seven straight appearances, from 1975 through 1981, in a predecessor national tournament run by the Association for Intercollegiate Athletics for Women. That streak started with Alabama's very first women's team in 1974–75, which finished seventh in the tournament. That's the best Alabama ever did in the AIAW competition. (For more on the AIAW, see "Queen of the 'Golfing Co-eds,'" page 333.)

Alabama women's golf does have an individual national champion. Way back in 1941, Alabama's Eleanor Dudley won the first-ever intercollegiate women's golf championship, played at Ohio State. (Again, see "Queen of the 'Golfing Co-eds,'" page 333.)

Alabama's women share with the men some of the best golf facilities in the country: the Ol' Colony Golf Complex home course and the Jerry Pate Golf Center, the university's private practice and training facility at Ol' Colony.

They also share a bright future. Meadow already owns Alabama's career record for best scoring average, 72.11, and fellow senior Hannah Collier ranks eighth at 75.22. Sophomore Emma Talley averaged a sizzling 73.00 during her 2012–13 Crimson Tide debut.

Alabama AIAW Nationals Appearances

1975 7th		**1978** 20th		**1981** 22nd	
1976 17th		**1979** 18th			
1977 23rd		**1980** 18th			

Alabama NCAA Finals Appearances

1987 9th		**2008** tied for 12th		**2011** tied for 8th	
2006 24th		**2009** 11th		**2012** 1st	
2007 23rd		**2010** 3rd		**2013** 7th	

Southeastern Conference

Team Championships

11 Georgia		**2 Alabama**		**1** Vanderbilt	
9 Auburn		**1** LSU			
8 Florida		**1** South Carolina			

Individual Champions

8 Florida	**2** Arkansas	**1** LSU
8 Georgia	**2** South Carolina	**1** Mississippi State
5 Auburn	**2** Vanderbilt	
3 Tennessee	***1 Alabama**	

**Stephanie Meadow, 2013*

Queen of the 'Golfing Co-eds'

In 1941, Gladys Palmer, chair of the women's department at Ohio State, took it on herself to organize the first women's intercollegiate golf championship. Eleanor Dudley, who had just graduated from Alabama (the tournament was in July), beat Eddell Wortz of Stephens College in Columbia, Missouri, in the final. "The nation's golfing co-eds crowned their first queen today," said a story in *The Blade* newspaper of Toledo, Ohio.

"The event was one of the most see-saw affairs ever produced by a big-time tourney, but the outcome finally hinged on Miss Dudley's superior hitting power," the newspaper said. "Miss Wortz, with all her finesse and putting ability, could not overcome the tremendous distance advantage gained by her huskier foe."

The tournament came under the auspices of the Division for Girls' and Women's Sports of the American Association for Health, Physical Education and Recreation. Golfers competed as individuals representing their schools; there were no teams. After a four-year break because of World War II, the championship resumed in 1946. It remained at Ohio State through 1952, then continued at other venues under the DGWS and its successor organizations, the Commission on Intercollegiate Athletics for Women (starting in 1966) and the Association for Intercollegiate Athletics for Women (starting in 1972).

In 1970, the CIAW added a team competition to the golf tournament. The AIAW retained both the team and individual components when it took over the tournament in 1972. The AIAW also sponsored championships in many other sports. But in 1982, the NCAA began offering women's championships of its own. That year, the NCAA and the AIAW held competing women's collegiate tournaments in several sports. Following the 1982 tournaments, the AIAW, unable to compete against the NCAA's power and financial resources, ceased operations.

HEAD COACHES

Ann Marie Lawler, who coached the first two seasons of Crimson Tide women's golf beginning in 1974–75, became Alabama's women's athletics director and then associate athletic director for women's sports at Florida. Bob Montgomery, a local golf pro and assistant at the university, took over for a year, and then men's golf coach Conrad Rehling (see page 326) added the women's team to his portfolio for two years.

Starting in 1979–80, Lynn Kurth took the reins for five seasons. Kurth was a young former Iowa State golfer who earned a master's degree in physical education at Alabama. She also taught physical education. Kurth, later Lynn Kurth Shaffer, went on to be a club pro at courses in the Birmingham area. She died in 2002, age 48, of cancer.

The Alabama team reached the Association for Intercollegiate Athletics for Women national championship tournament in each of the first seven years of the team's existence, despite having four different head coaches during that period.

Dick Spybey, an assistant coach for the men's golf team, became women's head coach starting in 1984–85, guiding the team to a ninth-place finish in the 1987 NCAA championships. He left to become the men's head coach after the 1987–88 season.

The Betty Palmer Era

Betty Palmer grew up in Tuscaloosa and lettered in golf for four years at Alabama, starting in 1978–79. (She was Betty Buck then.) She became head coach in 1988–89 and stayed through 2004–05, when she retired and moved with her family to Jacksonville, Alabama, where her husband had accepted a teaching position at Jacksonville State University.

Palmer served on the NCAA Women's Golf Committee from 1995 until 1998 and coached the U.S. team in a women's collegiate tournament in Japan in 1998. Her Alabama teams posted five top-five finishes in the Southeastern Conference tournament but never won a championship, and she never took a team to the NCAA championships. Alabama's next coach wasted no time in changing that.

She didn't stay retired long. Palmer was athletics director and a history teacher at The Donoho School, a private school in Anniston, Alabama, from 2006 to 2008. After a year-plus selling sports equipment, she became athletics director and a coach and teacher at Faith Christian School, also in Anniston.

Mic Potter had already been named to the National Golf Coaches Association Hall of Fame before he came to Alabama in 2005.
University of Alabama Athletics

In June 2013, she took over as the women's golf coach at Birmingham-Southern College in Birmingham.

The Mic Potter Era

In 2005, Alabama hired Mic Potter away from Furman, where in 23 years as head women's golf coach he had built a career that earned him enshrinement in the National Golf Coaches Association Hall of Fame.

His impact at Alabama was immediate and spectacular. Since his arrival, the Crimson Tide has never failed to reach the NCAA championship tournament. And in 2012, the Alabama women's golf team won the national championship.

Potter had taken 21 previous teams to the NCAA championships and recorded eight other top-10 finishes. "He has been so close so many times," said Brooke Pancake, whose four-foot putt on the final hole won the title. "I'm so honored I got to be on the team that did it for him. For him to have hugged me with tears in his eyes afterwards, it was incredible."

List of Head Coaches

Golf coaches are sometimes ranked by total matches won and lost and sometimes by tournaments entered and won. Neither method is exceptionally precise, and complete records for some of Alabama's coaches are not available. So we're simply listing the Crimson Tide's golf coaches in chronological order:

1974–76 Ann Marie Lawler	**1984–88** Dick Spybey
1976–77 Bob Montgomery	**1988–2005** Betty Palmer
1977–79 Conrad Rehling	**2005–13** Mic Potter
1979–84 Lynn Kurth	

PRO PLAYERS

The first organization that tried to organize a U.S. women's pro golf tour, the Women's Professional Golf Association, strung together a few tournaments but survived only from 1944 through 1948.

In 1950, 13 golfers tried again, and this time it lasted. The lucky 13 players formed the Ladies Professional Golf Association. Today, the LPGA still runs the two dominant U.S. women's golf tours, the LPGA Tour and the developmental Symetra Tour (formerly called the Futures Tour; the top 10 money winners each year gain LPGA Tour membership). The LPGA also has an affiliation with The Legends Tour, formerly the Women's Senior Golf Tour, for women pros 45 or older.

In 2013 the top-of-the-line LPGA Tour encompassed 28 tournaments with an aggregate of nearly $49 million in prize money.

Alabama hasn't contributed nearly as many women to the LPGA Tour as it has sent men to the PGA Tour. And, so far, no Alabama golfer has won an LPGA event. Kathleen Ekey and Brook Pancake, the only Alabama alumnae who currently play on the LPGA Tour, may change that. Or some of the golfers currently competing for the Crimson Tide may beat them to that first win. Considering the amount of talent that Alabama has produced in the past decade, and continues to produce, attention-getting feats on the pro circuit seem just a matter of time.

PLAYER BIOS

College years are years receiving a varsity letter unless otherwise noted.

Tour years are years playing in one or more tour events through 2013.

CT: Champions Tour

LPGA: LPGA Tour

PGA: PGA Tour

HOF: Hall of Fame

JASON BOHN

COLLEGE: 1992 (on squad; did not compete)

PGA: 2004–2013, 2 wins

On November 1, 1992, Jason Bohn was a nonscholarship redshirt freshman golfer who had not yet played in an official match for Alabama. Groggy after several Halloween parties the night before, he nevertheless took a swing at a 135-yard hole-in-one contest.

The ball went in the cup. He won $1 million.

Bohn immediately forfeited his amateur status in favor of a $50,000 check every October 1 for 20 years (the last coming in 2012). But he didn't leave school. He graduated in 1995 with a degree in, appropriately, finance.

The guaranteed income allowed him to grind out a living for several years on the Canadian Tour and the PGA's second-tier Nationwide Tour (winning a tournament on each) before he finally made the big time—the PGA Tour itself—in 2004.

A single lucky swing led Jason Bohn to leave the Alabama golf team before he'd officially even started competing..

Credit: KeithAllisonPhoto.com

He's been there ever since. He won the B. C. Open in 2005, the nontour Callaway Golf Pebble Beach Invitational in 2006, and the Zurich Classic of New Orleans in 2010. He's also earned a reputation as the tour's nicest guy.

Altogether, the 6-0, 180-pound Bohn has won more than $10 million on the PGA Tour. Not counting that $50,000 each October.

BUD CAULEY

COLLEGE: 2008–11 . . . . **PGA:** 2010–13

After his junior year at Alabama, Bud Cauley qualified for the 2011 U.S. Open. All three of his years with the Crimson Tide, he had been a semifinalist or finalist for the Hogan Award as best college golfer. He had played in a couple of professional tournaments as an amateur in 2010, missing the cut each time but playing respectably.

So Cauley decided to turn pro. He made the cut in the Open, eventually tying for 63rd place, and hasn't looked back. He finished as high as third in a tournament that year (in the Frys.com Open) and performed well enough to be one of only a handful of golfers to go directly from college to the PGA Tour, bypassing qualifying tournaments.

Despite his compact size (5-7, 150 pounds), Cauley is a big hitter, averaging more than 292 yards per drive. In the 12 months following his PGA Tour debut, he won more than $1.5 million.

GARDNER DICKINSON

COLLEGE: 1950–51 (in school, but Alabama didn't have a golf team)
PGA: 1952–82, 7 wins; **CT:** 1980–91; Alabama Sports HOF

The young Gardner Dickinson could be crusty. He patterned his game after that of his mentor and friend, Ben Hogan, and adopted some of Hogan's gruffness as well. "With few exceptions," he said in his entirely self-written 1994 memoir, *Let 'er Rip,* "the most successful players are selfish, egotistical, combative and utterly indifferent to the well-being of their fellow man."

But the Dothan, Alabama, native they called the Slim Man (because he stood 5-10 and weighed 130 pounds) also could play golf. He won seven PGA tournaments from 1956 through 1971—even though he could never tell from the leaderboard where he stood. He was colorblind, so he couldn't distinguish red numbers (under par) from green (par or over).

Dickinson had been a star golfer at LSU in the late 1940s. He attended graduate school at Alabama in 1950 and 1951, playing in amateur tournaments around the state, but Alabama didn't start a golf team until 1952.

In the 1970s, he wound down his tournament schedule and focused on teaching. Successful students included Ladies Professional Golf Association stars JoAnne Carner and Judy Clark, the latter of whom became his second wife. In 1980, he helped organize the Senior PGA Tour, now called the Champions Tour, for golfers 50 or older.

Dickinson did mellow with age (and, by all accounts, with his second marriage). The strongly opinionated *Let 'er Rip* contains far more kind words than disapproving ones. He suffered a stroke in 1994 and died in 1998 at his home in Tequesta, Florida, age 70.

KATHLEEN EKEY

COLLEGE: 2007–09 . . . . **LPGA:** 2012–13

After finishing at the top of the money list for the LPGA Futures Tour (now the Symetra Tour) in 2011 and being named the tour's Player of the Year, Kathleen Ekey stepped up to the big league in 2012: the LPGA Tour. The 5-foot-7 Cleveland native played at Alabama her last two years in college after transferring from Furman. She ranks fourth among all Crimson Tide golfers in career scoring average (73.50). When she's back home in Ohio, she works with children, participating in the LPGA-USGA Girls Golf and The First Tee of Cleveland programs.

After two years at Furman, Kathleen Ekey followed coach Mic Potter to Alabama. Potter had recruited her at Furman.
Credit: David Eschmann

STEVE LOWERY

COLLEGE: 1979–83 . . . . **PGA:** 1988–91, 1993–2012, 3 wins; **CT:** 2010–12; Alabama Sports HOF

Big (6-2, 230 pounds), friendly Steve Lowery has been transitioning from the PGA Tour to the Champions Tour since he qualified for the latter by turning 50 in 2010. He didn't reach the PGA Tour for good until 1993, but he's been a solid performer ever since, consistently finishing among the top 100 on the money list and winning three tournaments along the way—all in playoffs. Most recently, he beat Vijay Singh to take the 2008 AT&T Pebble Beach National Pro-Am.

Steve Lowery, one of the most easygoing guys on the PGA Tour, signs autographs during the 2004 British Open at Royal Troon in Scotland.

Credit: Patrick Micheletti

Lowery played on two Alabama teams that reached the NCAA championships. His 1981–82 average score of 71.65 was an Alabama single-season record that stood for two and a half decades until Michael Thompson beat it with a 71.39 average in 2007–08. A flood of great young golfers followed Thompson and has bumped Lowery's mark down to 11th on the list.

Lowery remains an avid Crimson Tide football fan. After a 1999 fire while he was traveling destroyed his Florida house and its contents (thankfully with no injuries to his wife and children), he moved his family back to his native Birmingham. He lives in the Greystone golf community.

HUNTER HAMRICK

COLLEGE: 2008–12 . . . . **PGA:** 2012

Disappointment ended a steady four-year Alabama career for Hunter Hamrick, who posted the seventh-best career scoring average in school history. In 2012, at the end of his senior season, the Crimson Tide lost the NCAA Championships on one agonizing final-hole putt—although Hamrick had earlier done his part, winning his own final match, 6 and 5.

Things improved at a U.S. Open qualifying tournament later that same week. The 5-9, 155-pound Hamrick qualified for the Open, where he tied for 46th. The following month, he tied for 10th in the True South Classic in Madison, Mississippi—his best showing in a PGA tournament. In 2013, Hamrick played on the NGA Professional Tour, a developmental series not affiliated with the PGA.

SPIKE MCROY

COLLEGE: 1986–90 . . . . **PGA:** 1996–2010, 2012, 1 win

These days, Spike McRoy plays the PGA Tour only when he gets a call about an open spot in a tournament. Otherwise, he stays home with his family in his hometown of Huntsville, Alabama, where he's putting his 1991 Alabama degree in corporate finance to use as a financial adviser. He also hosts a weekly show on a Huntsville sports-talk radio station. He and his wife, an optometrist, have three children.

McRoy, 5-11 and 155 pounds, had a good run in the late 1990s and early 2000s, winning $2.8 million combined between the PGA Tour and the lower-level Nationwide Tour. His one PGA victory came in 2002 at the B. C. Open. At Alabama, he finished second on the team in scoring average his freshman year and led the next three years, even when his teammates included David Kirkpatrick, who also played on the PGA Tour for three years.

BROOKE PANCAKE

COLLEGE: 2008–12 . . . . **LPGA:** 2012–13

What a year! As a senior in 2012, Brooke Pancake sank the putt that gave Alabama its first NCAA women's golf championship ever. The 5-7 native of Chattanooga, Tennessee, won the Honda Sports Award as the top female collegiate golfer, then played in four tournaments on the developmental Symetra Tour, peaking with a sixth-place tie in the Eagle Classic in Richmond,

> ## Handicap? What Handicap?
>
> Charley Boswell, a football halfback for Alabama in the late 1930s and a promising baseball prospect, got drafted early in World War II. During a 1944 battle in Germany, Boswell was pulling a wounded comrade from a burning tank. An explosion blinded him. Permanently.
>
> At a rehabilitation hospital, Boswell tried golf for the first time. In his memoir, *Now I See*, Boswell said he was skeptical until, after getting help lining up his stance, he whacked a ball 200 yards down the fairway.
>
> Boswell returned home to Birmingham. He became an insurance executive and the world's best blind golfer (using a caddy or sight coach to help direct shots). He won 16 national blind-golf championships and 11 international championships. He founded the Charley Boswell Celebrity Golf Classic, which raised $1.5 million for Birmingham's Eye Foundation Hospital. From 1971 to 1979, he was Alabama's state revenue commissioner. In 1972, he was inducted into the Alabama Sports Hall of Fame, one of many honors and accolades he received. He died in 1995, age 78.
>
> Around Birmingham, you still hear Charley Boswell stories. Supposedly, he once met Ben Hogan on a golf course and cajoled the reluctant golfing great into playing a round together, for money. Hogan didn't want to take advantage of Boswell, but finally agreed, saying, "Name the place and time."
>
> "Right here," Boswell replied, "at 10 o'clock—tonight."

Virginia. In December, she tied for 11th at the LPGA Qualifying Tournament, making her eligible the following year for the top-tier LPGA Tour.

She struggled early in 2013, working on her swing and adjusting to the demands of tour life. Her game started coming together in June, when she tied for 13th place at the Walmart NW Arkansas Championship, earning $32,258.

JERRY PATE

COLLEGE: 1971–75 . . . . **PGA:** 1976–2003, 8 wins, 1 major; **CT:** 2003–13, 2 wins; Alabama Sports HOF

The University of Alabama's greatest golfer has made his mark all around the world. Jerry Pate has won tournaments in Japan, South America, and Canada and has designed courses across the United States as well as one in Germany. (Among his designs is Ol' Colony Golf Complex, a municipal layout in Tuscaloosa that is the University of Alabama's home course.) He also operates turf and irrigation businesses.

And he finds time to play a little golf. Left-knee surgery in 2010 curtailed his appearances on the 50-and-older Champions Tour, where he has two wins, in 2006 and 2008. On the PGA Tour, the 5-11, 180-pounder won the U.S. Open in 1976, his rookie year, and added seven other victories, all by the time he was 28. He remains the only Crimson Tide golfer ever to have won one of the four "major" pro tournaments (U.S. Open, British Open, Masters, PGA Championship). He was also a member of the Ryder Cup–winning U.S. team in 1981.

In 1982, he got his last PGA win (the Tournament Players Championship, which he famously celebrated by jumping into the water and pulling PGA Tour Commissioner Deane Beman and course designer Pete Dye in with him). That same year, Pate finished tied for third at the Masters. Then, hitting balls at a driving range, he hurt his shoulder. His swing would never be the same.

Pate cut back on playing in favor of designing courses. He also began doing golf commentary for broadcast networks. And he returned to the University of Alabama to complete his administrative science degree. He and his daughter, Jenni, received their diplomas at the same graduation ceremony in 2001.

During his first stint at Alabama in the early 1970s, he won both the U.S. Amateur and World Amateur championships while still an undergraduate. He helped lead Alabama teams to three straight NCAA championship tournaments (1973–75).

When he became eligible for the Champions Tour in 2004, Pate resumed playing with renewed enthusiasm. True to form, when he won his first Champions tournament, the 2006 Outback Steakhouse Pro-Am, he grabbed the tournament chairman and jumped into the nearest pond.

DICKY PRIDE

COLLEGE: 1988–92 . . . . **PGA:** 1994–2013, 1 win

After almost two decades of scuffling on the PGA Tour, Dicky Pride pulled his game together in 2012, the year he turned 43 (on July 15). His string of solid performances peaked with a second-place finish in the HP Byron Nelson Championship. He lost by one stroke when former Auburn golfer Jason Duffner knocked down a 25-foot putt for a birdie on the final hole. Altogether, Pride won more than $1.2 million during the season. That put him 70th on

> **Nicknames**
>
> > *Bonehead, Brisky, Cottonhead, Cottontop, The Lip, Mouth of the South, Whitey* (Jerry Pate)
>
> > *Dicky* (Richard Fletcher Pride III)
>
> > *The Slim Man* (Gardner Dickinson)
>
> > *Spike* (Robert McRoy Jr.)
>
> > *Tab* (Travis Hudson)
>
> > *Yogi* (Steve Lowery)

the money list, earning him a full tour card for 2013—automatically qualifying him for all tournaments, even the exclusive invitationals.

He had spent considerable time the previous year raising money for victims of the April 27, 2011, tornadoes that devastated his hometown of Tuscaloosa and killed 248 people in Alabama.

The 6-foot, 175-pound Pride won the Federal Express St. Jude Classic in 1994, his PGA Tour rookie year. He birdied the first extra hole in a playoff to beat Hal Sutton and Gene Sauers. Just two years previously, he had capped his three-year career on the Alabama golf team by winning the Paul W. Bryant Scholar-Athlete of the Year award as Alabama's top male athlete.

Serious health problems knocked Pride off the tour for four months in 2002. He suffered from gallstones and pancreatitis and had to be fed from a tube for two and a half months.

Pride's first golf coach was his father, Dick Pride, who played (1956–59) and later coached (1960–64) at Alabama and for years was one of the state's top amateur golfers.

MICHAEL THOMPSON

COLLEGE: 2006–08 . . . . **PGA:** 2011–13, 1 win

After storming from behind in the final round of the 2012 U.S. Open to tie for second, a single stroke behind the winner, Michael Thompson earned his first PGA Tour win in March 2013. At The Honda Classic in Palm Beach Gardens, Florida, he compiled a score of 271, nine under par and two strokes ahead of Geoff Ogilvy.

Alabama has Hurricane Katrina to thank for bringing Thompson to Tuscaloosa. He played for two seasons at Tulane University. Then Katrina struck in August 2005 and flooded half of Tulane's main campus in New Orleans. The school disbanded its men's golf team (although it still has a women's team).

Thompson transferred to Alabama for his final two years of college. Solidly built at 6 feet tall and 185 pounds, he set school records for single-season and career scoring averages (71.39 in 2007–08 and 71.66, respectively; both have since been surpassed). He finished second in the 2007 U.S. Amateur tournament and was low amateur in the 2008 U.S. Open, finishing in a tie for 29th.

In his first two and a half years as a PGA Tour regular, he won nearly $4 million.

Others on the PGA, LPGA, or Champions Tour

NAME	COLLEGE	TOUR YEARS
Sam Farlow	1966–70	PGA 1974, 1977
Tom Garner	1979–83	PGA 1994
Barry Harwell	1975–79	PGA 1980–82
Tony Hollifield	1971–75	PGA 1978–80
Travis "Tab" Hudson	1972–76	PGA 1978
Gordon Johnson	1973–76 (did not letter)	PGA 1984
Rick Karbowski	1973–77	CT 2005–12
David Kirkpatrick	1988–92	PGA 1996, 1998, 2000
Peggy Kirsch	1978–82	LPGA 1989–92
Mårten Olander	1990–94	PGA 2003–04
Alan Pate	1971–75	PGA 1977
Judi Schneider Pavon	1986–90	LPGA 1991–92
Lee Rinker	1981–83	PGA 1983, 1995–2001
Leslie Spalding	1988–92	LPGA 1996–2005
Gary Trivisonno	1975–79	PGA 1981

Alabama Men's Top 10 Scoring Averages

Single Season (Minimum 15 rounds)

70.39	Justin Thomas, 2011–12	**71.32**	Bud Cauley, 2009–10
70.75	Bud Cauley, 2010–11	**71.39**	Michael Thompson, 2007–08
71.08	Cory Whitsett, 2012–13	**71.39**	Cory Whitsett, 2010–11
71.11	Justin Thomas, 2012–13	**71.44**	Cory Whitsett, 2011–12
71.29	Bobby Wyatt, 2012–13	**71.50**	Bobby Wyatt, 2011–12

Career (Minimum 45 rounds)

70.73	Justin Thomas, 2011–13	**72.36**	Nick Rousey, 2000–02
71.28	Cory Whitsett, 2010–13	**72.65**	Hunter Hamrick, 2008–12
71.36	Bud Cauley, 2008–11	**72.91**	Lars Brovold, 2000–04
71.66	Michael Thompson, 2006–08	**73.18**	Mark Harrell, 2004–08
71.73	Bobby Wyatt, 2010–13	**73.38**	Matthew Swan, 2005–09

Alabama Women's Top 10 Scoring Averages

Single Season (Minimum 15 rounds)

71.24	Stephanie Meadow, 2012–13	**72.61**	Jennifer Kirby, 2011–12
72.15	Stephanie Meadow, 2010–11	**72.69**	Stephanie Meadow, 2011–12
72.29	Brooke Pancake, 2010–11	**73.00**	Emma Talley, 2012–13
72.46	Brooke Pancake, 2011–12	**73.06**	Jennifer Kirby, 2009–10
72.59	Camilla Lennarth, 2009–10	**73.35**	Camilla Lennarth, 2010–11

Career (Minimum 45 rounds)

72.11	Stephanie Meadow, 2010–13	**73.66**	Jenny Suh, 2005–07
73.10	Brooke Pancake, 2008–12	**75.08**	Kathryn Cusick, 1996–98
73.45	Jennifer Kirby, 2009–13	**75.22**	Hannah Collier, 2010–13
73.50	Kathleen Ekey, 2007–09	**75.89**	Sarah Johnston, 1998–2002
73.59	Camilla Lennarth, 2007–11	**76.07**	Helena Blomberg, 2006–10

OLYMPICS

Kirani James (see page 374), winner of a gold medal in the 2012 Olympics and the fastest man at the University of Alabama, has spent the past couple of years sitting in business-school classrooms rather than competing for the track team.

Before his 400-meter Olympics victory—at age 19—James performed sensationally for two seasons with the Crimson Tide. He won the NCAA Outdoor Championship 400-meter title in 2010 and 2011, and the latter year was named the Southeastern Conference Indoor and Outdoor Men's Runner of the Year.

After his sophomore season, the young man from the Caribbean island nation of Grenada went pro. He ran in races all over the world and kept training under Harvey Glance (see page 360), the coach who had brought him to Alabama. But he also continued his studies. In 2012, he told *Tuscaloosa Magazine,* "I have promised myself and my parents that I'm going to finish school and graduate. My training base is here. It's an honor to represent my people. Winning for them is the feeling that I live for. I just try to replicate that feeling on and off the track."

The Olympics victory made James an international celebrity and an idol back home. Grenada named a stadium after him and put his picture on postage stamps. Still, he quietly resumed the pursuit of his business degree. Pretty cool.

When James became Alabama's fourth winner of a track-and-field gold medal (see Alabama Medal Winners chart, page 350), he single-handedly made 2012 a good Olympics year for the Tide. Ten athletes with Alabama ties competed—counting swimmers Karolina Szczepaniak (see page 381), Kristian Golomeev (see page 379), and Anton McKee (see page 380), who all committed to attend Alabama only after the Games. The other Tide representatives were sprinter Tahesia Harrigan-Scott (see page 383)

In 1987, Lillie Leatherwood was named the Southeastern Conference Female Athlete of the Year.
Paul W. Bryant Museum/The University of Alabama

and swimmers Alec Coci (see page 378), Hunor Mate (see page 380), Vlad Polyakov (see page 380), Arlene Semeco (see page 381), and Kristel Vourna (see page 381). All 10 represented countries other than the United States. Only James won a medal.

You may wonder what Olympics sports are doing in a book called *Gone Pro* anyway. Well, for most sports, a professional major league represents the pinnacle of competition. But for such pursuits as swimming, diving, and what's known as "athletics" (track and field and other walking and running events), the highest level of competition occurs every four years at the Olympic Games.

So we're counting participation in the Olympics as having "gone pro." Besides, these days almost all Olympics athletes are professionals anyway (see "Modern Olympics History," page 366).

Only relatively recently has Alabama produced Olympics-caliber athletes. Actually, it's more accurate to say that Alabama has attracted such athletes. In swimming, diving, and track and field, the Crimson Tide recruits all over the world. Of the 97 Alabama athletes who have competed in the Olympics through the 2012 Games, only 16 did so as members of the U.S. team. That doesn't count the one who competed for the U.S. Virgin Islands and the five who competed for Puerto Rico. Both of those geographic entities are part of the United States but send separate teams to the Games.

The Crimson Tide's first Olympians competed in the 1972 Games at Munich, in what was then West Germany. Tragically, those Olympics are chiefly remembered for the terrorist attack that resulted in the deaths of 11 Israeli athletes and coaches, five Palestinian terrorists, and a German police officer.

Alabama swimmers Colin Herring (see page 379) and Jacques Leloup (see page 379) competed for New Zealand and Belgium, respectively. Jan Johnson (see page 383), who had just finished his Alabama career, competed for the United States in the pole vault.

Also in those Olympics were three swimmers who would later attend Alabama: Robin Backhaus (see page 377) of the United States, Mark Crocker (see page 378) of Hong Kong, and Christine Jarvis (see page 379) of Great Britain.

If you give retroactive credit to Alabama, then Backhaus won the Crimson Tide's first medal, a bronze, in the 200-meter butterfly event. Otherwise, Johnson's bronze medal, won four days later, would be the Tide's first. Alabama's first gold medal came in the 1976 Olympics when swimmer Jack Babashoff anchored the U.S. men's 4x100-meter medley relay team.

Jon Olsen has the most Alabama medals: four golds and a bronze. Altogether, Alabama athletes—including softball player Kelly Kretschman (see page 230) and basketball player Antonio McDyess (see page 308)—have won 14 gold medals, 7 silver, and 11 bronze. All were earned in the Summer Olympics. Not surprisingly, given the state's climate, the Crimson Tide has never been represented in the Winter Olympics.

Alabama Medal Winners

■ *Gold*

1976: Jack Babashoff, USA, men's 4x100-meter medley relay swim

1980: Mark Tonelli, Australia, men's 4x100-meter medley relay swim

1984: Lillie Leatherwood, USA, women's 4x400-meter relay run

1984: Jon Sieben, Australia, men's 200-meter butterfly swim

1984: Calvin Smith, USA, men's 4x100-meter relay run

1992: Jon Olsen, USA, men's 4x100-meter freestyle relay swim

1992: Jon Olsen, USA, men's 4x100-meter medley relay swim

1996: Jon Olsen, USA, men's 4x100-meter freestyle relay swim

1996: Jon Olsen, USA, men's 4x200-meter freestyle relay swim

2000: Pauline Davis-Thompson, Bahamas, women's 200-meter run

2000: Pauline Davis-Thompson, Bahamas, women's 4x100-meter relay run

2000: Antonio McDyess, USA, men's basketball

2004: Kelly Kretschman, USA, women's softball

2012: Kirani James, Grenada, men's 400-meter run

■ *Silver*

1976: Jack Babashoff, USA, men's 100-meter freestyle swim

1988: Lillie Leatherwood, USA, women's 4x400-meter relay run

1988: Liz Lynch McGolgan, Great Britain, women's 10,000-meter run

1996: Pauline Davis-Thompson, Bahamas, women's 4x100-meter relay run

2004: Terin Humphrey, USA, women's gymnastics team all-around

2004: Terin Humphrey, USA, women's gymnastics uneven bars

2008: Kelly Kretschman, USA, women's softball

Bronze

1972: Robin Backhaus, USA, men's 200-meter butterfly swim

1972: Jan Johnson, USA, men's pole vault

1980: Max Metzker, Australia, men's 1,500-meter freestyle swim

1984: Cam Henning, Canada, men's 200-meter backstroke swim

1984: Justin Lemberg, Australia, men's 400-meter freestyle swim

1984: Jon Sieben, Australia, men's 4x100-meter medley relay swim

1988: Calvin Smith, USA, men's 100-meter run

1992: Faith Idehen, Nigeria, women's 4x100-meter relay run

1992: Jon Olsen, USA, men's 4x200-meter freestyle relay swim

2004: Anne Poleska, Germany, women's 200-meter breaststroke swim

2004: Susan Bartholomew Williams, USA, women's triathlon

Alabama Olympics Athletes by Sport

Swimming and diving 58	**Basketball** 1	**Triathlon** 1
Track and field 32	**Gymnastics** 1	
Tennis 3	**Softball** 1	

Alabama Athletes per Olympics

1972 6	**1988** 19	**2004** 15
1976 11	**1992** 22	**2008** 12
***1980** 5	**1996** 16	**2012** 10
1984 31	**2000** 12	

Boycotted by the United States and other countries because of the host Soviet Union's invasion of Afghanistan

Numbers add up to more than Alabama's total of 97 Olympians because some participated in multiple Olympics.

SWIMMING AND DIVING

In 1959, founding Alabama swimming and diving coach John Foster, just hired by athletics director Bear Bryant, arrived on campus to find a brand new pool and no swimmers. "We took what volunteers we could get," Foster said later.

During Foster's 14 years as coach, Alabama finished among the top three in the Southeastern Conference 11 times and was runner-up four times—but never champion. Still, not bad for a new program in a state that had almost no organized youth swimming programs until Foster started creating them. "Coach Bryant said when he hired me that he wanted a respectable program," Foster said, "and that's what he got."

Foster's successor as head coach, Don Gambril (1973–90), took the program from respectable to powerful. His men's teams won SEC titles in 1982 and 1987, and his women's team did the same in 1985. He also took Alabama to a second-place finish in the NCAA Division I national championships in 1977.

But Alabama's swimmers have never won a national title. Coach Dennis Pursley, hired for the 2012–13 season, started slowly, with dual-meet records of 2-4 (men) and 2-5 (women). For 2013–14, he signed 23 scholarship athletes, including 2012 Olympics swimmers Karolina Szczepaniak of Poland, Kristian Golomeev of Greece, and Anton McKee of Iceland. The Alabama athletics website quoted Pursley as saying, "This group of student-athletes is really going to help us take a leap forward next year."

Men's Southeastern Conference Championships

(Through 2013)

34	Florida	**3**	Georgia
18	Auburn	**2**	**Alabama**
10	Tennessee	**1**	LSU
4	Georgia Tech		

Women's Southeastern Conference Championships

(Through 2013)

17	Florida	**5**	Auburn
10	Georgia	**1**	**Alabama**

HEAD COACHES

Since 1979, when men's coach Don Gambril added the women's team to his domain, a single head coach has overseen both programs. Gary Ilman, who won two gold medals as a member of the U.S. 4x100-meter and 4x200-meter freestyle relay teams at the 1964 Olympics, got the women's program off to an excellent start, compiling a 14-5 dual-meet record from 1974–75 through 1976–77. Alabama brought in young Amateur Athletic Union swim coach Harold Lanier to succeed him. His teams did even better, going 11-3 in two seasons until Gambril took over.

Before them both, John Foster created the Alabama swim program from scratch.

The John Foster Era

John Foster launched Alabama's swim program—at first, just a men's program—starting with the 1959–60 season. Until he got the call to Tuscaloosa,

Foster was coaching age-group swimming in Atlanta and working with the Georgia Tech physical education department. He was born in Birmingham, competed as a diver in his youth, and had promoted aquatics throughout Alabama before moving to Georgia.

He really did start with nothing except a pool. "When I first got to Alabama, I felt like I was in a boat in virgin territory with one oar," he told an interviewer years later.

In addition to coaching swimming and diving, he was aquatics director, supervisor of intramural and recreational swimming, and assistant professor of physical education. "He had a very fine record," said his successor, Don Gambril. "He brought a lot of great teams through here and did a great job with very few resources."

A very fine record indeed: his 122 dual-meet victories and .697 winning percentage trail only Gambril's records among those of Alabama's men's coaches.

Two of Foster's swimmers, Colin Herring and Jacques Leloup, were the first to go from Alabama to the Olympics in 1972. Three other swimmers in those Olympics eventually competed for Alabama.

In 1973, Foster stepped down from coaching, but not before making the genius move of bringing Gambril from Harvard to be his successor. He continued teaching and supervising the aquatics program at the university until he retired in 1981.

He moved to Nokomis, Florida, south of Sarasota. He died in February 2003, age 84, after a long illness.

The Don Gambril Era

In the United States, the most famous Alabama coach is obviously Bear Bryant. Internationally, it may be a man that few U.S. sports fans have heard of: Don Gambril.

Athletes from all over the world came to compete for the Crimson Tide in the 1970s and 1980s, drawn by Gambril's reputation for getting the most out of swimmers. Gambril left Harvard to take over coaching the Alabama men beginning in 1974. He added the women in 1980.

Gambril turned a strong program into a national power. His dual-meet records were 170–21 with the men and 100–26 with the women. His teams won three Southeastern Conference titles (men in 1982 and 1987, women in 1985). Fifteen times they finished in the national top 10. He also coached

A Diver with True Grit

Bob Webster won his first collegiate diving competition representing a school that didn't have a pool. He trained by diving off a board into a sand pit in the back yard of Olympic champion, coach, and physician Sammy Lee.

That was in 1957 at Santa Ana Junior College in Santa Ana, California. Webster went on to compete for the University of Michigan, which actually had a pool. He took to water so well that he won the 10-meter platform diving gold medal at both the 1960 and 1964 Olympics. Between those Olympics, he won every platform diving event he entered.

After retiring as a competitor, Webster became a highly successful diving coach at Minnesota, Princeton, and, from 1975–76 through 1984–85, Alabama. He has been inducted into the International Swimming Hall of Fame.

the very successful 1984 Olympics swim team—which featured an astounding 31 Alabama swimmers and divers. Gambril was assistant U.S. Olympics coach in 1968, 1972, 1976, and 1980.

He is a member of the International Swimming Hall of Fame and the Alabama Sports Hall of Fame. In 2001, the university named the pool at its aquatics center for Gambril, who had overseen the center's construction in 1980.

Gambril retired from coaching in 1990 and became an associate athletics director. He retired from that too in 1996 but has kept ties to the university. In 1996, he was elected to the board of the United States Anti-Doping Agency.

Meanwhile, the Alabama swimming and diving program has, frankly, drifted. From Gambril's retirement through the 2011–12 season, the men's team's cumulative record was 98-89, and the women's was 99-99-1.

In May 2012, Alabama hired Dennis Pursley to be its new swimming and diving coach. Pursley is originally from Louisville, Kentucky, and swam for Alabama from 1968–69 through 1971–72. He was national team director of USA Swimming for 14 years, starting in 1989, and was the head coach of British Swimming through the 2012 London Olympics. Briefly (2007–08), he was even director of swimming and diving operations at Auburn.

During and after a disappointing first season, Pursley recruited around the globe, signing up athletes from Australia, Poland, Greece, Cyprus, Iceland, Russia, Switzerland, and Great Britain—as well as New York, California, Michigan, Ohio, Tennessee, Florida, Texas, Mississippi, and Alabama. In recruiting, at least, he seems to be emulating Gambril. Now we'll see about the coaching part.

Men's Head Coaching Records

(In chronological order)

YEARS	COACH	RECORD	WINNING %
1959–73	John Foster	122-53	.697
1973–90	Don Gambril	170-21	.890
1990–94	Jonty Skinner	16-16	.500
1994–98	Chuck Horton	21-19	.525
1998–99	Ed Reed (interim)	0-6	.000
1999–2003	Don Wagner	15-14	.517
2003–12	Eric McIlquham	46-34	.575
2012–13	Dennis Pursley	2-4	.333

(Ranked by victories)

RECORD	COACH	YEARS
170-21	Don Gambril	1973–90
122-53	John Foster	1959–73
46-34	Eric McIlquham	2003–12
21-19	Chuck Horton	1994–98
16-16	Jonty Skinner	1990–94
15-14	Don Wagner	1999–2003
2-4	Dennis Pursley	2012–13
0-6	Ed Reed (interim)	1998–99

(Ranked by winning percentage; a tie counts as half a win, half a loss, per NCAA practice)

WINNING %	RECORD	COACH	YEARS
.890	170-21	Don Gambril	1973–90
.697	122-53	John Foster	1959–73
.575	46-34	Eric McIlquham	2003–12
.525	21-19	Chuck Horton	1994–98
.517	15-14	Don Wagner	1999–2003
.500	16-16	Jonty Skinner	1990–94
.333	2-4	Dennis Pursley	2012–13
.000	0-6	Ed Reed (interim)	1998–99

Women's Head Coaching Records

(In chronological order)

YEARS	COACH	RECORD	WINNING %
1974–77	Gary Ilman	14-5-0	.737
1977–79	Harold Lanier	11-3-0	.786
1979–90	Don Gambril	100-28-0	.781
1990–94	Jonty Skinner	16-16-0	.500
1994–98	Chuck Horton	25-16-0	.610
1998–99	Ed Reed (interim)	3-4-0	.429
1999–2003	Don Wagner	15-16-0	.484
2003–12	Eric McIlquham	40-47-1	.460
2012–13	Dennis Pursley	2-5	.286

(Ranked by victories)

RECORD	COACH	YEARS
100-28-0	Don Gambril	1979–90
40-47-1	Eric McIlquham	2003–12
25-16-0	Chuck Horton	1994–98
16-16-0	Jonty Skinner	1990–94
15-16-0	Don Wagner	1999–2003
14-5-0	Gary Ilman	1974–77
11-3-0	Harold Lanier	1977–79
3-4-0	Ed Reed (interim)	1998–99
2-5-0	Dennis Pursley	2012–13

(Ranked by winning percentage; a tie counts as half a win, half a loss, per NCAA practice)

WINNING %	RECORD	COACH	YEARS
.786	11-3-0	Harold Lanier	1977–79
.781	100-28-0	Don Gambril	1979–90
.737	14-5-0	Gary Ilman	1974–77
.610	25-16-0	Chuck Horton	1994–98
.500	16-16-0	Jonty Skinner	1990–94
.484	15-16-0	Don Wagner	1999–2003
.460	40-47-1	Eric McIlquham	2003–12
.429	3-4-0	Ed Reed (interim)	1998–99
.286	2-5-0	Dennis Pursley	2012–13

TRACK AND FIELD

Whatever happened to track and field?

Just a generation ago, running, jumping, throwing, and vaulting occupied a much more prominent place in the sporting public's consciousness, at least in the United States. Sure, people still pay attention to the Olympics every four years. But in between?

Casual sports fans used to know the names of the world's top mile runners, such as Sebastian Coe in the 1980s and Jim Ryun in the 1960s. Sprinters Carl Lewis, Florence Griffith-Joyner, Marion Jones, and Ben Johnson showed up regularly in sports coverage, as did pole vaulter Sergey Bubka and barefoot distance runner Zola Budd.

Now, who knows the world record holder in the mile? Or the "metric mile"—the 1,500 meters? As of this writing, Hicham El Guerrouj of Morocco has owned both marks for more than a decade.

Maybe that's the problem. We've edged so close to the physical limits of the human body that records don't fall nearly as often as they used to. A mere win draws much less attention than a world record.

Anyway, whether or not the word has gotten out, Alabama has a track and field program. Men's and women's programs, in fact, as well as men's and women's cross-country teams. The 2013 track and field schedule featured five indoor meets, including the Crimson Tide Indoor Opener in January, and six outdoor meets, including the Alabama Relays in March. In addition, the team competed in the Southeastern Conference Indoor Championships in

February, the NCAA Indoor Championships in March, the SEC Outdoor Championships in May, and the NCAA Outdoor Championships in June.

The cross-country team competed in four fall events, including the Crimson Classic in October 2012, plus the SEC Championships later that month and the NCAA South Region Championships in November.

Alabama's track and field program draws top athletes from around the world. Two qualified for the 2012 Olympics. Kirani James competed for his home country, Grenada, and won the gold medal in the 400-meter run. Tahesia Harrigan-Scott, under the British Virgin Islands flag, ran the 100-yard dash for the second straight Olympics but, as in 2008, failed to win a medal.

Alabama also has boasted a world record holder. Sprinter Calvin Smith lettered for the Crimson Tide from 1980 through 1983. At the 1983 U.S. Olympic Festival he set a 100-meter dash world record (9.93 seconds) that lasted until 1987. The following year, he helped the U.S. Olympics team set a world record in the 4x100-meter relay.

And Harvey Glance, the Tide's track coach from 1997 through 2011, held world records in the 100-meter and 100-yard dash events in the 1970s, although back then he wasn't wearing crimson and white. He was a student at Auburn.

Men's Southeastern Conference Track and Field Championships

(Indoor, through 2013)

19 Arkansas	5 **Alabama**	1 Kentucky
18 Tennessee	4 Auburn	
6 Florida	4 LSU	

(Outdoor, through 2013)

25 Tennessee	4 Auburn	3 Georgia Tech
22 LSU	4 Florida	1 Georgia
18 Arkansas	3 **Alabama**	1 Mississippi State

Women's Southeastern Conference Track and Field Championships

(Indoor, through 2013)

12	LSU	4	Arkansas	**1**	**Alabama**
7	Florida	4	Tennessee	1	Georgia

(Outdoor, through 2013)

13	LSU	3	Arkansas	2	Georgia
5	Florida	3	South Carolina	1	Texas A&M
4	Tennessee	**2**	**Alabama**		

Southeastern Conference Cross-Country Championships

(Men, through 2012)

25	Tennessee	6	Auburn	**3**	**Alabama**
20	Arkansas	5	Mississippi State	2	Florida
10	Georgia Tech	4	Kentucky		

(Women, through 2012)

13	Arkansas	5	Tennessee	**2**	**Alabama**
6	Florida	3	Kentucky	1	Vanderbilt

GYMNASTICS

Alabama's 2013 gymnastics team drew an average crowd of 13,422 to Coleman Coliseum. The 2012–13 men's basketball team, en route to a 20-11 regular season and the quarterfinals of the National Invitation Tournament, played in the same venue but averaged only 11,159.

Granted, it's an unfair comparison. The basketball team played 20 home games, winning 16. The gymnastics squad had only five home meets (and won all five). On the other hand, the gymnasts reached the NCAA Championships, finishing a close third (with 197.350 points) to Florida (197.575) and Oklahoma (197.375). Not bad—except that the Tide had finished first in 2011 and 2012.

That 2012 title was Alabama's sixth national gymnastics championship. The team has reached the NCAA Championships every year since 1983—31 years in a row. In 2013, Alabama went 7-2-1 in the regular season, including a 5-2-1 mark in the Southeastern Conference. For the second straight year, Alabama finished second to Florida in the postseason SEC Championships.

For all of its success, Alabama gymnastics can claim just one Olympics representative—Terin Humphrey (see page 376) in 2004—and she came to Alabama only after competing in the Games. (In the world of gymnastics, that's a typical story; see "Missing Rings," page 364.)

Alabama, like other Southeastern Conference schools, competes in women's but not men's gymnastics. The economics of college sports and the gender parity requirements of Title IX (see "Title IX and Women's Sports," page 27) make it unlikely that the Crimson Tide will add a men's program.

However, never say never. Over the past three decades, one Alabama athletics program stands unmatched for sustained brilliance. Only one sport has contended for a national championship every single year. And it's not football.

Women's National Championships

(Through 2013)

10	Georgia	**6**	UCLA
9	Utah	**1**	Florida
6	**Alabama**		

Women's Southeastern Conference Championships

(Through 2013)

16	Georgia	**7**	**Alabama**
9	Florida	**1**	LSU

HEAD COACHES

Bear Bryant himself hired the Bear Bryant of gymnastics coaches. Before the 1979 season, Bryant, as Alabama athletics director, invited Sarah Campbell to take over the gymnastics team. Campbell was 22 years old and just out of Slippery Rock State College in Pennsylvania. To that point, Alabama's gymnastics program, created in 1975, had stumbled to a cumulative record of 14-25 under four coaches, each of whom lasted just one season.

Campbell's first team went 7-7. That was her last season without a winning record.

Missing Rings

Why has Alabama's gymnastics team, a perennial powerhouse with six national championships (1988, 1991, 1996, 2002, 2011, 2012), included only one Olympics athlete, Terin Humphrey (see page 376), in its history? Because the very best female gymnasts begin full-time training at very early ages and compete in the Olympics before they're old enough for college. At the 2012 Olympics, for example, the U.S. female gymnasts ranged in age from 15 to 18.

Gymnasts in training for Olympics-level meets have little time for anything else, including college classes. A few Olympics gymnasts, such as Humphrey, do go on to compete in college. Many others either remain in full-time training for the international circuit or quit competition to move into coaching or other pursuits.

The coach, who became Sarah Patterson in 1984 when she married her assistant coach, David Patterson, has taken Alabama to six national championships—in 1988, 1991, 1996, 2002, 2011, and 2012. That matches the number that Bryant won in football (though, to give Bear his due, he did it in 25 years compared to Patterson's 35). Alabama has reached the NCAA championships for 31 straight years, and it packs Coleman Coliseum for home meets (thanks in part to Patterson's tireless marketing).

Patterson's teams also earned seven Southeastern Conference championships in the postseason tourament, in 1988, 1990, 1995, 2000, 2003, 2009, and 2011.

In recognition of that record, the Alabama Board of Trustees in June 2012 announced that a new $2.8 million monument to the success of all Crimson Tide sports programs would be called the Sarah Patterson Champions Plaza.

For years, Alabama carried on a great gymnastics rivalry with Georgia, given extra fuel by the mutual dislike between Patterson and Georgia coach Suzanne Yoculan. Yoculan came to Georgia in 1983 and achieved even more success than Patterson: an 831-117-7 record, 10 national championships, 16 SEC titles. Since her retirement in 2009, Georgia has failed to reach the NCAA championships while Alabama has thrived.

Patterson stresses life outside the gym as well. Gymnasts are expected to excel in the classroom and work for the betterment of the community. The team was active in helping Tuscaloosa recover from the devastating April 27, 2011, tornado. Patterson also designates one meet a year as the Power of Pink meet to raise awareness in the fight against breast cancer—earning her the nickname "The Pink Lady." The other Alabama women's sports programs and a local Toyota dealer have joined in the promotion.

The Bear died in January 1983. Later that year, the gymnastics team made its first national championships appearance. Five years later, it won its first national title. You know he's proud.

Head Coaching Records

(In chronological order)

YEARS	COACH	RECORD	WINNING %
1975	Riki Sutton	4-4-0	.500
1976	Sheila Hill	3-7-0	.300
1977	Phyllis Draper	1-7-0	.125
1978	Tom Steele	6-7-0	.462
1979–2013	Sarah Patterson	423-95-3	.815

(Ranked by victories)

RECORD	COACH	YEARS
423-95-3	Sarah Patterson	1979–2013
6-7-0	Tom Steele	1978
4-4-0	Riki Sutton	1975
3-7-0	Sheila Hill	1976
1-7-0	Phyllis Draper	1977

(Ranked by winning percentage; a tie counts as half a win, half a loss, per NCAA practice)

WINNING %	RECORD	COACH	YEARS
.815	423-95-3	Sarah Patterson	1979–2013

WINNING %	RECORD	COACH	YEARS
.500	4-4-0	Riki Sutton	1975
.462	6-7-0	Tom Steele	1978
.300	3-7-0	Sheila Hill	1976
.125	1-7-0	Phyllis Draper	1977

MODERN OLYMPICS HISTORY

Nostalgia and a colonial-era notion that physical education leads to political power created the modern Olympic Games.

The ancient Olympics took place at Olympia in Greece every four years from at least 776 BC until they were banned in AD 393 by the Roman Emperor Theodosius. They consisted of a series of athletic competitions to honor the Greek god Zeus, though originally there was just one competition, a stadium-length sprint of somewhere around 200 meters. Any Greek-speaking free man could compete. Greece's city-states suspended any wars they had going at the time in order to allow passage to and from the competitions.

Other sports were added: boxing, chariot racing, horse racing, other running events, wrestling, pankration (an ancient version of mixed martial arts), and pentathlon (discus, javelin, jumping, running, and wrestling). Athletes generally competed naked except for one footrace run in some 50 pounds of armor. Winners got a wreath of laurel leaves.

To 19th-century intellectuals who idealized the glories of ancient

The Alabama gymnastics team anoints coach Sarah Patterson with confetti during an on-campus celebration of Alabama's 2012 national championship.
University of Alabama Athletics

Greece and Rome, it all seemed so noble and, well, manly. Several Olympics-style competitions took place as early as 1796 and at various places in Europe throughout the 1800s. In 1890, French Baron Pierre de Coubertin founded the International Olympic Committee. In 1896, it held its first modern Olympic Games in Athens. The Games have gone on every four years since, except for interruptions during World War I and II. In 1924, the IOC added a Winter Olympics for cold-weather sports in the same year as the Summer Olympics. Starting in 1994, the IOC shifted the Winter Olympics schedule so that it alternates with the Summer Games every two years.

Coubertin admired the British system of physical education at schools. He and other aristocrats of the time thought the lessons learned by the upper classes on the playing fields of Eton had contributed greatly to the worldwide expansion of British power and colonization. Not wanting to confine sports to a small coterie of professionals, he conceived of his Olympics as a competition for amateurs. Unlike many of his peers, he thought physical education—and Olympics eligibility—should be available to the working classes as well as the aristocracy.

Drawing Crowds

Alabama's gymnastics team finished second in average attendance among all 2012–13 college women's programs, regardless of sport. The Crimson Tide outdrew every gymnastics team, basketball team, softball team, rowing team, whatever, except for Utah in gymnastics.

Utah led with an average crowd of 14,349 (just shy of the NCAA record of 14,352 it set last year) in five home meets. Alabama averaged 13,422 in five meets—all of which it won. Next closest in women's college sports was the Tennessee basketball team, which averaged 11,993 per game. No other collegiate women's program topped 10,000 in average.

Here are the 2013 top 10 schools in average women's gymnastics home attendance:

Utah, 14,349	Auburn, 4,408
Alabama, 13,422	UCLA, 4,071
Georgia, 8,721	Missouri, 3,715
Florida, 5,865	Oregon State, 3,707
LSU, 5,353	Arkansas, 3,440

The modern Olympics remained open only to amateurs—theoretically—for most of the 20th century. As the Games became more popular and, thanks to television and corporate sponsorship, more lucrative, ways of subsidizing athletes within the rules proliferated. Critics increasingly dismissed the IOC's attempts to preserve the ideal of the 19th-century gentleman athlete as "shamateurism." Starting in the 1970s, professional athletes gradually were granted eligibility. Today, boxing, wrestling, and soccer still exclude professionals on a limited basis; for all other events, income source is irrelevant.

Much earlier, the old boys began allowing women to compete, though grudgingly. The 1900 Paris Olympics included women's events in the genteel sports of lawn tennis and golf. Women's sports were gradually added over the years until, with the debut of women's boxing in 2012, no Olympics sports remained restricted to men only.

Political controversies, boycotts, accusations of drug use to enhance performance, scandals involving bribery by cities hoping to become Olympics hosts, massive cost overruns, and other issues have dogged the modern Olympics.

Still, the Games draw avid public interest and global TV audiences estimated at close to 5 billion people. Whatever the reason—national pride, love of sport, or perhaps even the purity of athletic competition that so enthralled the Games' founders—the Olympics continue to thrive.

The IOC frequently tinkers with the Games, adding and subtracting sports between Olympiads. (Bring back tug of war!) TV networks have struggled with time-zone differences and the rise of the Internet. How do you maintain suspense for a delayed broadcast of an event that took place in the middle of the previous night local time, especially when everything that happens goes online as soon as it occurs?

Still, some marketing options remain unexplored. Imagine the boost in TV ratings if, in a bow to ancient tradition, athletes competed naked. Don't think it hasn't been considered.

Summer Olympics Games

1896	Athens	*1906	Athens
1900	Paris	1908	London
1904	St. Louis	1912	Stockholm

1916	Berlin; canceled because of World War I	**1968**	Mexico City
1920	Antwerp, Belgium	**1972**	Munich, West Germany
1924	Paris	**1976**	Montreal
1928	Amsterdam	**1980**	Moscow
1932	Los Angeles	**1984**	Los Angeles
1936	Berlin	**1988**	Seoul, South Korea
1940	Tokyo; canceled because of World War II	**1992**	Barcelona, Spain
1944	London; canceled because of World War II	**1996**	Atlanta
		2000	Sydney, Australia
1948	London	**2004**	Athens
1952	Helsinki, Finland	**2008**	Beijing
1956	Melbourne, Australia, and Stockholm	**2012**	London
1960	Rome	**2016**	Rio de Janeiro
1964	Tokyo		

**No longer recognized by the International Olympic Committee as official Olympics; now called the 1906 Intercalated Games*

Winter Olympics Games

1924	Chamonix, France	**1972**	Sapporo
1928	St. Moritz, Switzerland	**1976**	Innsbruck
1932	Lake Placid, New York	**1980**	Lake Placid
1936	Garmisch-Partenkirchen, Germany	**1984**	Sarajevo, Yugoslavia
1940	Sapporo, Japan; canceled because of World War II	**1988**	Calgary, Alberta, Canada
1944	Cortina d'Ampezzo, Italy; canceled because of World War II	**1992**	Albertville, France
		1994	Lillehammer, Norway
1948	St. Moritz	**1998**	Nagano, Japan
1952	Oslo	**2002**	Salt Lake City
1956	Cortina d'Ampezzo	**2006**	Turin, Italy
1960	Squaw Valley, California	**2010**	Vancouver, British Columbia, Canada
1964	Innsbruck, Austria	**2014**	Sochi, Russia
1968	Grenoble, France	**2018**	Pyeongchang, South Korea

ATHLETE BIOS

College years are years receiving a varsity letter unless otherwise noted.

HOF: Hall of Fame

Swimming and Diving

JACK BABASHOFF

COLLEGE: 1974–77 . . . . **OLYMPICS:** 1976, 1 gold medal,
1 silver medal

On July 22, 1976, at the Montreal Olympics, swimmer Jack Babashoff won the first gold medal ever by a University of Alabama Olympian. He swam the anchor (final) leg for the U.S. men's 4x100-meter medley relay team, bringing home the victory in world-record time. Two days later, the 6-3, 185-pound swimmer took a silver medal in 100-meter freestyle race.

Despite that success, Jack's sister Shirley upstaged him in the same Olympics. Shirley had already won two gold and two silver medals in 1972, at age 15. Four years later, she added four more silvers. And she anchored the gold medal–winning U.S. team in the 4x100-meter freestyle relay.

Jack competed in only one Olympics. He swam one more season for Alabama, achieving All-America status (top eight in the NCAA championships) in three events. In later years, the native Californian competed in masters swimming events with the San Diego Swim Masters.

JON OLSEN

COLLEGE: 1988–91 . . . . **OLYMPICS:** 1992, 2 gold medals,
1 bronze medal; 1996, 2 gold medals

Still the Alabama school record holder for the 100-meter and 200-meter freestyle, Jon Olsen collected five Olympic medals. In 1992 at Barcelona, he helped the U.S. team win gold medals in the 4x100-meter freestyle and 4x100-meter medley relays, and a bronze in the 4x200-meter freestyle relay. In 1996 at Atlanta, he added two more gold medals in the 4x100 and 4x200 freestyle relays.

Olsen, 6-5 and 180 pounds, now lives in the Florida Keys, where he coaches swimmers and triathletes.

JON SIEBEN

COLLEGE: 1985 . . . . **OLYMPICS:** 1984, 1 gold medal,
1 bronze medal; 1988; 1992; Sport Australia HOF

Australians still celebrate one of the greatest Olympics swimming upsets ever: their Jon Sieben's victory over West Germany's Michael Gross in the 200-meter butterfly in the 1984 Games in Los Angeles. Gross, 20 years old, stood 6-7, weighed 194 pounds, and was nicknamed "The Albatross" for his 7-foot-plus arm span. During most of the 1980s, he was the best butterfly swimmer in the world. In contrast, the 5-9, 163-pound, 17-year-old Sieben was known as "The Shrimp."

But The Shrimp came from behind in the last 50 meters to set a world record. He added a bronze medal in the 4x100-meter medley relay. For his feats, he was named Young Australian of the Year 1984.

The year after that triumph, Sieben spent a season on the Alabama swim team, setting team records (since surpassed) in the 100- and 200-meter butterfly. He returned to Australia, where he and his wife, also a swim teacher, operate a swimming venue at the beach city of Townsville in the state of Queensland.

MARK TONELLI

COLLEGE: 1976–79 . . . . **OLYMPICS:** 1976; 1980,
1 gold medal

Despite scholarship offers from Harvard and Stanford, Australian swimmer Mark Tonelli chose Alabama in order to train under coach Don Gambril. After his first college season, he competed for Australia in the 1976 Montreal Olympics but failed to win a medal. At the end of three more years at Alabama, he ended his college career with an exclamation point as an All-American (top-eight finisher at the NCAA championships) in five events.

In the 1980 Olympics at Moscow, Tonelli swam the butterfly leg of the 4x100-meter medley relay in a personal best time that would have placed him second in the individual butterfly event. Australia took the gold.

Tonelli, 5-11 and 145 pounds, retired after the Moscow Games and embarked on a colorful career as, among other things, a TV commentator and host, a member of the Australian Sports Commission, the operator of a swimming school, a real-estate agent, and a motivational speaker.

Track and Field

PAULINE DAVIS-THOMPSON

COLLEGE: 1986–89 . . . . **OLYMPICS:** 1984; 1988; 1992; 1996, 1 silver medal; 2000, 2 gold medals;
Central American and Caribbean Athletic Confederation HOF

Sprinter Pauline Davis-Thompson improved with age. The 5-foot-6, 126-pound Davis-Thompson, who competed for her native Bahamas, didn't win a medal until her fourth Olympics, in 1996 at Atlanta. She earned a silver in the women's 4x100-meter relay.

In 2000 at Sydney, Australia, age 34, she helped the 4x100-meter relay team win a gold medal. Back home, it was a cause for national celebration. Ever since, the team has been known to Bahamians as the Golden Girls.

Davis-Thompson also finished second in the 200 meters. Nine years later, after winner Marion Jones was stripped of the title following her admission that she used banned drugs, Davis-Thompson's silver medal was upgraded to gold.

Davis-Thompson founded a track club where she trained post-collegiate athletes. She is a member of the International Association of Athletics Federations Council and has marketed sports tourism to the Bahamas. She also has been an assistant track coach for the University of Tennessee.

In 1998, she married Jamaican Olympics hurdler Mark Thompson, whom she had met at the 1992 Olympics. In 2011, thieves stole some of her medals from her house in the Bahamas. She had earlier presented her gold medal for the 200-meter race to the Bahamian prime minister.

The then–Pauline Davis (left) leads the field in a meet during her 1980s Alabama career.
Credit: Paul W. Bryant Museum/The University of Alabama

LILLIE LEATHERWOOD

COLLEGE: 1983–87 . . . . **OLYMPICS:** 1984, 1 gold medal;
1988, 1 silver medal

A homegrown star out of Tuscaloosa County High School, Lillie Leatherwood
won a gold medal as part of the Olympics record–setting U.S. 4x400-meter
relay team during the 1984 Los Angeles Olympics.

At the Seoul games four years later, the team almost duplicated the feat,
settling for a silver medal. Leatherwood didn't run in the final; coaches
replaced her at the last minute with Florence Griffith-Joyner. She did get a
medal because of her work with the team in earlier heats.

Leatherwood, 5-6 and 123 pounds, came back to Tuscaloosa after her
track retirement and is now a city police officer, directing Police Athletic
League programs. The annual Lillie Leatherwood 5K run raises money for
the league. She also works for other charitable causes, including the Special
Olympics.

LIZ LYNCH MCCOLGAN

COLLEGE: 1986, 1991–94 . . . . **OLYMPICS:** 1988, 1 silver medal;
1992; 1996

Liz Lynch McColgan (Liz Lynch when she first came to Alabama) likes running long distances. During the 1986 NCAA track and field championships,
she won the mile run. She left Alabama for international competitions—and
longer races. During the 10,000-meter run in the 1988 Olympics, she couldn't
hold off the closing sprint of the Soviet Union's Olga Bondarenko and had to
settle for a silver medal.

After time out of training to have her first child (of five), she returned to
Alabama but never recaptured her national-championship form. McColgan,
5-7 and 100 pounds, did compete in two more Olympics. She finished fifth in
the 10,000-meter run in 1992 and 16th in the marathon in 1996.

Injuries finally forced her retirement from competition in 2004. She and
her husband, former steeplechase runner Peter McColgan, whom she met
when both competed for Alabama, ended their 26-year marriage in March
2013 after a messy battle over property and an assault accusation (of which
she was cleared). She is now a running coach and TV and radio personality.
Her oldest child, her 22-year-old daughter, Eilish McColgan, competed for
Great Britain in the 3,000-meter steeplechase in the 2012 Olympics.

KIRANI JAMES

COLLEGE: 2010–11 . . . . **OLYMPICS:** 2012, 1 gold medal

In interviews, Kirani James comes across as polite, thoughtful, and quietly determined. When thrust into the spotlight, he handles it calmly and well. But at Alabama, where he continues to work toward a business degree, he's pretty much just another student. He may be an international track superstar and the first person ever to win an Olympics medal for the Caribbean nation of Grenada, but, well, it's not as if he plays football.

"Most of the time, people see me and recognize me, but they're too shy to say anything," he told *Tuscaloosa Magazine*. "People who follow track and field get excited seeing someone like me do what I do. That's why I like Tuscaloosa and this campus. I can really stay grounded."

James powers through his favorite event, the 400-meter dash, in a long-limbed lope that befits a man nicknamed The Jaguar. He has posted the fastest 400-meter times ever for a 14-year-old (46.96 seconds) and a 15-year-old (45.70). He reached a personal best time of 43.94 during his Olympics win, less than a month before his 20th birthday. As he gains strength—he's listed at 5-11 and 146 pounds—and refines his technique, he could be a force on the track scene through two or three more Olympics. After all, retired U.S. sprinter Michael Johnson was 18 days shy of his 32nd birthday when he set the current 400-meter record of 43.18 seconds.

Kirani James says he expects to compete in the 2016 Olympics in Rio de Janeiro.
Credit: Erik van Leeuwen

CALVIN SMITH

COLLEGE: 1980–83 . . . . **OLYMPICS:** 1984, 1 gold medal; 1988, 1 bronze medal; National Track & Field HOF

For four years, Calvin Smith was the world's fastest man. In 1983, at the U.S. Olympic Festival at Colorado Springs, Colorado, he set a 100-meter dash world record of 9.93 seconds. It lasted until 1987.

Smith was a slender (5-10, 150 pounds), graceful runner, in contrast to such bulkier and flashier contemporary sprinters as Carl Lewis of the United States and the Jamaican-born Ben Johnson of Canada. In the 1984 Los Angeles Olympics, Smith won a gold medal as part of the world record–breaking U.S. 4x100-meter relay team.

At Seoul in 1988, he eventually was awarded a controversial bronze medal in the 100 meters. Johnson finished first, Lewis second, Linford Christie of Great Britain third, and Smith fourth. But Johnson later tested positive for banned anabolic steroids and was stripped of his medal. Lewis got the gold, Christie the silver, and Smith the bronze. Lewis later admitted he had tested positive for stimulants in the Olympic Trials, and Christie also tested positive for metabolites of a banned substance. No wonder Smith, who never failed a drug test, described himself as "the best clean runner" of his generation.

Smith, known in the track world as a quiet, charming man, is now a social worker in Tampa. He follows the exploits of Calvin Smith II, his son, also an international sprinting star.

Nicknames

- *Cam* (Cameron Henning)

- *Casey* (Keith Cawthon Converse)

- *The Golden Girls* (Pauline Davis-Thompson and her gold medal–winning relay teammates)

- *The Jaguar* (Kirani James)

- *Little Scoob, Sis* (Terin Humphrey)

- *The Pink Lady* (Alabama gymnastics Coach Sarah Patterson, because of her work for breast cancer awareness and prevention)

- *The Quietly Confident Quartet* (Mark Tonelli and his gold medal–winning relay teammates)

- *Ragga* (Ragnheiður Runólfsdóttir)

- *The Shrimp* (Jon Sieben)

- *Siggi* (Sigurður Einarsson)

Gymnastics

TERIN HUMPHREY

COLLEGE: 2004–08 . . . . **OLYMPICS:** 2004, 2 silver medals; U.S. Gymnastics HOF

Terin Humphrey came home from the 2004 Athens Olympics with two silver medals, one for the women's team all-around competition and one for the uneven bars. She joined coach Sarah Patterson's always-powerful Alabama gymnastics team and won the NCAA uneven bars championship as a freshman and a junior.

But injuries started to add up. She had surgery on both elbows in 2006. Back problems forced her to retire from gymnastics during her senior year, 2007–08.

Humphrey got her degree in criminal justice and is now a police officer in Raymore, Missouri, in suburban Kansas City. Despite her size—5 feet tall and 110 pounds—and surgeries, she finished first in her police academy class in physical training. She remains involved in gymnastics and helped select the 2012 U.S. Olympics team.

Terin Humphrey performs her floor exercise routine for Alabama in 2005.
Credit: University of Alabama Athletics

Other Alabama Olympians
(All in Summer Olympics; through 2008)

Swimming and Diving

NAME	COLLEGE	OLYMPICS	COUNTRY	EVENT	MEDAL
Ricardo Aldabe	1984–87	1984	Spain	100- and 200-meter backstroke	
Rafael Álvarez	1994–95	1992, 1996, 2000	Spain	Platform and springboard diving	
Brendan Ashby	2001–04	2004	Zimbabwe	100-meter backstroke	
Oren Azrad	1998–2001	2000	Israel	4x100-meter freestyle relay	
Robin Backhaus	1977	1972	USA	200-meter butterfly	Bronze
Laurence Bensimon	1985–86	1984	France	200- and 800-meter freestyle, 200-meter individual medley, 4x100-meter freestyle relay	
Jens-Peter Berndt	1985–87	1988	West Germany	100- and 200-meter backstroke, 200- and 400-meter individual medley	
Carlos Berrocal	1976–79	1976	Puerto Rico	100-meter backstroke	
Spyros Bitsakis	2002–06	2000, 2004	Greece	100-meter freestyle, 4x100- and 4x200-meter freestyle relay	
Kathryn Bomstad	1985–87	1984	Norway	200-meter butterfly, 200- and 400-meter individual medley	

NAME	COLLEGE	OLYMPICS	COUNTRY	EVENT	MEDAL
Carole Brook	1985–86	1980, 1984	Switzerland	100- and 200-meter butterfly, 4x100-meter medley relay	
Cătălina Casaru	2001–03	1996	Romania	200-meter backstroke, 4x100-meter medley relay	
Carmel Clark	1985–88	1984	New Zealand	100- and 200-meter backstroke, 100-meter freestyle	
Alex Coci	2011–12	2012	Romania	200-meter butterfly	
Filiberto Colon	1983–86	1984	Puerto Rico	100- and 200-meter butterfly	
Casey Converse	1977–78	1976	USA	400-meter freestyle	
Mark Crocker	1975–78	1972, 1976	Hong Kong	100- and 200-meter freestyle, 100- and 200-meter backstroke	
Mike Davidson	1985–87	1984	New Zealand	200-, 400-, and 1,500-meter freestyle	
Agustina De Giovanni	2006–10	2004, 2008	Argentina	200-meter breaststroke	
Anna Doig	1985–87	1984	New Zealand	100- and 200-meter butterfly, 100-meter freestyle	
Rania Amr El-Wani	1996–97	1992, 1996, 2000	Egypt	50-, 100-, and 200-meter freestyle, 100-meter backstroke	
Igor Erhartić	2004–06	2004	Serbia and Montenegro	200-meter freestyle	

NAME	COLLEGE	OLYM-PICS	COUNTRY	EVENT	MEDAL
Rita Garay	1990–93	1988, 1992	Puerto Rico	200-, 400-, and 800-meter freestyle, 100- and 200-meter backstroke	
Ştefan Gherghel	2002–03	2000, 2004, 2008	Romania	4x200-meter freestyle relay, 100- and 200-meter butterfly, 4x100-meter medley relay	
Kristian Golomeev	2013–14	2012	Greece	100-meter freestyle	
Cam Henning	1979–81	1984	Canada	200-meter backstroke	Bronze
Colin Herring	1970–73	1972	New Zealand	100- and 200-meter freestyle	
Franck Iacono	1985–88	1984, 1988	France	400- and 1,500-meter freestyle, 4x200-meter freestyle relay	
Christine Jarvis	1976–77	1972, 1976	Great Britain	100- and 200-meter breaststroke	
Marcelo Jucá	1982–85	1980, 1984	Brazil	400-meter freestyle, 1,500-meter freestyle, 4x200-meter freestyle relay, 4x100-meter medley relay	
Angelika Knipping	1983–85	1984	West Germany	100-meter breaststroke	
Jacques Leloup	1971–74	1972	Belgium	100- and 200-meter butterfly	
Justin Lemberg	1985	1984	Australia	200-, 400-, and 1,500-meter freestyle, 4x200-meter freestyle relay	Bronze

NAME	COLLEGE	OLYMPICS	COUNTRY	EVENT	MEDAL
Hunor Mate	2005–07	2008, 2012	Austria	100- and 200-meter breaststroke	
Anton McKee	2013–14	2012	Iceland	400-meter individual medley, 1,500-meter freestyle	
Ellen McGrath Owen	1982–85	1992	USA	Platform diving	
Max Metzker	1981	1976, 1980	Australia	400- and 1,500-meter freestyle, 4x200-meter freestyle relay	Bronze, 1980
Stavros Mikhailidis	1991–94	1992, 1996, 2000	Cyprus	50- and 100-meter freestyle	
Hanna Miluska	2005–06	2004	Switzerland	200-meter freestyle, 4x200-meter freestyle relay	
Felix Morf	1983–86	1984	Switzerland	100- and 200-meter breaststroke	
Anne Poleska	2001–05	2000, 2004, 2008	Germany	200-meter backstroke	Bronze, 2004
Vlad Polyakov	2003, 2005–07	2004, 2008, 2012	Kazakhstan	100- and 200-meter breaststroke	
Tony Portela	1985–89	1984	Puerto Rico	100-meter freestyle, 4x100-meter freestyle relay	
Enrique Romero	1984–87	1984	Spain	100- and 200-meter breaststroke	
Mark Rourke	1988–91	1984, 1992	Canada	Platform and springboard diving	

NAME	COLLEGE	OLYM-PICS	COUNTRY	EVENT	MEDAL
Ragnheiður Runólfsdóttir	1990–91	1988, 1992	Iceland	100- and 200-meter breaststroke, 200-meter individual medley	
Karolina Szczepaniak	2013–14	2008, 2012	Poland	400-meter individual medley, 800-meter freestyle, 4x200-meter freestyle relay	
Arlene Semeco	2004–05	2004, 2008, 2012	Venezuela	50- and 100-meter freestyle	
Andreas Schmidt	1982–85	1976, 1984	West Germany	400-meter freestyle, 4x200-meter freestyle relay, 4x100-meter freestyle relay	
Helga Sigurðardóttir	1992–94	1992	Iceland	50- and 100-meter freestyle	
Apostolos Tsangarakis	2003, 2005–07	2004, 2008	Greece	50-meter freestyle	
Jeff Van de Graaf	1978–79	1976	Australia	200-meter butterfly, 400-meter individual medley	
Kristel Vourna	2011–13	2012	Greece	100-meter butterfly, 4x100-meter freestyle relay	
Glen Walshaw	1997–2000	2000	Zimbabwe	100- and 200-meter freestyle	

Tennis

NAME	COLLEGE	OLYMPICS	COUNTRY	EVENT	MEDAL
Juan Carlos Bianchi	1993	1996	Venezuela	Doubles	
Constantinos Efremoglou	1986–89	1992	Greece	Doubles	
Ellis Ferreira	1988–91	1996	South Africa	Doubles	

Track and Field

NAME	COLLEGE	OLYMPICS	COUNTRY	EVENT	MEDAL
Evelyn Adir	1984–88	1984	Uganda	800-meter run	
Laura Agront	1984–87	1984	Puerto Rico	High jump	
Solomon Amegatcher	1990–94	1992, 1996	Ghana	400-meter run, 4x400-meter relay	
Katie Anderson	1990–92	1988, 1992, 1996, 2000	Canada	4x100-meter relay, 100-meter hurdles	
Trish Bartholomew	2007–08	2008	Grenada	400-meter run	
Samuel Boateng	1991–93	1988, 1992	Ghana	4x100-meter relay, 200-meter run	
Eggert Bogason	1986–87	1988	Iceland	Discus	
Tim Broe	1996–2000	2004	USA	5,000-meter run	
Grace Buzu	1990–92	1988	Uganda	4x100-meter relay	
John Crist	1976–78	1984	USA	Decathlon	
Siggi Einarsson	1984–86	1984, 1988, 1992	Iceland	Javelin	
Diane Francis	1991	1996	St. Kitts and Nevis	400-meter dash, 4x400-meter relay	
Disa Gisladdottir	1981–85	1976, 1984	Iceland	High jump	
Iris Gronfeldt	1983–86	1984, 1988	Iceland	Javelin	
Pétur Guðmundsson	1983	1988, 1992	Iceland	Shot put	
Vésteinn Hafsteinsson	1981–84	1984, 1988, 1992, 1996	Iceland	Discus	

NAME	COLLEGE	OLYMPICS	COUNTRY	EVENT	MEDAL
Hreinn Halldórsson	1980	1976	Iceland	Shot put	
Kristján Harðarson	1983	1984	Iceland	Long jump	
Tahesia Harrigan-Scott	2005–07	2008, 2012	British Virgin Islands	100-meter dash	
Flora Hyacinth	1986–89	1996	U.S. Virgin Islands	Long jump, triple jump	
Faith Idehen	1992–94	1992, 1996	Nigeria	4x100-meter relay	Bronze, 1996
Jan Johnson	1969–72	1972	USA	Pole vault	Bronze
Eduardo Nava	1989–92	1988, 1992	Mexico	100-meter run, 4x100-meter relay, 4x400-meter relay	
Andrew Owusu	1992–96	1996, 2000, 2004	Ghana	Long jump, triple jump	
Miguel Pate	2000–02	2008	USA	Long jump	
Clive Wright	1990–91	1988, 1992	Jamaica	200-meter run, 4x100-meter relay	
William Wuycke	1982–85	1980, 1984	Venezuela	800-meter run	

Triathlon

NAME	COLLEGE	OLYMPICS	COUNTRY	EVENT	MEDAL
Susan Bartholomew Williams	1988–90, 1992	2004	USA	Triathlon	Bronze

TENNIS
TENNIS
TENNIS
TENNIS
TENNIS

Keep an eye on the Alabama men's and women's tennis teams. One or both just might be next to bring a "secondary sport" national championship to Tuscaloosa.

That's a bold prediction. Alabama has never won a national championship in tennis, or even come closer than the NCAA tournament's round of 16. You have to go well back into the previous century just to find the Crimson Tide's lone Southeastern Conference championship. The men posted it in 1975–76—and even then, they shared it with LSU. But new athletics director Bill Battle has carried on the work of his predecessor, the late Mal Moore, in trying to spread Alabama's winning tradition to all varsity sports, not just the traditional powerhouses of women's gymnastics and, of course, football. When Bear Bryant was athletics director, he was content if teams in sports other than football were competitive. Moore and Battle have sent a clear message: that's not good enough anymore.

Alabama has long recruited worldwide. Its most successful tennis graduate in the professional ranks, Ellis Ferreira (see page 404), came from South Africa. The 2012–13 teams included men from South Africa, Canada, the Netherlands, Cyprus, Bolivia, and Estonia, and women from Germany and Egypt.

And the athletics department has invested in first-class facilities. The $4.2 million Alabama Tennis Stadium, opened in 2004, won a U. S. Tennis Association Outstanding Facility Award in 2006. It contains 12 hard courts and overhead seating for 2,000 with views of all courts. Next door, the university in 2012 opened the six-court Roberta Alison Baumgardner Indoor Tennis Facility, named for a woman who played varsity tennis for Alabama a decade before the school had a women's team (see "Play Against a Girl? Ewwww!" on page 397). "This is the finest indoor tennis facility in the country," said women's Coach Jenny Mainz at the building's dedication. "Roberta Alison Baumgardner would be very proud of it, and we are going to work very hard at winning championships in this building."

The women's program has been building momentum the past couple of years. New men's Coach George Husack came to Alabama after three straight years as associate coach for national championship teams at the University of Southern California. So we'll see.

MEN

Alabama had a men's tennis team for at least a decade or two before it became an official varsity sport. In a 1981 *Tuscaloosa News* interview, Donald Smith, PhD, then a chemistry professor at Alabama, recalled being invited to Alabama for a match when he played for the tennis team at the University of Chattanooga (now the University of Tennessee at Chattanooga).

"We played against Alabama in 1934, and at that time they didn't have a coach," he said. "It was just a bunch of boys who got together. They paid us $10 total to come and play them.

"They looked like a bunch of guys who had gotten together to play each other and have a good time. They were a fairly good team too. They skunked us pretty bad back then."

Even after tennis achieved varsity status in 1948–49, Alabama didn't exactly emphasize the sport. The second Crimson Tide coach, C. de la Manardiere (1950–53, 1955–56) was primarily a professor of French. His successor, Rafael del Valle (1953–55, 1957–60), taught Spanish.

Alabama has sent a few players to the pro circuit. One, Ellis Ferreira, even earned the number two ranking in the world and won titles in two Grand Slam tournaments. But he did so in doubles, not the more glamorous singles. So he never made much of a splash among casual tennis fans.

The best Alabama graduate currently touring as a pro is Saketh Myneni, a 6-foot-4 right-hander who played for the Crimson Tide from 2006–07 through 2009–10. The native of India has won several tournaments on the International Tennis Federation Futures tour, two steps below the top-level

Association of Tennis Professionals World Tour. He's not getting rich; Futures tournaments max out at $15,000 in prize money. But they do offer the possibility of ATP rankings points. As of mid-2013, Myneni, age 25, had made it as high as 263rd in singles and 301st in doubles.

HEAD COACHES

The Jason Morton Era

Lee Shapiro got the Alabama tennis program off to a great start in the 1948–49 season, finishing 8-1 in dual meets and 4-0 in the Southeastern Conference. Unfortunately, he lasted as coach only one more year, during which his team slumped to 7-8. Things continued downhill from there. In the first dozen years of Crimson Tide tennis, even including that 8-1 start, Shapiro and four successors struggled to an overall record of 55-93—and 23-57 in the SEC. In the nine seasons from 1951–52 through 1959–60, the Tide won a total of only nine SEC dual meets.

To the rescue in 1960–61 came a force of nature named Jason Morton, who for several years had been the pro at the Tuscaloosa Racquet Club (where he mentored Jean Mills, who became Alabama's first women's tennis coach; see page 394). After an 8-10-1 start (3-4-1 in the SEC), his teams ripped off records of 13-2, 15-5, and 15-3, and SEC marks of 7-0, 7-4, and 4-2. The Tide's third-place SEC finish in 1963 remained its best conference showing until Bill McClain's team finished second a decade later—and Morton accomplished it with the help of a 19-year-old woman (see "Play Against a Girl? Ewwww!" on page 397).

Morton was an organizer, an innovator, a teacher, a motivator, a promoter, and a heck of a player himself. After leaving Tuscaloosa, he added to his legend. He umpired at major tennis tournaments and other matches, including the famous "Battle of the Sexes" victory by Billie Jean King over Bobby Riggs in September 1973. He earned induction into the Texas Tennis Hall of Fame for his playing in high school and college (at the University of Houston) and his later work as a pro at several clubs in the state. He helped design a tennis club in Sun Lakes, Arizona, his last home. He kept playing until almost the end of his life, winning the International Tennis Foundation world singles championship in 2008 in the men's 80-plus age-group division.

Morton died of pneumonia in 2011 at age 82, survived by his wife of 64 years, Edith.

The Bill McClain Era

The three coaches who followed Jason Morton all posted records at or below .500 in stints of one or two years, although Morton's immediate successor, Earl Baumgardner, who also succeeded him as the pro at the Tuscaloosa Racquet Club, did marry women's tennis pioneer Roberta Alison (see "Play Against a Girl? Ewwww!" on page 397). Then, starting with the 1969–70 season, Bill McClain came over from South Carolina, where two years previously his team had won the Atlantic Coast Conference championship.

McClain stayed for eight years, taking the team to the second-most dual-meet victories of any Alabama coach—142, behind only the 148 wins posted by Billy Pate in two more seasons. McClain also ranks second in winning percentage to Morton (.705 to .715). Under him, Alabama achieved its first 20-win records: 27-7 in 1971–72 and 23-3 in 1975–76. Also in 1975–76, McClain led the Crimson Tide to its only Southeastern Conference championship, men's or women's, with a perfect 7-0 SEC mark. Along the way, he picked up a doctorate in education at Alabama.

In 1977, McClain left to coach at Southern Methodist University, where in three seasons he won two Southwest Conference titles. He remains the only coach to win conference tennis championships at three different Division I universities. After leaving the collegiate ranks, he spent many years as a teaching pro at private clubs in the Los Angeles area.

The Armistead Neely Era

Armistead "Armi" Neely, a globetrotting, glasses-wearing, 30-year-old touring pro with a handlebar mustache, thought he'd give college coaching a try. Succeeding McClain, he managed one 20-win season in five years (20-4 in 1980–81). In 1982, he left Alabama to move to Atlanta, giving way to Tommy Wade. He has been based there ever since as a player (he still competes on the international senior circuit), administrator, and teaching pro. For fun, he even plays in local recreational leagues.

The Tommy Wade Era

In six years, Tommy Wade's Alabama teams won 20 or more dual meets four times. Each year, his teams achieved national end-of-season top 20 ranking by the Intercollegiate Tennis Coaches Association (now the Intercollegiate Tennis Association); no other Alabama coach can say that.

When he left in 1988 to become tennis director at Cherokee Country Club in Knoxville, Tennessee, he said, "If there is one thing of which I am most proud, it is the fact that we have had a tremendous graduation rate among our athletes." Under Wade, Alabama tennis players had the highest grade point average of all Crimson Tide men's teams and achieved a graduation rate of more than 90 percent.

Since 2004, he has been director of tennis for the city of Decatur, Alabama, and teaching pro at the Jimmy Johns Tennis Center in Point Mallard Park. There, he has presided over an expansion from six courts to 12 outdoor hard courts, 4 outdoor soft courts, and 2 indoor hard courts in a soft-walled inflated enclosure called The Bubble.

The Billy Pate Era

The three coaches who succeeded Tommy Wade had some peaks, notably the ninth-place Intercollegiate Tennis Association ranking—the Crimson Tide's highest ever—achieved by John Kreis in the 1991–92 season. But Alabama couldn't sustain success at a high level, a problem that also plagued Billy Pate. In his best season, 2006–07, Pate coached Alabama team to a 22-8 dual-meet record and a national ranking of 14th. But Alabama managed only a tie for third in the Southeastern Conference that year. In his other nine seasons, the best Pate's teams could do in the SEC was fifth. Overall, he posted five winning and five losing records. His last three marks were 13-14, 10-12, and 10-15.

In May 2012, Princeton hired Pate to coach its men's tennis team. "Billy has guided a very successful program in Alabama for the last decade, and we are fortunate to be able to bring someone with such a winning background to Princeton," said athletics director Gary Walters.

Alabama replaced Pate with George Husack, who was the 2012 Intercollegiate Tennis Association National Assistant Coach of the Year at Southern California. "Here I want to be a championship contender for a national title and a conference title," he said. "How long that is going to take I'm not too sure, but I like what I see." More than one year, at least; his initial dual-meet record was 14-14.

Men's Head Coaching Records

(In chronological order)

YEAR	COACH	RECORD	WINNING %
1948–50	Lee Shapiro	15-9-0	.625
1950–53, 1955–56	C. de la Manardiere	22-31-0	.415
1953–55, 1957–60	Rafael del Valle	15-45-0	.250
1956–57	Eugene Lambert	3-8-0	.273
1960–64	Jason Morton	51-20-1	.715
1964-66	Earl Baumgardner	13-15-0	.464
1966–67	Bill Mallory	7-7-0	.500
1967–69	Dale Anderson	12-16-0	.429
1969–77	Bill McClain	142-59-1	.705
1977–82	Armistead Neely	73-41-0	.640
1982–88	Tommy Wade	115-56-0	.673
1988–94	John Kreis	79-69-0	.534
1994–97	Joey Rivé	32-45-0	.416
1997–2002	Adam Steinberg	69-58-0	.543
2002–12	Billy Pate	148-120-0	.552
2012–13	George Husack	14-14-0	.500

(Ranked by victories)

RECORD	COACH	YEARS
148-120-0	Billy Pate	2002–12
142-59-1	Bill McClain	1969–77
115-56-0	Tommy Wade	1982–88
79-69-0	John Kreis	1988–94
73-41-0	Armistead Neely	1977–82
69-58-0	Adam Steinberg	1997–2002
51-20-1	Jason Morton	1960–64

RECORD	COACH	YEARS
32-45-0	Joey Rivé	1994–97
22-31-0	C. de la Manardiere	1950–53, 1955–56
15-9-0	Lee Shapiro	1948–50
15-45-0	Rafael del Valle	1953–55, 1957–60
14-14-0	George Husack	2012–13
13-15-0	Earl Baumgardner	1964-66
12-16-0	Dale Anderson	1967–69
7-7-0	Bill Mallory	1966–67
3-8-0	Eugene Lambert	1956–57

(Ranked by winning percentage)

WINNING %	RECORD	COACH	YEARS
.715	51-20-1	Jason Morton	1960–64
.705	142-59-1	Bill McClain	1969–77
.673	115-56-0	Tommy Wade	1982–88
.640	73-41-0	Armistead Neely	1977–82
.625	15-9-0	Lee Shapiro	1948–50
.552	148-120-0	Billy Pate	2002–12
.543	69-58-0	Adam Steinberg	1997–2002
.534	79-69-0	John Kreis	1988–94
.500	14-14-0	George Husack	2012–13
.500	7-7-0	Bill Mallory	1966–67
.464	13-15-0	Earl Baumgardner	1964-66
.416	32-45-0	Joey Rivé	1994–97
.415	22-31-0	C. de la Manardiere	1950–53, 1955–56
.429	12-16-0	Dale Anderson	1967–69
.273	3-8-0	Eugene Lambert	1956–57
.250	15-45-0	Rafael del Valle	1953–55, 1957–60

Men's Southeastern Conference Championships

(Through 2013)

26	Georgia	**5**	LSU	**2**	Auburn
18	Tulane	**5**	Mississippi	**2**	Kentucky
9	Florida	**3**	Georgia	**1**	**Alabama**
9	Tennessee	**3**	Mississippi State		

Men's SEC Tournament Championships

(Through 2013)

8	Georgia	**3**	Tennessee	**1**	Mississippi State
4	Florida	**2**	LSU	**1**	Vanderbilt
3	Mississippi	**1**	Kentucky		

WOMEN

Alabama's women's tennis teams have been regulars this century in the NCAA Tournament, qualifying every year since 2001 except 2007, 2008, and 2010. In 2013, the team advanced the furthest in school history, to the round of 16. The Crimson Tide finished both 2011–12 and 2012–13 ranked 11th in the country.

The team has come a long way from its first season in 1974–75, when only two players had scholarships (for $300 apiece) and the players had to return their skirts to the university at the end of the season. They did get to keep their shoes.

No Crimson Tide women have gone on to make a dent on the pro tour—although the first women's coach might have except for her father's notions about femininity; read on for the details.

HEAD COACHES

The Jean Mills Era

A tennis prodigy, Jean Mills ranked third in the country as a 14-year-old. Then her father pressured her to get off the tournament circuit. "He didn't want me to turn into a muscular woman athlete," Mills told the *Tuscaloosa News* in March 1975. "I disagreed with him, but gave up competitive tennis anyway. I never had second thoughts about it until six months ago, when the women pros started getting a lot of money. Now I wonder if I could have made it."

Mills, a Tuscaloosa native, made it in other ways. At the time of the interview, she was coaching Alabama's first-ever women's tennis team. Her players finished 6-5 in dual meets that year and 44-26 in her four years as coach. She never had a losing record.

She resigned from Alabama after the 1977–78 season, saying, "I feel like I need to leave Tuscaloosa. This is my home. It's been my life. I'm ready for a new experience." She became the first executive director of the Professional Tennis Registry, headquartered at Hilton Head Island, South Carolina. It describes itself as the largest global organization of tennis teachers and coaches. Since 1985, she has been director of tennis operations at the Polo Club of Boca Raton in Florida.

The Karin Gaiser Era

Mark Heinrich, a doctoral student at Alabama in counseling and guidance who also taught tennis classes at the university, succeeded Mills. In two years, Heinrich's teams went 39-14 in dual meets; his .736 winning percentage leads all Crimson Tide tennis coaches—including those of the men's team. He is now the chancellor of the Alabama Community College System.

Lewis Lay posted a 9-21 record during one season as coach. Peter Heffernan did better until he resigned for personal reasons during the middle of the 1983–84 season. He was credited with an overall record of 67-50, including the 1983–84 matches completed after his departure. Karin Gaiser, an Alabama graduate student who had been the assistant coach the previous year, took over as interim coach and got the permanent job after the season.

Under Gaiser, Alabama first broke into the Intercollegiate Tennis Coaches Association national team rankings (1991–92, finishing 25th) and first reached the NCAA Championships (as an alternate in 1993). Alabama had its first All-America players, the Dutch doubles team of Marouschka van Dijk and Titia Wilmink in 1993, and its first representatives on the Southeastern Conference Academic Honor Roll. In her nine seasons, Crimson Tide players achieved SEC academic honors 29 times. Her dual-meet record was 126-104.

After the 1992–93 season, Gaiser resigned to return home to Ohio and work for her father's Dayton-based company, Encon Inc., which created the modern plastic beverage bottle. She is now president and chief executive officer of Eco-Groupe Inc., which owns Encon and several other manufacturing companies. It's based in Vandalia, just north of Dayton.

The Jenny Mainz Era

Jim Tressler, who was an assistant coach at perennial tennis power Florida when the Gators went undefeated and won the national championship in 1991–92, led the Crimson Tide from 1993–94 until he resigned in February 1997 to take a position with sports equipment company Nike. Assistant coach Michelle Morton became interim coach for the rest of that season. Tressler now directs Atkins Tennis Center at the University of Illinois. The Illinois website says his Alabama teams "consistently finished among the top 20 in the country," which is true if by "consistently" one means "once in three and a half seasons, and then just barely." (Alabama was ranked 20th in 1994–95.)

Jenny Mainz, by far Alabama's longest-serving tennis coach (men's or women's), began her tenure inauspiciously, with an 0-21 dual-meet record in 1997–98. The next two years brought slow improvement—3-18, 7-15— before Alabama went 16-10 in 2000–01 and finished with an Intercollegiate Tennis Association rank of 26th. Mainz continued solidly but unspectacularly, putting up a record over the next decade of 115-116.

But lately, she has had Alabama tennis on a roll. In 2011–12, The Crimson Tide finished 18-5 in dual meets and 10-1 in the Southeastern Conference. The Tide achieved both its best-ever SEC finish (second) and best ITA end-of-season ranking (11th).

Alabama did even better the next year, advancing to the NCAA Championships round of 16 and having players reach the semifinals in singles (Alexa Gurachi) and doubles (Gurachi and Mary Anne Macfarlane), all for the first time. The final record was 21-6. Mainz was named the Wilson/ITA National Coach of the Year to go with her back-to-back SEC Coach of the Year honors in 2011 and 2012.

Before the 2012–13 season, Mainz said, "We are certainly capable of winning an SEC championship and even a national championship in the coming years, and I think we're really moving in the right direction to be able to do that." Bold words, but she's backing them up.

Play Against a Girl? Ewwww!

In 1963, Roberta Alison became the first female scholarship athlete for both the University of Alabama and the Southeastern Conference—playing on the men's tennis team.

Alison was a 19-year-old sophomore from Alexander City, Alabama. Crimson Tide Coach Jason Morton discovered her at the Tuscaloosa Racquet Club, where he was the tennis pro. Alison was training for national women's competition, which was played on grass, and Tuscaloosa had the nearest grass courts to Alexander City.

Morton talked her into enrolling at Alabama, saying that he'd try to get her onto the men's team but that at the very least, practicing against men would improve her game. Meanwhile, enlisting the help of football coach and athletics director Bear Bryant, Morton successfully lobbied for a new SEC rule allowing women to play on men's teams if their school had no women's team in their sport. In her first match, Alison whipped Rick Wise of Spring Hill College in Mobile, Alabama, 6-0, 6-0.

At least he showed up. Several opponents forfeited rather than risk losing to a girl—which, of course, guaranteed that they would lose to a girl. Mississippi State Coach Tom Sawyer protested unsuccessfully to SEC Commissioner Bernie Moore. "It is no honor for a man to beat a woman," he said, "but the humiliation of a man beaten by a woman would be of great dimension."

"That's a lot of bunk," Morton responded. "Can I help it if other teams don't get good players? What am I supposed to do, bench Roberta because she happens to be able to beat many of the men players? No, sir, she will play!"

And play she did, earning three varsity letters. The *Tuscaloosa News* interviewed her more than 20 years later and reported that her records were 15-5 as a sophomore (freshmen couldn't play varsity sports at the time), 15-3 as a junior, and 9-5 as a senior. Alison, who became Roberta Baumgardner when she married Earl Baumgardner, her senior-year coach, said Mississippi State's Sawyer was the only coach who wouldn't allow his players to compete against her. "We all felt like it was ridiculous," she said. "The SEC had passed a special rule letting women play on teams if they made the team, and every time he defaulted, that automatically gave us two wins."

Her teammates, she said, were very supportive, and many became lifelong friends.

Some sources say she started playing number four singles and moved up to number two and sometimes even number one by her senior year. That's likely a product of the same process by which a birdie becomes a hole in one after a few decades of telling and retelling. The Southern Tennis Hall of Fame, which inducted her as a member, says she played number four singles all three years and number two doubles for two years. Regardless, she was a great player, winner of the United States Lawn Tennis Association National College Girls' Tennis Championships in singles in 1962 and 1963, and doubles (with Justina Bricka of Missouri) in 1963.

In the 1960s, she played on the American tennis circuit, which was then strictly amateur for women. But she became a mother to two sons, and her tennis career stalled. She virtually gave up the game, saying later, "I found that I have never been able to make the transition from playing competitive to playing social tennis."

Buamgardner continued to live in Alexander City, where her grandfather Benjamin Russell had founded the sports apparel company that eventually became the Russell Corporation (now part of Berkshire Hathaway). Heir to a significant amount of Russell Corporation stock, she became known for philanthropic work and civic activities and founded the Lake Martin Humane Society. She died in 2009, age 65, from injuries sustained during a fire at her home.

Women's Head Coaching Records

(In chronological order)

YEAR	COACH	RECORD	WINNING %
1974–78	Jean Mills	44-26	.629
1978–80	Mark Heinrich	39-14	.736
1980–81	Lewis Lay	9-21	.300
1981–84	Peter Heffernan	67-50	.573

YEAR	COACH	RECORD	WINNING %
1984–93	Karin Gaiser	126-104	.548
1993–96	Jim Tressler	29-34	.460
1996–97	*Jim Tressler/Michelle Morton	13-12	.520
1997–2013	Jenny Mainz	180-191	.485

*Jim Tressler resigned as coach February 1, 1997; assistant coach Michelle Morton finished the season as interim head coach.

(Ranked by victories)

RECORD	COACH	YEARS
180-191	Jenny Mainz	1997-2013
126-104	Karin Gaiser	1984–93
67-50	Peter Heffernan	1981–84
44-26	Jean Mills	1974–78
39-14	Mark Heinrich	1978–80
29-34	Jim Tressler	1993–96
13-12	*Jim Tressler/Michelle Morton	1996–97
9-21	Lewis Lay	1980–81

*Jim Tressler resigned as coach February 1, 1997; assistant coach Michelle Morton finished the season as interim head coach.

(Ranked by winning percentage)

WINNING %	RECORD	COACH	YEARS
.736	39-14	Mark Heinrich	1978-80
.629	44-26	Jean Mills	1974–78
.573	67-50	Peter Heffernan	1981–84
.548	126-104	Karin Gaiser	1984–93
.520	13-12	*Jim Tressler/Michelle Morton	1996–97
.485	180-191	Jenny Mainz	1997-2013
.460	29-34	Jim Tressler	1993–96
.300	9-21	Lewis Lay	1980–81

*Jim Tressler resigned as coach February 1, 1997; assistant coach Michelle Morton finished the season as interim head coach.

Women's Southeastern Conference Championships

(Through 2013)

26 Florida	**8** Georgia	**1** Kentucky

Women's SEC Tournament Championships

(Through 2013)

9 Florida	**4** Georgia

PRO TENNIS PLAYERS: FROM OUTCASTS TO IDOLS

Before 1968, the world governing body of tennis considered professional players to be . . . well, if not pariahs at least tainted by their insistence on getting paid for their efforts. In contrast, noble amateurs played simply for the love of the game.

Theoretically.

In reality, full-time tennis players whose training and travel schedules left no time for any other job could hardly have afforded to compete in tournaments around the world without under-the-table appearance fees. The tennis world finally bowed to reality in 1968, when professionals were allowed to compete in theretofore amateurs-only tournaments, including the prestigious Grand Slam events: Wimbledon (founded in 1887) in England, the U.S. Open (1881), the French Open (1891; opened to all nationalities in 1925), and the Australian Open (1905).

Professional tennis more or less officially began in 1926 when promoter C. C. "Cash and Carry" Pyle signed up a group of American and French players—men and women—to put on a series of exhibition matches before paying crowds. Professional tournaments did evolve, but the "tour" model, in which a group of players barnstormed around the world playing exhibitions among themselves, dominated the pro world for male players. Women's pro events were much fewer and farther between.

After the Open Era dawned in 1968, such rival professional tours as the National Tennis League, World Championship Tennis, the International Lawn Tennis Association's Grand Prix, the U.S. Indoor Circuit, and the European Spring Circuit sprang up, merged, unmerged, banned each other's players, and generally attempted to savage each other. In 1972, a group of male pros formed the Association of Tennis Professionals. In 1990, the ATP Tour became the top professional league and brought order to the world of men's tennis.

The National Tennis League also included women, as did tournaments run by the International Lawn Tennis Federation (now the International Tennis Federation; it consists of a couple of hundred national tennis associations and is the sport's international governing body). But the women got much less prize money. So in 1971 several top players helped put together the much better-paying Virginia Slims Circuit (sponsored by a cigarette brand, which caused intermittent controversy during the tour's existence). The circuit eventually became today's worldwide WTA Tour, operated by the Women's Tennis Association (founded in 1973).

Both the ATP and WTA also operate other circuits in addition to their marquee tours. The ATP World Tour tournaments and the four Grand Slams, which the International Tennis Federation administers, comprise the top level. The ATP Challenger Tour is a notch below. The ITF Futures tournaments constitute the entry level for touring pros. Players can earn ATP ranking points at all levels—the higher the level, the greater the number of points available. The singles players and doubles teams with the most points at the end of the season play in the ATP World Tour Finals.

The WTA has a similar points system and a similar season-ending tournament, the WTA Tour Championships. Its top level consists of Premier tournaments and the Grand Slams. Below that are, in order, International tournaments, Challenger tournaments, and the entry-level ITF Women's Circuit.

Back in the 1970s, some promoters thought tennis could become a big team sport. So World Team Tennis debuted in 1974. Teams consisted of at least two men and two women representing 16 localities: Baltimore, Boston, Buffalo, Chicago, Cleveland, Denver, Detroit, Florida, Hawaii, Houston, Los

Angeles, Minnesota, New York, Philadelphia, Pittsburgh, and San Francisco. The founders dreamed that kids in, say, Philadelphia who followed the Phillies in baseball, the Eagles in football, the 76ers in basketball, and the Flyers in hockey would also make room on their bedroom walls for posters of their favorite players from the Philadelphia Freedoms.

That didn't happen—although Elton John did write a hit song, "Philadelphia Freedom," about his favorite team. WTT folded after the 1978 season. A more modest version reappeared as TeamTennis in 1981. In 1992, it reassumed the World Team Tennis name. Today, it consists of eight teams: the Boston Lobsters, New York Sportimes, Orange County (California) Breakers, Philadelphia Freedoms, Sacramento (California) Capitals, Springfield (Missouri) Lasers, Texas Wild (of Irving), and Washington (DC) Kastles. The season takes place during July, and some pros take a break from the tours to participate.

On July 28, 2013, the Washington Kastles (featuring Martina Hingis) won their third straight WTT title, beating the Springfield Lasers (featuring Andy Roddick), 25-12, in front of a sellout home crowd at Kastles Stadium at The Wharf. But you knew that, right?

Two other sets of team competitions, both involving national teams, stir more interest. The Davis Cub began in 1900 as a match between U.S. and British teams. The United States won in three straight matches. One of the players, Dwight Davis of the Harvard tennis team, spent some $1,000 of his own money on the sterling silver trophy that the winner has received from the beginning. Davis later became U.S. secretary of war and governor-general of the Philippines.

Today, the annual Davis Cup competition involves male players from 130 nations. The ITF administers both it and the women's equivalent, the Fed Cup, which began as the Federation Cup in 1963.

Every four years, dozens of countries send tennis teams to the Summer Olympics. Tennis was part of the first modern Olympics in 1896 but was discontinued after 1924 because of disputes involving how amateurism should be defined and whether the International Lawn Tennis Federation or the International Olympic Committee should be in charge. It was played again as a demonstration sport in 1968 and 1984 and returned as a full medal sport in 1988. Today's Olympic tennis events are men's and women's singles and doubles, and mixed doubles.

PLAYER BIOS

College years are years receiving a varsity letter unless otherwise noted.

Pro years are years playing in top-level pro events, including Grand Slams, the ATP Tour/ ATP World Tour, the Davis Cup, and the Olympics, all through 2013.

Records are match records.

Titles are top-level tournament championships, including Grand Slams and ATP Tour/ ATP World tour events.

Grand Slams are the Australian Open, the French Open, Wimbledon, and the U.S. Open.

JUAN CARLOS BIANCHI

COLLEGE: 1992–93, doubles All-America 1993

PRO: singles 1989, 0-2; doubles 1994, 1996, 0-4; Davis Cup: singles, 1989, 0-2; doubles 1991, 1996, 0-2; Olympics: doubles 1996, 0-1

An All-America doubles player for Alabama in 1993 (with teammate Rick Witsken; see page 405), Juan Carlos Bianchi represented his native Venezuela in Davis Cup singles (1989) and doubles (1996) and at the 1996 Atlanta Olympics, his last hurrah in international competition. As a pro, his peak Association of Tennis Professionals rankings were 384th for singles in 1994 and 171th for doubles in 1996. The right-hander now directs junior competitive tennis at Midtown Athletic Club in Weston, Florida.

At age 7, Juan Carlos Bianchi began playing tennis in Maracay, Venezuela.

Credit: Courtesy of Juan Carlos Bianchi

CONSTANTINOS EFREMOGLOU

COLLEGE: 1986–89 . . . . **PRO:** singles 1986, 1989–90, 1993–94, 1996, 10-13; doubles 1984–86, 1988–89, 1992–96, 13-16; Davis Cup: singles 1986, 1989–90, 1993–94, 1996, 10-10; doubles, 1984–86, 1988–89, 1992–96, 12-11; Olympics: doubles 1992, 1-1

Athens native Constantinos Efremoglou played sparingly in pro tour events. Instead, the 6-2, 163-pound right-hander concentrated on representing his country. He competed for Greece in 43 Davis Cup matches from 1984 through 1996 and in the 1992 Olympics.

ELLIS FERREIRA

COLLEGE: 1987–91; doubles All-America 1989, 1990, 1991
PRO: singles 1992–95, 4-8; doubles 1993–2004, 314-201, 18 titles, 2 Grand Slam titles; Davis Cup: doubles 1996–98, 1-3; Olympics: doubles 1996, 2-1

The Association of Tennis Professionals once ranked him second in the world. He won 18 top-level tournaments, including at least one a year for seven straight years, 1995–2001. He claimed two Grand Slams titles. And yet Ellis Ferreira never became a household name (except in very tennis-centric households).

Why not? Because he specialized in doubles. He hit number two in the rankings early in 2000 after he and Rick Leach won the Australian Open title, and he added the Australian Open mixed doubles championship, with Corina Morariu, in 2001. He earned a career total in prize money of $2,378,295.

Ferreira, a 6-2, 190-pound South African who plays left-handed, followed older brother Clinton (see page 405) to Alabama. In 1989, the Ferreiras teamed to win the Southeastern Conference doubles title and achieve Intercollegiate Tennis Coaches Association All-America status in doubles.

Ellis Ferreira plays at Wimbledon in 2001, when he and partner Rick Leach reached the quarterfinals.
Credit: Carol L. Newsom

Ellis Ferreira earned both his marketing degree from Alabama and his first pro win in 1992. After stepping away from the tour grind in 2003, he developed a line of children's tennis clothing, then operated the Eagleton/Ferreira junior tennis academy on Longboat Key, Florida. In 2013, he became the head of the tennis department at the Life Time Fitness center in Vestavia Hills, Alabama, a suburb of Birmingham.

FRANCISCO RODRIGUEZ

COLLEGE: 1996–2000; singles All-America 1998, 1999
DAVIS CUP: singles 1998–2000, 2002–04, 2006–07, 14-5;
doubles 1999–2000, 2003, 2006–07, 5-1

Playing for his native Paraguay, Francisco Rodriguez was a Davis Cup stalwart for most of a decade in both singles and doubles. On the pro tour from 2001 through 2006, the right-hander primarily played the third-tier Futures circuit, peaking in the Association of Tennis Professionals rankings at 373th in singles and 545th in doubles. He achieved his greatest fame after his career ended. In 2008, he became the first (and so far only) touring male tennis pro to come out as gay.

Others in the ATP Tour, Davis Cup, or Olympics (S=singles, D=doubles)

NAME	COLLEGE	PRO
Clinton Ferreira	1985–89, D All-America 1986, 1989	D 1994–97, 3-21
John Stimpson	1987–90, S and D All-America, 1990	S 1991, 1-3; D 1991, 1-1
Rick Witsken	1990–93, D All-America, 1991, 1993	D 1993, 1996, 1999, 0-3

Men's Records

Singles Wins, Season

34	John Stimpson, 1989–90	31	Cecil Brandon, 1992–93
33	Andy Solis, 1982–83	30	Ellis Ferreira, 1990–91
32	Gregg Hahn, 1984–85	29	Francisco Rodriguez, 1998–99
32	Michael Jung, 2008–09	29	Jarryd Botha, 2012–13
31	Gregg Hahn, 1982–83	29	Becker O'Shaughnessey, 2012–13

▪ *Doubles Wins, Season*

29 Daniel Buikema-Mathieu Thibaudeau, 2008	**20** Joseph Jung-Saketh Myneni, 2007
23 Ellis Ferreira-Rick Witsken, 1991	**19** Gregg Hahn-Andy Solis, 1985
23 Clinton-Ellis Ferreira, 1989	**18** Billy Mertz-Saketh Myneni, 2009
23 Rick Witsken-Juan Carlos Bianchi, 1993	**17** Gregg Hahn-Clinton Ferreira, 1986
22 Alin Taranga-Rashid Hassan, 1996	**17** John Stimpson-Ellis Ferreira, 1990

Women's Records

▪ *Singles Wins, Season*

37 Myke Loomis, 1981–82	**30** Alexa Guarachi, 2011–12
34 Mary Anne Macfarlane, 2011–12	**29** Sophie Cremers, 2002–03
32 Lori Smith, 1992–93	**29** Natalia Maynetto, 2012–13
30 Beth Marrow, 1989–90	**28** Jane Phillips, 1989–90
30 Amanda Ballinger, 1996–97	**28** Baili Camino, 1996–97

▪ *Doubles Wins, Season*

29 Alexa Guarachi-Courtney MacLane, 2010–11	**23** Alexa Guarachi-Courtney McLane, 2009–10
28 Titia Wilmink-Marouschka van Dijk, 1992–93	**23** Ashley Bentley-Robin Stephenson, 2003–04
27 Ashley Bentley-Robin Stephenson, 2005–06	**22** Alex Clay-Taylor Lindsey, 2010–11
27 Antonia Foehse-Mary Anne Macfarlane, 2010–11	**19** Jane Phillips-Rachel Marrow, 1989–90
27 Alexa Guarachi-Mary Anne Macfarlane, 2012–13	**19** Marouschka van Dijk-Hilde Otterman, 1993–94
	19 Antoniua Foehse-Mary Anne Macfarlane, 2011–12

FIGHTING

century ago, three pastimes dominated the American sporting consciousness: baseball, horse racing, and boxing. Starting with John L. Sullivan in the late 1800s, boxing champions, especially the heavyweights, achieved towering popular celebrity. On September 23, 1926, when Jack Dempsey lost the heavyweight title to Gene Tunney, 120,557 people packed the Sesquicentennial Municipal Stadium in Philadelphia to watch the bout.

Boxing's popularity permeated all strata of society. Even as late as the 1930s into the 1960s, A. J. Liebling wrote regularly about what he called "the sweet science" in that most self-consciously literary of magazines, *The New Yorker*. In 1919, with matches between Pennsylvania and Penn State, boxing debuted as a college sport.

The National Collegiate Athletic Association held its first boxing tournament in 1932. In 1940, a match in Madison, Wisconsin, between Wisconsin and Washington State drew a crowd reported at 15,000. As late as the 1950s, more than 200 schools had boxing teams.

In 1985, the most famous member of the University of Alabama's boxing squad recalled his collegiate experiences of the late 1930s and early 1940s: "I remember boxing being the second most attended sport at the University of Alabama and at other schools in the Southeastern Conference. It outdrew basketball, baseball, and track. At Alabama, you had to line up two or three hours ahead of a fight to be able to get into Foster Auditorium."

So wrote George Wallace (see page 411) in a letter to E. C. Wallenfeldt. Wallenfeldt quoted from the letter in his book *The Six-Minute Fraternity: The Rise and Fall of NCAA Tournament Boxing, 1932–60*.

History is vague as to when the Alabama athletics department officially adopted boxing, but the Crimson Tide's team dated back at least to 1930. After 1940, the Southeastern Conference dropped the sport. "Boxing was outlawed in 1940 by the conference as being too brutal," Wallace wrote in his letter. "I believe it was discontinued because of a jealousy that existed due to boxing being more popular than all other sports except for football."

Boxing took a further hit from World War II. Many colleges and universities suspended their programs during the hostilities. At some schools, the sport never resumed. Even LSU, which dominated boxing in the South, dropped it as a varsity sport after the 1956 season, partly because it was getting hard to find opponents within a reasonable traveling distance.

Except for a World War II–related hiatus from 1944 through 1946, the NCAA continued to hold a national boxing championship meet. But in 1960, Charlie Mohr of Wisconsin died a week after being knocked out during the championships. The NCAA withdrew its sanctioning. Boxing withered.

But it didn't die. At a few colleges, students continued to compete on a club basis—meaning that the students themselves, rather than the school, ran the teams. In 1976, the clubs formed the National Collegiate Boxing Association under the auspices of what was then the United States Amateur Boxing Federation, known since 1978 as USA Boxing.

Thirty-four schools currently compete. The service academies dominate. Of the 37 championships from 1976 (the NCBA's first year) through 2012, Air Force won 19 (1980–81, 1983–86, 1988–90, 1992, 1994–95, 1999–2004, 2012), Navy 5 (1987, 1996–98, 2005), and Army 4 (2008–11). The Coast Guard Academy also has a team.

Army left the NCBA in 2012 to join a new club boxing organization formed that summer: the United States Intercollegiate Boxing Association. It's affiliated with NIRSA, a collegiate recreation organization formerly known as the National Intramural-Recreational Sports Association. The USIBA counts 30 schools as members, including a few two-year institutions. Its inaugural national championships in April 2013 saw Army win the women's team title and UC Davis win the men's.

Until 2009, Alabama had no state boxing commission to sanction professional fights. Unsanctioned fights did occur, and officials from other states sometimes put on sanctioned pro bouts. After passage of the enabling legislation, it took a while for the Alabama Athletic Commission to get organized. But by early 2011, Deontay Wilder, a Tuscaloosa heavyweight who won a bronze medal at the 2008 Summer Olympics, became Alabama's first licensed pro boxer.

In February 2011, Wilder headed the card at the state's first sanctioned boxing matches, which took place at Shelton State Community College in Tuscaloosa. He beat DeAndrey Abron on a technical knockout. As of June 2013, he had run his professional record to 28-0, winning every bout by a knockout or technical knockout. Along the way, he had collected a minor bauble among boxing's many championships: the World Boxing Council's Continental Americas regional heavyweight title.

Meanwhile, another kind of fighting has roared past boxing in public popularity: mixed martial arts. It involves punching, kicking, wrestling, and just about every other kind of hand-to-hand combat. The Alabama Athletic Commission in early 2012 granted the first state-sanctioned promoter licenses for the sport. Some matches had taken place before then, but legal uncertainty created after the Legislature adopted mixed martial arts legislation had caused many promoters to suspend activities.

In this age of safety consciousness (not to mention lawsuit consciousness), it's hard to imagine the NCAA ever sanctioning intercollegiate mixed martial arts competition. But that doesn't mean athletes who play other sports in college can't turn to it as pros once they've left their alma mater. One Alabama football player has already taken that path. We expect more to follow as the sport continues to grow.

ATHLETE BIOS

College years are years receiving a varsity letter unless otherwise noted.

IFL: Indoor Football League

MMA: Mixed martial arts

HOF: Hall of Fame

ERYK ANDERS ■ *Mixed Martial Arts Fighter*

COLLEGE: 2007–09 . . . . **IFL:** 2011; **PRO MMA:** 2012–13

Eryk Anders shows off the Tennessee state championship belt he won at an International Sport Karate Association match in May 2012.   Credit: Curtis B. Photos

After his quarterback sack forced a fumble and helped seal Alabama's 37–21 national championship victory over Texas in January 2010, linebacker Eryk Anders couldn't get his professional football career going. Anders, short for a linebacker at 6-0 and weighing at most 240 pounds, had used his quickness to become a starter for the Crimson Tide his junior and senior seasons. Undrafted after his college career, he tried out, unsuccessfully, for National Football League and Canadian Football League teams before playing a season with the Colorado Ice of the Indoor Football League.

In summer 2011, Anders began mixed martial arts training. Helped by his high school experience as a state champion wrestler, he learned quickly. A year and a half after his professional career began in early 2012, he had compiled an 11-3 record and picked up three championships: the Strike Hard middleweight title, the V3Fights light heavyweight title, and the International Sport Karate Association light heavyweight title for Tennessee.

GEORGE WALLACE ■ *Boxer*

COLLEGE: 1938–40 . . . . **PRO:** Late 1930s–early 1940s; Alabama Sports HOF

George Wallace, a 118-pound bantamweight from Clio, Alabama, entered the University of Alabama School of Law directly from high school in 1937 and captained Alabama's freshman boxing team. He fought for the varsity the next three years. In 1939, he went undefeated in dual meets. In 1940, Wallace reached the Southeastern Conference bantamweight title bout, losing to Al Michael of LSU. Years later, he called it his best collegiate fight. Wallace also boxed professionally to help pay his way through law school. Most if not all of those bouts were pretty informal, and his professional record appears lost to history.

He made his name, of course, as Alabama's fiery segregationist governor in the 1960s and '70s and a presidential candidate in 1964, 1968, 1972 (when a gunman's assassination attempt left him paralyzed below the waist), and 1976. In the late 1970s, Wallace became a born-again Christian and renounced white supremacism. During the last of his four terms as governor, 1983–87, he appointed a record number of African-Americans to government positions. He died of heart failure in 1998, age 79.

The Golden Gloves and college boxing career of George Wallace (right, with a boxing partner) foreshadowed his pugnacious approach to politics.

Credit: The W. S. Hoole Special Collections Library, The University of Alabama

Index

Note that there are many names of former University of Alabama athletes who had pro careers that are listed in alphabetical tables at the end of each chapter. Those names are not replicated in this index. For football, see page 181; baseball and softball, page 248; basketball, page 315; golf, page 345; Olympics, page 377, and Tennis, page 405.

C

Note that there are many names of former University of Alabama athletes who had pro careers that are listed in alphabetical tables at the end of each chapter. Those names are not replicated in this index. For football, see page 181; baseball and softball, page 248; basketball, page 315; golf, page 345; Olympics, page 377, and Tennis, page 405.

Note that there are many names of former University of Alabama athletes who had pro careers that are listed in alphabetical tables at the end of each chapter. Those names are not replicated in this index. For football, see page 181; baseball and softball, page 248; basketball, page 315; golf, page 345; Olympics, page 377, and Tennis, page 405.

Note that there are many names of former University of Alabama athletes who had pro careers that are listed in alphabetical tables at the end of each chapter. Those names are not replicated in this index. For football, see page 181; baseball and softball, page 248; basketball, page 315; golf, page 345; Olympics, page 377, and Tennis, page 405.

Note that there are many names of former University of Alabama athletes who had pro careers that are listed in alphabetical tables at the end of each chapter. Those names are not replicated in this index. For football, see page 181; baseball and softball, page 248; basketball, page 315; golf, page 345; Olympics, page 377, and Tennis, page 405.

About the Author

Steve Millburg got his start as a professional journalist on the night sports desk of the *Omaha World-Herald* newspaper in Nebraska in 1973, while still in college. He quickly became the official typewriter ribbon changer for the crusty old night sports editor, who after 35 years on the job remained wary of such newfangled technology.

Millburg spent 16 years working for newspapers and 17 more working for magazines before becoming a freelance writer and editor in 2007. Along the way he was on the staff of the *St. Petersburg Times* newspaper (now the *Tampa Bay Times*) and *Southpoint, Cooking Light, Travel South, Southern Living,* and *Coastal Living* magazines. He has been a copy editor, city columnist, movie reviewer, rock concert reviewer, theater reviewer, sportswriter, travel writer,

Credit: Melissa Springer

medical writer, advertising copywriter, fitness writer, food writer, teacher, fact checker, musician, and wedding officiant, and in fact still is many of those things.

He lives in a suburb of Birmingham, Alabama, with his wife, Pamela, an elderly dog, and an elderly cat. He plays softball and ultimate Frisbee, more slowly than he once did, and is president of the Birmingham Ultimate Disc Association.